YOU LOOKED AT ME

The Spiritual Testimony
of
CLAUDINE MOINE

affection. Ie fus donc adressée au R. P. _____ qui m'ecouta auec beaucoup
de patience et de charité, me fit beaucoup de questions et demandes auxquelles
aiant repondu auec grande naiueté, il me promit sur l'heure d'auoir soin de
nous, ce qu'il a fait auec vne charité tres pure, puisque iamais nous ne lui auons
été recommandées de personne. Ie m'arreste a lui pour me confesser plus par
interest temporel que par aucun autre desir, et ie n'auois encore iamais eu de
confesseur arresté. Ce qu'il nous donnoit, auec ce que nous pouuions gagner de
notre trauail nous faisoit subsister tout doucement: nous menions vne vie fort
retiré, trauaillant continuellement tant que nous pouuions auoir de l'ouurage, et
vous l'ordonniez ainsi, mon Dieu, que ie fusse reduitte a cela en punition de mes
faineantises qui auoient été si grandes iusques alors que ie ne faisois pas d'ouurage
en vn an ce que l'on en pouuoit faire en vn mois trauaillant raisonnablement. Il
y auoit enuiron vne année que nous étions a Paris quand O Mon Dieu, vous me
regardâtes des yeux de votre infinie et extraordinaire misericorde dont ie vous rends
graces infinies. Monseigneur Ie ne sçai quel iour ni quel mois ce fut, mais ie sçai
bien que tout d'vn coup ie ressentis de grands desirs de la vertu et perfection. Vous
me fistes connoitre l'enormité de mes crimes, et l'abus que i'auois fait de vos
graces, ie vis la peine des damnez et sur tout celle du Dam. La veüe de cette peine
du Dam me dura enuiron 15 iours, et ie ne sçai comme ie ne mourus pas
voiant vne chose si terrible. I'auois vne si grande confusion de mes pechez que
ie n'osois leuer les yeux auec vne si viue douleur que i'etois toujours a vos pieds
sacrez, Mon Iesus, comme vne Magdelaine a pleurer et detester les desordres de
ma mechante et miserable vie. La veüe de l'enfer ne me fit point de peur car
vous ne m'auez pas conduitte par la crainte mais par la voie d'amour, et de bon
coeur i'y eusse voulu estre, et ne vous auoir iamais offensé. La connoissance
que i'auois comme misericordieusement vous ne m'y auiez point precipitée
vous y aiant prouoqué mille et mille fois, me preseruant de cet horrible malheur
d'estre en votre haine pour iamais, car tous les autres maux ne me touchoient point
et me donnant encore le temps de vous aimer et de vous seruir allumoit dans mon
coeur vn si ardent amour que i'en etois toute consumée. I'eusse volontiers fait

Manuscript page showing 'vous me regardâtes' (you looked at me);
MS1409, Archives of Missions Etrangères, Paris.

YOU LOOKED AT ME

The Spiritual Testimony
of
CLAUDINE MOINE

Translation, Introduction and Notes
by
Gerard Carroll, DD, PhD

Preface by Jean Guennou

James Clarke & Co
Cambridge

James Clarke & Co Ltd
P.O. Box 60
Cambridge CB1 2NT

British Library Cataloguing in Publication Data

Moine, Claudine, *fl. 1618*
    1. Christian life. Spirituality - Personal observations
    I. Title II. Carroll, E. Gerard III.
       La couturiere mystique de Paris. *English* 248.4'092'4

ISBN 0-227-67907-5

Published in French as *La Couturière Mystique de Paris* by Editions Pierre Téqui

Translation copyright © Gerard Carroll 1989

First published in English by James Clarke & Co

Printed in Great Britain by St Edmundsbury Press Ltd,
Bury St Edmunds, Suffolk

TO THE MEMORY OF

MY FATHER AND MOTHER

We were about one year in Paris when, O my God, with those eyes of infinite and extraordinary mercy, you looked at me; for which, my Lord, I am exceedingly grateful to you. I do not know what day or month it was. But well I do know, that all of a sudden I felt a great desire for virtue and perfection.

Claudine Moine

Contents

Preface

Claudine Moine is not totally unknown to readers in the English language. *The New Catholic Encyclopedia*, published in 1967, consecrated a short biographical note to her (vol. IX, p. 1006). The entire text of her writings, however, has only been available up to the present in the French language. But thanks to the great care with which Father Gerard Carroll has applied himself to this first translation into another language, English-speaking people will now be able to have direct access to this treasure.

It might be difficult to appreciate the remarkable value of the original text in translation. Despite some traces of the preclassical era in the use of the present participle, to give one example, the language of Claudine Moine carries with it all the characteristics of the great classical period in France: clarity, sobriety and exactitude of expression, without an overstudied style or affectation. However, the present translation succeeds admirably in capturing the style of expression. But it is not simply the style of the work that is striking; the content is even more exceptional. There are many authors who have described their spiritual journey from a life of sin or indifference to that state of union with God we normally refer to as 'spiritual marriage'; but when Claudine takes up the pen in 1652 on the behest of her confessor, she has already spent four years in this last state. When she ceases writing she has spent seven years in it. For her the spiritual journey continues; changes manifest themselves. And the description of the later states is of the greatest interest.

Moreover, the visions she recounts are nearly all intellectual; to characterise them amounts in effect to an exposition of Christian doctrine. This already suggests that for her the essentials of the mystical life are to be found elsewhere, that is in living and acting under the movement of the spirit. She tries hard to describe the nature of this experience, which she seems to have discovered in herself suddenly, without reference to any other previous experiences of that kind. This explains the prudent course she adopts in writing: a certain fear of being wrong allows her to persist, despite everything, in the profound confidence she has of being on the right road.

One of the more frequent expressions in her writings is 'the movement that drives me' or 'the instinct that directs me'. This concept is entirely biblical. Thus Simeon comes to the Temple 'prompted by the Spirit' (Luke 4:1-2; Matt. 4:1), and Paul on his way to Jerusalem is 'a prisoner already in spirit' (Acts 20:22). Another time the spirit prevented Paul and his companions from crossing the frontier into Bithynia (Acts 16:7-8).

The agent of spiritual progress for Claudine is the Eucharist, whose action is 'transforming'. And when this word takes on its full force for her, her 'soul acts hardly any more except from the motive of love'.

Briefly, the presentation which Claudine gives of her personal experience makes it possible for us to see in it a spiritual theology inspired by the Bible. Her spirituality is no longer taken from the experience of the great mystics of the sixteenth century, although she never disparages them in any way.

While Claudine Moine brings us back in her spirituality to the origins of Christianity, she is also very relevant for today. She found herself in the situation of having to earn her living by the work of her hands. She led a very normal existence (although celibate) in the world and lived out her exceptional experiences in the midst of the many domestics who worked for the important people of this world, without causing anyone to comment on her.

She also bore witness to the fact that the gifts of God can blossom and bear fruit well beyond our wildest imagination in the most humble of circumstances.

Despite the exceptional character of the favours she received, she never considered herself as commissioned with a message. Her writings, however, relating - as far as one can say this - the mystical life in its pure state, bear a testimony. They are edifying and stimulating, and they can help every one of us, without any risk of leading us astray, because they bring us back always to the essentials, so much so that one could entitle them: 'If you only knew what God is offering' (John 4:10).

Jean Guennou

Acknowledgements

A work of this kind is never completed without expertise and generous help from people whose names I now wish to acknowledge here. It is my pleasant duty to express my indebtedness first to Father Jean Guennou for his very fine edition of the French text, and also my thanks to him for the many conversations we have had together about its translation into English. The principal task of an editor being to facilitate the reading of the text, the work already accomplished by him on this seventeenth-century French manuscript made my task as translator more easy when I came to prepare this present English edition of the writings of Claudine Moine.

Destined for the general reader and not exclusively for the experts, the editing of this text posed a problem for Father Guennou, in so far as the manuscript consisted of an ensemble of four separate accounts of which only the fourth carried a title: 'De l'Oraison'. He therefore found it necessary to add titles and subtitles throughout the text. He also subdivided the generally long paragraphs of the manuscript in accordance with present usage, and, with every possible fidelity to the sense indicated in the manuscript itself, modernised the orthography and punctuation. This present edition retains the titles and subtitles supplied by Father Guennou. I have treated as an integral part of the text the expletive words indicated by the symbols < > in the French edition. In addition to retaining the square brackets [ ] employed by Father Guennou to restore words left blank in the manuscript, usually of proper names, I have introduced more square brackets in order to insert certain words and phrases I considered necessary to supply apparently missing words and furnish a more accurate reading of the text.

To this acknowledgement I now add my expression of gratitude to Adrian Brink, David Game, Mrs Linda Yeatman, and Richard Burnell, of James Clarke & Co. Ltd for their generous offer to publish this present edition and for the meticulous care with which it has been printed. In particular I extend my indebtedness and thanks to Mrs Jenny Knight for her dedicated commitment to the preparation of this manuscript for publication. I also thank Father Guennou for providing the frontispiece, and the Bibliothèque Nationale for permission to reproduce the two Seventeenth-century engravings. Finally, I am conscious of my good fortune in having friends notable for their interest in Claudine; in particular I think of Father François Brune, Father Georges Montabert, Father Theophane Cooney, Mr and Mrs Michael Crowe, Mrs Daphne Rae and Mr Enda Gearty, whose encouragement sustained me in my endeavours as a translator to put the heart of this text into your hands and render its soul visible to your eyes.

Gerard Carroll

Seventeenth-century engraving of the interior of the church of St Louis during a sermon preached in the presence of the King, the Queen, and the whole Court.

Introduction[1]

It is now, my dear and Reverend Father, that I can truly say I have put my heart into your hands and rendered my soul visible to your eyes

From behind the awnings of time, at last is revealed in these words a spiritual beauty curtained from history since the seventeenth century. Taken from MS 1409 of the archives of La Société des Missions Etrangères in Paris, they spring from the pen of a young woman who arrived in Paris in 1642 as a refugee from her homeland, to lead a secluded life in the Marais quarter of that city, plying the needle and thread so as to earn a living as a dressmaker. Finally, reaching for the heights of spiritual perfection and in obedience to the behest of her confessor, she recorded her spiritual experience in writing. Unsigned, and with all proper and place names left blank (except for a few: Paris, Dijon, Annonciade, Ursulines), MS 1409 was found only in the past thirty years by the then archivist of the Missions Etrangères, Father Jean Guennou; the relatively recent discovery of this hitherto unknown text determines the following way of introducing this, its first English translation: *You Looked at Me: the Spiritual Testimony of Claudine Moine.*

The imagination of those interested in the fabulous is easily excited by the discovery of an unknown manuscript without an author. They ask: 'How old is the manuscript?' and 'Who wrote it?' It is these questions that are discussed in this Introduction, for it is generally accepted that a story not vouched for by a principal participant defies belief. A certain contract, it would seem, is arrived at between the writer and the reading public; they take on the role of members of a jury who must hear what happened from the witness's own lips and who will accept neither hearsay evidence nor inspired guesses. But the words of Claudine are no fable. It is true that God usually reserves for himself the knowledge of the high summits and profound depths of some privileged souls who will only be known to us in Heaven. For example, what do we know of St Joseph and the many saints devoted to the hidden life? But occasionally, a grille is unsealed, a gate broken open in front of us; and the time arrives for some Sleeping Beauty to come back to life among us, putting their heart into our hands and rendering their soul visible to our eyes. The author of the above words, who awakes for us at this moment in history, has slept for over 300 years and speaks the French of the mid-seventeenth century.

Anxious as we always are to identify ourselves with some form of life that is real and historical, that has a true heart and soul in it, the words of Claudine evoke in us something of the author's own deep sense of identity and the unmitigated truthfulness

1

of her soul's experience as she writes about it. Writing with authority - for she evidently experiences in her person what her heart and soul had revealed to her confessor - she displays in these words to her confessor the fortunate, albeit uncommon, combination of a spiritual vision and a writer's ability. She was as dexterous with the pen, it would seem, as she was with the needle and thread, and these words illustrate the dual characteristic of spiritual depth and literary ability reflected in her writings as a whole: a very special blend of spiritual vision and theological understanding - a rare fortune nowadays, which can only be something of a treat for the reader.[2]

Generally, in presenting to the public a work of a writer, it is customary to begin with a biography, trying to clarify the thought of the author through the circumstances of the author's life and the historical influences of the times in which he or she lived; then to treat of the work in question in the context of the author's general output, if any; and finally to move on to discuss the sources and leading ideas of the work. But in this present case we are forced to do the reverse: we must try to work out the biography from the content of the work itself. This means that, notwithstanding the fact that a cursory glance at the first few pages of the manuscript will tell us that the author was born in 1618, is a woman and is the eldest of three children in her family, that she lost her mother when she was 8 or 9 years of age and that her family had considerable private means, for all intents and purposes we are confronted here with an unknown work and an unknown author.

What air of authenticity, then, has this manuscript? How credible is the experience described in it? For in the above words the author is saying to her confessor that she has completed the work of recounting for him the great favours God granted her in her life. It was on one day in Paris - most likely sometime around the feast of All Saints 1642 - that she perceived in herself a presence, that is the experience of a force new to her. She will guard the impression forever after that her life consisted of two very distinct phases: the one before and the other after that moment when, as she says, 'you looked at me'. This is how she describes it:

We were about one year in Paris when, O my God, with those eyes of infinite and extraordinary mercy, you looked at me; for which, my Lord, I am exceedingly grateful to you. I do not know what day or month it was. But well I do know, that all of a sudden I felt a great desire for virtue and perfection.

No Christian theologian has ever denied that the elect will have a vision of God in the state of final beatitude. Is it not the cherished yearning of every Christian believer to know and see God in himself, as he is? It is in fact a fundamental truth attested to by scripture: 'My dear people, we are already the children of God but what we are to be in the future has not yet been revealed; all we know is, that when it is revealed we shall be like him because we shall see him as he really is' (I John 3:2). But the same scriptures, the same Epistle of St John (4:12), affirms that 'No one has ever seen God.' And St Paul himself points out that God 'alone is immortal, whose home is in inaccessible light, whom no man has seen and no man is able to see' (I Tim. 6:16). Is this vision of God as he is, then, reserved exclusively to the eternal life, or can it have its beginning here below, in this life? And moreover, the question that challenges us all today, is there a personal God who truly loves us and draws us to himself as to our final end? Not the projection of her own imagination, nor the result of the activity of her own mind, Claudine Moine's awareness of a new presence and force within herself is a testimony to the fact that God really exists and that a true union with him is possible, even in this life. With her eyes open to vision beyond the range of normal sight, she testifies to the fact that she has seen God and that her word is true. But Dante in the first Canto of the *Paradiso* points out that the person who has been in Heaven and seen things has neither the knowledge nor the power to relate them when he descends from there, because, as Dante says, as it draws near to its desire, our intellect enters so deep that memory cannot go back upon the track (cf. *Paradiso*, Canto I, lines 6-9). And again in the *Paradiso*, Dante, confessing that his vision was greater than his speech could show (Canto XXXIII, lines 55-6), says that, through abounding grace, he presumed to fix his look through the Eternal Light so far that all his sight was used up, and that in its depth he saw gathered together there, bound by love in one single volume, that which is dispersed throughout the whole universe (ibid., lines 82-7). He was experiencing the Trinity, in which, as in a knot (line 91), he now saw the meaning of all existence. Speech is scant indeed, and how feeble is one's conception when it is a question of relating such wonderful things. This is indeed Claudine's task also.

To say whether her testimony is true or not we rely solely on the integrity of her own word; and, as in the case of our acceptance of the Apostles' testimony to the risen Christ, its verisimilitude can only be attested to in the positive by those who find in her a kindred spirit by testifying with her, and with all the witnesses in the life of the Church down the ages, to having had the same experience in their own lives. We may be navigating on a stormy sea; but, 'Behold, he who keeps Israel will never slumber or sleep' (Ps. 121:4). It is true, God has eyes; he looks at us, and everything is changed - all is calm. 'How beautiful you are, my love,/ how beautiful you are!/ Your eyes behind your veil,/ are doves;/ your hair is like a flock of goats / frisking down the slopes of Gilead' (S. of S. 4:1). 'Is the inventor of the ear unable to hear?/ The creator of the eye unable to see?' (Ps. 94:9.) For God indeed looked at Claudine: 'those eyes of infinite and extraordinary mercy' gazed upon her, and she awoke spiritually to behold his form, Christ. Bearing testimony in these words to this real experience of God, Claudine also echoes the same sentiments of St John: 'Something which has existed since the beginning,/ that we have heard,/and we have seen with our own eyes;/ that we have watched / and touched with our hands:/ the Word, who is life - / this is our subject./ That life was made visible:/we saw it and are giving testimony,/ telling you of the eternal life / which was with the Father and has been made visible to us' (I John 1:1-2). 'We are writing this to you,' says St John, 'to make our own joy complete' (I John 1:4). So intimately connected with her spiritual vision was Claudine's need to bear testimony to it, that it would falsify it entirely if she could not speak about it.

Speak about it she did, to her confessor; and, under obedience to him, she agreed to write about it.

This so far is the history, and this the life, of Claudine Moine; now perceiving within herself a presence on a day in Paris in 1642, looked at by those eyes of infinite and extraordinary mercy. This is the history, and this the life, of Claudine Moine, appearing from behind the awnings of time to put her heart into our hands and render her soul visible to our eyes. For the reader who has never entered the world of seventeenth-century France, it has to be a revelation; and for the reader who is familiar with this area, it can only be praised for its unique example of everything that was great in the spirituality of seventeenth-century France. Not a history, not a treatise in theology, not even the traditional spiritual autobiography or story of a soul, this work presents us with a word that depicts the most simple spiritual ideas with the utmost accuracy, to which the above words of her conversion testify. Perhaps her experience is too private, has too personal a value to be of much interest to a wider public. But this is a judgement readers must make for themselves if they will read Claudine's fascinating testimony with an open mind. Some may feel that this text would have done better had it been written as a treatise rather than in its present form. But the author of this manuscript is speaking from the inside out, from her own experience, and reflecting in a very definite way upon this very special action of God in her life. Claudine in a sense becomes her own parent spiritually, in so far as, being reborn, it is this time a question of her own choice.[3] She also becomes her own theologian in as much as she reflects upon her spiritual experience. This is its fascination, its invitation to us to bring us beyond language into the truth, beyond the story into the real, and finally beyond the self into God. Its content, then, is its true biography, a spiritual testimony: the Spiritual Testimony of Claudine Moine.

It is important therefore, as an attempt to answer the above questions, to point out the following characteristics of the text as a key but not a hindrance to the reading of this translation. For I believe that a close and informed reading of the text will reveal the author, and that the wise reader will find that the surest guide to Claudine Moine is her own words. But first, the history of the text; then some words on the possible sources behind it; and finally, I shall comment on the opening words of the manuscript as a key to the understanding of the author's spirituality.

The dressmaker of Paris

There is scarcely a repository of ancient documents, above all in Paris, that does not contain some spiritual writings. Since their creation in 1658, the rich archives of La Société des Missions Etrangères in Paris have acquired a significant number, from many different provenances. Many of these writings are, of course, very commonplace and trivial, and would not merit publication. But MS 1409 is an entirely different matter.[4] First, however, two important matters must be clarified: How old is the manuscript? Who wrote it?

Introduction

The last page of the manuscript answers the first question. On this page is written:

This manuscript belongs to Abbé de Choisy, who lent it to Madame la Marquise on 14 July 1686; then to Madame la Présidente de Némod on 25 August 1696; then to Monseigneur l'Evêque de Rosalie on 9 September 1706.

The handwriting of Abbé de Choisy can be authenticated from the many examples of it that are to be found in the archives of the Missions Etrangères. Any mystery about the presence of this manuscript in the archives can be eliminated by pointing out that the Bishop of Rosalie, Monseigneur Artus de Lionne, returned to the Missions Etrangères, where he died in 1706. Further, Abbé de Choisy had retained an apartment there from about 1686. One way or the other, the presence of the manuscript (which belonged to Abbé de Choisy) in the archives of the Missions Etrangères does not pose any great problem; and the attendant information at least establishes the fact that it goes back to the seventeenth century, the century of the lost original.[5] But who wrote it?

At the end of the first part of the manuscript two capital letters, 'N.N.', substitute for the Christian name and surname of the author. It appears, then, that this manuscript stems from a lost original and is, so far, the only manuscript available. All further research undertaken to find the original has been unsuccessful. But this should not deter us from considering the second question: Who wrote it?

In the Marais quarter of the busy city of Paris of the seventeenth century, somewhere between the Place des Vosges and the then newly-built baroque church of St Louis, in which she attended daily Mass and listened to the great sermons preached there, lived a dressmaker. Clothed in the simple dress her poverty limited her to, she plied the needle and thread to earn her living. Yet, this is the kind of person in whom is revealed to us the rich spiritual heritage of seventeenth-century Paris: Claudine Moine.[6] As we looked at MS 1409 together, Father Guennou pointed out to me the following passage as the one that launched him on his research to find this Sleeping Beauty.[7]

Finally, not seeing our way of putting our affairs in order, we, that is my sister and myself, desired to leave home and work as domestics while waiting for a peaceful end to the war. With this in mind, I took the opportunity of writing to the Ursulines. For it happened that, some people from [Vesoul], who were sent as hostages to the Count of [Grancey] until such time as the amount of money which had been agreed upon with him was paid, had to pass through [Langres]. For on account of the war, and all communications having been destroyed accordingly, it was about four years, I believe, since I had last let the Ursulines have any news about me. I conveyed to them, then, the state of our affairs and the plan we have to work as domestics.

This passage matches up with an episode in seventeenth-century French history.[8] 'The year 1618', writes C.V. Wedgwood, 'was like many others in those

5

uneasy decades of armed neutrality which occur from time to time in the history of the Empire.'[9] On 17 January of that year, the author of this manuscript was born; and on 23 May of the same year the revolt in Prague took place, the date traditionally assigned to the outbreak of the Thirty Years War.[10] During the Thirty Years War the city of Vesoul,[11] already ruined by the demands and taxes of the war, was summoned by the Count of Grancey, in September 1641, to pay a thousand crowns (*écus*) ransom under the penalty of being pillaged by the French troops. Vesoul capitulated; but not being able to get together the necessary amount of money, the city had to provide twelve hostages whom the Count of Grancey convoked at Scey-sur-Saône, on 30 September, before dispatching them to his castle, situated to the south-west of Langres. The author of this manuscript, then, wished to take advantage of this situation in order to have a letter sent to the Ursulines, where she had been a boarder at school. She had no idea when writing her letter to the Ursulines that it was going to lead eventually to her coming to Paris.

From these pieces of information, we come to two conclusions about the identity of the author: she lived in Scey-sur-Saône, where the Count of Grancey had summoned his hostages before conveying them to his castle at Langres - the only town on the route of the hostages where a convent of the Ursuline sisters is to be found; and her name was Claudine Moine - for it only remained to consult the parish register of Scey-sur-Saône to find out that she was the daughter of Mathias Moine and Jeanne la Brune. A thorough investigation revealed also that Claudine had a younger sister and a younger brother - all of which precise information corresponds exactly to the data given in the text. In the first page, in fact, she writes:

It pleased God to take my mother from this world when I was about 8 or 9 years of age and, even so, the eldest of three children she left behind.

The war and its severe consequences began to make themselves felt even among the well-to-do, and in the long run Mathias Moine and his family found themselves battling against great difficulties, possibly financial. Claudine, being the eldest, was sent by her father to Besançon (that, from a hypothesis based on the timetable of her return journey, was in all probability the town in question) to carry out some business transaction. Because of the insecurities the roads presented, the young Claudine was not able to return to Scey-sur-Saône until a period of three months had passed. Eventually a safe route home presented itself. But on her way home she had an accident that resulted in her losing consciousness, which she sustained because of a horse that leaped and knocked her to the ground on a pile of rocks. Regaining her consciousness, however, and resuming her journey, she finally arrived home, but she was confined to bed for fifteen days. She was not long recovered from this illness when she was stricken with another one; this one lasted almost fifteen months.

The material situation of the family was deteriorating more and more almost daily, and Claudine and her sister Nicole thought they should enter someone's service as domestics until the war was over and peace was re-established. As stated above, the

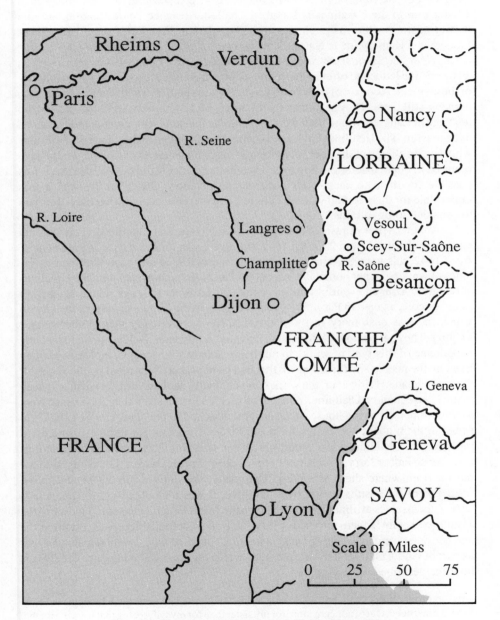

Franche-Comté at the time of the Thirty Years War

occasion for them to obtain such a position presented itself when a convoy of hostages from Vesoul passed through Scey-sur-Saône, making it possible for Claudine to have a letter sent to the Ursulines at Langres. The letter reached its destination, and the former mistress who was in charge of the boarders in Claudine's time there, Sister Françoise d'Hémery (de la Nativité), later superior of the house (see *Directoire pour les novices du Monastère Sainte-Ursule de Langres*, Lyon, 1642, pp. 510-14), answered the letter and offered the young women from Scey-sur-Saône the hospitality of the convent. A cousin of theirs who was a religious had been in the convent and was, perhaps, still there. They set out on their journey on 12 February 1642 and arrived the next day at Langres, where they were received by the nuns with great demonstrations of friendship. The Ursulines envisaged keeping them hidden in the quarters of the nuns who were in charge of the door for as long as the circumstances of the war would have required it; out of discretion, however, Claudine and Nicole did not believe that it was possible for them to accept this generous proposition. Owing to the war it was impossible for them to find work at Langres, and therefore, come what may, they had to consider going to Paris.

Another series of research brings us in the footsteps of Claudine to Paris, to find out where she lived from 23 April 1642, the date given for her arrival in Paris. On 17 April 1642, this young woman from the provinces, forced on account of the misfortunes of war to quit her homeland, set out for Paris after a short stay with the Ursulines at Langres. After an eventful journey, which lasted about six days, Claudine and her sister, Nicole, arrived in Paris. They found a room in the Marais quarter of the city; in which, as was customary in those times, there were already many other people lodging. They set out to look for domestic work, but in vain. Neither of them had any experience of this type of work, so not being able to find proper employment, they lived by the needle and thread, work that had been procured for them by the sisters of the Annonciade.[12] However, the work was very badly paid and did not suffice to keep them. Consequently, Claudine, more out of concern for her sister than for herself, went to present herself to the house of the Jesuits, attached to the church of St Louis,[13] to speak to them about her distressful position. So it was not for totally disinterested motives that Claudine, a few months after her arrival in Paris, took as a director of conscience Father Jarry,[14] procurator of the house of profession of the Jesuits, situated not far from where she was staying. Obviously, she did not present herself to the residence of the Jesuits on her own initiative. It was undoubtedly the Annonciade sisters, themselves affiliated in some way to the Jesuit Order, who sent Claudine to the Jesuits to explain to them the terribly miserable and materially deprived condition she and her sister were in. Looking back on her life, Claudine will always recall this event as part of God's plan for her - his providence, his constant watching over her. This is how she described the event:

After some months in Paris, and not having brought with us there very much money, we began to be in great need. Out of concern more for my sister than for myself, seeing that we were unable to earn enough from our work in order to feed and house ourselves, I resolved to find someone who could help us in our need. At last, beginning to put all my confidence in you, my God, with great affection I asked your help. I was directed hence to Father [Jarry], who listened to me with great patience and charity.

Such, then, was the providential guidance of God that was about to launch Claudine Moine on the path of an astonishing spiritual journey by putting her in contact with her first regular confessor. Father Jarry himself had been involved in the foundation of the convent of the Annonciades célestes, and, as procurator of the house of profession, he was also in charge of the charitable works of mercy. The young Claudine told him her whole story; then asked him if she could present herself regularly to him in his confessional, which he agreed to. That it was indeed the said Father Jarry is proved all the more by the fact that she herself gives some indication in her writings about the time of his death; for that corresponds more or less with the date engraved on the tomb of Father Jarry (and on his alone) in the crypt of the church of St Louis, where all the Jesuits who died at the adjoining residence were buried. The inscriptions on those vaults, or tombs, have been restored many times,[15] and these permit us to identify even the second confessor of Claudine, Father Pierre de Sesmaisons.[16] Finally, the rather distinguished career of her third confessor, such as it is described in the manuscript, seems to correspond to that of Father André Castillon, celebrated as a preacher at the beginning of the reign of Louis XIV:

All the repugnances and difficulties which I had with virtue were dispelled in an instant; and I well experienced that which I have since heard said by the greatest preacher of the century, that when it pleases you [God] to act according to your extraordinary power, your graces are infallible in their effect, without encroaching upon the freedom of man.

Castillon himself was regarded as one of the foremost preachers of his time. It was also to him that Claudine Moine addressed herself in October 1648. Furthermore, she gives more information about him in the following passage:

But another thing that will help one understand better this conduct (because, for once and for all, I would really like to state it openly), is that I was going to the confessor of whom I have spoken for only a short time, and to whom I believe it was our Lord himself who directed me in the manner in which I have explained, when, on the order of his superiors, he changed places and went to be superior very far from here.

And true enough, at the end of December 1648, Father Castillon was appointed rector of the Jesuit college at Orléans, where he remained until 1651. He exercised the same functions at Rennes for a year, and then he came back to Paris in September 1652. Three weeks after his return to the residence of St Louis, his old penitent, Claudine, made a general confession to him. As a result of this, it seems, Father Castillon believed it was his duty to ask Claudine to relate in writing the principal favours she had received from God since the time of her birth.

9

Claudine Moine: we have only to contemplate her life's history to anticipate that what comes from her pen can only delight us and strike us with wonder as it clothes and exemplifies a meaning that transcends it. An historical document as well as a spiritual testimony, her manuscript commands the interest of historian and theologian alike. The ingenuousness of its appearance among us and the story it tells eschews all the frenzied claims to authenticity and the extraordinary lengths to which some authors go to make plausible not only the writing of a true confession, but also its subsequent discovery and publication: the yellowing manuscript discovered under lock and key in an old, empty house, or in a trunk abandoned in an inn by a traveller who never returns to reclaim it. The setting for Claudine's story needs no such setting for authenticity. The historical climate in which she lived out her spiritual existence - between struggling with the vagaries of war and the religious thinking of seventeenth-century France - had just been shaken by the stormy onslaught of many philosophical and theological upheavals in the lives of people. Although we have very little biographical information about Claudine, apart from what she chooses to reveal to us and what can be gleaned from the historical evidence offered in the manuscript, the recorded events surrounding her life demonstrate at least the simple fact that Claudine is an historical character. But whether belief in the credibility of her story commands assent or not depends less on this than on the spiritual climate that sustains it. And if her written word is the progeny of her soul, we are invited by her, as by all writers of good spiritual literature, to transcend the historical - that is our own story - and transfer to our lives what she contemplates through the spiritual interpretation of the things spoken literally.

She is dignified and refulgent in her language as she puts her heart into our hands and renders her soul visible to our eyes, and that ranks her with Augustine, Teresa of Avila, Catherine of Genoa and Mary of the Incarnation, according her a rightful place in the history of Western spirituality. It is not overestimating her importance to place her among the writers identified with the history of Christian thought and renowned for their spirituality and sound doctrine. So this is the history, and this the life of Claudine Moine; recounting for Father Castillon on some day in the year 1652 the favours she received from God in her life, plying the needle and the thread, passing on to the church of St Louis, and flitting in at its open door some time around the end of 1653 to give to Father Castillon the finished first account of her spiritual experience. And indeed this history and this life of Claudine Moine furnish us with much that is fascinating in the political and religious history of seventeenth-century France in general and of Paris in particular.

The generation preceding the Thirty Years War was certainly more devout, although not necessarily more virtuous than those before it. As a reaction to the materialism of the Renaissance which was prevalent in the middle years of the previous century and had now reached its peak, a spiritual revival had now penetrated to the very roots of society and religion and was now a reality among those to whom politics were meaningless and public events unknown.[17]

Wedgwood goes on to say:

Theological controversy became the habitual reading of all classes, sermons directed their politics and moral tracts beguiled their leisure. Among the Catholics the cult of the Saints reached proportions unheard of for centuries and assumed a dominant part in the experience of the educated as well as of the masses; miracles once again made the life of everyday bright with hope. The changes of the material world, the breakdown of old tradition and the insufficiency of dying conventions drove men and women to the spiritual and the inexplicable . . . . Before Galileo's discovery the antithesis between faith and science had been partly admitted. Luther had cried out against the 'harlot'. Philosophy, science and the processes of reasoned thought were felt to be safe only so long as they were guided by revealed religion. Truth sprang from direct and divine revelation; scientific facts, for which man had no better evidence than that of his own faculties, might be merely the calculated deception of the devil. The natural conservatism of the human mind helped the churches in their opposition to the new outlook. Men wanted certainties, not more causes for doubt, and since the discoveries of science perplexed them with strange theories about the earth on which they walked and the bodies they inhabited, they turned with all the more zeal to the firm assurance of religion.[18]

The churches had never seemed as strong as during the opening decades of the seventeenth century. But one generation alone was to witness their fall from political dominance, and this fall was embryonically contained within the events of 1618. The fundamental issue was between revealed and rationalised belief,[19] for the lesser issue between Catholic and Protestant had only obscured the greater and more crucial crisis of the seventeenth century.[20] Born also in 1618 was Claudine Moine, and, since her accounts of her spiritual experience are bound to reflect something of the time in which they were written, the intellectual and spiritual crises of the century will undoubtedly feature in her history and life.

The religious history of France in the seventeenth century revolves around the progress of the Counter-Reformation. Almost every issue which came up during the century may be related to this central fact. Its influence is to be seen in the foundation of new religious orders and the expansion of old ones; in the growing influence of the Jesuits; in the movement of Jansenism; in the provision of seminaries for the secular clergy; and in particular in a whole renewal of the spiritual life that made of seventeenth-century France one of the high moments in the history of Christian mysticism.

Towards the end of the month of October 1642, around the feast of All Saints, Claudine was 'touched' by God. Thus began to unfold, under the shadow of the church of St Louis, a mystical experience of the most interesting kind in the history of the Church. In this church Claudine attended daily Eucharist. And here, too, she made her frequent confession. Also in this church, she would have been able to see many times, as she says, 'the King, the Queen and all the Court', if she had so wished. The King, the Queen, and all the Court used to go to this church of the Jesuits for the feast of the name of Jesus,[21] and on 25 August for the feast of the patron of the church, St Louis.[22]

Moving into the quiet and calm of this church from a noisy and busy twentieth-

Seventeenth-Century engraving of the Church of St Louis

century street, we enter as it were into a great theatre where the glorious theological dramas of the seventeenth century were presented. In the last transept, as you approach the high altar, lies the body of Bourdaloue (1632-1704), whose voice at one time confounded the congregations with great learning and oratory. We have only to evoke his sermons, from 1669, of which it is said, from 5 o'clock in the morning, the valets took themselves to St Louis and held places for their masters for the sermons at 3 o'clock in the afternoon. Or one can also recall Madame de Sévigné, a faithful listener to his sermons, who wrote to M. de Bussy-Rabutin about Bourdaloue's funeral oration for the Grand Condé, in 1687: 'I am charmed and transported by the funeral oration for the M. le Prince, given by Bourdaloue. He surpassed himself. This is saying a lot.' In the same pulpit other illustrious people were heard, such as Jean-François de Gondi, the future Cardinal de Retz, who, in 1648, gave, in the presence of the King and the Queen, the panegyric for St Louis. Claudine was present, more than likely, at that sermon.

Throughout the seventeenth century the preachers in St Louis were followed assiduously by the population. Accordingly, conceived very specially for preaching, this church is lit by very large windows and has only one nave, which is capable of gathering together an attentive congregation. The zeal of the Jesuits would have attracted the crowds there. To facilitate preaching, then, the pulpit is well in view; the large nave and the important tribunes can hold a very substantial congregation; and the side aisles are reduced to simple passages consisting of various side chapels. This beautiful edifice plunges you into the heart of the Grand Siècle, again evoked by the

Marais quarter of the city of Paris. Reaffirmed in its faith and its mission by the Council of Trent (1545-63), the Catholic Church of the Counter-Reformation, of which the Jesuits constituted one of the principal driving forces, desired an architecture full of grandeur and majesty. Right from the beginning of the seventeenth century, when the Counter-Reformation was blooming, the Jesuits of the house of profession attached to the church of St Louis proved themselves capable of carrying out their educational task. When they returned to Paris in 1606,[23] they immediately instituted courses in the Catechism for children, which were very soon attended by adults; and this was imitated in the other parishes of the city. To their work as preachers was added that of directors of conscience and confessors; notably that of kings: Father Cotton was confessor to Henry IV, Father Caussin to Louis XIII, Father Annat and Father La Chaise to Louis XIV, and Father Pérussault and Father Lignières to Louis XV. Their success in this domain was so great that often the faithful were obliged, on account of the great number of penitents, to wait many days before having their confessions heard. This does not seem to have been the case with Claudine; for the dressmaker of Paris was immediately given the sacrament the first time she asked for it from Father Jarry.

And moreover, the Jesuits forced themselves, in every way, to develop the piety of the people. In this task, they were following the Council of Trent which declared that the nature of man being such that he cannot easily, and without some external help, raise himself to the meditation of divine things, on account of this, the Church, as a good mother, has established certain uses such as lights, incense, ornaments and many other such things according to the discipline and tradition of the Apostles. And this in order to render more commendable the majesty of such a great sacrifice as the Mass and to excite the minds of the faithful by those sensible signs of piety and religion to the contemplation of the great things which are hidden in that sacrifice. So, in order to permit the people to participate actively in the liturgy, there is no rood-loft in the church of St Louis; the choir, of one row, opens immediately on to the altar, and the apse is abundantly decorated in order to capture the eye. The lay people, who were more and more instructed, were obliged to follow the divine office in their missals; therefore the windows of the church were large and the panes reduced to simple frames so that the light, reflected by the naked stone, was abundant. The sculpted and painted decoration presents with great insistence the most controversial aspects of doctrine of the reformed religions: the Eucharist, the cult of the Virgin, the angels and the saints. The greater part of the original works there in Claudine's time have since disappeared.

Very characteristic of the spirit of the Counter-Reformation and of the company of Jesus, this church was for Claudine a stage, as it were, upon which were acted out all the religious and theological dramas of the time, and in which she lived out her spiritual development. It vibrated with the many battle cries that accompanied the various theological controversies which prevailed at the time between the Jesuits and the Jansenists. The long line of Jesuit preachers was specially chosen from among the best quality of the Jesuit Order. Claudine would have been present in this church at

13

some of the great sermons preached by them. And remember Claudine's own words referring to her confessor, Father Castillon, as the foremost preacher of his day.

This was an age when religious eloquence flourished more than ever before; many of these preachers would have taken part personally in the theological controversies of the time, particularly the controversy between the Jesuits and the Jansenists over the Eucharist. So Claudine Moine, present at some of these sermons, would have been exposed to many of the theological issues that rattled the religious world of seventeenth-century France. In no part of Paris, as it existed then in the middle years of the seventeenth century, did French religious history wear a more spiritually rich and intellectually exciting garb than it displayed in the Marais quarter of the city; an area in which the Théâtre Marais was the literary centre, and the church of St Louis might be considered the spiritual one. Indeed, as we have discovered earlier, it is this combination of theology and literary ability that characterises most of Claudine Moine's writings.

Descartes had published his well-known *Discourse on Method* in 1637. In 1640, two years before Claudine's arrival in Paris, Jansen[24] published his *Augustinus*, a work that later became the controversial text which eventually launched the movement known as Jansenism, after the name of the author. The year after Claudine's arrival, 1643, Louis XIII died and Louis XIV acceded to the throne. Antoine Arnauld, a great champion of Jansenism, published that same year his treatise entitled *De la fréquente communion*,[25] which was an attack on the Jesuit attitude to the reception of Holy Communion and was in favour of the Jansenists, who recommended a less frequent reception. This work was to be the centre of conflict between the Jesuits and the Jansenists. And because one of Claudine's Jesuit confessors, Father de Sesmaisons, was the target aimed at by Arnauld in his work, it is not surprising that this conflict features also in the writings of Claudine. Indeed, perplexed at the whole affair, she will have some interesting things to say about it.

Not very far from where Claudine was staying, the atmosphere of Corneille's plays was breathing heroic grandeur in the Théâtre Marais. The plays were mainly concerned about the clashes between passion and duty and about self-mastery as the epitome of virtue. This included duty under all its forms: subservience to a high ideal, whether honour, loyalty or faith; to glory, or to feminine pride in chastity. Everything in Corneille's plays works itself out in terms of the decisions of the soul. In *Poleucte*, in particular, which would have been playing in the Théâtre Marais very shortly after Claudine's arrival in Paris, we see acted out the war between attachment to a fellow human being and the exclusive claims of Heaven. And almost as a public testimony on stage to the lived, Christian reality of the hidden life of Claudine Moine, Poleucte points out how baptism liberates in us whatever idealistic urge there may be, and stimulates us to live nobly: 'But to receive its [baptism] sacred character, which washes our crimes in a salutary water, and which, purging our soul and opening our eyes, gives us back the first right we had in Heaven.'[26] Indeed in her own life and work, her own spiritual awakening in which her eyes were opened to the sight of God,

Claudine was living in reality what Corneille was writing about. For she was writing about something that did happen to her; God looked at her and changed her life - a change that can only be regarded as a spiritual rebirth as distinct from natural birth. This she alludes to in the opening words of her writings: 'I was born, or baptised in any case'.

Immediately after October 1642, when she was 'touched' by God, there began for her, as she herself would see it, a season in Paradise, one that was characterised by intellectual visions, above all after receiving Holy Communion. But from 1643, she had to submit to the 'great trials', uniting the night of the senses with that of the spirit, which St John of the Cross talks about. In autumn of 1644, physical and moral sufferings that were due to sickness and false accusations were joined to this. The following year, her change of spiritual director coincided with the deliverance from these sufferings and her entry into what we can regard as the Illuminative Way. She was living alone then, her sister, Nicole, having left her to take up employment elsewhere; and she considered this period in this little room as a little Sinai, a little desert. After Nicole's unwilling departure, Claudine had remained in the room she had shared with two or three other young women plying the needle and thread all day long, but never making enough money to earn her living. Despite her poverty, however, she rented a little room in 1645, not for herself, but in order to take in her sister who had been exposed to certain difficulties in her new employment and wanted to quit it for reasons which Claudine herself was in agreement with. Finally the conflict died down, and Nicole remained in her employment while Claudine remained alone in her little room, with poverty for company, as she says, in the way that St Francis lived.

Great lights on her own evil inclinations were then given to her; followed by perceptible consolations and infused visions; these removed her need for food. These consolations were, she says, 'without form, image, or representation, as if unaware and without giving it any thought, one sees someone before their very eyes'. The visions concerned the Trinity and the Eucharist and prepared Claudine for the Unitive Way in which, as if in a mystical anaesthesia, the powers of the transformed soul expire, and in which a veritable divine possession is produced in their place. So, since the time when God 'touched' her, Claudine Moine experienced six months of consolations, two years of temptations and three years of great lights which finished in a transforming union. Even so, this was not the last state of her soul. There then followed the Great Darkness. However, experiencing the weight of divine action in her life, this left a profound peace in the soul.

It was under the direction of Father Castillon that Claudine Moine was introduced to the Great Darkness. In this darkness she was no longer conscious of her body or her soul. For, after the gifts of God there also follows 'a way of faith stripped of sentiment if not, at intervals, of some little lights'. Looking into herself, Claudine does not know if this state is good or bad. And she can surely doubt it, all the more that her natural inclinations are awakened again. The only thing that remains to her now is union in the night through mortification, patience and resignation, for she puts her 'sovereign contentment in doing in everything the will of God'. Her writing ends here; and, no external piece of information coming forth to complete it, we are ignorant after that of everything concerning the dressmaker of Paris, Claudine Moine. When, on the behest of her director, Father Castillon, she put down the needle and thread and took up the pen at the end of 1652, Claudine Moine had already been raised to that state which we normally refer to as the 'spiritual marriage'. Towards the end of 1655, she finished her task. From that moment on we lose sight of her until, like some Sleeping Beauty, she awakes historically and spiritually for those who read this testimony from the seventeenth century; a testimony which would not have been written if she had not considered it an absolute law to comply with the wishes of her confessor.

It is through the wishes of her confessor that she adopts the particular plan she follows in her writing; she says in the Preliminary Oblation to her work:

And to you, my dear and Reverend Father, I give this report as the greatest witness of my submission to and respect for your desires and wishes, which indeed to me are orders, laws that are absolute.

In this Preliminary Oblation of her work, Claudine affirms that she writes her spiritual report, that is 'describing the mercies of God in her life', in order to fulfil the will of God manifested to her through her confessor. It was not rash or foolhardy on her part to think of the demands of her confessor in such a way, given the fact of her concern for total obedience to him. When she had finished this written account, she gave it to him, thinking that she had responded entirely to his wishes. But her confessor ordered her to continue writing and 'bring to the light of day the most hidden graces she has received'. So she then writes again, and this time more amply, more fully (123 written pages this time, as against 90 the first time); and at the end of this second written account, she asks to be dispensed from writing any more. Father Castillon's response was again the same: an order to continue writing. Claudine mentions this at the beginning of the third account. In terminating the second account, Claudine wrote that it remained for her to speak about how 'union with our Lord Jesus Christ guided me, brought me into the mysteries of his life, and raised me to the knowledge of his divine attributes', and the different 'ways of prayer' which it pleased him to communicate to her. All these were to be topics and subjects dealt with in the third and fourth accounts. What we see emerging here, then, is a kind of plan that Claudine was to follow in the course of writing the third and fourth accounts.

Either the order of Father Castillon confirmed the plan given by Claudine, or he had already given this plan to her and at the end of the second account she had asked him all the same to be dispensed from it in grace. But his order having been final after the second account, at the end of the third account there is no asking for exemption for the 'ways of prayer', the fourth account. One can conclude then, that in completing the third account, Claudine knew that it remained for her to write the fourth one, which, besides, is the summit of the four but presupposes the other three. So, to summarise, Claudine began writing her first account sometime in 1652. And in July 1653, forty-five paragraphs had already been written. At this pace, the first section of the work was undoubtedly finished before the end of the same year. But, as we explained above, it did not end there. She believed that she had completely satisfied what Father Castillon had asked her to do. He was not completely satisfied, however, and he encouraged her to take up the pen again in order to give a more thorough and detailed account of God's action in her life, without referring back this time to the external, one might say the more biographical, events of her life. This explains the writing of the three remaining accounts: the second in 1654, the third in 1655 and, immediately after that, the fourth, entitled 'De l'Oraison' (On Prayer), the only one of the four with a title. Such, then, are the simple origins of this text and the plan the author followed in the writing of it. It remains for us now to say something of its content and general outline.

The first account, composed between the month of October 1652 and the end of December 1653, tells the story of Claudine's life from her young age till the time she put herself under the direction of Father Castillon. This is where we find more or less all the information she gives of her childhood, her family, her homeland, her conversion, her arrival in Paris in 1642 and the material difficulties she had up to the time she went to live with her benefactors. But the interior events of her life, which occurred between 1642 and 1648, are also related here in this first account. In it she describes the infused lights she received concerning the grandeur of God, the nothingness of man and the enormity of sin. The visions happened, for the most part, between 1645 and 1648. She then retraces her spiritual itinerary from 1642 to 1653, characterising the successive states through which she passed, but focusing principally on the one in which she still found herself. She then goes on to speak about the Holy Sacrament. It would have been possible for her to do this earlier on in her writing when she was speaking about the lights received from God between 1645 and 1648, above all the effects produced in the soul by the clarifications from above. However, the author preferred to describe the different phases of her spiritual life before treating of the Eucharist, which she considered to be the reason for her sanctification. Finally, she ends this first account with details of the rule she followed throughout the days, weeks, months and years. So it is convenient to give to this first account the following title: 'Autobiography'.

The second account was written in 1654, and its composition must have taken the greater part of the year. Avoiding for the most part a harping back, a reverting to the exterior, biographical events recounted in the first account, Claudine concentrates her attention now on the different phases of her interior evolution, from the day when she was 'touched' by God, right up to the moment she began to write. Beginning with a deepening reflection on her spiritual combat, she then moves on to consider the effects produced by the infused lights, the Eucharist again, and, finally, the Great Darkness. She ends this second account with a slightly developed conclusion, explaining the way she writes. The following passage, then, is an interesting description in her own words of her methodology - being led by the spirit in everything, she writes:

But I saw nothing distinctly, and almost did not know where to begin, having nothing ordered in my mind. Yet, resolved simply to obedience, I set about writing; and right from the beginning up to the end, our Lord gave me a ray of light that made me see clearly and distinctly not only the external and perceptible things, but also the interior affections which I have had to write about in many places, having no other ways of describing my sentiments and my disposition, all of which are expressed through the words I use. For I do not think that of all the words used in this writing, even twelve of them are changed (and never with any change in their meaning); and if they are confused, it is as they occurred to me in my mind, and because they occurred in the soul without doubt in this same confusion. One takes little care in arranging what one says, except to say it with respect and love. As I wrote it on the paper, it was accordingly erased from my mind, making no longer any impression; as if what it stood for did not happen to me, or I did not do it. And sometimes when I began writing, I myself would have difficulty in trying to remember things. But, not being able to do anything without the help of that ray, and doing nothing but fatiguing my mind and being unable to stir almost from my place, I was obliged to stop writing. And the other paper which I have already given to your Reverence has been done in the same way.

The third account would be dated very accurately by the expression, 'since the twelve years that God touched me', if Claudine recalled with precision the moment when the event she invokes happened; which is not so.[27] For indeed, the above passage testifies to the fact that Claudine was not particularly conscious of external details. The second account having occupied more than likely the greater part of 1654, this third account must be dated 1655. In it the author speaks about the mysteries of the life of Jesus Christ and the mysteries of God. From a contemplation of Providence, she then passes to a consideration of the Trinity and the effects and value of the divine action in her life. Claudine retraces anew the spiritual itinerary she has followed, insisting on the lack of knowledge she found in herself with regard to the exceptional character of these states. She has only become aware of them quite recently, because of the effect the different changes brought about in her soul, in particular a slight reawakening of the passions.

The fourth and final account, entitled 'De l'Oraison' in the manuscript, seems to have followed closely on the preceding one; for the slight reawakening of the passions mentioned above is presented here as dating from about a year before, the same indications which were furnished in the third account. Consequently, it seems that one must equally date the fourth account from the year 1655. In it Claudine speaks of the three states of prayer; the familiarities and intimacies of Jesus Christ with the soul; how God speaks to the soul; what disposes one to prayer; the effects of prayer; and the excellence of the divine communications. She had already announced that she would treat in the last place 'of the degrees of obedience in which the soul is tested'. So she speaks finally of 'the communications of God with the soul and of the soul with God'. The last pages of the fourth account serve as a general conclusion to the ensemble of the four accounts.

Of the four separate accounts of her spiritual experience that constitute the full testimony of Claudine Moine, only the first one concerns her life. As we move on in our reading of the other three, we shall see that they are no longer a narrative continuation of the first, but are shot through with doctrinal passages of progressive difficulty in language and thought, each giving way to a continuous and ever deepening reflection on the events of the first account, especially the moment of 'you looked at me'. This, of course, raises the question of whether or not there is an underlying plan to be found in these writings, a plan that is born in the intention of the author from the effort involved in trying to put into language the various levels of personal awareness and spiritual growth. Apart from the basic plan outlined above as coming possibly from her confessor, it is difficult to say whether or not Claudine herself had any plan in her head before setting down to write. She wrote under obedience. However, a very obvious progression in thought is clearly detectable from one account of her writings to another, a development that corresponds respectively to four different levels of meaning. This gives the text its exceptional quality; and of course is not too far removed from the great medieval composition of a work that started off with the historical, or literal account, and then went on through the various stages of the spiritual commentary on it. Hence, we give the following titles to the four accounts which go to make up the spiritual testimony of Claudine Moine: 'Autobiography'; 'Deepening'; 'Light'; and 'On Prayer'.

The question of the authenticity of the text merits attention indeed for anyone who reads it. It could be asked if the only known copy we have is in fact the same as the original. Could it have been touched up by Father Castillon or Abbé de Choisy? This is highly unlikely. For if we look at the various corrected mistakes of the copyist, we see that the document does not carry any trace of having been tampered with. We find no correction written in any other ink or handwriting. Everything gives the impression of a copyist who was attentive and faithful in reproducing the text he had under his eyes. Despite her talent as a writer, Claudine made many syntactical and grammatical errors; she shows herself little concerned about the arrangement of phrases. She cannot have ever re-read what she wrote! As she herself states, she loses immediately the memory of what she writes. She also repeats the same words at very short intervals; she often abuses the present participle; and it is difficult at times to distinguish the personage designated by the possessive pronoun.

A further indication that the manuscript has remained intact is that it is highly unlikely that either Abbé de Choisy, himself a member of the French Academy, or the Jesuits, representing one of the principal foyers of humanism in the seventeenth century, would have tolerated the like of such errors and negligence, if it were not for the fact that they wanted to keep the manuscript as it stood. Father Castillon himself, the addressee of Claudine's writings, would at least have suppressed the passage in which he was referred to as the greatest preacher of the century. Another observation unfavourable to the hypothesis that corrections might have been made to the text would be the fact that the chronological data have not been unified. Claudine, as we shall see later on, lived in a sort of continuous present, and her propensity for exactness in describing her spiritual journey does not always coincide with historical detail. Even the description of her states of soul is at times very vague. The element of repetition may disconcert or irritate the modern reader. But this must be seen as a necessity not merely to put across with maximum impact the moral and doctrinal content, but in Claudine's case to underline the subtle gradations in her spiritual ascent. All in all, the question of the authenticity of the text takes us beyond the obvious into the less obvious, and can only be judged ultimately by a personal savouring of the integrity of Claudine's own word and an expeditious reading of it. And the attitude of people like Abbé de Choisy and Father Castillon to this manuscript at least attests to the fact that these writings have a place in the canon of spiritual literature. Although not a treatise, this spiritual testimony still abounds in rich doctrinal analysis while at the same time satisfying the need for works of popular appeal. Given the dual nature of this work, that is, its spiritual and theological appeal, and in order to assign to it its exact place in the history of spirituality, measuring correctly the originality it contains, two questions must be asked. What were the author's sources? How did she use them? The first question takes us on to ground as mysterious as the text itself. We shall tread warily, then, avoiding every unnecessary investigation of sources, and attempt to outline their presence as helpfully as the history of the text would allow and the reading of it warrant. The second question brings us into a contest with the author and the text, which I shall deal with in the last and final section of this Introduction, struggling with the question of Claudine's spirituality; for, if we believe, like Clement of Alexandria, that the word is the progeny of the soul,[28] then we shall realise that in discovering Claudine Moine we shall find the true source for her work. But first, what were the sources?

Admittedly, no one writes words of this kind on the spur of the moment. But if we want to understand Claudine Moine, it seems that the problem of sources does not present itself to her. For she writes:

I have not learned the mysteries of the faith and religion, and above all, the life of our Lord, from anyone except him alone.

I have not learned by human means nor by the intermediary of any creature the truths which are contained in my writings! Our Lord, in his infinite goodness, has taught them to me himself. That he may be blessed for this forever!

Despite the astonishing claim expressed in these words, one has to assume that Claudine's mind had been formed and her spiritual vision fashioned by all sorts of external influences, some of which she will remember and disclose, and others which, because they are now part of her, she has forgotten. This is quite normal and does not detract whatsoever from the veracity of the above claims. These latter sources can be just as revealing, and patient and often detailed research will discover what they are. Consequently, we are able on occasion to point to particular sources that have contributed to the writings of Claudine Moine. At other times we are reduced virtually to guessing or determining similarities. But some sources are identifiable.

What we have already said concerning the plan suggested to her by her confessor, that she wrote out of obedience to his demands and believed that she was taught by God himself, does not resolve by any means the question of sources. But it does furnish at least the essential indications. Whatever the sources were, by the time she wrote she had so made them her own that they were redolent of her thinking, or she had in fact assimilated their teaching from the prevailing mystical heritage of her day. This brings us first of all to the question of writing through obedience to her confessor and not from dependence on her literary ability. This makes us wonder whether she was influenced by St Teresa of Avila in this: for there are striking parallels. On the question of the inability to write, and writing nevertheless under obedience, the following are some passages to be considered. Claudine disclaims her literary ability - which of course is not justified - and says:

If these writings were to fall into other hands than those of your Reverence, one could be scandalised that a person like me had written them.

More or less the same apprehension is expressed by St Teresa at the beginning of her *Life*:

May He who waited so long for me be blessed for ever. I beseech Him with my whole heart to give me the grace to write this account of my life, according to my confessor's command, with complete clarity and truthfulness. The Lord Himself, I know, has long wished it to be written but I have not presumed to write it.[29]

Indeed, at various stages throughout the writing of her *Life*, Teresa refers often to the fact that she is a person of very little value intellectually and that the work she is doing is well beyond her ability. Of course, the implication is that it is God who is writing through her, once she places herself under obedience. On the task of writing under obedience, Teresa says:[30]

Few tasks which I have been commanded to undertake by obedience have been so difficult as this present one of writing about matters of prayer.

The same difficulties are expressed in the following words of Claudine:

These writings are the greatest proof of it, for I do not know if there has been anything more difficult for me than that, having no inclination for it, and moreover, having lost my memory for all things.

There is a very obvious parallel between Claudine's Preliminary Oblation to her work and the sentiments expressed by Teresa in the first page of her *Life*. And there are two very striking passages from both Teresa and Claudine, displaying their fidelity to the teaching of the Church in their writings. Teresa writes in the *Interior Castle*:[31]

And if there is any error in it, this is due to my lack of understanding, for in all things I submit to what is held by the Holy Roman Catholic Church in which I live, and protest and promise that therein I will live and die. Praised and blessed for ever be God our Lord. Amen, Amen.

And Claudine:

That is all I can say about it [prayer]. I would never have undertaken to make a stroke of the pen on this subject, nor on all that which is contained in this present report if it had not been enjoined on me, because all this is infinitely beyond my reach. And if anything contrary to the faith and the great doctrine of the Church is found there, I disown it entirely, completely ready to retract and to take back what I said, because, through the mercy of God, I am a daughter of the Church and hope to live there and die. Amen.

Claudine mentions St Teresa twice in her work. This is one reason why there is all the probability in the world that she knew about the works of Teresa. This may also account for the striking parallels in methodology between the two writers. But the similarities stop there. For, although Claudine's 'transverberation'[32] is almost a word-for-word repetition of that of Teresa's, as we shall see later, Claudine's spirituality is by no means that of the Carmel reformer. The similarities are no indication, either, that Claudine copied from Teresa. They merely point out that any authentic account of one's own spiritual life must satisfy these two qualities: it must be written under obedience and must not say anything contrary to the teaching of the Church. In fact, these two qualities you find in almost all of the great mystics and their writings.

There is much to be gained from discussing the literary sources of Claudine. She was brought up and nourished in the Catholic religion, and was a boarder with the Ursuline sisters for two and a half years even, but we must first of all say that Claudine came to know about the mysteries of religion through the ordinary means and channels. And although we must marvel at the ingenuity of her words when she says 'there is a great difference between that which men teach us and that which God teaches us', indicating by that, of course, that she herself was taught by God, nevertheless we must not rule out the fact that personal contacts and books were not lacking in her life. They must have influenced her somewhat, providing her with themes and, more important still, a vocabulary with which she was able to describe her spiritual and personal experience although she herself was unaware of it. Further, she confesses to the fact that she read many romances and comedies when she was young. Corneille's Le Cid (1636)[33] was certainly not unknown to her. We have already noted in passing the Corneillean presence in the Marais quarter of Paris where Claudine lived. We shall not be surprised to find the accent of Corneille in her declarations on the spiritual combat she carried out, as she says, with much 'heart'; that is probably a result of her having spent, as she says, a good part of her time reading Corneille's romances and comedies during her younger days, or worldly life. At every instance one finds under her pen words such as honour, generosity, courage and glory, and also others which were in vogue under Louis XIII. In brief, you cannot separate Claudine from her cultural milieu. The text itself abounds in marvellous passages and prayers composed by herself, not the less remarkable for their style than for their strength of thought. It seems, then, contrary to Claudine's own disclaimer of her literary ability, that one must attribute to the dressmaker not only the temperament of an exceptional writer, but also the mind of a thinker.

Towards 1653, she tells us that her daily routine consisted among other things of one or two periods of reading a day. It is legitimate, then, to seek out those authors who could have furnished her either with means of expression (vocabulary, images, etc.) or themes and ideas. The only title of a work mentioned in her writings is the *Introduction to the Devout Life* by St Francis de Sales. Claudine recounts in her writings how, while convalescing after her accident, a Jesuit priest gave her this book to read. Inspired, no doubt, from having read the preface to that work, Claudine will come up in her own writings with the following: 'And if it is true what is said, that veins of sweet water flow through the salted water of the sea without being spoiled'. Following Pliny, Francis de Sales writes: 'Towards the Celandine Isles, there are indeed fountains of sweet water in the midst of the sea.'[34] The dressmaker is indeed less unaffected than the Bishop of Geneva in her use of this image. Another passage from the *Introduction to the Devout Life* which Claudine has possibly made use of is that which concerns the 'retreats'. St Francis de Sales counselled that one should retreat into the wounds of our Lord in order to be safe from temptations.[35] This was the constant practice of Claudine.

But her formation took place above all at church. In Paris, after her conversion, she went to Mass twice daily. It was the liturgy, then, that formed her. The Latin language does not seem to have presented any great obstacle to her participation in the liturgy, for she understood many Latin prayers, which she used to recite by heart. Of course this speaks very commendably for the excellent kind of liturgy presented by the Jesuits in the church of St Louis. On Sundays and feast days, she never missed attending Vespers and, with the élite of Parisian society, listening to the sermons preached at the church of St Louis by the foremost preachers of the day. Ten years of regular listening to the greateast preachers and conferences of the classical period are bound to have left their traces.

Her culture is essentially biblical. The liturgy itself would have provided her with a constant reference to the Bible. Assuredly Claudine would have had a very profound biblical sense, for she had perfectly assimilated the essential elements of the holy books. She names Adam, Moses, Jacob, Job, Tobit, Melchizedek and Isaiah. She uses Genesis, Exodus, Numbers, Deuteronomy, Kings, Tobit, Job, the Psalms, Ecclesiastes, the Song of Songs, Wisdom and Isaiah; and four times she applies to herself the response of Samuel: 'Speak, Yahweh, your servant is listening' (I Sam. 3:10). But the greater part of Claudine's biblical sense goes back to the New Testament, as it should: the Acts of the Apostles, St Paul, sometimes St James and the First Epistle of St John; but above all, the Gospels. One half of her third account is consecrated to the mysteries of Christ. Did Claudine read the Bible directly? There is nothing to prove this one way or the other. A simple missal would have contained these biblical texts, all of which, besides, would have been found in any catechism of the time. And of course we must not forget that Claudine would have been a keen listener to every sermon she heard during Mass on Sundays or feast days.

Would a spiritual person of such calibre as Claudine have totally escaped the attention of her contemporaries, or at least of those who came in contact with her personally? Certainly not that of her confessors! And this brings us to a very definite source in her spirituality. The direction she found with the Jesuits corresponded with the grace she had received, seeing that it was through the Eucharist she says that God had drawn her. Father Castillon had asked her to put in writing the great mercies the Lord had shown her. But even the other confessors were fully aware, as he was, that they found themselves confronted with a privileged soul, a person full of the grace of God. One has only to read Claudine's own words:

My confessors used to say to me that this state was extraordinary and very particular . . . It seemed to me that my state was common and ordinary, like that of everyone else in the world . . . I noticed that my confessors, when I would speak to them of it, would make a case of it, esteeming it very much, and say to me that this state was supernatural and that God gives it whenever he wishes and how he wishes.

There are many indications that this young woman went regularly to the sacrament of confession, although it is not possible to determine with what frequency she did so; that, of course, could vary considerably, depending on what her spiritual need was. All the spiritual directors at the church of St Louis to whom she addressed herself showed themselves to be very understanding and clear about Claudine's need. Their direction of Claudine corresponded exactly to the grace she had received. Her good fortune was to meet a disciple of the famous Father Louis Lallement (1587-1635)[36] when, having arrived at the abstract phase[37] in her spiritual evolution, she began to be troubled about not being able to apply herself any more to the mysteries of Christ. Father Castillon, the disciple in question, did not have to form her; she had already reached a high state of sanctity. But straight away he recognised in her the guidance of the Holy Spirit, about which his master, Louis Lallement, would have spoken to him a great deal during his second novitiate. Lallement was well known by everyone as a great spiritual director.

It was in their knowledge of spiritual matters that Claudine's confessors must have rendered the greatest service to her. And Claudine praises all her confessors for having approved of the way in which she behaved in this regard. For example, immediately after her conversion, which she described so simply in the words 'you looked at me', and finding herself as she says 'constrained by an interior voice to accomplish all her actions through obedience', she wrote a short account which she gave to Father Jarry in order to let him see the state of her soul. She does not mention explicitly any other writings; but as she assures us that she proceeded in this way every time she changed confessor, it is very unlikely that she would have acted differently, for the simple reason that, if one can judge from her own words, the response of her confessors was the same in each instant:

With regard more particularly to the guidance of the heart and the spirit, they [her confessors] only said to me to follow simply the appeal of God.

So, in the guidance of this soul 'touched' by God, a soul simply following the appeal of God, the question must be raised here as to the spiritual sources these confessors of Claudine would have drawn from. She herself writes:

With these feelings, so sweet, so loving, it seems to me that for the first six months I was hardly able to speak, even say vocal prayers without doing great violence to myself. I was ordered to omit such prayers and not to worry about them.

It had to be Father Jarry, her first confessor, who gave her this advice, and who took the responsibility for such a clement and wise solution in a domain that was indeed very delicate. It is not unreasonable to assume that Father Jarry, whose special function in the house of profession attached to the church of St Louis was the responsibility for the material running of the house (this is why Claudine was advised by the sisters of the Annonciade to go and see him when she first arrived in Paris), would have consulted some confrères beforehand. On the assumption that Father Jarry did consult someone, and not just give the advice on his own accord, a reasonable hypothesis would be for him to choose Father de Saint-Jure,[38] one of the principal specialists in these matters in Paris at that time. Conjecture and not certitude seems to be the only basis for this; but there are good reasons for believing that Father de Saint-Jure knew of Claudine's case.

In 1642, the year Claudine arrived in Paris, de Saint-Jure was the master of novices for the first year in Paris, after having directed for sixteen years the colleges of Alençon, Amiens and Orléans. Eight years previously he had published his most elaborate work: *De la connaissance et de l'amour du Fils de Dieu, Notre Seigneur Jésus-Christ*. A number of spiritual writings followed that first work: *Le livre des Eluz* and *Méditations* in 1643; *L'Exercise de la mort et les Conduits pour les principales actions de la vie Chrétienne* in 1644. The following year, 1645, Father Jarry died and Claudine went to Father de Sesmaisons as her confessor. By then Father de Saint-Jure had become the spiritual prefect of the college of the Jesuits in Paris, which might well have facilitated consultations between him and his confrères resident in the house of profession. If Father Jarry in 1642 and Father de Sesmaisons in 1645 had recourse to this specialist in spiritual questions and possibly submitted Claudine's report to him, it is not inconceivable, in fact it is a probable and attractive hypothesis, that he, de Saint-Jure, would have incorporated it into his writings. For Father de Saint-Jure published in Paris, in 1646, a book entitled *L'Homme spirituel*, in which he introduced a report which had been communicated to him, and whose every line and expression have an echo in the writings of Claudine Moine. The account runs as follows:

A pious soul, according to what I have been told, used to practise exactly what follows on this subject. The first thing I perform every day, she says in the report she gave of her behaviour, is an interior act of honour and adoration towards Jesus Christ, whom I recognise to be true God and true man. Then, illumined through faith, and with a profound respect, I look at him with the eyes of the soul, as my sovereign Lord, as my Saviour, my Redeemer and the source of all my good. Afterwards, I fall down before him and I humble myself, lowering myself into the bottom and abyss of my own nothingness. I then abandon myself absolutely to his love, to his wisdom and his power, so that he may accomplish in me and through me whatever he wishes for his glory, remaining in a state of indifference and independence towards all things in the universe, be they in the order of nature or in that of grace, so that I may put myself in a state of being able to receive freely his directions and not be subject to anyone but him. I keep myself as best I can in a naked and pure readiness for all his designs, binding myself through submissions and consent to everything he would wish to bring about in me, be that of joy or privation, repose or pain, light or darkness, riches or poverty, honour or disdain, and yielding to him on that account all the rights I have on my life and my freedom. I declare to him, and I protest from the bottom of my heart that I belong to him and wish to be his, and in all my actions I only act with regard to his purpose; and I do not pretend to have any other will apart from his. Finally, I ask him that I may participate in his spirit, appealing to him to put me into the necessary disposition to accomplish perfectly in me and through me everything he had resolved to do.[39]

Obviously written some time prior to 1646, when de Saint-Jure inserted this report into his book, this short note compares favourably with the writings of Claudine, which were handed over to Father Castillon some years later. Whether it is a question in either case of exercises of piety or ardent love, one will find not only the same ideas but also the same way of expressing them. There is no passage in Claudine's writings that corresponds exactly with this short note, written by a woman, in de Saint-Jure's *L'Homme spirituel*. However, be that as it may, Claudine is certainly included in an allusion in a contemporary text, even if it is not an exclusive reference to her sister or herself. The passage in question is found in *La Vie de la Vénérable Mère Marie-Agnès Dauvaine* (edited in Paris in 1675 under the direction of the Annonciade nuns, who asked Father de la Barre, a Jesuit priest, to revise the work written by them).

Born in 1602, Agnès Dauvaine spent three years at Court in Lorraine before entering, in 1618 - the year Claudine was born and the year in which the Thirty Years War began - the convent of the Annonciades célestes at Nancy, which had been recently founded. Designated four years later for the new foundation in Paris, at the age of 21 she was the first mistress of novices there and in 1635 she became the prioress. When the daughters of Mathias Moine, Claudine and Nicole, settled in the Marais quarter of Paris in 1642, where the house of the Annonciades célestes was situated, she held the office of sub-prioress; two years later, she found herself again elected superior of the community.

This good mother, her biographers say, did not limit her great charity to within the confines of the convent, that is to the refugee nuns [see above for reference to the Annonciades de

Champlitte] who were staying there, but extended it outside beyond its walls to succour those many other people of standing who were reduced to begging because of the social havoc wars bring with them. And so as not to miss out on the principal assistance she wished to give them, she brought them through her exhortations to make a holy use of their afflictions in taking these afflictions from the hands of the Lord who wished to guide them to their salvation through the sure way of the Cross. This is what she taught them in word, while in deed she devoted herself to relieving them in their distress and making their burden that bit lighter. (See *La Vie de la Vénérable Mère Marie-Agnès Dauvaine*, Paris, 1675, p.160.)

All this corresponds with what we know of Claudine and her sister, young women 'of standing', as testified to in Claudine's text, and reduced in effect to having to beg. Every month Claudine and her sister would come to this house, where the Ursulines at Langres had recommended them to go when they arrived in Paris, to receive some help and alms. When Claudine was eventually alone, Nicole no longer with her, instead of entering the house as she did before, she would wait her turn and willingly receive this charity before the eyes of everyone. She would often go to this Annonciade convent to bring back her finished dressmaking work and procure some more assignments to complete. Regularly she would go to fetch water at the fountain in the grounds of the convent. The nuns in charge of the door, who had taken a great affection for her, helped her in whatever way they could. But were there in the vicinity of this convent other refugees answering completely to this description given in *La Vie* of Mother Agnès? We cannot be sure about that. The influence on Claudine of this notable mystic, as Mother Agnès herself was, seems indisputable. And this brings us directly to the problem of sources. As stated above, conversations and books were not without their influence on Claudine; they furnished her with themes and, still more, the vocabulary which she used to describe her personal experience. Apart from the Lord who 'looked at' her and who alone, according to her, taught her, her principal teachers seem to have been, through conversation, Mother Agnès and her confessors, particularly Father Castillon; and through books, Father de Saint-Jure and Catherine of Genoa. The other influences are minor ones, except for the Bible and the liturgy (her daily attendance at Mass and her listening to the sermons preached in the church of St Louis).

Whatever Mother Agnès was able to say to Claudine is the secret of God. But the parallel between the two lives is astonishing. They both followed the same spiritual journey, from the first favours received from God up to the Great Darkness; they both considered the Eucharist as the centre of the whole Christian life; and they both loved the hidden life and prayed especially for the intentions of prelates as well as for the ministers of the word. In the biography of Mother Agnès, there are innumerable passages which could be applied equally as well to Claudine: for example, 'Her maxim was that the whole science of the soul that wishes to please God alone must be to hide oneself entirely from the world; for all that which manifests itself externally in the life of the saints is not what makes them saints' (see above, *La Vie*, p. 3; also, see below, at the end of this Introduction, for the same sentiments expressed in a quotation from

Claudine). This influence of Mother Agnes was probably the first spiritual one for Claudine in Paris, perhaps even the most decisive, for it was only at the end of a certain amount of time that Claudine had recourse to a definite confessor. Her confessors' direction of her merely fitted in with the grace she had received, for she states that it was by means of the Eucharist that the Lord guided her. In this respect, it must be remembered that Father Pierre de Sesmaisons, who directed her from 1645 to 1648, served as the target of criticism for the principal doctor of Jansenism, Antoine Arnauld, who criticised de Sesmaisons for admitting the faithful too easily to communion (see below for reference to Antoine Arnauld's treatise *De la fréquente communion* and how it features in the writings of Claudine). And Father André Castillon, the addressee of Claudine's writings, has left us two works on the Eucharist. His knowledge of spiritual matters did indeed render a great service to Claudine. But like his predecessors, he merely directed the path followed by Claudine more than orientating it in any one way. The initiatives in Claudine's case always came back to the spirit.

With regard to books, however, there is some evidence to suggest that it is more than possible that *L'Homme spirituel* of Father de Saint-Jure was one of the greatest influences on the language of Claudine Moine. In saying this, we are stating that Claudine Moine, when writing the account of her own spiritual journey, was at least acquainted with the leading ideas of de Saint-Jure if not in fact fully conversant with the contents of his book. She may even have read it. In the following passage from Claudine's writings it is easy to give for every expression of hers references in de Saint-Jure's book:

O my Jesus, because you are my prototype,[40] and my model,[41] I wish to enter into the same affections of love, of respect, of dependence,[42] which your very great soul and holy humanity had in letting themselves be led to your divinity[43] . . . Govern me as my head, use me as the cause does its instrument.[44]

The parentage of certain texts is even more obvious from the following:

De Saint-Jure	Claudine
As it is said, the tyrant Mézentius used to put dead bodies to lie with living men whom he wanted to die.[45]	My spirit restrained and enclosed in my body was suffering something of that form of torture which, it seems, they used to make certain people endure, attaching them while alive to a dead body.[46]
All the people of the world with all their pomp, with all their grandeur and all that which renders them commendable, are before God only a droplet of water which remains	Finally, I saw, in an ineffable way, the truth of that word which God said to Moses: 'I am who I am' (Exod. 3:14) and also knew, through the same light, how it is true what

28

at the bottom of a bucket after it has been drained, or as a small grain of dust on scales which is not seen on account of its smallness, and does not weigh anything because of its lightness. They are even in his presence as if they were not there at all, and disappear as mere nothings. (Isa. 40:15.) [47]

Isaiah said, that all the things of the world are, in his presence, only like a small drop of water left in a bucket after it has been purified or, better still, as if they were not really there at all. [48]

In reproducing this gloss of de Saint-Jure, we are able to indentify one of Claudine's principal sources. Moreover, there are in *L'Homme spirituel* many other expressions which Claudine also uses in her writings; too many to point out here. How can one account for this source in Claudine? A possible explanation is to be found in her confessor, Father Castillon. His piety, his knowledge of spiritual matters and his talent as a preacher all contributed to make him Claudine's choice as confessor. And he himself seems to have had, to put it in her own words, 'a very special affection' for directing her. He most certainly directed her reading. Before 1647, the dressmaker was too poor to buy any books. But from the day when her benefactors began to give her her daily meals, she would have been able to put by a little bit of money; and from the time she went to live with them, her modest earnings would have been entirely at her disposal to do with as she wished. Did she buy books? One can never be certain of this. But in the Grand Siècle, in the great houses of that time, works of devotion would have filled the shelves of the libraries. Claudine would have found some of them in her benefactors' house, perhaps the very ones that were recommended to her. As her director, Father Castillon must have broached the question of what she should read right from the first days of his guidance of her. It is highly probable, then, that Father Castillon would have recommended to Claudine a work that was very much in vogue at the time, and also written by one of his own confrères who had assimilated the best elements of French spirituality of the seventeenth century. This then probably accounts for the dozen or more times that Claudine puts into her writings the ideas and expressions of this Jesuit, dispersed in about fifty different passages or more.

Another possible source is St Catherine of Genoa.[49] We mentioned earlier that Catherine's spirituality was a common source for the Annonciade sisters and the Jesuits. So it would not be at all out of the question that the writings of this great mystic influenced Claudine also. The experience of Claudine and of Catherine have many points in common: union and transformation, mystical anaesthesia, sufferings comparable to those of Purgatory, desire for death, divine possession, etc. One cannot avoid the impression that Claudine must have been impregnated with the work of Catherine, to the point perhaps of making unconscious expressions which appear to be reminiscences of her readings, or at least quotes from some of her spiritual directors who themselves, maybe, had read the works of St Catherine.[50] If we were to compare all the expressions of St Catherine of Genoa that correspond to those of Claudine, we would need many pages. Now and then we come across in both writings, as if a refrain, the two words 'union' and 'transformation', used instead of the more usual expression among mystics, 'spiritual marriage'. The parallelism is at times very evident, as for example the following indicates:

Catherine	Claudine
I was so immersed and sunk in the fur-nace of love, so great and surpassing all measurement that, as if I was in the sea, right at the bottom of the water, I was not able, from any side, to touch, see, or feel anything but water.[51]	Thus, the soul, plunging into God, drowns itself and is immersed there all the more. And as that person who would have thrown him-self thus into the water, so the soul sees nothing but God; and in him, through him, and no longer through the medium of creatures, as it used to do beforehand, touches and feels nothing but him.[52]

But there are also considerable differences between them. And possibly this arises from the fact that Catherine did not write her own text; others wrote about her. Hence we find Catherine's text abounding in the account of extraordinary phenomena, which at times is very tedious to read and which attracts too much attention to her. That is not the case with Claudine, and is probably the reason why her writings are characterised by a sober inebriation that brings us closer to her true spirituality.

In investigating the sources, I have avoided drawing any unnecessary conclu-sions, attempting to outline the historical genesis of the text as helpfully as possible for the reader. We have seen at least that this text reflects to a certain extent the spiritual impact that certain people had on the author and probably, in certain literary aspects, the author's acquaintance with particular spiritual writers and mystics. We have detected very striking parallels between Claudine and Teresa of Avila in their similar attitudes to the writing of the text. Both of them strongly disclaimed their ability to write about such exalted matters, and went to great lengths to show that they were writing out of obedience to their confessors. And this last point accounts for the plan followed by Claudine in her writing, a plan born of obedience. Claudine definitely knew about Teresa, for she mentions her twice in her writings. We have also shown how certain people such as Mother Agnès influenced Claudine spiritually, and in particular her Jesuit confessors who had an immediate impact on her day-to-day life and spiritual formation. And lastly, we have considered the spiritual writings which most likely influenced Claudine: L'Homme spirituel by de Saint-Jure, and the life and works of St Catherine of Genoa. But this remains external to the real source, which she herself so gently hints at when she says that, despite the personal contacts and books in her life, 'there is a great difference between that which men teach us and that which God teaches us'. Considering herself to have been taught by God, then, Claudine not only concludes here with the last word on the historical question of sources but, delicately describing the action of the Holy Spirit in her life, opens up a more fascinating one of her spiritual source. So much is her word and herself in her thinking, to recall Clement of Alexandria - where the word is considered to be the progeny of the soul[53] - in other words, where so much of her personality is in her writings, that if we find her true spiritual source, we find the real Claudine Moine. We know that she was born on 17 January 1618, but the fact that she was not sure whether it was the day of her baptism or the day of her birth raises many interesting questions about this spiritual testimony of the dressmaker of Paris.

A spiritual testimony

I was born, or baptised in any case

With these opening words Claudine Moine begins her writing. In them we have the first intimations of her spiritual awakening. An oblique suggestion, they evoke in us something of her own intuition, conveying to us from the start that she has witnessed a new birth in herself, and that her testimony is true. 'Your new birth', we read in I Peter I:23-4, 'was not from any mortal seed but from the everlasting word of the living and eternal God'. Gregory of Nyssa makes a similar observation when he says: 'Such a birth occurs by choice. We are in some manner our own parents, giving birth to ourselves by our own free choice in accordance with whatever we wish to be, whether male or female, moulding ourselves to the teaching of virtue or vice.'[54] Other beings who are born owe their existence in effect to their parents, whereas spiritual birth depends on the will of the person who is born. So, Claudine is telling us that spiritually she has become her own parent, and that also she is going to become her own theologian: her own parent, in so far as she is giving birth to a new life, virtue, a new self, a new home; her own theologian, in so far as having seen God, she can afford to speak about him,[55] thus giving rise to a language that is a reflection on her own spiritual experience, a true testimony to having seen God. Depending therefore on how one reads this text, it can be a guide to the spirituality of Claudine Moine.

Claudine's spirituality is hidden in the very narrative itself. We must search for it. Her writings do not constitute a treatise of any kind; so we do not have a clearly defined doctrine in them. But in discovering her plan we discover her thought. And I believe her plan is to be found embryonically in her opening words, 'I was born, or baptised in any case', and that all her spirituality hangs on the correct understanding of them.[56] For they announce a work that describes the normal experience of a complete mystical development. Beginning with baptism, the whole spiritual life can be regarded as a never-ending restoration of the image of God in the soul.[57] And this restoration can be envisaged in different stages, the first realisation of which results in death to sin and to the passions; the second in death to the natural ways of knowing, perceptible and conceptual; and the third in death to self as the final stage in the restoration of the image of God in the soul, a state in which the soul is as if torn away from itself through love. These three stages of spiritual experience are traditionally referred to as the three ways: the phases of penitence and self-discipline (Purgative Way), illumination and dereliction (Illuminative Way) and, finally, that ecstatic union with divine nature (Unitive Way).[58]

Beginning with these opening words, then, Claudine Moine is announcing not an historical account of her life, but a spiritual testimony to the restoration of this image of God in her life, which had already begun in the event of 'you looked at me', foreshadowed in the opening words of Claudine's testimony: 'I was born, or baptised in any case'. The point is that Claudine's work is not an historical narrative recounting chronologically the various stages in her earthly, human life, as it were, but a spiritual reflection on a reality that has already taken place in her life and has achieved a very high state of perfection within her. Like Dante's person in the *Paradiso* who had been in Heaven and seen things which he had neither the knowledge nor the power to relate, Claudine is going to venture forth in her testimony to recall for us a spiritual journey that challenges every intellect and even her own memory. This accounts for the peculiar nature of her work that brings us in thought and language through all the stages of the spiritual life into the world beyond all knowledge and where only love reigns supreme. This explains the underlying plan in Claudine's writings, bringing us from the Purgative Way, through the Illuminative, into the Unitive, where we are restored to the true image of God in us and become one with the Beloved of our hearts.

Of the four separate accounts of her spiritual experience that constitute the complete work of Claudine Moine, only the first concerns her life. These four constituent divisions of her writings are linked in such a way that the sequential accounts intimate both in language and thought a reflection on a true religious experience, the progress of a soul which only the reader can authenticate. The whole work is a narrative of great complexity in which the main adventures of her life (before her conversion) are interwoven and broken off, and their threads picked up again and knit together repeatedly after what sometimes seems to be an interminable contemplation and reflection on that moment when, 'you looked at me'. In fact, the chronology and underlying pattern of the four accounts in these writings are far more rigorous than a superficial examination might allow. Picking up the threads of thought left hanging in one account, she weaves another episode into the tapestry of her spiritual life. Within each account, though, the narrative is further broken up with passages of commentary or interpretation, frequently in the manner of prayers composed by herself. The reader's interest is sustained throughout by a method involving a series of flashbacks, constantly relating past events to the present, enlightening them with the present knowledge. The style itself is direct, at once dignified and unpretentious. It is a style perfectly adapted to its purpose, clear subtle, analytical, reminding one of much that was magnificent in the spiritual literature of seventeenth-century France.

A mistress of the pen as she was of her passions, Claudine knows how to manage the most elevated ideas without flinching in the slightest and how to paint a tableau uncluttered with useless detail. She does not indulge in flamboyant descriptions. Her intellectual nature would be opposed to that. She is content to describe for us, as best she can, the impressions which the lights she was favoured with by God produced in her. But like all mystics, she has the sense of the symbol. For example, the passions are compared to famished and yelling dogs; she herself to a broken reed. The greatest number of her images[59] are taken from nature: the tulip bulb, the tree which pushes up its roots, the straw, fire, the sun, sea, storm and, particularly, light and darkness. The soldier, the bearer of arms and the horse-rider provide her also, in the context or perspective of her times, with noble images.

Most spiritual literature can be read on more than one level, that of the story proper and that of the meaning it serves to illustrate. The author of these writings, therefore, was not doing anything exceptional in using her own story to clothe and exemplify a meaning that transcended it; she merely did it with exceptional single-mindedness and took it to unusual, even extraordinary, spiritual, nay mystical, conclusions. One can fairly say that she did not write a single paragraph for the pleasure of the story telling. And, it is by no means boring to read what she wrote on that account. On the contrary, it is fascinating; for she tells her story remarkably well, and the fact that every line is subordinated to her central theme, her conversion, enabled her to avoid many of the death-traps of story telling. These writings have a place in the canon of spiritual literature; and although not theological treatises, they still abound in rich doctrinal analysis while at the same time satisfying the need for works of popular appeal. Not unlike Gregory of Nyssa's *The Life of Moses*, Claudine's writings move from the literal or historical stage in the autobiographical section to an ever more deepening spiritual commentary in the three accounts that follow. That is precisely what happens in Gregory of Nyssa's work, where the historical events of the life of Moses are treated in the first part, and a spiritual commentary on those events follows in the second part. So, moving from Claudine's autobiographical account, we see her as living in her vision and her thought in the remaining three accounts that follow. Hence those merely historical aspects of her life with which her writings open and which are contained in this first account, touching upon the ensemble of her life, serve only for further reflection in the three remaining accounts, and for all intents and purposes are the fruit of meditation upon that vision of God: 'you looked at me'.[60] But this plan, if there is one, is, as we have stated earlier, born out of obedience.[61] This we have seen to be the case in the Preliminary Oblation to her work, and it is why, in the general conclusion to her writings, she could utter those remarkable words to her confessor, the addressee of her writings: 'It is now, my dear and Reverend Father, that I can truly say I have put my heart into your hands and rendered my soul visible to your eyes.'

In the true and authentic tradition of all the great contemplatives in history who have written about their lives, Claudine renders her soul visible to our eyes, and tells us in every page of the text how God watched over her at all stages in her spiritual journey. What more should we want from a text? In giving us her written word, she gives us herself, her true self. It is precisely this realisation that establishes in our minds the underlying plan of this text and its exceptional quality as a work elucidating the internal movement of thought and language, the revelations growing ever more intense and acute as one progresses from account to account. And when word and self are espoused to one another in a form of union, the result is an invitation to a journey that seems to shun the obvious and whisper words of warning into our ears against the wordly and materialistic mind, the reductionist attitude that puts all belief in a name, all meaning in a word. For, when looked at from the reader's eye, this text evinces the delicate alliance that exists between word and meaning, and at the same time, while being linked indissolubly in strict contract, recognises that the permanency of the spiritual message to be gleaned from this alliance derives its strength and credibility from the fact that the writer relinquishes claim to the full possession of the reader.

On the assumption, then, that the word is the progeny of the soul,[62] from behind the awnings of time we shall indeed be able to transfer to our own lives what is contemplated through the spiritual interpretation of the things spoken literally[63] in this spiritual testimony from the seventeenth century. 'If these writings were to fall into other hands than those of your Reverence,' writes Claudine, 'one could be scandalised that a person like me had written them.' 'Who could believe what we have heard', says Isaiah, 'and to whom has the power of Yahweh been revealed?' (Isa. 53:1.) Our intellect has gone so deep, says Dante, that our memory cannot go back on it (*Paradiso*, Canto I, lines 6-9), for now only love remains (*Paradiso*, Canto XXXIII, lines 55-6). As in the case of Moses, without any tombstone to mark his grave,[64] the only memory we have of Claudine is her own word; a word like that of Moses in the book of Exodus, which brings us through all the stages of the way of perfection, from the literal to the spiritual with its allegorical, moral and anagogical meanings of the goal of the virtuous life.

To arrive at the goal of the virtuous life involves memory and forgetting, the thesis and antithesis of every conversion or spiritual awakening: for we must recall 'those eyes of infinite and extraordinary mercy' while forgetting the past, as St Paul says in his Epistle to the Philippians (3:13), and striving (*epectasis*)[65] to what lies ahead. But forgetting the past[66] will require a complete turning about[67] so as to face the blinding light, towards the cloud of unknowing. 'Show me your glory, I beg you', asked Moses of Yahweh (Exod. 33:18). Yahweh answered him: 'I will let all my splendour pass in front of you', but 'you cannot see my face . . . for man cannot see my face and live' (Exod. 33:19-20). Then Yahweh placed Moses in the cleft of a rock and shielded him with his hand as he passed by (Exod. 33:22-3), for as Yahweh said to Moses: 'Then I will take my hand away and you shall see the back of me; but my face is not to be seen' (Exod. 33:23). Seeing the back of God and not his face is allegorically understood as the true way to the knowledge and love of God - following through darkness into the light. And for Christians, the same is true of Christ.[68] Led by the spirit and, as she says, taught by God and not by men, Claudine's text embodies its allegorical and moral meanings in the credibility of the story told and the edifying nature of its testimony. Its anagogical meaning is to be seen in Claudine's own written accounts that correspond respectively to the reality of this eternal progress (*epectasis*) in her life as the result of grace, a real witness to the vision of God.

'To be known by God and to become his friend', is the way Gregory of Nyssa describes the goal of the virtuous life.[69] But one does not become the friend of God without paying a price: Abraham was put to the test through many trials before becoming the friend of God (Judith 8:25-7); Moses was spoken to by Yahweh as a man speaks with his friend (Exod. 33:11). To arrive at this state of serenity (*apatheia*) and boldness (*parresia*)[70] before God involves a whole period of testing, as it were a purification and illumination, before being finally united with the beloved of your heart.[71] 'When the Lord has given you the bread of suffering and the water of distress', writes Isaiah, 'he who is your teacher will hide no longer, and you will see your teacher with your own eyes. Whether you turn to the right or left, your ears will hear these words behind you, ''This is the way, follow it'' (Isa. 30:20). This is the way Claudine Moine follows. This is borne out from the very start when Claudine says that 'all of a sudden I felt a great desire for virtue and perfection'. For Claudine Moine, all could be summed up in the words of Gerard Manley Hopkins: 'I am all at once what Christ is, since he was what I am.'[72]

'Purity, simplicity, sanctity, are the luminous rays of the divine nature through which we see God.'[73] The only knowledge of God that we have is that which we have in knowing that we are made in the image of God; and it is purity of heart that shows us that image: 'Blessed are the pure of heart, for they shall see God' (Matt. 5:8). Following Christ is the only way for Claudine to the knowledge and love of God. For 'He is the image of the unseen God / and the first-born of all creation' (Col. I:15). But as Christ 'did not cling / to his equality with God / but emptied himself / to assume the condition of a slave' (Phil. 2:6-7), so Claudine must empty[74] herself in order to find the way and restore the lost image of God in herself. This is the goal of the virtuous life - through serenity and boldness, leading to vision where knowledge concedes to the superiority of love (*Paradiso*, Canto XXXIII, lines 55-6) as the only language capable of describing 'those eyes of infinite and extraordinary mercy' that looked at her and changed her whole life.

Purity united to incorruptibility and to sanctity denotes the participation of the soul in the life of Christ through which it recognises Christ in itself.[75] So this death to sin and to the passions, the *apatheia*, signifies the divine life of the soul in its generality - sanctifying grace, deifying grace. This grace results in the supernatural organism of the virtues. Often virtue evokes in our mind the idea of moral perfection rather than of a spiritual quality. The real idea is that virtue is an emanation of the divine life: 'The rays of true and divine virtue shine in the life purified by *apatheia* which emanates from it: it is the same thing, besides, as speaking about the rays of the sun, the emanations of virtue or of the good odour or perfumes.'[76] We see clearly in this context that virtue is a participation in the life itself of God: and it permits us to recognise him in ourselves. Purity has no meaning; virtue has no meaning except as a participation in the divine life. This doctrine constitutes, in a sense, the foundation of mystical knowledge - being conscious of grace in ourselves: the doctrine of the knowledge of God in the mirror of the virtue, because virtue is the life of God in us. This, it seems, is what Claudine is conscious of when she says that she felt a great desire for virtue and perfection. It was the beginning of the Purgative Way for her. And this launched her on a whole journey of restoring the lost image of God in her soul. For this presence of God dwelling in the soul is proportionate itself to the transformation of the soul in God, that is the restoration of the image. And remember how Claudine, after God 'looked at' her, felt a presence and a power in herself that was new to her. She writes:

I was placed in a new country where I saw so many, such great things that my spirit was as if completely transported.

This new country is the effect of grace, not of philosophy or reason; it is a participation in the life of Christ, a participation in his divine nature. God looked at Claudine first. Gregory of Nyssa says:[77]

Thus, if someone, having gathered all the perfumed flowers in the mottled fields of virtue, has made of his whole life a perfume from the good odour of the works of every virtue, and that he has become perfect, he would not have on that account the capacity of fixing his eyes on the God as on the disk of the sun, but in himself, as in a mirror, he sees the sun.

So Claudine's desire for virtue and perfection comes as a result of God having first 'looked at' her, thus revealing to her his image in her soul; and that image is Christ. Consequently, from this experience, and the subsequent effect of death to sin and the passions (*apatheia*) that follows, comes another aspect of the spiritual life, namely the *parresia*, or familiarity with God.[78] On account of this restoration of the image of God in the soul, the soul now turns to God with confidence; from a Paradise Lost the soul now comes to a Paradise Regained, removing all fear and being now at home with God. The passions that previously troubled the flesh do not exist any more, but enter into a peaceful state where the thought of the flesh does not combat the soul any longer.[79] And another fruit of the ascetical life will be the suppression of shame which took hold of Adam and Eve after the Fall: they will find again the *parresia*, the filial confidence, the familiarity with God.[80] To know and love God, becoming the friend of God, involves the *apatheia* (the death to self and the passions) - leading to knowledge - and the *parresia* (death to any fear or shame in the presence of God) - leading to familiarity.[81] Foreshadowed in her opening words, 'I was born, or baptised in any case', is the birth of a new individual, transformed into the image of God in Christ through baptism; leaving home for a new country, restoring in us the image of God that was lost in the dust of our own existence. Led by the spirit, then, and taught by God and not men, Claudine forgets the past, as St Paul says, and strives to a new country that lies ahead.

The contemplation of Christ, our friend, should accustom us to look at others as Jesus looked at them - that is, from the perspective of their eternity. This all-embracing look of love reaches into the void which is in each one of us and which only God can fill. The hearts of those people consumed with this love are a proof of this. In them we see that a mysterious dialogue takes place between infinite being, truth and love, and his creature. For every mind that is ready to understand it, this fact remains an irrefutable sign that there is a personal God who truly loves us and draws us to himself as to our final end. This, then, is the spiritual testimony of Claudine Moine; and I believe that her word is true. A friend of mine asked me if there was any movement to canonise Claudine Moine. But in answering 'No', I was reminded of Gregory of Nyssa's *The Life of Moses* in which he shows how Moses left behind him on the earth no sign nor any grave as a memorial of his departure from this life.[82] We do not know when Claudine died, and there is no grave indicating where she lies. Her only tombstone, then, is her written word, the only memorial she would wish to be remembered by. And indeed we are indebted to her confessor for asking her to leave this memory of herself, putting her heart into our hands and rendering her soul visible to our eyes. What other canonisation do we need? For her written word frees us to take this text and make it our own, moving from the literal to the spiritual, as Claudine did, beyond home and language to where the self is lost in God, transcended, and the soul is made visible to the eye.

So, a parent of new life, it becomes clear that Claudine's personal encounter with infinite reality in Christ was only one of the two movements which constitute her full life. She must now turn back to pass on the revelation she has received, she must mediate between the transcendent and her fellow human beings. She is in fact called to be a theologian in her own right; and only when she is such does she fulfil her duty to the human race. This is what a spiritual testimony is all about. As her own parent, Claudine felt herself to be an exile in Paris, and considered herself among those strangers and voyagers on the earth who, like the ancient monks, abandon their fatherland and family in their search for their heavenly home. It is the theme of the pilgrim who follows in the footsteps of Abraham, a theme which Origen, influenced by Philo, had strongly developed. Origen says:[83]

Of old it was said by God to Abraham, 'Come out of your land' (Gen. 12:I). But to us in a short while it will perhaps be said, 'Come out from the whole earth.' It is good to obey Him, so that He may presently show us the heavens in which exist what is called the kingdom of heaven. Now we can see that life is filled with contests for many virtues, and we can see the contestants.

Philo writes:[84]

Under the force of an oracle which bade him leave his country and kinsfolk and seek a new home, thinking that quickness in executing the command was as good as full accomplishment, he [Abraham] hastened eagerly to obey, not as though he were leaving home for a strange land but rather as returning from amid strangers to his home.

In the *Spiritual Meadow* of Jean Moschus, we read: 'No matter where you shall be, always say: "I am a stranger."'[85] As in the opening words of Claudine's writings, we also find in St Athanasius's *Life of Antony* the same oblique, suggestive language, showing that his (Antony's) real race was other than indicated: 'Antony was an Egyptian by race.'[86] Antony was indeed an Egyptian by race; but the implication is that he belonged to God by choice. So in the case of Claudine becoming her own parent, she belongs to God by choice. What it is important to point out here about the lives of Antony and of Claudine is that there is a spirituality between them, a spiritual life that transcends all time and space in their respective lives, both witnessing to the one spiritual tradition that has characterised the Christian life down the ages. Whether it was in a deserted fortress on a mountain in fourth-century Egypt or in a room in the Marais quarter of seventeenth-century Paris, we have here in both of these lives real examples of authentic Christian asceticism, witnessing to the spiritual pilgrimage of the soul's journey to God.

Being her own theologian, Claudine is forced to use a religious language to describe her spiritual journey. For, in a text which sets before us the various stages in the story of a soul, outlining the providential action of God in her life, she moves from the literal or autobiographical account to an ever-deepening spiritual commentary on it in the remaining three accounts. The simple description of her conversion, which is narrated in the first of her four accounts, and which takes place almost imperceptibly, denotes a complete transformation in knowledge and love of God. It must be seen as the inspiration, the driving force behind every word of her writings, as she desires to confess, as it were, to the whole world what marvels God had achieved in her soul - her spiritual testimony: 'that unity of witness, which is one of the most impressive facts in the history of mysticism, may reasonably be regarded as evidence of the reality of that world of spiritual values which contemplatives persistently describe'.[87] Thus we are introduced to the mystical theology of Claudine Moine. But let us conclude with Claudine's own words, where she sums up for us what the spiritual life is for her, and conveys to us more than anywhere else the spiritual and theological depth of her knowledge since the time when God 'looked at' her:

I have often thought to myself, that in writing the lives of the saints, people write about everything but what makes saints saints. For they write about the saints' vigils, fasting, prayers, penances, austerities, exercises of exterior devotion and suchlike; and this is not what makes them saints; being nothing more than means of arriving at sanctity. For sanctity in no way consists in these things, seeing that they can be practised by people who are very evil, and often with a greater appearance of devotion than by the people who are truly virtuous. That which makes saints saints is the communications of God with the soul and the soul with God; for it is that which purifies, sanctifies, deifies, unites and transforms the soul into God, in which consists our perfection and our sanctity.

Conclusion

Two reasons guided me in my decision to translate this work. The first is a simple one: the enormous spiritual satisfaction I gained personally in reading it. And if the above commentary on Claudine's words of conversion is any indication of the spiritual richness that can be derived from them, what might be gleaned from the reading of the full text? The work translated in this book is the echo of a personal and authentic spiritual experience. It is personal, indeed, in so far as this work is the private testimony of a seventeenth-century person's experience of God, who, as a child of her time, and describing it to us in her own idiom, reflects the hopes and fears of her own day; but authentic to the degree that it is the inheritor of a whole Christian tradition which makes it possible for those reading this work to feel that they are in contact with a kindred spirit. If this personal experience of God is to be communicated to others for their edification and instruction, and hence to be worthy of being put into writing and therefore helpful and true to the receiver - that is, to those who read it - it must in some way be an expression in accord with the teaching of the Church and must commend itself to Christian reason.[88] On the assumption, then, that this work does square up, as it were, with all these demands, we can be assured that we are witnessing to, and reading the spiritual testimony of, a genuine Christian experience of God that is in tune with, and not a substitution for, the teaching of the Church. In fact, the reader will notice that in the case of Claudine Moine, as in that of Teresa of Avila, the author is always anxious to submit her experiences and interpretations to the judgement of the Church and determined that her full intention be completely orthodox. This is why Claudine regarded her confessor as vital to her spiritual life, and would only write out of obedience to him.

The second reason is this: while pursuing a more thorough investigation of this text's historical background, and delving more and more into an analysis of its spirituality, I have been variously struck by the deep theological significance of the author's thought. This adds even greater interest to her writings: they are couched in the words of a thinker. In a culture like ours today, whose imagination leaves very little breathing space for the use of spiritual language and Christian belief, the genuine analysis and description of the central paradoxes of our Christian understanding and experience become almost impossible. The problem is partly in the area of language and partly in that of belief. In language we see it above all with theologians who do not possess the writer's ability to convey to the world the religious truths they believe in. In belief we notice it in the modern mind's inability to believe any longer in the possibility of a true union between God and man and the sanctification of the world. But it is the combination of these two areas that is the greatest achievement of this text. For both these reasons, then, this English edition of the manuscript will attest, I hope, to the importance of the text, first of all for those who will look for some spiritual nourishment from the reading of it, and secondly for those who will savour even further the theological significance of its author.

So my first duty in translating is to give as reliable a translation as is possible, while being fully aware that there is an obvious loss when any text is deprived of its original language; but hoping, nevertheless, that the inevitable inadequacies of the translation will not obscure the spiritual beauty and theological depth of this seventeenth-century work. Any translation of this kind is bound to imply a certain amount of personal choice, as one cannot include everything; its size alone prevents one from aiming at giving all the experts in the various fields of spirituality the historical background and textual analysis they may look for or need. Because it must aim at providing adequate help for the reader of a general book on spirituality as well as for the reader of a major theological work, I have had in mind the reader who is concerned not only with the reading of texts, but who also wants to benefit spiritually from the reading of such a work. For either type of reader about to begin this work, the most profitable remarks in this Introduction were probably those which best satisfied these two needs.

So the reader has been foremost in my mind in introducing this translation of the writings of Claudine Moine. I have in no way laid down hard and fast rules for the reader to follow in his or her interpretation of the text. The text is too rich for that, and offers to every reader endless possibilities for finding him or herself in every page. In pointing out various aspects of the text as a whole, I have been delineating the particular characteristics of the text that inspired me as I worked on this first English translation. I have aimed, first, to present this fine seventeenth-century French mystic to the English-speaking world; and secondly, to place this important and as yet unknown writer within the history of spirituality. As regards the first, my effort has been to give a faithful rendering of Claudine's text within the limits that a clear English style permits. I have therefore approached my task as a translation of equivalencies: the translation presented in this book has been made with an eye towards being as true as possible to the text while also giving a readable and intelligent English version. I have also tried to remain true to the author's style where possible; but, as the stylistic problems of the French text itself indicate, I have had to rearrange much of the syntax in order to bring out in English a correct meaning of what the author is saying. As every translator is aware of the dangers of traducing the original, I must point out again that many works of this kind imply a certain amount of personal choice. In other words, the translation itself entails a certain interpretation on my part, which means that it is not always easy to be faithful. While striving sincerely not to misrepresent the author, I am also fully aware that, when translating a work of another period, especially one from as far back as the seventeenth century and only recently discovered, I can attempt merely an approximation, a neutral English prose, as it were, that belonging to no specific period, cannot hope to convey the essential vitality of a work which enjoys both unity of word and spirit. Every language has its peculiar ways, and these seldom correspond; so that to be faithful to the content, one is forever augmenting, or diminishing the form. However, in order to facilitate a close reading of the text, and to protect the reader from possible confusion, I have decided to illustrate the text by retaining the titles and subtitles used by Father Guennou in the French edition. Thanks to these, the thought of the author reveals itself more clearly, and her concepts are the more luminous.

As regards the second aim, my Introduction and Notes constitute my own commentary on a text that I consider to be an extremely important addition to the corpus of classics in the history of spirituality. But I hope that I have demonstrated in this Introduction, despite its length, and in the Notes that follow, my own conviction that any ponderous annotations of these writings would in fact severely restrict their meaning. Presumably, in saying this, I am giving the green light to the reader to forget my Introduction and Notes if he or she so wishes, and read the text alone; for, as I pointed out earlier, the best guide to Claudine Moine is her own word. As Bremond says about his task: 'to distinguish the principal religious works of the seventeenth century (texts of devotion and biographies), to savour them, observing them in such a way that they render present and living to us the religious genius which inspired them and whose victories they show us', so I humbly wish to accomplish the same here in presenting this seventeenth-century French mystic to the English-speaking world for the first time; and to do so - seeing that Bremond himself was unaware of Claudine Moine and her work - is for me an inexpressible privilege. I am certainly thankful to Father Jean Guennou for choosing me as translator.

It is exciting beyond words to think that the young Claudine Moine from Franche-Comté, while living in utter poverty and almost complete anonymity, was being nurtured on such food for thought and recollection that forged within her a character of exceptional spiritual strength and vision. When Corneille was trying to portray on the stage of the Théâtre Marais the spiritual life, Claudine, not too far distant, was living that life in reality. This is a fact which her contemporary, Pascal, on the other side of the city would have marvelled at if ever he had known her. They never met. Yet they shared that mystic vision of the seventeenth century which, although they were in opposing camps (Jesuits versus Jansenists), placed them above all controversy by uniting them in that one and abiding knowledge that the heart, united to God, speaks a language the mind knows nothing about.[89] So I wish to present the spiritual testimony of Claudine Moine, mystic: first, in gratitude to her for having put her heart into our hands and rendered her soul visible to our eyes; and, secondly, in thanksgiving for having been given the chance to place this marvellous work among the annals of the greatest classics of Western spirituality, hoping that the reader will find as many, if not more, spiritually enriching discoveries as I have in the life of this great mystic, the dressmaker of Paris, Claudine Moine.

FIRST ACCOUNT

Autobiography

Preliminary Oblation

O my God, God of love and infinite goodness, aid me with your grace to fulfil your will and accomplish now what you desire of me. Accept from my hand all I write as acts of praise and thanksgiving for all the favours I have received from you. It is with confidence in your help, my God, that I undertake to reveal the great mercies you bestowed on the most unworthy of your creatures. And to you, my dear and Reverend Father,[1] I give this account as the greatest witness of my submission to and respect for your desires and wishes, which indeed to me are orders, laws that are absolute.

How God watched over me

Infancy

I was born, or baptised in any case,[2] on 17 January, in the year 1618, in a small town of [Franche-Comté] called [Scey-sur-Saône], of a father and mother of good family and considerable private means. It pleased God to take my mother from this world when I was about 8 or 9 years of age and, even so, the eldest of three children she left behind. My father took great care to make sure that we were given all the education needed to fit us for the world. But he prepared us with much indifference with regard to piety and virtue; for, between the age of reason and that of 12 years, I had already committed more sins than I could ever recall.

My natural inclinations were wanton; so much so that only you, my God, were able to deliver me from them. I loved to play at cards. And as might be expected, to anyone who was willing to play with me I would give all the time I could find. I had a penchant for oaths such as 'My faith!' 'My soul!' and, sometimes, 'The devil!' I would say all sorts of abusive things to the domestics and even beat them; and I would get angry both with them and my brother and sister. Most days I was untruthful and vain, and made light of those who were like myself. And with regard to that which directly concerns the service of God, how often did I fail to hear holy Mass on feast days and Sundays! For remaining in bed late out of an appalling laziness, I would miss the last Mass which, in a little town like ours, was at 10 o'clock. Since I flouted my obligation in this regard, one can imagine my attitude to less rigorous duties.

I received Communion when I reached the age for it. I believe now, that, apart from the required number of years, I did not have what was necessary to do this. I do not remember if I ever had any particular instruction for it; other than, perhaps, being told to read a few prayers in some book. Also, on account of the sins I had not confessed, a confessor I once had said to me that this first Communion was a sacrilege. But others said this was not true, because I had not committed these sins voluntarily. For, O my God, you have always protected me from consciously hiding anything in confession; and it is you alone who know if I have ever had the misfortune of falling into this horrible sin.[3] My God, look at me in pity and have mercy on me.[4]

The beginning of my life having been so wretched - since I cannot see that there was any particular inclination to the good in me then, except for the odd time when, in secret and not too often, I said my rosary and some few prayers, what would have been its continuation and end if you had not looked at me with eyes of mercy?[5] But your divine Providence, already watching over me as a father, ordained, and indeed inspired in me the desire, the desire of a child, that I be sent to a convent school. It was more a desire born out of curiosity, and a wish to change my country, than a desire born from any good inclinations.

School

For several years I had asked if I could be sent to the Ursulines at [Langres] where I had a cousin who was a religious. And so, towards the end of my twelfth or at the beginning of my thirteenth year I was sent there.[6] What gratitude must I show you, my God, for having taken such care of me! Before it was even possible for me to be lost in my bad habits, you made sure you let me know about goodness and virtue; of which as yet I had no knowledge. For, by an act of your particular kindness, you made me love them almost as soon as I knew them.[7] Through your grace, and because of my docile spirit, in less than no time I accepted quite well all the instructions that were given me, despite all my bad habits. For you brought about in me affections that were completely different from what I had known up to then. My God, you were already developing in me a special attraction to mental prayer. My schoolmistress told me of the difficulties involved, but permitted me to practise it sometimes, together with other little exercises of penance and mortification; which I did, it seems to me, with great pleasure. And I am indebted to you, my God, for having given to her a loving concern for my well-being: and indeed for all the other affections I was to receive later.

Desire for the religious life

The first year I stayed there had not passed by before I desired ardently to be a religious. I wrote several times to my father about this, to see if he would allow me to be admitted among the novices, but he never gave his permission. Seeing my desires thus frustrated, I fell ill out of sadness. I was sick for almost three months.

I remained in that little Paradise for very nearly two and a half years.[8] Around the time of my fourteenth birthday,[9] I took a vow of chastity, of which I spoke to no one. It is true that I have since doubted whether that vow was ever valid. But God permitted me to make it then, and in that manner, as a foil to the danger I was to find myself in later. Subsequently, and thanks to God, I made the vow in due form; and I renew it now with all my heart.

Although I was still only a boarder, the sisters had given me their word that they would let me take the habit when my father was willing. But your divine Providence, my God, ordained it otherwise; for you knew well that I would make a very bad religious. My father, having informed the sisters that he wished to be sure about my desires, asked many lay and religious people if he should remove me from there; and there were those who were for and those who were against. But finally, he resolved to take me home for some time in order that I might test my vocation; and he promised to bring me back in three or four months. On his word, then, I returned home with him because it was impossible to do otherwise. And so, with pitiful tears and great chagrin, I said goodbye to those dear sisters.

Worldly life

I spent three or four months in my father's house, continuing my exercises of devotion and leading a rather secluded life.[10] But after that time, my father was asked if he intended to bring me back to the convent as promised. He let me have an answer[11] that shocked my very spirit, for I was told: 'Tell her I will marry her off!' But when I asked if I could have some clothes made for myself - for I only wanted the most modest kind - he did not dare refuse me that.[12]

All I needed now was to go and look for companions elsewhere; as if I did not have enough with him![13] And so, little by little, not having much steadiness in virtue, I returned to the world. For my evil inclinations - which were never really dead, and had not appeared while at the convent for the simple reason that they did not have the opportunity to do so - soon carried me away wherever they wished. Card playing, the reading of romances and comedies, useless or perhaps harmful company - all these were my daily occupations, enthralling me more than I care to mention. No trace of true Christian piety appeared in me any more; and sometimes, if one were ever to speak to me about my previous state,[14] I would become red with anger. For, although I sometimes mentioned that I would have wished to be reinstated into the religious life, I was now completely against that thinking and did, I believe, wish that I had never been there.

Forgetting God

I was for about seven years at the beck and call of that miserable existence,[15] living in such a forgetfulness of God and of the good instructions that had been given me, that I passed entire days without remembering him. I did not serve him any better - I would say, worse - on feast days than on other days, since I still often failed to hear Mass. In this I committed the gravest of sins. After all, my God, who but you would have suffered the dissoluteness of my life and not have abandoned me, hurling me a thousand times into Hell?

War

At this time war was declared between the Kings of Spain and France,[16] and the neutrality which had always been observed in our country[17] was now broken.[18] We were a long time at war before we began to feel the inconveniences of it ourselves; but in the long run we also began to suffer. And when I deeply felt poverty and need, I began to open my eyes and see the deplorable state of my life. O my God, was it not on account of the depravations of my life that I caused the war in our country and the particular ruin of our family? Yet, instead of chastising me according to the rigours of your justice, you let me feel the effects of your great mercy!

'I had my mind elevated to God'

I was in [Besançon][19] then,[20] where my father had sent me on some business. And having been touched in my heart, I made a general confession of my life since the time I had left the convent. Our Lord granted me many graces. From that moment on I began to feel very strongly attracted to prayer. I stayed in that town for three to four months, not being able to return home from there on account of the danger the various routes presented. But just a few days after I made my confession, such a safe way home did present itself that I was unwilling to pass it over.

On leaving the town fairly late, we had only gone a league or so of the road when the Providence of God took extraordinary care of me, in ways which I cannot fully describe because it would take too long. But what I cannot omit saying is, that for the whole night - which we[21] spent without sleeping in a barn in the middle of a courtyard, for we did not wish to enter the dwellings for fear of coming upon the people there unexpectedly - I had my mind elevated to God, and this without anyone, or even the commotion of the journey, hindering me in the slightest.[22] And the prayer I made was to say to him: 'Lord, that your hand may serve me as a pillow, so that, if I happen to fall, I should not hurt myself.'[23] It is possible I repeated this more than a hundred times during the night. I do not know from where I took these words; neither do I know why I said them. But whatever happened to me explains that I had need to make that request. When morning arrived, the whole convoy got ready for departure. Missing the articles I thought I had brought with me for making the journey, I was obliged to accept the travelling case of a captain, who offered it to me with much civility. Not all people of war are bad! But his horse leaped and knocked me to the ground onto a pile of rocks which I did not see as I fell backwards. I was as if dead for more than two hours, so I was told. It is here, my God, I experienced that care of your Providence; for, the whole convoy having gone, I was left alone with people whom I did not know. But you prompted those soldiers not to leave me there. One of them took me in his arms; and without seeing in me, I believe, any sign of life, unless perhaps a little breathing, he carried me straight on for about two leagues of the journey. Later, on opening my eyes, and directing my first thought to God, I said to him from the bottom of my heart: 'I abandon myself within the arms of your Providence.'[24] During my loss of consciousness I saw nothing, I mean in mind any more than in body. But when I came back to myself, our Lord filled me with great light.[25]

I finished my journey in the most remarkable of circumstances. About two hours after I had regained consciousness, and after such a serious accident, I went seven leagues on foot without the slightest inconvenience.[26] But I had to go straight to bed on arrival at my father's house; and there I remained sick for about fifteen days to three weeks. The doctors consulted with one another; and concluded that they should perforate the skull. But I was resolved to die rather than suffer that; and so they left me in peace. Since then, thanks to our Lord, I have not had any further trouble.

During my illness a good Jesuit priest - a holy religious - came to see me and gave me *The Introduction to the Devout Life*[27] to read. This did me a certain amount of good. But in no way did I begin to put my life in order; for through lack of direction, and there being nobody to encourage me, I was very faltering in virtue. But I thank you, my God, that you removed me from the occasion of sin because of the poverty which prevented me from re-establishing myself in company and in my former ways of vanity.

Sickness

Soon after I was cured of that sickness it pleased God to visit me with another one. On the feast of the Exaltation of the Cross,[28] the good Jesus let me participate in a portion of his Cross. But, O my Saviour, I still did not know well enough the value of that treasure, even though you had already planted in my mind some slight knowledge of it. As it happened, I was taken with a fever[29] that lasted till November, so that I had it for about fourteen and a half months. I experienced this illness in every possible way during that time; unremittingly once or twice; and on one particular occasion it lasted for eighteen days. I felt the cold so strangely for the first seven months that the shivering and trembling used to last for six or seven hours at a time. I do not understand how a body like mine was able to withstand it. There were many people sick that year. But they were sick off and on, sometimes being well for a complete month or so and then falling ill again. But if I had really understood it then, my Saviour, I would have realised that you treated me much better than all of them; for I never had one day of respite.

This sickness was accompanied by such great poverty that I was without any relief whatever; for the affairs of the family were becoming worse and worse as the days went by. My Jesus, you gave me the grace to endure this patiently, and all its circumstances. And also, for almost ten months of my sickness, I do not think I desired a cure even once. Eventually, however, I did prepare some rather drastic treatments; but did not have the means to continue with them.

I suffered that pain, my God, with a virtue that was indeed mediocre; for I did not accept it with that great joy, that love with which one must receive suffering. Through your great mercy, however, you prevented me from committing any sin in this! Having been rid of the sickness, I was left however with its after-effects; which I felt for a long time and, perhaps, still do.

Letter to the Ursulines

Finally, not seeing our way of putting our affairs in order, we, my sister and myself, desired to leave home and work as domestics while waiting for a peaceful end to the war. With this in mind, I took the opportunity of writing to the Ursulines. For it happened that some people from [Vesoul], who were being sent as hostages to the Count of [Grancey] until such time as the amount of money which their town had agreed upon with him was paid,[30] had to pass through [Langres]. For on account of the war, and all communication having been destroyed accordingly, it was about four years, I believe, since I had last let the Ursulines have any news about me. I conveyed to them, then, the state of affairs and the plan we had to work as domestics.

The sister who was superior then had been my schoolmistress when I was there. She always had a great affection for me. Although she was sick when she received my letter, she wrote back to me herself, saying that we should get someone to take us to her and that, while waiting for a situation to be found for us, we could stay with the sisters in attendance.[31]

Having got this assurance, we prepared ourselves for the journey. And the sisters on their part summoned some men from the town to find out from them whether our being received there would present any difficulty.[32] The gentlemen informed the sisters that we would not be allowed to enter. This troubled the sisters very much, and they wrote me many letters, telling me not to leave our country. But our Lord - who knew well what he wanted to do - saw to it that I did not receive any of the letters apart from the one in which the sisters[33] had advised me and my sister to come.

Departure

We left home, then, in February, on the twelfth day of the month, I think it was, in the year 1642. On our journey there, the good God let us be robbed by peasants. The person who was driving us, on seeing this, fearing that once at [Langres] we would raise objections and not pay him, because we were saying that he was on the side of those who robbed us, left my sister and myself - together with two young women who had come along with us on leaving our homeland - completely destitute in the middle of the countryside. We did not have the least idea of which road to follow.

I accepted this setback without any worry, at least, not that much. And, already being accustomed to turn to divine Providence, we now had full recourse to it; for with regard to human assistance, we saw no trace anywhere. O my God, that you may be blessed for ever, for the care you take of those who hope in you!

A man came along who brought us to the nearest village,[34] which had only a few inhabitants. Fortunately, inquiring if any people of good birth were there to whom we could speak, we found a young lady who was living in that place with her father and who happened to have been at the Ursulines with me. When I introduced myself to her and told her my name, she recognised me and received us all with the utmost expression of charity and friendship. But she and her father, having lost everything, were so poor that our hearts went out to them. She gave us whatever she could, and with such heart that even that alone would have been sufficient for us. We spent the night there. The next morning, she and M.   ,[35] her father, having conducted us a certain distance along the road and offered us what little money they had, sent us on our way. We said our goodbyes to one another, feeling deeply our mutual afflictions. And thus your divine Providence, my God, succoured us in that need. May you be ever praised for that!

Arrival at Langres

We had only four or five leagues to go to [Langres], part of which we did on foot; for, passing through a certain village, we took a cart which brought us to within one league of the town. That good young lady had given us a guide to lead us; and it was you, my God, who were directing us, you who were waiting for us at the gates of the town in order to let us enter. For we entered without anyone saying even one word to us.[36] We arrived at the sisters; seeing what pitiful state we were in, they were deeply touched. They received us there with all the demonstrations of love and charity possible; and they gave us whatever clothes and linen they could, for we had nothing.

After we had remained there with them for five or six weeks, I urged the superior to give some thought to what was going to become of us. The whole community, and she in particular, had so much charity in them that they offered to keep us permanently; but, for good reasons we did not wish to accept. They had at least the intention of sending my sister to Dijon, where we had a relative who was a religious; and when they wrote to him about my sister, he offered to take care of her. They intended keeping me with themselves. But having only recently come out of our homeland and away from all our relatives, my sister and myself could not agree to this separation.

Those good sisters said many prayers and offered up their Communions to know where they should direct us. And one day the superior came to me and said that it would be necessary for us to go to Paris since we did not wish to stay with them; and that we would find there - more than in any other place - what we were looking for. Paris has such a bad reputation in the provinces - but without reason - that this proposal troubled us greatly. But after some encouragement, our voyage was decided upon. The sisters summoned some gentlemen from the town, who were to leave in the same coach as we were, to come to speak to them. They beseeched the gentlemen with great affection to take care of us. Having relatives in religion, these men received well the request made to them. Your divine Providence, my God, ordained it that the sisters had this foresight. In this way you wished to deliver us from the peril which, as you only knew too well, we were bound to find ourselves in.[37] For although they were people of position and honour, if these gentlemen had not known us at all, perhaps they would not have helped us as they did. For this may you be always blessed!

Dangers on the road

So we left [Langres] on Holy Thursday, 17 April 1642. On Easter Sunday,[38] in a market town,[39] where our coachman had stopped to feed the horses, we met with a great number of soldiers who came at once to speak to the gentlemen and the coachman about having us. Dismissing completely such a proposition, the gentlemen let them know that we were ladies of position and honour and entirely different from what they imagined. And they had sent a soldier to us to come and ask us to stay with them, and to tell us about the attractive qualities of their lieutenant, on whose behalf they were bringing us this message.

We trembled with fear at such a horrible proposal and immediately rid that soldier of the hope of having from us what he desired. He said to us as he went away: 'Since you do not wish to comply out of friendship, you will be made to do so out of force.' The people from the inn came to us to tell us that we were done for and that the soldiers had resolved to carry us off. O my God, only you knew the anguish of our hearts! And I believe that never before had I prayed to you with such affection and confidence as I did then. Not knowing really what to do, all in the coach were greatly distressed by all this.

As we left, there were fifteen or sixteen men on horseback, and as many on foot, who accompanied us; for they did not wish to treat us violently in the village, but at a half league or more from there, where we would not be able to have any help. On seeing this, the gentlemen in our carriage made them return immediately; one remaining in the coach to look after us, while the other, who had found out where the lieutenant was, went to him - for it was he who was responsible for initiating all this, although he himself never appeared - and complained about the disgraceful intention of his soldiers, saying boldly to him: 'If any dishonour is intended, it will be necessary to kill us all, because we shall never fail to complain about it to the King, and nothing less than your head will be at stake.'

The lieutenant was greatly taken aback, made many excuses and wished to come and apologise to us. But this gentleman said to him that it was not necessary, and that he should merely prevent the evil the soldiers intended doing to us. The lieutenant then gave an order to his soldiers that no one was to be so bold as to dare approach the coach, and that they should leave us to go in peace. Thus, my God, you delivered us from that peril through the care of your paternal Providence; for which I render you infinite thanks.

Paris

We arrived happily in Paris, on 23 April[40] where as ever you took care of us by directing us to a good place, seeing to it that we happened upon good people for our lodgings. Also, that was what we needed most; for it was said to us that this is where we would run up against the greatest dangers. The sisters had given us many letters of recommendation so that some position could be procured for my sister. This did not help in any way. And seeing the difficulty there was in finding something which would suit her (because, never having been a domestic, she was unable to do much of what had been asked of her), we sought work in order to earn our living. This we have had for a long time now, all because of the sisters from our own homeland who are here.[41] We, my sister and myself, found accommodation which we paid for monthly. We lived like that for two years.

'You looked at me'

After some months in Paris,[43] not having brought with us very much money, we began to be in great need. Out of concern more for my sister than for myself, since we were unable to earn enough from our work in order to feed and house ourselves, I resolved to find someone who could help us in our need. At last, beginning to put all my trust in you, my God, with great affection I asked your help.

I was directed hence to Father [Jarry],[44] who listened to me with great patience and charity. He put many questions and requests to me, to which I responded with great innocence. Out of pure charity - for we had never been recommended to him by anyone - he promised to take care of us from that very moment. I then stayed behind to make my confession to him, more from temporal interest than from any other desire. For besides, I never had a regular confessor.

What he gave us - together with the little we were able to gain from our work - helped us to survive and no more. We led a very retired life, working continually as long as work was available. You decreed it so, my God; you reduced me to this in punishment for my laziness, which had been so great up to then that I was incapable of doing in a year what one, working moderately, could easily have done in a month.

We were about one year[45] in Paris when, O my God, with those eyes of infinite and extraordinary mercy, you looked at me;[46] for which, my Lord, I am exceedingly grateful to you. I do not know what day or month it was. But well I do know, that all of a sudden I felt a great desire for virtue and perfection.[47]

You made me see the enormity of my crimes and the abuse I had made of your grace. I saw the punishment of the damned; I saw above all the pain of damnation.[48] The sight of this lasted with me for about fifteen days; and I do not know why, in seeing such a terrible thing, I did not die. Such great confusion had I about my sins, I dared not lift my eyes; such a living sorrow, I was always at your sacred feet, my Jesus, like a weeping Magdalene, hating the chaos of my evil and miserable life. This vision of Hell did not frighten me; for you have never guided me by fear, but by the way of love. Truly, I would have preferred to be there rather than have offended you.

51

Knowing that it was because of your mercy you did not hurl me there, kindled in my heart such a fervent love that I was completely consumed by it. Though I provoked you to it a thousand times over, you preserved me from that dreadful evil of being forever the object of your hatred (for I was not in the least concerned about the other evils) and gave me time still to love and serve you. I would willingly have made my public confession before the whole world.[49]

The knowledge I had of my weakness, after having received so many graces, gave me a great fear of falling into my sins again; and, developing an acute distrust and despair of myself, I put all my confidence in you.

You made me see the excellence of suffering and poverty, and how you had introduced me to these out of an excess of love. From that very moment I loved my plight, my condition, but was unable to thank and praise you enough for it.

I would dearly have wished to enter again upon all the afflictions of my life, bearing them all with the knowledge I now had; and turning them over in my spirit, I would have suffered them now out of longing and with affection, desiring for my whole life no other portion than the Cross. I would have seen them, not as a punishment, but as very great blessings and special favours in those whom you inflict them upon. This has stayed with me up to the present. I have been unable to see what one calls punishment and affliction as anything more than a very great blessing.

If I had a thousand crowns and as many sceptres, even a million worlds, I would have left them all in order to embrace holy poverty; and seeing myself placed there by you, my God, I would have felt myself all the more your debtor, taking great joy in observing it at your pleasure and in holding fast to your preference for me.

You made me see the care your divine Providence took of me, to the point that my physical disabilities were seen by me as signs of your love; for, having a strong propensity for flattery and vanity, these bodily deficiencies kept me very firmly back from committing sins I would have otherwise committed; and ever since, I have loved those deficiencies very much.

In order to serve you, O my God, so rich in mercy, you made my intention so pure that I have not turned my eyes since to myself or my interests of body or soul, temporal or spiritual, of time or eternity; for in offering myself to serve you, it was without condition or reserve that I said to you: 'My God, do with me what pleases you. If you wish, give me something or give me nothing; to me both are the same. I know well, and I believe it, that you have a Paradise and a Hell, but I want to ignore them both in serving you. It is not to have one and avoid the other that I serve you.'

My sovereign Lord, you placed my will in your will so that I could wish for nothing else but the accomplishment of your good pleasure in all things.[50]

You infused me with an ardent longing for Communion. This was the means whereby you drew me to yourself and granted me many graces.

I received also, from your generosity and infinite goodness, the desire to avenge you of the injuries I did you; and putting a stop to all my evil inclinations, with resolute courage I undertook the destruction of my evil nature.

You gave me such great light to see this evil nature, its meanderings, even down to its smallest movements, that I was incapable of ever being surprised by it; you gave me such great strength to resist and subjugate it, that I have no recollection of ever having yielded to it. Whenever it did oppose me, I became so emboldened, chiding it all the more, that next time it did not dare disapprove, fearing indeed a worse treatment.

In short, my God, you granted me so many graces, I would be unable to recount them all.[51]

I began therefore to regulate my life. And having been in that state for some time, I was pressed upon by an interior voice to seek guidance and let my actions be led by obedience. So I wrote a report, which I gave to my confessor, letting him know the state of my soul.[52]

I asked him if I could receive Communion on the Thursdays that were not feast days, which he permitted. But, because of the ardent desires I had for Communion, this was not enough for me. So he also permitted me to go more often. However, for as long as he lived, I only went regularly to Communion three times a week, and sometimes four.

Continuous prayer

I began to practise mental prayer; but only for a half-hour every day. At first my confessor raised some objections as to whether he should allow me to do it; but in the end he was willing. O my God, you were my master in this holy exercise; for, although I had been given some start in this when I was in religion,[53] I can truly say that I learned it only from you. And it is here, O supreme Goodness, that you made me feel the effects of your greatest mercies, elevating my mind from then on in a continuous prayer. I was almost two and a half years, or so, in that initial stage. And I do not believe that, during all that time, I was twenty-four hours in all without being continually in prayer, united to you through a mental activity that was personal and intense - although in different ways - and which nothing in the world could keep me from. With those feelings, so sweet, so loving it seems to me that for the first six months I was hardly able to speak, even say vocal prayers, without doing great violence to myself. I was ordered to omit such prayers and not do myself any harm.

Favours from God

But your caresses increased, my Saviour, when I approached you in that most Holy Sacrament, allowing me so many liberties[54] with your divine Majesty that I suffered an extreme confusion because of them. Lovingly, and with great strength, you would draw me sometimes into the wound of your sacred side so that I could make my abode there; and other times you would allow me to put my hand into your sacred heart so that I could fetch there the virtues that were necessary for me. And asking these virtues of you with respect and confidence, I immediately made interior acts of them; and at once this habit remained in my soul. Moreover, I must really say, my God, that it was you who performed these acts in me, there being nothing there of my own apart from my consent. And to tell the truth, I did not even know what was meant by interior acts. But through your mercy - since I had given myself completely to you so that you could do with me, in me, to me, and through me whatever would have pleased you - you made up for my ignorance and poverty.

Activity of mind

One day, my dear Master, you said to me: 'Think of all the things in the world that could give you pain, and be resolved to suffer them.' Picturing to myself, then, all the misadventures that could happen to me, I saw, among other things, how being sick in hospital would have disturbed me most intensely. For although I was in love with poverty, I would have feared it in this way. To have been accused of theft and my honour thereby questioned, would have been very distressing to me. To see my homeland[55] entirely ruined would have been something very hard for me to bear, not having been divested yet of that natural affection. And others still! But these were the principal ones you wished me to work on. Immediately, through interior acts, I began to dispose myself to accept with good heart these misadventures, whenever it would please you to send them to me. All this was happening inside myself; but see, it pleased God to arrange for them to come true!

I hardly spoke to anyone any more. I was not able to do so on account of that great activity of mind I was involved in. I constantly tried to keep myself in the background; but living in one room with many other people, the only chance I had was in the evening when, under cover of darkness, I could sigh and cry without being noticed. For, from that time on, my Lord, you gave me the gift of tears; which has stayed with me ever since. My sister, however, seeing a great change in me, used to say to me sometimes: 'I don't know what has come over you, but you are becoming silly!' Indeed she could well say this, and with much truth; and especially since they themselves held no other state than that which, at the time, I only held in name, leaving their condition to enter into that of the angels.[56]

Separation

A new position turned up for my sister which we had not looked for.[57] But divine Providence wished to take her from me so that it could complete within me what it had begun. My sister accepted the position with much reluctance. Willingly, I resigned myself to this separation, and indeed to be separated from all other creatures whenever God would have wished it. On the day she was about to leave, I fell ill. The previous day, if I recall, I had the first indications of it, so my sister did not want to leave me at all. But urging her strongly not to lose the opportunity through any delay, I made her agree to go.

Sickness and poverty

So I was sick with a continuous fever, with shivering and vomiting, on and off experiencing it with a great intensity; it lasted for seven days. I had but little money; and after the first and second broth that was given to me, I could afford no more. My landlady had the good heart to go and speak on my behalf and ask that I be admitted to the parish charity.[58] But she was told that, since I did not have a room on a permanent basis (for I only paid for my room monthly), no such charity could be given to me; that it is never distributed to those who live as I did, and that I should see to it that I be brought in to hospital.[59] When this word came back to me, I received it with great joy. Having been well prepared beforehand for this misfortune, I did not fear it in any way, but rather desired it with great longing, taking unprecedented pleasure in seeing myself sleeping in a bed with five or six poor people - which is ordinarily the case - or on a piece of straw in some corner of the street. However, it was only the desire for this that our Lord asked of me. Whatever it was my landlady said to those ladies concerning me, I do not know; but they must have changed their minds, for they sent one of their sisters round to see me, and following on this the doctor came, and then the ordinary services which it is their custom to give were sent to me. The Reverend Father[60] was in the country and did not return until after I was cured.

Calumnies

Not long after that sickness some old clothes were stolen from the landlady, for which she blamed me. Not that she said that it was I who had taken them; but seeing how well I got along with those who did steal them, which was one and the same thing, she threatened that she would make me pay for them or else have me put into prison. I went to find my confessor, who said to me very coldly: 'Enough! Let this chatter drop! Are you incapable of suffering a harsh, evil word?' I said to him: 'It is not because of this that I have come to you. But she is threatening me with prison.' 'Ah well!' he said, 'when she arrives at that point, we shall apply the remedy to it.' And thus he dismissed me. How salutary, my dear Master, your warnings were to me! Not even one ounce of its tranquillity did my spirit lose. In my defence I said what truth obliged me to say; and then I remained in peace, being well satisfied to suffer that. I even had sentiments of affection for that woman; and I would have served no one more willingly than her.

I have continued ever since to have these feelings of affection for those who are unpleasant to me. And for a long time now I have never failed to pray to God every day in particular for those people who have offended me - intentionally or unintentionally; be they even my close relations. For in truth, the injury done to themselves in offending is often greater that that done to us who are offended. While praying for the souls in Purgatory I have a particular inclination to pray for those who, if indeed there are any of them there, would have been disagreeable to me in any way. The motive which inspires me to do this is to imitate our Lord praying on the Cross for his enemies.

The only way I could be of some service to that woman was, in the morning when she was out, to clean her bedroom and wash her dishes. And ever since the time of our quarrel, whenever I met her little boy, and precisely because his mother had offended me, I would give him great kisses and sometimes money so that he could buy something for himself. I was drawn to this with feelings so strong, so loving, that I would do it with great jubilation of heart.

For my honour's sake I must say that a certain person, to whom we[61] had never given the slightest cause for displeasure, and whom we just barely knew, spread the blackest scandals imaginable about my sister and myself. My heart and mind were the same in this mishap as in the others.

One day I was told that [Scey-sur-Saône] had been burned. As a matter of fact, the suburbs were.[62] I was as sad about this, as doleful I suppose as one should be about the sufferings of one's neighbour. But seeing it as part of God's plan, I accepted it gladly.

Fearing nothing but sin, and desiring nothing more than that the will of God be always accomplished, I cannot imagine anything that might happen to me or take place in the world that would trouble me.

Temptations

After that, our Lord changed the state of my soul.[63] He permitted me to be assailed by the greatest and most furious temptations, so that for the space of about two years, I was as if in Hell. The first was against faith. I felt that there was no God. Then anger, despair, blasphemies so horrible assailed me that, sometimes, I dared not open my mouth in prayer to God, fearing that I would curse instead of praise him. Unseemly temptations of such strength and violence even assailed me so that I was reduced to inconceivable straits. The exercises of devotion were as horrible torments to me. I believed myself to have been abandoned by God. But however, my Saviour, that was not so. For never have you guarded me so well and held me in your all-powerful hands, preventing me from falling, as during those crushing torments. I did not understand that then; I could not even have imagined it.

You gave me great weapons to fight the powers of Hell which you had released against me. At first I wished to argue against the temptations - which is what one should never do. But our Lord, having pity on me, inspired me to fight them through their opposing acts of virtue - which is what one should always do. In this way I remained ever in prayer; and although it seemed to me that these acts had no vigour, they had the force of preventing me from succumbing to temptation. My God, you also gave me a great simplicity in telling my confessor the troubles I had, without disguising anything, no matter what shame or confusion I might have had concerning them; such a great desire and firm resolution to obey him and do whatever he would ask of me that, doing exactly that, through your mercy, I was delivered unharmed from those dangers.

You put at the bottom of my heart such a hatred of sin and such a firm resolve to die a thousand and one times rather than commit one, that all the furies of the demons could not make me fall. This did not rule out the fact that I suffered cruel torments as a remedy for this temptation against modesty.[64]

56

O my sweet Jesus, what shall I say about your loving kindnesses but that they are extravagant and infinite! For the first seven or eight months - mainly when the temptation was at its fiercest - you kept me continually in the wound of your sacred side without the slightest possibility of my moving from there.

From the moment I woke on the morning of the feast of St Thomas the Apostle, I was in such extremities because of this temptation that I cried out inwardly with all my force: 'O my God! where are you?' Seeing myself in such a strange state, I thought I was abandoned. Rising promptly from bed, I was not any better during prayer. In church I found myself even worse. And during Mass - at which I intended receiving Communion, and now had in mind not to, all of a sudden someone spoke to me in my heart: 'Courage! This is only to prevent you!' And being urged on more and more, I ardently longed for Mass to finish so that I could receive Communion and have some help.[65] Our Lord did not appease in any way this horrible tempest, but, to add to it, rather let me be further tormented with the thought that I had committed a sacrilege. All that day was terrible for me. When evening came, I saw Jesus Christ on the Cross; and he, drawing me to himself and putting my mouth into the wound of his side, said: 'Drink and take from here the forces that are necessary for you to overcome all the pain and suffering that may come your way.'[66]

To dwell in God

Another time, as I longed to receive Communion - or having received it; I do not remember precisely - I felt myself to be elevated to Heaven above all the choirs of angels and presented before the throne of God where Jesus Christ was. Through my enchantment, he first pulled at my heart. Then, this enchantment intensifying, he had me placed in the midst of his sacred heart; and finally, the enchantment increasing for a third time to the very depths of that same heart, I said: 'I shall remain here so that I may save myself from the persecutions of the devil and the flesh.' And you shut me up there so that I might never again leave. My Saviour, that is the way you helped me with your great mercies. May they be always praised! Consequently, because of the confidence I had through union with you, three or four times you allowed me to see all Hell under my feet.[67]

Destitution

During that mental affliction I was also thrown into a state of extreme poverty. For our Lord permitted that the Reverend Father [Jarry] would not continue to give alms to me any longer. For my entire food I only had a little bread and water, and some fruit and a little cheese which I still used to buy so that I would not give any reason for talk to those with whom I was living. They might have said that the only thing I ate was bread. When I first went to Father [Jarry] he ordered me to tell him whenever I was in need of anything. This I did from time to time in order not to disappoint him in what he asked me to do. And whenever he had nothing to give me - which happened fairly often - I had as much joy in this as when he had something to give me, all my pleasure and contentment coming from the fact that I was completely destitute and depended from day to day, or rather from moment to moment, on divine Providence.

I did not speak about my needs to anyone, not out of shame, but because they were dear to me. And if I had the choice of all kinds of life, I would have taken none other than the one I was in; which was all the more pleasing to me because it was God who put me there. Seeing in this the order of his Providence, and that it was he who arranged those plans for me, I had no difficulty in accepting them and seeing them fulfilled. Sometimes I asked for bread, having none; and in finding some for dinner,[68] I did not worry about the evening, quite happy to have nothing in order to depend on and to hope continually in you, my God. I was like this at various times for about a year to fifteen months. And yet, my God, out of your goodness there was increased within me a desire to suffer, so great that I do not think I could ever describe it. With such a vehement desire, all troubles are delights; and when one desires to suffer, one suffers no more.

Mortifications

To these unsolicited afflictions I was driven on instinctively to add some that were voluntary. For about two or three winters I rarely went near a fire. I was always dressed as if it were in the middle of summer, having only one outfit for all occasions. If it was only some water I had, I would have had what was sufficient for me. Yet, O my God, how strange your ways are! You granted me such a great desire for mortification that I even rationed what water I did have. So that I could cut back on the water, I bought a little container especially to drink from. Though I was seven or eight years without ever drinking any wine, I was ordered to colour the water in order to drink it. In this way I managed - or at least very often - not to satisfy my thirst for about two years. And what is more, I drank nothing at all on Fridays. At meal times I would say to the Eternal Father: 'Receive, if it pleases you, this little water which I offer you with the purest blood of my heart, and the greatest affection of my soul, and give it to drink to your only Son who died from thirst on the Cross. Receive it also with his precious blood that it may clean the stains and blemishes of my soul.' I was nearly eighteen months without drinking at all on Fridays. Thirst is a very painful suffering. I do not know on which occasion it was that I spoke of it to my confessor. But well I do know that he rebuked me very fiercely for it; forbidding me to do it again, he commanded me to drink to the full satisfaction of my thirst. And so our Lord wished that I suffer that martyrdom no more.

I had a great longing to do penance. He[69] only permitted me to do very little, which distressed me a lot. But the desire to obey has always prevailed over all the desires which God has ever granted me. Never did I find anything as difficult as having to obey in this; particularly when, seeing all the sickness, poverty and suffering of people, and I myself having such a strong desire to suffer, I would have wished to wrest it all from them by force and bring it all down on myself. So I have had no envy since then for anyone other than for those who are suffering more than I am. Realising sometimes that there would be no Cross in Paradise, I felt no desire to be there. Ordinarily I would say to myself: 'To suffer is preferable to Paradise.'[70] I was frightened of death, for fear of losing out on suffering. Well, my God, may you be blessed forever for all the graces you have granted me!

I believe it was about towards the end of those two years of spiritual suffering - during all that time I had my lodging on a monthly basis - that our Lord put me in a bedroom all by myself. I had real evidence that such was his will. It was not, however, so that I could be there alone that I took the room, but in order to take back with me my sister who was anxious to quit her position for a very understandable reason, and on account of which I myself also thought she should leave. However, the problem resolved itself and she did not leave; and I was alone. Your divine Providence, my God, ordained it so in order to complete more easily what you had already begun.

Torments

Before shutting myself up in that bedroom which was a Paradise for me, I must say how our Lord put an end to my internal pains. So I was beaten down strangely by those temptations - and also by gluttony, which I have forgotten to mention. But our Lord used to give me powerful help for this from time to time - rays of that light with which the angels sometimes console the souls in Purgatory. I believe that I was more or less in my pains as they are in their torments; where, because they wish entirely what God wants, they are in peace and content - although cruelly tormented - and their joy does not diminish their sense of pain in any way. I was more tormented than troubled. I said before, that sometimes I was able to fight these temptations with opposing acts of virtue; but very often it was not in my power to do so. I suffered then the most extreme anguish; and it was with this bitterness I resisted temptation, without doing anything beyond sometimes speaking out loud a few words of renunciation.

Insight into the Lord's way

Our Lord finally gave me an insight into his behaviour towards me. For these temptations had been in order to punish me for the sins I committed related to them. Having lived as an atheist and without Christianity, it is reasonable that I should be persecuted in the truths of the faith and afflicted with dreadful thoughts that there was no God; with those blasphemies, for all the swearing I did; with those impurities, for having lived with so little self-control and modesty. And so for the rest.

Seeing now with what great kindness God prevented me from being lost, I could not understand how it was possible for anyone to be damned, saying to myself: 'Certainly, if God acts thus for everyone, how is it possible for one to be lost, seeing that he puts so many impediments in the way?' I was for many days with that insight; following which, however, God let me see the malignant character of our nature. O, how I was seized with astonishment on seeing such a terrible thing! I could no longer imagine how anyone could be saved. I realised very well what is said so often, that those who are damned are damned from their own malice - for God certainly abounds in such infinite kindness towards us and care for our salvation that we can never excuse ourselves in his presence - and that those who are saved are saved out of the mercy of God alone.

From that time on, God took from me both the vision of my sins and the knowledge of how he guides me. Since the time he touched me I had this vision of my sins almost continually, and with such a sharp and extreme pain that I am astonished I did not die because of it. I have never seen these sins again, except for the time I made a general confession to Father [Castillon].[71] For immediately after confessing my sins (which God made me do, I believe out of a particular providence, so that this man could know, according to his heart, the state of my soul) I had no more knowledge of them.[72]

In solitude

It is time, my God, that I enter that bedroom which your divine and loving Providence prepared for me. When they brought me the key, you, O my sweet Jesus, put into my head the idea that I should go off in front of the most Holy Sacrament and present it to you, declaring that I have received it from your hand and beseeching you fervently to be so kind as to enter that bedroom with your Holy Mother and your foster-father, St Joseph; that I should enter that room as your poor, little servant with the sole intention of serving you and fulfilling scrupulously all your wishes. Having made my offering, I went off with myself to that bedroom as the servant of the divine family.

As long as I remained there on the strength of my intention and the declaration I had made, whenever the time for paying the rent would come, some days beforehand I would say to the Master of the house with simplicity and very great trust: 'Lord, if you would, please pay the rent! It is not I who owe it; because the servant who runs up the debt on the order of the master is in no way responsible for it! It is up to the master to release the servant from such a debt! I am here because it pleases you, and not on account of any reason of my own. What do you want me to do? Should I beg? Indeed I am quite prepared to do so. Is it necessary that I should work? In that I shall not spare myself. Just give me your order, and I will carry it out to the full.'

What a strange thing it is, the way Providence takes care of those who confide in it and who, out of a good heart, wish to depend on it! Money was always there, just when I needed it. And yet, even when I was worried about it, I never asked for any. It is my belief that if my rent money had been given to me before the date due, I would not have taken it, so much had I the joy and pleasure of waiting for it from the goodness of God. I would dearly wish that all poor people would avail themselves of this method. Indeed, it is the best of all ways that one might take.

Now I was so poor that, when I myself would go to seek water at the Annonciade,[73] and sometimes at the fountain,[74] I did not even have the money to buy it; not even something to put it into, except a bottle which had been given me. I took great pleasure in this exercise of poverty and humiliation; for God made me recognise his own good pleasure in that. Nevertheless, after one year in that place,[75] as some means had been given me whereby I could buy the room, I was planning to do so. But our Lord on one side and my confessor on the other prevented me from this, pointing out to me that I should always hold on to the natural practice of poverty and humility in the way I had always done during the period of the three years I was alone - except, during that time, for the few months I was with M. de   .[76]

Many times there[77] I had no bread. In that case, bowing low on my knees, and abandoning myself completely to him, with profound respect and great love I would adore God's designs for me; I used to say to him: 'What does it matter to me, my God, what does it matter to me what state I am in, provided that your will is done and all your plans accomplished!' O ineffable goodness of God, how great you are! If only I could make you known to the whole world, so that everyone could render you infinite acts of thanksgiving! By means of a powerful attraction, God drew me to himself; and I could really say: 'My God, my all![78] You are everything to me!' For indeed, God was my food, my fire, my clothes and all my fortune; and in an indescribable way I found in him all things. For about one year or so, and without any help from anyone else, God himself provided for all my necessities. Often I would ask of my body if it was content with this way of living.[79] It would respond: 'Yes', and that it longed for no other one. It is not that I was completely without food - although sometimes I had nothing at all - but I had so little that, in human terms, I was unable to live on it.

Sometimes, my good God, you granted me the grace of seeing myself in your arms, being showered with kisses and embraced more closely and lovingly than a mother or nurse,[80] crazy with love, would do for her little infant. You made me understand that, as long as I would confide in you I would never want for anything. Moreover, I feared nothing. Not even now do I fear anything except the turning away, no matter how little, from the fulfilment of your wishes.

The death of the spiritual father

It was around this time that Father [Jarry] died.[81] I felt this so deeply that the loss of all my goods, the removal from my homeland, and generally all the losses I ever suffered did not affect me as profoundly as this did. Consequently, I suffered a great loss; not with regard to worldly goods - for he no longer gave me anything - but because he took great care of my progress and perfection, doing me the kindness of never letting me live according to my own sense and judgement. Thus, because of the care he had taken of me, with our Lord's grace, throughout the whole period of my temptations I never let up in any way on my devotional exercises. I loved him in a very unique way, and feared him a great deal. His charity was great, entirely selfless; for in all the assistance he gave us,[82] we had never been recommended to him by anyone.

For a long time, his death was painful to me. I thought that this wound would never heal. But it was also for me an occasion for exercising submission to the orders of God, conformity to his will, and detachment from all creatures. And no matter how afflicted I was, even if only one word was needed from me to bring him back to life again, I would never have spoken against the will of God. This is indeed horrible to contemplate! But I would not have given one hair of my head, if it meant that in so doing the will of God would have been fulfilled less, no matter how little. For my wish is that it be accomplished perfectly. I think I had been with him for about three years, or a little more.[83]

Second confessor

I had been going to confession to Father [de Sesmaisons] for about seven months when he[84] died. He had gone on a journey and remained away for almost four months. And immediately after his return, he fell ill and was sick for a long time. I returned to Father [de Sesmaisons] during his illness, and remained with him after his[85] death; with much difficulty, however, because I found a great difference in his[86] treatment of me from that of Father [Jarry's]; not that it was not good, but everyone to his own way! He allowed me to receive Communion more often,[87] and ten months before his death,[88] he let me do so every day. He was more liberal in his penances for me than the person I had lost, which pleased me, I must say, a little. I am very much indebted to his charity; for greatly did he give it to me. And after I had become more accustomed to his way with me, I would not have changed it for anything in the world.

So I dwelt thus in my little room (I have described it elsewhere),[89] not leaving it at all except to go to church and sometimes to the Annonciade, where the sisters who looked after the door used to help me in whatever way they could. At all times, apart from my time for prayer, I was working; and in my work my spirit was exceedingly united to God.

Providence

One day it happened that a lady for whom I was working went off to the countryside without giving me anything to do, and having worked for her for a long time, I said to myself: 'What am I going to do? I have nothing at all!' Nature is so evil, it is always asking for something. All of a sudden, our Lord, responding to that question, said to me: 'What are you afraid of? Since the time you took on responsibility for my service and left me as the one who was to provide all the necessities of your life, have you ever lacked anything? Have I not provided for all your needs with a providence that is very special and particular? If you are not happy with what I have done, tell me what you wish me to do, and I will do it.' This reproach made me look into myself and take note of my thoughts; for it was part of my nature not to reflect much. Blushing with shame before our Lord, I said to him: 'My God, I am indeed very miserable for having had those thoughts, especially after so many proofs of your kindness! Well I can say to you, as your Apostles did, that I have wanted for nothing since I put all my trust in you.[90] Well, my God, never again do I want to have any more concern for myself, leaving it entirely up to you!' And it pleased you, my God, to grant my request. So much did you take away from me any care or thought for myself that, if the essential things were not given to me, I would have been incapable of seeing to them.

A desire of nature

As I am very disabled (being in continuous pain for the past fifteen years except for about fifteen days, yet, I do not think, perhaps, I have ever been forced to stay in bed any more than a few times) I know that I once said to myself: 'I must go into partnership with someone!'[91] Indeed, this was so that someone could take care of me. This is not contrary to devotion. And likewise, responding again to my thought, my dear Master, you said to me: 'Who is this that desires this in you? The flesh or the Spirit?'[92] This made me see clearly that it was a desire of nature. I said to you: 'O my God, I do not wish to become partners with anyone but you!' And, by your goodness, you drew so much to yourself all my affections that I have never been able to have a particular friendship with anyone, neither to love nor to desire anything of a purely natural or human affection.

End of the solitude

It was during my first year, it seems to me, when I was living in that room, that my name came up when the sisters in attendance at the Annonciade (where I went very often) had been to visit Madame de   . I do not know how; for I never made myself visible to the world. Her ladyship,[93] who is a very wise and honest young woman, asked them to beseech me to come and see her. I had never seen her; neither had I ever heard one word spoken of her or her house, which is a very significant one indeed.[94] But this is because I did not frequent anyone. I was troubled a great deal by this, not knowing how I was going to resolve it. I had never sought any new acquaintances, being quite content the way I was. Nevertheless, since they insisted upon it, I went there. Her ladyship gave me a great welcome, making me promise to come back - which I did, in order not to renege on my word. Madame came into the room where the two of us were, and her ladyship said to her that I was the person about whom she had spoken. Madame, who had a truly Christian virtue, gave me a great embrace. I left that house very afflicted indeed, and with the intention of never going back there again, seeing that they made too much of me.

But your Providence, my God, ordained it otherwise. For, a few days after that, they resolved to send me my daily meal, which I accepted; but subsequently I cried, fearing that I had contributed something to a withdrawal from the poverty in which I lived. I went to them to beseech them not to do it, for fear that it would do harm and cause their servants to complain. But my prayer had no effect whatsoever. Everyone in that house, without exception, was so partial to this that each person contributed individually whatever he or she could to it; although I still had not seen them or they been obliged to me in any way. The daughter who had charge of all this carried it out with wonderful charity, as if despite me, or at least without my having to do anything other than accept. I was provided for well beyond my needs. I gave much of it to the poor; which I did heartily. They gave me this charitable help for a year or a year and a half before I went to stay with them.

Madame gave me work to do,[95] which necessitated my having to go there now and then. Finally, wishing to go to the country with a daughter of hers,[96] Madame asked me if I would ever come and stay in their house in order to look after things when she was not there; which I did. I was there for three months. The very day they returned from the country, I returned to my room, even though they wished me to stay on with them. The following year I was also caretaker of the house in the same way. Their charity to me grew and grew every day; and finally they kept me there in their house permanently. Worrying little as to whether I should or should not have accepted, as long as I was where it pleased him, I pass over in silence all the resistances I made to this and the many tears with which I beseeched our Lord to reduce me to eating grass like the beasts, if it were really necessary, rather than be in a position where I would have to accept something contrary to his wishes for me.

Father [de Sesmaisons] died at this time.[97] And having been directed by your divine goodness to Father [Castillon],[98] I learned from his mouth your will; which was all I wished to know. It is true that I loved that little solitude. But I also had no attachment to it. For all places and situations are the same to me as long as I am put there by your hand.

The spirit of poverty

I thank you, my God, for the sentiments and intentions you inspired me with then, and for the graces you granted me afterwards. And abandoning myself entirely to your directions, my God, with profound respect I adored then the orders of your Providence for me. I entered that house so that your wishes for them[99] and for me would be fulfilled. For them they were fulfilled since it pleased you that I serve them as an example of one who, while suffering, exercised continually the virtues of humility and patience; and while being at ease, charity, generosity and mercy. For myself they were fulfilled since it also pleased you to arrange my needs in that way, so that I could submit myself to your sacred orders and receive them in a spirit of poverty without seeking there in any way my own interests and comforts. I have not noticed, even since I have been there, that I have changed place, employment or dwelling; because attaching myself strongly and entirely to the accomplishment of your good pleasure, I have neither seen nor felt anything else. I render you a thousand acts of thanksgiving, my Lord, that these sentiments and intentions have not left me in the slightest.

All the feelings of my nature were such that they were submitted to your orders; and my soul, attached to you, did not communicate with its natural sentiments.[100] Just as when I had nothing to eat and you fed my body with a meat[101] that was not its normal sustenance, I could not complain; so in the same way, when in fact you did give my body everything that was natural for it in order to sustain it, through your grace you attached my soul so strongly to yourself and to the fulfilment of your will, that looking for nothing, and throwing away whatever was left over, I felt no taste, no delight whatsoever for all things visible and of the senses. That, my God, is one of the great mercies you showed me; and for it may you be always blessed![102]

You put me in a state in which I saw, spoke, conversed, drank, ate and yet did all these things without feeling or satisfaction from nature; but in what way they made an impression on my soul, I do not know. You put me in the world and at the same time conserved me in solitude. Creatures were to my eye as if they did not exist. So I was not concerned with the thought: 'What will one say?' I did what I saw to be your desires for me; and since it seemed to me that there were only the two of us in the world,[103] there was no going back to what I had left.

My God, I feared that I would lose poverty. But you taught me how to practise it continually. Everything that was given to me I received in that spirit of not belonging to me. And never even once have I been at table that I did not go there as a poor person to take as charity whatever was given to me, recommending the poor to you and thanking you for having provided for me so generously in all my needs. In the beginning I preferred the coarser pieces of meat, not indeed out of mortification, as was said of me sometimes, but because they were the poorest pieces. You then made me realise that I should not exercise any choice, all the time like a true, poor person who has no choice at all, but who takes whatever is given to him, avoiding in this way any sign of being different - which is what one should always do.

After all, my God, when you put us somewhere, there is nothing to fear. You know well how to keep us there without any harm. I thank you also that I had no disagreement there with anyone, except what amounted in the end to less than nothing. But I lived in great friendship with everyone.

Transition

This has been the brief summary of how God, from the interior and the exterior, watched over me.

Imprinting certain truths on my soul, elevating it and placing it in a state of great purity; he let me realise that once they were acknowledged and practised by me they would cut the roots of sin. I do not pretend to speak about them in order, how they came to me - not being able to remember; but only how they present themselves to my mind now.[104]

I received in my mind a very great light

God, the sovereign Lord

Many times I have seen God to be the source of all goodness, the eternal and necessary good. This vision gave to my soul wonderful feelings in making me detest with horror all the sacrilegious thefts that are committed in regarding creatures as good, or in attributing any good to them. I used to suffer with great pain when I would hear it said, or when I myself would say, 'This person is good, is holy', or something of that kind. Of course this is our miserable way of speaking! For it seems to me that one should say instead: 'God is good and holy, and he makes a little ray of his goodness and of his sanctity shine', or any other attribute you would wish, 'in such a person, his creature.' I thought that, by some miracle, if it were possible to find in a creature some good he could regard as his own, I would wrest it from him with a lively force and replace it in God, its proper abode - where it belongs. In him I see the good; in him I wish it to be. I indulge in extreme self-satisfaction in knowing that it, the good, is there, and that he himself is the sovereign Good.

The supreme grandeur of God

About three years had passed when it pleased you, my God, to fill my mind with the knowledge of the perfections and attributes of your divinity; and of your supreme grandeur, above all. Now about this vision - I can say nothing that would make one understand, except by way of the sentiments and effects which it produced in my soul.

Since then I have always been amazed that it is considered such a great act on man's part to submit himself to God freely and offer himself to do his will. I do not understand the foolishness that makes it necessary to think in such a way in order to be induced to this act. On the contrary, it would be up to us to speak about it to God so that he may deign to accept our services and homage; seeing that - having regard for his grandeur and our baseness, and he being an object of very great admiration - it is only right that such a majesty should have plans for us. O how I adore with a profound respect all the designs he has for me! I consider myself to be fortunate, holding it to be a great honour that they be entirely fulfilled, no matter what they might be. If it were to be for me like Job, on a heap of dung[105] until the end of the world, it would always be a matter of the greatest honour that God would even deign to think of me!

I have a very great joy in seeing the distribution God makes of his gifts to his creatures, in nature and grace as much as in glory; for in that shines forth his magnificence and his sovereignty. But in so far as it concerns me, it is incomparably preferable for me to be the last among all creatures, and to be entirely submissive to him, than to have that which they consider to be great and excellent and yet to render him less submission. And you know, my God, how often I have said to you, that if you were to give me the choice of all bodies, of all souls, conditions and employments, in short, of all things, I would not wish to have any of them other than those you have given me, considering it a great honour to have what I have through your choice rather than by my own election.

And moreover, I say, that in order to acquire all the graces, virtues, degrees of perfection, sanctity and glory, and to have them to the extent in which God would wish to give them to me, there is no sort of pain or labour I would not willingly suffer. But, if only one word was necessary in order to have all the perfection and glory of the saints, I would not pronounce it, preferring indeed to be at his service and disposal, to be the last of all creatures than to be the first and thereby lack in this, no matter how little.

To serve through love

This vision of the sovereign grandeur of God kindles such a great love in the heart, purifies it so much of all self-interest, that if one had never received or never would receive any benefit from God, one could never refrain from wishing to serve him, and would feel sufficiently recompensed that he deigns to suffer the fact that one adores him and loves him. If I knew through some divine revelation that I was damned, and if I believed in this as firmly as I believe in the truths of faith, I would in no way wish to leave the service of God, so that I could accomplish at least in time what I would so unhappily be unable to do in eternity.[106] How often have I desired and asked God that he put me at the gates of Hell until the end of the world so that I could keep them closed and prevent the demons from leaving there and coming to tempt people. And through the magnanimity of that ordeal, in thus preventing people from falling in, I might contribute something to their knowledge of God so that they would be as submissive to him through love as they are through necessity. Sometimes I have even desired, and would still heartily wish it at the present moment, to be stripped of all the gifts and graces which God has given me - provided I would not offend him - and that they be given to Kings, Princes and persons who have the power to demand that he be served, so that they would do so.

These, then, are some of the effects which this divine vision has produced in my soul, effects which remain imprinted there, never to be erased. Immediately, and for some years, this vision continued to last for me; and having no words for it, I can say nothing about it. Sometimes however, I had this vision with such intensity that I felt myself to be melting away like wax before a fire; and throwing myself on the ground out of love and respect, I would say to God: 'Stop, my God! Stop! This is not bearable for a person in my mortal condition.'[107]

Man's final end

I have seen how this great Majesty has created man to serve him and to love him. O, how this knowledge has given such generous sentiments to my soul! This truth, understood correctly, not only detaches one from, but endows one with such disregard for all the things of this world that one cannot look upon them any more without holding them in contempt. O man, if you but knew your excellence and the end for which you are created,[108] you would see how you pull yourself down and demean yourself infinitely as you go in pursuit of the things of this world, be they crowns or empires! For, what is all that for the person who can possess God?

If one wished to give me the empire of Heaven and sovereign domination over all the angels and inhabitants of that grand kingdom, it would not touch my heart! Desiring him as he is, all perfect and infinite, I say that my heart would not be happy even if - although impossible - there could be some diminution in any one of God's perfections and I were to possess it in that less perfect state. But also, having him, I freely and willingly give up all the rest to whosoever wants it, holding all other things to be so much beneath me, my esteem and my love, that I would regard them as pure nothings.

O, what astonishment seizes me, my God, when the thought enters my mind that you have made man principally to love you, asking of him nothing beyond that! Sometimes I say to you: 'O God of majesty, do you know who you are and who we are?[109] If you had made us to serve you with all the baseness and abjection possible, keeping us grovelling and crushed before you, like serpents and worms, would we not be highly indebted to you? But having made us to love you, you also ordered us expressly to do so - that is what I cannot understand; and it fills me with such love that I am really distressed that I have only one heart, one body and one soul to be employed in this! For if I had all those hearts, bodies and souls that you have ever formed and will for all time to come, I would dearly wish to use them all in loving you.'

Jesus Christ, Master and model

Another truth, my God, which you have wished to let me know about, and which caused in me great sentiments of love and gratitude, is that you have given us your Son to be our Master and model for the practice of virtue and sanctity. This infinitely restores man. If God had declared to us his will and given us his commandments only through a fly and an ant, we, without doubt, having regard for his infinite grandeur, would be obliged to pay strict attention to them and to die a thousand times rather than contravene this. But to have given us his Son instead is a witness of his love to us and an inconceivable honour for us! I knew, then, that all our good, our honour and our glory consisted in becoming more like Jesus Christ, since he is our Master and our model. I cannot understand, therefore, the actions of those Christians who desire and pursue with such assiduity the things which put them in a state that is quite different from his.

I know well that the goods, the dignities and the honours of this world have to be possessed by someone, divine Providence ordaining it so; but those who do possess them must, it seems to me, be in great confusion, being in a state that is so dissimilar from that of our Lord who, instead of making a vain display of them, has shown such disdain for all such things. When I hear that certain people are praised because they are comfortably rich and magnificently housed, or that they are fine persons, it seems to me that I blush with shame for them; for what relation have all these things with the life and example of our Master, who was born in a stable, who led a life that was so humble and hidden and who died on the Cross with such pain and infamy? Certainly none.

That is why, if God were to permit me - which I beseech with all my heart his great mercy to prevent - to attach myself firmly to a state which would be considered important in the world, I would doubtless have more shame and confusion that I can say. And moreover, I can only think that one might say: 'The poor shameful people.' What, my Saviour - to be ashamed of marching behind you and carrying your livery?[110] Such is the excess of our misery. For my part, Lord, I wish, through your grace, to follow you step by step, embracing with all my affection your poverty, your suffering and the contempt the world has for you. And if one asks why do I do this, I shall answer that it is out of honour and because of the great esteem I have for your doctrine and example, and in order to render myself entirely true to you in love and gratitude for what you have deigned to show me as your will in what I should do and in what I must abandon.

Pure nothingness

One day, as I drew near to receive Holy Communion, I saw a great abyss before me. Looking at it attentively, I penetrated it with my eyes right to the centre of the earth. I did not know what it meant when it was explained to me that in such a way God wished to construct an edifice of perfection in my soul, and that it was necessary to have a deep foundation; that what I saw was the image of my misery and my nothingness. In that vision, throwing myself thus into the abyss of my nothingness, I had this thought and said: 'Lord, may this puny grain of dust be placed at the feet of the whole world, and may this nothingness remain in nothingness and never become visible!' O my Saviour, I thank you infinitely, because since that time - and although it must be already more than eight years - it has pleased you to hear my prayer. You have always kept me in that nothingness so that, especially at the beginning, if someone had asked me, 'Who are you?' I would have answered, 'Nothing! - What is your name? - Nothing!' And so for all questions that were asked of me.[111]

And it is also true that we have nothing of our own except pure nothingness. When one says of man, in order to humiliate him, that he is a worm and a grain of dust, one surely says more of him than he is; for even his nothingness he cannot call his own. This knowledge is the cause of great good, absolutely preventing one from ever attributing anything to oneself. This knowledge was given to me in such a forceful way that I was no longer able to see - and still do not see - whether I have a body or soul, being, substance, form or measure.[112] But submerged in that nothingness, I often said to God: 'Since it is a peculiarity of yours, O great God, that from nothing you create something, make of this nothingness something great for your service, some rare work of art from your hands, a finished and accomplished portrait of your Son.'[113]

Self-knowledge

It was already some time after this had happened to me that, all at once, I received in my mind a very great light. It made me understand, that to be so in the presence of God - in that feeling of nothingness - was a sort of pride, and that of myself - since nothingness does not resist God and is in no way evil - I had nothing but sin, which is much worse and infinitely more contemptible than mere nothingness.

O God of goodness, it pleased you to open my eyes in order to make me see that which belonged to me, that which I could call my own, what I was capable of doing - which is sin. For I see and confess innocently before Heaven and earth, that I have in myself such a great core of malice and corruption, and that left to myself I would commit all the sins that have ever been committed. So if I do not fall into sin, it is entirely due to your goodness and mercy which prevent me from doing it. For this I am infinitely grateful to you.

Since that time too, I began to consider myself to be below not only all rational creatures, but also beasts - for through sin I have debased myself more than they; and even more, below Lucifer in Hell. For although I have not committed all the sins necessary for that place, I know perhaps that I could have; and indeed I am still capable of committing them, if it were not for the fact that God has held me by the hand. Consequently, no matter what fault or dissoluteness I hear about, I have never the slightest contempt for anyone. But it humbles me before God to know that I myself could have committed them. For if God had let me have my way as much as he did with those people, doubtless I would have done worse. Indeed I have great compassion for them.

One must confess that vainglory and complacency only come from great blindness; because on account of how little we know of ourselves, we are always safeguarded against the slightest trace of them in us. I have often had difficulty in understanding what is said about St Paul, namely that he was tempted in order to keep him humble, for fear that, on account of the great knowledge he had, he would have exalted himself.[114] For it seems to me that there is nothing which should humble us more than those favours and gifts which God grants us - for he deigns to throw the precious stones of his grace into our mud and mire which is for him an extreme goodness, a supreme kindness; and for us - receiving as we do that which does not belong to us - a reason for very great humiliation. O, what fear I had that I might see these graces, experience them and regard them as in any way belonging to myself! But God granted me the grace which I constantly asked of him - that I return them to him as pure as he gave them to me; for which may he be blessed! I would dearly prefer never to have them at all than to be a thief.

Nature and grace

Another intimation which has been given to me on that subject is this: we cannot have one good thought or accomplish the slightest action by ourselves. This shows how unjust and evil we are when we attribute to ourselves the good which we do; or to put it in another way, that which God accomplishes in us. For it is he who gives us the thought, the desire, the strength, the body, the soul and all that is necessary to carry it out. It is true that, of our own will, we make use of all these things in order to do this good; but we put so little of our own into it that it is indeed reasonable enough to give all the glory for it to God, since he wants all the profit from it for us. Let us add to all this, that the merit of our works is due to grace; for no matter how good our thoughts may be naturally, if they are not ennobled by grace they have no value and are in no way conducive to our holiness.[115]

I have elaborated upon these thoughts which God gave me of my baseness and extreme misery; because I value this grace more than any other he has granted me, for it has been the cause of great good for me and has guarded me against very great evils. I have known through experience that, provided that we have confessed frankly and with openness our poverty and our misery, he holds us strongly by the hand to prevent us from falling. And whenever, feeling any movement of passion or anything else, I had recourse to him, I would say to him: 'O my God, I realise that if you were to give me all the graces you have given to all the saints, it would still take only one moment for me to fall from that state and maliciously become Lucifer! This is why, Lord, keep me always in your protection; protect me from such a fall and punish my sins with such chastisements as please you, but preserve me from having them punished through other sins, which is so terrible! My God, if it is to make me fully aware of the fact that of myself I can do nothing but fall - that I know well; and I have enough experience of it.' Whenever I had recourse to him in this way, our Lord has never let me fall. Confidence in him and distrust of ourselves will always secure us against all sorts of dangers and preserve us from every fault.

We can conclude that we should never attribute to ourselves any good, since it is very true that a creature who in no way participates in the goodness of God would almost be as evil as he [God] is good, so great is the malignancy and corruption of our nature.[116]

St Paul is very right in calling humility the virtue that is proper to Christ.[117] It seems to me also that it is only Christ who humbled himself. All his grandeur and outstanding features are proper and essential to him as God and rightly his due as man on account of his unity with the divinity. He lowered himself, took on our infirmities and the appearances of sin. But I do not see how we - who possess only nothingness, a powerlessness to do good, an inclination to evil and where the value of any work we do is due to grace - are able to practise this virtue. Humility, according to what I think, is to lower oneself more than one is obliged to do - which is what in fact we can never do. But what we can do is to practise justice and truth, to touch nothing of what appertains to God, and to recognise our misery. It is extremely important to be well aware of this and to practise it. The more one does this, the more one has confidence in God, and the more one enjoys a purity of conscience.[118]

The enormity of sin

I have had unusual insights into the enormity of sin. God has made me see one thing for which I would heartily have given the last drop of my blood in order to write about and put it well to the fore in the minds of everyone; and which I would wish all preachers to speak aloud about often in order to make it vividly understood. I saw, I say, that the greatest and most horrifying chastisement that God gives for sin is not Hell, but that it is given at the hour and moment when the sin is committed. The sinner becomes the object of God's hatred and is disgraced before him. O, God's hatred! How this has not been really understood! It has been imprinted on my mind in such a way that I would prefer to be damned eternally, and bear alone all the torments of Hell and the fury of the demons, than to be for one instant the object of God's hatred. May no one think that I exaggerate as I speak! I am saying the truth; and he who will understand well what it is about will not find what I say to be strange, but will believe it easily. If ever the thought that I might have been in that unhappy state enters my mind, the blood in my veins runs cold, and I am seized by such horror and suffering that, if it does not disappear promptly, I would die of it.

As regards venial sin - which does not cause us such a great evil, but freezes charity - O, how terrible this is to the soul that loves and only wishes to live so that it may make the degrees of its love grow in equal proportion to the moments of its life, and to whom a thousand years of punishment would be delightful in order to acquire even one degree of love! For how many years, my God, have I desired and yearned for death in order not to fall into that extreme evil! And how often, Lord, have I said to you, completely brimming over with tears and my heart pierced with a sharp pain: 'I beseech you, my God, by the purity and sanctity which is essential to you, all your perfections, all the virtues of your sacred humanity, the merits of your holy death and passion, through the hatred you have for sin and through everything you have done in order to destroy that evil, to destroy it entirely in me. Lord, make me suffer through mercy what you would wish me to suffer through justice, making me endure the pain in order to preserve me from sin; ten times, a hundred times, even a thousand times more pains would I endure if it is necessary in order to be punished for my sin! I love these punishments, since they are as glorious to you as the effects of your mercies. But I detest their cause, my sins; and I would heartily dwell for centuries in Purgatory in order to avoid even one of them.'

It gives me great pain to hear it said: 'Just little sins!' That is a horrifying error: there are no small sins!

This vision of sin is so terrible to me that the minute I see it, either in myself or in anyone else, my eyes never stop crying and my pain is so acute that I am unable to express it. This is why, I believe, God does not permit me to see it. Otherwise, I do not think I could live.

Three states of my soul

Itinerary

As I write this now I realise that I have been eleven years and three months in Paris.[119] Apart from the first year, or at least the first nine or ten months, which I am not clear about at all, from the moment it pleased God to touch me deeply, all this time could be reduced to three states in my soul. My first concern was to be the person who suffers and is a pilgrim in the world; the second, to have my mind always in Heaven; and the third, to be in solitude with God alone.[120]

First state: the suffering pilgrim

One day, while complaining to our Lord as I looked up to Heaven, and thinking that if I had been in my own homeland and among my close relations a certain thing would not have happened - for they did something to me which had distressed me terribly,[121] I said to him: 'When will it be, Lord, when will it be that you will take me away from these strange places[122] and put me back in my own country and among my relations?' And an interior voice, through words very well articulated at the bottom of my heart, answered me: 'Poor creature! Is not the whole world a strange land to you? What does it matter where or how you pass your days of pilgrimage? Your country is Heaven.'[123]

These words did not make a great impression on my soul at the time, for I was too deep in sadness. But not long after that, they caused great changes there. I understood this truth, and I began from then on to walk as a pilgrim on the earth, not desiring any longer any establishment, regardless of how small it might be; which meant that, no matter what state of poverty I was in, I never procured for myself anything that was secure, preferring only the things which divine Providence provided me with, putting all my joy in depending on them from moment to moment. I had from then on a certain desire to make a vow of poverty; but my sins rendered me unworthy of it!

The human and natural love I had for my homeland and relatives was taken away from me. I only loved them now in God and for God, as he wished, and for as long as he wished. The dwelling places in the whole world were all the same to me, since I was a stranger everywhere;[124] and desiring nothing more than God, being able to find him everywhere, I was content.

This was the way I existed in the world for about four years, or a little more; and - these words[125] having been uttered to me almost from the beginning, from the moment I was touched by God - these affections and sentiments were mixed with the difficulties I had.

Second state: my mind in Heaven

One day after Holy Communion, our Lord gave me to understand that he wished me to be a stranger in this world in a manner quite different from the way I had been. And right from that moment the world was unknown to me. I had no knowledge of or dealings with anyone, beyond one only person,[126] who was then far away from me. And I have remained like this ever since.

But with regard to the rest of people, they were as wild savages to me, whose ways and speech I did not understand. The whole world seemed to me to be one great hospital for mad people, possessed with all sorts of follies, the folly of honours, riches and pleasures, or with the love for some fellow-creature. I saw clearly how all the passion one has for these things is nothing but pure folly. I saw those who are violent and frenetic, who kill others and themselves too; those who are attached to sin and are a scandal to everyone. There were among them, however, those who were wise and who tried to restore the mind of those poor, demented people. These were the preachers and the people who were truly Christian. But even those, it seemed to me, had some grain of madness also; but it did not show.

This lasted with me for several months. And being very distressed with other people's company and extravagances, I began to desire to die! I saw them cry when they should have been rejoicing, call evil what was good, and on the contrary consider good to be evil. I did not understand in any way their manner of behaving; which meant that, not being able to dwell on the earth, I always had my mind in Heaven, conversing with those blessed spirits. Feeling deeply the pain of my exile, I used to say often to our Lord: 'Since, O my God, I am only here to obey and follow the orders of your divine Providence, grant me the favour of beginning, at least, to serve perfectly my apprenticeship[127] to that exercise which - through your grace - I desire and hope to do during all eternity, which is to praise you and love you perfectly. It is indeed hard for me to be separated from you without suffering and discontinuity in this holy exercise!'

So I exercised almost all the time those continual acts of praise, love, benediction, and the like, uniting myself to the blessed.

I saw at once the folly of malice. I saw the contempt everyone has for Jesus Christ and how they take no more notice of his doctrine, his examples, and his Cross than if they were the product of some worthless man who had uttered nothing but foolishness and mere reveries. For many months while that vision lasted in me, I cried with such bitterness that I thought I would die from it. And outraged by a severe sorrow, I used to say sometimes: 'O my God, what do you intend by making me see these things? I am only a sickly young woman, and can provide no remedy for them! Do you take pleasure in seeing me consumed by tears? If this pleases you, Lord, I would dearly wish to have my eyes shed all the blood in my veins!'

I was given a great affection for praying to God on behalf of preachers, confessors, superiors of religious communities, and generally for all those who are employed in the direction of souls. I asked him, with untold love, to bless their work so that they might save those poor, insane people by restoring judgement and reason to them. This affection has remained with me ever since, being much stronger, however, during Advent and Lent than at other times.[128]

Towards the third state

This diverse knowledge I had produced different effects in me according to the things I saw. But bit by bit all this was taken from me, including the great light I had received right from the beginning for the direction of my actions. That light had made me see down to the least thing I had to do or avoid, saving me from being deceived or misled by the cunning and malice of nature. Desires were no longer in me with that same force and vigour as they once were; and I began to find myself in a certain darkness where I no longer saw anything.[129] It seems to me that, strictly speaking, I had hurled all my actions, even the more physical ones, to the bottom of the sea in order not to see them again;[130] for, as was previously not the case, an instinct in me pushed me to do things without forethought, without knowledge, and without returning to them once they were done. In the midst of all this I had such a calm and tranquil conscience that sometimes I would try to worry myself about something which really did not exist.

I say that I tried to do this. But I did not succeed. Despite myself, remaining in such a great tranquillity of body and soul, I did not feel the slightest movement of passion[131] or of anything else that might in the least trouble me. In so far as I did feel any movements of passion at all, they were always to me a reason for exercising virtue, and in no way a worry or an occasion of sin. But with all this I was also stripped of the gifts of God. At least I did not see them to be in me any longer, which astonished me. Not knowing what I could have done to occasion this, I said to myself: 'I wish to give myself in exchange for all this. I would not mind, my God, I said to him, for I wish for nothing else but you.' Now this dark and tranquil state has always remained with me, and has indeed increased.[132]

Solitude with God alone

One morning, while kneeling and having put myself in the presence of God to say my prayers, suddenly I saw all the crowns, all the sceptres, honours and grandeurs of the world before me as a small puff of wind[133] or a little smoke, or even less than that. Looking with great wonder at these honours and their folly, how people esteem them and seek them so assiduously, I said: 'Poor chameleons, turncoats, who only feed on the wind; you poor people who only blacken yourselves and smother in the smoke of these vanities!' This lasted for about half an hour, following which I saw that these vanities, which are called the pleasures of life, are veritable torments; and I wondered all the more how often must it be that we are charmed[134] into pleasure by throwing ourselves into those bushes of thorns, to be torn to pieces there and for all parts of us to be soaked in blood, before we can see that there is nothing that is greater and more conducive to happiness than service of God! This gave me the desire of wanting to have a stomach of iron and a voice as strong as thunder in order to cry throughout the whole world: 'Everything is vanity[135] outside of loving and serving God!' And this lasted a long time with me.

At the end of my prayer, God, imparting to my heart a great desire to see this fulfilled, said to me: 'I want to take all these things from your vision, so that nothing may come between you and me.' Now I saw this not only once; but over a period of many, many months, even many years for it is more than three years since this first happened to me. It is true that although I have not always had a vision of this, these truths have always remained imprinted on my soul, in such a way that I would no more make a fuss of anyone than I could of a grain of dust; and strictly speaking, of anything even less than that. For my mind having been rid of all forms, figures and images so that none remains, and being in a solitude so great that I cannot see anything any more, nor know anything of these things, I do not know if there is such a thing even as a grain of dust.

Furthermore, I say that the knowledge of spiritual things had also been taken away from me. Even the Holy Virgin and the saints I loved and honoured with a very great affection, no longer in order to see them through the light of knowledge, but through an instinct and feeling which brought me to them.[136]

The presence of the visible and perceptible God was changed for me into an impression which I have of him in my soul; which fills it and occupies it so that nothing else can enter there, and welcomes me and holds me in great respect at all times, in every place, and at every encounter. I have no image of the divinity or humanity of God our Lord, except very occasionally, and then it does not last very long, and the state of my soul is such that it rejects immediately any form or figure, yearning for and desiring the original and not the representation.[137]

Filled with God

Speaking with the understanding I presently have of this state and the discernment I am able to make of it compared with the others I have been in, I can say that in the other two states the soul is filled with the gifts and light of God, whereas in this one the soul is filled with God himself.[138] Also, it is indeed a long time ago now since I said to Him: 'What did I desire, if not you yourself? I did not say to you: "Give me humility in order to prevent me from being proud, and poverty that it might make me have contempt for the things of the world; and so for the rest." But, O my God, give yourself to me, and put yourself between me and vanity, between me and all the things of this world, between me and sin! Submerge me in yourself; so that there I may be happily lost to all those things!'

Once while receiving Communion - it was a long time ago; it was before all these visions - I saw it as the sea and I myself as a drop of water. I was thrown there as a drop of water in the sea, in order to be lost.

The soul is then empty of all things and does them without forethought. But it applies itself to everything it is called upon to do, and does it with great love; and these things, be they spiritual or corporal, once done do not present themselves again to the soul. The knowledge of them having been completely taken away, the soul remains thus, always empty, always full.[139]

These then are the ways by which God has led me for the past ten years and a half; because, for the greater part of my first year in Paris, I did not understand what was happening to me. In all ways there are occurrences, many things that happen between God and the soul which would be impossible to speak about, above all in this last state, because it does not fall under the senses.[140]

I have scarcely ever received graces except through Holy Communion

Desire for the Eucharist and its effects

There still remains for me to say something concerning the most Holy Sacrament. It is a sea and an ocean upon which I fear to embark, because there is neither bottom nor shore. And yet, my Saviour, I owe my gratitude in this to your kindnesses, since it is your wish to make them known. One of the greatest desires you have given me, my Lord, is that for Communion! And the first years I had this desire so passionately - with such loving concern for this divine Sacrament - that I was sometimes on that account at the limits of my strength. When the evening of the morrow in which it was not customary for me to receive Communion came, I was unable to stem my tears; and it seemed to me as if my heart was going to melt away out of love and pain. It is in this way that you have drawn me to yourself!

This is why I have great difficulty when I hear it said that one must not approach this Sacrament often![141] It is true that it is not fitting for each person to approach it in the same way! But I know, of course, that it is only those whose will to sin is resolute, or who do not wish to avoid the near occasion of falling into sin, who must not approach the Sacrament. May they be prevented from receiving Communion! For this Sacrament of life would give them only death.[142] But those who have the right disposition, who are of goodwill, no matter what pain or infirmity they might be subjected to - that they may go there with humility and confidence! For that is the best means they can take in order to help themselves out of their predicament.

One wishes to be a saint! One should be, having the grace which justifies the soul. But with regard to this exalted state of sanctity, it is the special effect of this Sacrament to communicate it; and it is very difficult to acquire it otherwise. Although I had ardent desires for Communion at the beginning, I had fear almost in daring to approach it. And in my heart, someone was saying to me: 'Go to God as you are, and he will make of you that which he wishes you to be.' So I have scarcely ever received graces except through Holy Communion. If I have received them at other times, they have always grown in Holy Communion or been confirmed by it.

By means of the Eucharist

One day, Holy Thursday it was, I saw our Lord as a wet nurse[143] who, having her breasts exceedingly full of milk, cried plaintively because she had no infant to feed.

81

There are many persons who desire from our Lord temporal and tangible favours; but very few indeed who would long for true virtues and real, solid sanctity, which is what he, coming down to us through the means of the Sacrament, intends to communicate to us. Often I have strongly felt the urge to drink and suck at the two breasts, the one of God, the other of Jesus Christ; that is one, the purity and sanctity of God, the other, the humility of Jesus Christ. So filled was I with this desire that it caused great changes in my soul. Having received Communion, I attached myself now to one and then to the other; the only longing I had was to suck lovingly.[144]

The Lord's place

Once, on entering into me,[145] and without uttering anything else, our Lord said: 'Leave it to me!' With great affection, then, abandoning myself entirely to him, and beseeching him to satisfy completely his good pleasure, I was as I think more than seven or eight times at Communion.[146] It was at that time, it seems to me, that I began to receive Communion every day. I am not, however, very sure about this! So that he alone could remain in my heart and be the absolute Master of it, I considered all my Communions as ways of ejecting all things from me, particularly myself; for I was in greater conflict with him than they were. So it seems to me, my Lord, that you are that absolute Master entirely; and that it is you alone who dwells there! Then, one day he said to me: 'I wish to make here the dwelling place of my delights!'

Transformation

He gave me such a great love for death - which I did not understand - that I used to ask for it from him with unbelievable affection; and often he would say to me: 'I wish you were dead!' I was, and still am, unable to suffer the word 'mortification', wishing to be completely dead so that he alone could live in me.[147] I also rejected the word 'humiliation', longing and wishing instead to be annihilated entirely so that only he would appear in me and that I would have his divine being. And not being content to be united to him, I desired and asked fervently to be transformed into him.

Original purity

Consequently I say to him often while I approach that sacred feast: 'My Lord, I have eaten you so often! Eat me also once in a while, if you please! Convert me completely into your substance! Eat my heart, my soul, my senses, my internal and external strength, and transform me completely into you, making me one and the same thing with you!'

This accomplished wonderful results! Sometimes he drew me to himself with this thought and affection. Consider that our soul, leaving the hands of God all beautiful, all pure, is sullied at the very moment it touches the flesh of Adam, and is enveloped with so many miseries that it remains overwhelmed by them; and that his flesh, his sacred flesh, has indeed much more power and virtue to sanctify us than the other has to tarnish us. And I went to receive him, embracing him closely and lovingly, making

82

him touch my body, my whole soul, and all the interior and exterior parts of myself. It is true that he brings about such great effects of sanctity not only in the soul, but also in the body, that it seems that one returns to, or at least approaches, that first state of purity and innocence in which he created us.

Purification through the blood of Jesus Christ

More than seven years ago, I believe, I was once thrown into a bath of our Lord's blood and washed from head to foot by a hand other than my own, not knowing, however, whose hand it was. And it was given me to understand that the attachment to sin was taken away from me; and not only that, but also the affection for all things which tend towards it. And so, since then I have not had any such affection. The memory of this grace sometimes entered into my mind and made me throw myself yet again into that precious bath where, in addition to that first grace of having no affection for evil or for the things that are inclined towards it, was given to me also a horror of, and extreme aversion to, sin.

Divine effects

It would be to end where there is no end if, my Saviour, I had to speak of all the mercies you have shown me by means of this Sacrament, drawing me to it in so many different ways and by various affections that only you know about. For this, I am exceedingly grateful to you. But I will say, that as there are two ways of making oneself rich - one through some sort of trade deal, purchasing bit by bit; the other through the finding of some treasure or the liberality and magnificence of some Prince - there are also two for acquiring sanctity and perfection. First, through the exercise and practice of the virtues, where one acquires them little by little. Second, through Holy Communion, where one finds them all like treasure, and where that magnificent King gives them with such plenitude that one sole visit of his would mortify more passions, destroy more vices and fill one with more grace than would spending entire years trying to obtain this with any other method.

O my Saviour, is it not you who gives these generous sentiments to my soul so that, feeling myself deeply honoured by your visit, I might have contempt for everything that is not you? Is it not you who will banish sin from my soul forever? And could I ever savour any more the better things of this world, having tasted your delights in that divine Sacrament? No, my Lord; for you know that you are the only, unique object of all my love and all my joy.

Having received you, how often have I said to the blessed saints that I scarcely envy them; because I believe that I am as firm in my holding on to you as they are certain in seeing you. But I pray to them only to obtain for me this grace, and beseech you, my Saviour, to grant it to me - that I be such in receiving you as they are in seeing you; that your divine essence accomplish in me what your clear vision effects in them, uniting me to yourself, embracing me to the full with your pure and divine love, rendering me all beautiful, all pure, so that there is nothing left in me that might displease you. Do this, O my God, so that having seen you and adored you in that divine Sacrament by the light of faith I shall experience afterwards by the light of glory!

Lord, you often made this light shine so brilliantly in me, that on seeing your divine Majesty with such evidence and certitude, everything I saw and touched, and generally everything I could be sure of through the reality of the senses, seemed to me to be nothing but fables and lies compared with this truth. I thought I had almost lost the faith. You also paid me the honour, O God of infinite generosity, of imprinting so strongly on my soul all the truths of the faith that nothing could ever make me doubt them! And if I had been at the far end of the Barbary coast,[148] never having heard those truths spoken of, I would have been given enough knowledge by you in order to believe in them firmly and to live according to your holy law and Gospel.

My God, in your mercy do me the honour of producing in me the results which you expect from all this. O my God, since nothing remains for me now but to ask of you that I may see clearly what you have made me believe so strongly, break asunder, then, all my ties! Deliver my soul, therefore, from the prison in which it longs to see you!

O most holy and incomprehensible Trinity, Father, Son and Holy Spirit whom I believe to be only one God; and you, adorable Jesus, arrange it that I may see you soon in the splendour of your glory, so that, not having the obstacles of this miserable life any longer, I may never cease for one single moment to praise and love you.

O sacred Virgin, who, after God and your Son, is the object of my respect, my love and all my hopes, take me under your protection, guiding me to the safest harbour of my salvation. Great St Joseph, and you, all the saints of Paradise, receive me into your company, so that with you I may praise and love eternally he who can never be praised or loved sufficiently. So be it.

My exercises and occupations

Rising

It remains for me to describe then, my daily, monthly and yearly exercises and occupations.

The hour of my rising is never that well regulated, either for reasons of sickness or because of my hour of retiring to sleep, which is often very late. However, sometimes earlier and other times later, the general rule I have is to rise at 6 o'clock. But always on rising it is   [149] and for our Lord.

While dressing I say the office of the Holy Spirit with the Veni Sancte Spiritus, beseeching him to instruct me and to be my master; a prayer to the Holy Trinity, the Holy Virgin, my Guardian Angel, than an O Gloriosa in honour of the Immaculate Conception of the Holy Virgin, asking of her a perfect purity and sanctity of body and mind; the Ave Maris Stella, recommending to her and putting under her protection my closest relatives; a Salve Regina, doing the same thing for Monsieur and Madame de,   [150] their children, and generally for all those who live in their house.

After this, having dressed adequately, I go on my knees, kissing the ground in order to humble myself outwardly and inwardly before God. Then I make an act of adoration on behalf of myself and all those creatures who do not adore the most Holy Trinity, especially for all the persons in the house where I live, so that if I cannot make the Trinity known to and adored by all of them there, I myself may do it for them, making up for that defect as much as is possible for me. Likewise, I make an act of thanksgiving for all of God's kindnesses, and particularly all those for which no one (all creatures and myself in particular) gives thanks: the blessings of creation, redemption, conservation and others. And I give thanks especially for the fact that he has placed me in a state of poverty, in absolute dependence on the charity of others and the care of his divine Providence, to which indeed I abandon myself entirely, and forever, asking of him with great affection the grace to live and to die in that state. And I hope in his kindness that he will do this for me.

Oblation

I thank him for all the pains, sorrows and sufferings which it has ever pleased him to allow me be part of, either in body or in mind; and entering as much as it is possible for me into the sentiments our Lord has out of zeal for his glory, his justice and fulfilment of his plans, particularly that of the Cross, I offer to him my body and my soul as a blank document so that he may put on it such a death, such a condition, employment, sickness and circumstances as it pleases him, responding to everything: let his will be done; I am content as long as he takes from it his greatest glory.

Then I offer him all my thoughts, words, works and áctions, good or indifferent, planned or unplanned; such as he knows and foresees I must do, say, think, suffer or feel deeply for his greatest glory; uniting them all to those of all the just who are on the earth and the saints who are in Heaven, and to the praises which they will give him throughout eternity. I desire with them to honour him as they do, and more than they do, if it were in my power, wishing to perform all these actions in his own heart, his own mind and intentions, in order to be able to render him all the glory he awaits from this. And considering Jesus to be in myself, I abandon myself completely to him, and I beseech him to guide me in all these things as my chief, and to use me in them as the cause, his instrument, so that they will not only be done for him, but also through him, and that I be filled with the same motives and intentions as are his, and applied by him to everything that will be for his greatest glory.

Daily observances

After this I make an act of contrition and ask for his blessing, which I also do for all sinners, beseeching him to preserve them from sudden death and to give them the grace of a true conversion; for the just, that he may conserve them and make them grow in his grace; for all the perfect souls, so that, showering them with his greatest blessings, he may more and more take his delight in them; for my confessor in particular, so that he may grant him the grace of living and dying in a perfect observance of his vows and rules, and of changing his heart into a furnace of love; next, for all the poor and the afflicted, all the dying and other persons of this kind, that he may grant them the grace to recognise the happiness of their state and to make good use of it; and then my nearest relatives, and Monsieur and Madame   ,[151] their children, placing them all, in so far as I am able, under his holy protection. I greet the most Holy Virgin, imploring her to take me into her charge; St Joseph; my Guardian Angel; my holy patrons and protectors, entreating them all to help me never to offend God, but that in everything I may fulfil his holy will. Then I say five Paters and five Ave Marias, and one Miserere for all the needs of the Church, for the Pope, and generally for all those who are entrusted with the salvation of souls. Three days of the week I say these prayers with my arms crossed; the other days, no. I was not allowed to do so.

I spend a good quarter of an hour at that, after which I kiss the ground, say the Veni Creator and begin my prayers. These include the litanies of Jesus and a few other, small prayers, and they last a good hour. Having finished these prayers, I then say the Salutation of the Angel[152] if I had not said it at the beginning, which I almost never miss saying three times a day. Then kissing the ground, and asking a blessing from the Holy Virgin, I rise from my knees, make my bed, tidy my room and finish dressing. Then I go to Mass. Every day I follow two rules as I attend: the first is to prepare myself for Holy Communion, the other is to make an act of thanksgiving. After this I say the little rosary of the Holy Virgin, which consists of three Paters and twelve Aves, gain some indulgences for the souls in Purgatory, and return to the place where divine Providence has put me to see its plans fulfilled both for them[153] and for myself.

Sometimes I read a chapter from a book. Then I begin work, whatever that happens to be, doing it in a spirit of submission and obedience and united to that of the Holy Virgin and our Lord. When I have to do exhausting work, I do it more willingly, that being in keeping with poverty. My spirit is contemplative, or at least respectful before God.

The Lord granted me the grace as I sit down to eat of never failing to thank Providence for the care it takes of me. And as I go to table as a poor person, I recommend to him the poor, taking as alms, and indifferently, that which is given to me, avoiding thus any singularity. This is what one must always do.

After lunch I work, do a little bit of reading at an hour that is convenient, and, a good hour before dinner, retire some place to say my rosary and some other prayers, which are often enough interrupted by certain interior movements. But when they pass, I carry on with my prayers.

Dinner is taken in the same way as lunch. In the evening, I pray to God with all those in the house. Once in my room, I finish my prayers; which last a short half-hour, performing almost the same acts when I retire as when I arise. Then I take my subject for prayer for the following day. All ready to go to bed, I fall on my knees, entreating the Holy Virgin and the saints to bless God and Jesus Christ for me, because while asleep I would be unable to do so. I make an agreement with him, nevertheless, that all my breathing be regarded as acts of love and praise in order to glorify him while asleep as well as awake. Taking holy water, I go to bed; and after a few short prayers, I conclude them saying: 'Nos cum Prole pia, etc.'

During the night

When I wake up during the night, I go on my knees at the side of the bed to adore God and Jesus Christ in the Holy Sacrament of the altar. Offering him again my sleep, I return to bed. If I wake up many times, I do not kneel down. This I do only the first time. So that is the order of my day.

Sundays and feast days

The same routine takes place on Sundays and feast days. But in addition I say the office of the Virgin, the crown of our Lord, the seven penitential psalms, and the Vespers of the dead for the souls in Purgatory. I always attend Vespers and the sermon[154] or Catechism.

The rosary

The first Sundays of every month, and all the feasts of the Holy Virgin, I say the complete rosary.

Intentions

On the first days of the month it is my exercise to renew all my intentions for the greater glory of God.

Special days

For many years now I have had particular devotion to the Immaculate Conception of the Holy Virgin. And for the past four years, on the day on which it fell, as this year it has fallen on a Monday,[155] every Monday I offer Holy Communion to thank God for having preserved her from sin; and I say the office of the Immaculate Conception, beseeching the same Virgin to obtain for me the grace of a perfect purity and sanctity of body and mind.

I also take a day off each week when I offer all my prayers for the poor, so that it may please God to provide for them; and I give some little thing within my power in order to relieve them as much as I can and so that I myself grow that much poorer. The indulgences I gain that day, on that account, are for the soul that died in the exercise of the greatest poverty.

Orientations

The other days are also for various intentions. At the end of each month, when there are only three days left, I take the first of the three to receive Holy Communion and to do my exercises of devotion in order to thank God for all the graces, general and particular, temporal and spiritual, he granted and will grant to all creatures during the month. For it seems to me that there are so many people who receive these graces without ever thanking him for them that it is necessary to make up for this defect. The second, I use to thank him for all the graces he gave me that day and also throughout my whole life, imploring him that they produce in me the effects of perfection which he intends. The third I devote to doing my exercises in a spirit of penance, making a list for confession of all the sins I had committed during the month. And it seems to me that all these little exercises, practices, are of great value. The first Sunday of the month I offer Holy Communion and my other devotions to ask for the grace of a happy death, and to make up for whatever I might be lacking at the hour of my death.

From Epiphany to Lent

From the Epiphany to the three days which precede Ash Wednesday, I add a half-hour of prayer to my daily prayers, taking good care to withdraw myself all the more; because, since at that time comedies, ballets and general gatherings of people take place, I believe that I am obliged at this time more than at any other time to serve God, and also perform every week some particular mortification for this. I do the same in the period between Easter and Pentecost, all the more because everyone, weary from Lent, seeks only to enjoy themselves.

The forty hours

I renew with great care the vows of my baptism on the three days preceding Ash Wednesday, renouncing entirely the world, the devil, the flesh and sin. I recognise and take for my choice and election Jesus Christ as my Master. Uniting myself to all the saints and to the Trinity itself, and to all the praises to which the Trinity is devoted, I say 300 Gloria Patris every day to glorify the Holy Trinity in reparation for the dishonour shown it by sinners during those days. I also say the rosary in honour of the thirty-three years which our Lord lived, offering to the Eternal Father all the merits of the life of the Son, so that he may show these sinners mercy. I also give some alms in so far as I am able, setting myself against the extravagance and criminal spending which takes place during those days. In order to make amends to God for the offences committed against him each evening of the three days, on retiring to my room I take a stick in my hand, which I keep expressly for the purpose, and with the cord round my neck, as I have heard it said is the way it should be done,[156] in my nightdress I enact the discipline to do penance for all that. It is true that, since I have been with Monsieur, [157] I have not waited until the evening to do this, for fear of being heard, but choose some other hour and place for it. I have practised this without fail for a good eight years. On the feast day of the Holy Trinity, I also say 300 Gloria Patris, a hundred for each person.

Fasting and hair shirt

It is, as I believe, more than nine years since I made the vow to fast on Saturdays. For the first three or four years, I renewed the vow every year; but after that I was permitted to take this vow for my whole life. For more than seven years, I believe, one day in the week (usually it was a Monday), I wore a girdle of hair, putting it on when I rose and taking it off before retiring to bed. I also wore it on all the vigils of the feasts of our Lord and the Holy Virgin. For the past two years I have made no use of it.

Discipline

I think that all the time I was by myself (which was for three years), I fasted also on the vigils of those feasts on bread and water; but on entering where I am now, I stopped that; and in its stead I was permitted to replace it by performing some discipline. For the past nine years or so, especially since I stopped wearing the girdle, regularly I have done this twice every week, and more than often three times. But for the past nine months it is a great exception for me if I do it more than twice a week; and, although I am such a weak, cowardly creature that one would want to put the spur in my back, I am however kept very tightly in check.

Communion

As regards Holy Communion, almost immediately after our Lord touched me,[158] I received it two or three times in the week, and finally four times. Then, for a period of nineteen or twenty months I was allowed to receive Communion every day. But there being some difficulty with that, two days in the week were taken from me; for which I was the cause, and which really cost me many tears. Since that time, three and a half years now, I receive Holy Communion only five timés in the week. It is true that, for most octaves of the feasts of our Lord and our Lady, I received every day! And for the past nine months Communion has been permitted to me every day,[159] unless some inconveniences might prevent it.

Address to Father Castillon

Well, my very dear and Reverend Father, this is what you desired of me! And ending where I began, I pray you to receive this account as a mark of respect and submission I wish to render your desires, the least of which is for me, from now on, an indispensable law. And I beseech you also to believe that I place among the most special graces God has ever given me the fact that I have been under your direction. There was a very special Providence in the first time God sent me to you,[160] and in the second, when he brought me to you himself,[161] having put so many good things in you for me that everything led me to virtue. Also, he gave me such esteem and respect for your Reverence that I doubt if any more could be added. The facility and simplicity with which I was able to disclose to him, even down to the greatest secrets of my heart, is a proof to me that God absolutely wished it so, in order that he might receive from you - knowing the abundance of his mercies to me, of which I am unworthy - the acts of thanksgiving which my ingratitude was unable to render him; and that he could use you - knowing the enormity of my sins, my poverty and misery - for me to obtain pardon for my sins and find a remedy for them. That is what I ask of you with all the affection of my heart; and in exchange, if it pleases the Lord to show me mercy as I hope he will from his goodness, you tell me what it is you wish me to do, and I hope that I may never fail in this.[162]

N.N.[163]

Doxology

Glory be to our Lord Jesus Christ, to the Holy Virgin, and to the great St Joseph. Amen.

SECOND ACCOUNT

Deepening

Preliminary Invocation

O my God of ineffable goodness, since it pleases you that I continue to bring to the light of day the most hidden graces I have received from you; if it pleases you, therefore, give me enlightenment and the words to accomplish this according to your good pleasure, and receive my word in recognition of your favours. My God, I declare, and you know it, that I do not desire or lay claim to anything else by this avowal beyond obedience to your wishes - which are known to me on this matter, since he[1] who holds your place has ordered me so - and procuring for you in this all the glory which you desire to receive from it, which is the one and only thing I seek now, in the future, and for all eternity.

Spiritual combat

Other accounts of the first favours

After you had taken me away from my homeland, separated me from my parents, from every honour in the world through the loss of all the temporal goods I possessed, and put me in a position where need and the absence of all acquaintances - who could have succoured me - compelled me to have recourse to him, it was then, O my God, that you began to give me much more than I desired to ask of you. For at that time, I believe, all my pretensions were still only to have the things that were necessary for this present life. So I received through the pure goodness and liberality of God (for, on my part, I had no disposition whatsoever to it, but on the contrary much opposition) a great desire for Holy Communion, and so many caresses our Lord gave me in drawing me to himself that I was drowned and swallowed up in consolation.[2] I was hardly able to speak, drink or eat, particularly on the days I received Communion. Having eaten the bread of angels, I would hide myself away and cry when I had to take my meals, seeing myself now compelled through the misery of our nature to take this food which is the same for us and the beasts. These sweet moments, so great, did not last in me only during that sacred banquet; but for about six months they were almost continuous. I was placed in a new country where I saw so many and such great things that my spirit was as if completely transported. The slightest things that offered themselves to my eyes would elevate me to God and keep me sometimes three or four days in continuous prayer. Eventually, my God, when through those attractions and consolations our Lord had committed me well to the exercise of devotion, from which I could no longer withdraw, for a very just reason you wished to punish me and chastise me for all the resistances I had made to you. Now I do not intend to repeat any of the things I have already mentioned, but only say, as I did then, what at this moment comes back to my mind.

So that I may make God's kindnesses to me better known, I believe it is necessary to declare more particularly that, since the time I had left religion,[4] I led a life for six or seven years completely contrary to the maxims of Christianity, following in everything my evil inclinations. I was at that point of misery[5] in which, it appears to me, I didn't have any remorse of conscience. Seeing that I made no use of the means which God ordinarily uses to touch us, such as sermons, good readings and the like, I was unable to get out of that abyss of miseries without some complete and extraordinary act of the mercy of God. But in a word, touched by poverty and a sickness that lasted for fifteen months, I retreated into myself. O my God, how good you are! For, from the moment I had recourse to you, and you had shown grief over my evil life, you gave me more grace than I can say. My understanding was enlightened with great lights and my will filled with affections for virtue; and you drew me principally to the frequentation of the most august Sacrament. But for the want of direction - since it seemed to me that it was too often to receive Communion twice a week - I did not respond to your divine charms! And so, more through ignorance than through malice on this point, I rendered myself unworthy of the graces which you wished to grant me in order that I might extricate myself entirely from sin. I was about three or four years[6] in that way of life, making great protestations to God about serving him and being completely his. My mind was often elevated in prayer.[7] But I was so full of bad habits that my resolutions did not take effect. It is true that poverty and the curtailment in my companionship prevented me from falling again as gravely as before; but in fact I did not give to God all he desired of me. And during that time, O my God, instead of damning me to Hell through your justice, you, wearied from such long rebellions and resistances of mine, through an infinite goodness took the occasion of my malice as a way of making me experience the effects of your greatest mercies.

Suddenly you filled my understanding with such brilliant light, letting me know so many, such great truths - which I have made known elsewhere;[8] and gave to my will such strong, sweet and loving impulses to follow you, I no longer had any room for

repugnance and difficulties I experienced with virtue
..., and I truly experienced that which I have since heard said
by the greatest preacher of this century[9] - that when it pleases you to act according to
your great power, the effect of your graces is infallible and does not encroach upon
man's liberty. For indeed, I saw that my will was won over and not forced; that I was
voluntarily following my impulses, which had become so sweet and full of enchantment that not only did I give myself over to them willingly, but also with pleasure. I
know this through experience better than I am able to explain it. May your goodness
which taught me this in such a way, be forever blessed! I remained so full of shame
in your presence, so full of confusion, of sorrow and of love at the sight of these graces
and my ingratitude, that all I could do was to cry and groan. My soul was pierced by
an acute sorrow at the sight of my sins and at the same time filled with an extreme
sweetness through a feeling of love. Intoxicated with the delights of Paradise, I soon
lost the taste and affection for all things of the world. And I do not know how my heart
was able to endure all those caresses, those consolations which our Lord lavished upon
me to excess and unceasingly. Nevertheless, I accepted all of them without dwelling
on them, beholding much more the person who was giving them to me than the things
given. Such sentiments produced in me a profound humility and a complete distrust
of myself before the goodness of God. Through everything I had done, I saw what I
myself was capable of doing; and that, notwithstanding all the graces God had given
me up to then (which, it seems to me, would have been capable of converting the most
evil of all the Turks), I still persisted in my bad habits. This caused me much fear,
making me have recourse to God and put all my trust in him.

So I was about six months in that state in which, it appears, our Lord wanted to
overwhelm me with the weight of his favours. Often since then, and even now, these
favours become for me punishments and chastisements since I would rather be
punished than caressed in such a way. In the same way as when, having offended a
person who afterwards comes and showers you with graces, favours and all the
pleasures that are his to give, you would undoubtedly suffer greater shame and pain
in the presence of such a benefactor - because of the smallness of heart and mind of
the one obliged, and especially if one recognises that the benefactor might know about
one's malice and bad will - than if they had done some evil to you. Now this is the way
I was and often still am in the presence of God. For it belongs only to you, O God of
goodness and mercy, to revenge yourself by being indulgent with your kindnesses. But
the effects of your justice being no less glorious to you than those of your mercies, you
were able to glorify yourself in chastising as you deigned to do in pardoning me.

Temptations and torments

After these six months, or thereabouts, I then felt deeply a change within my soul. Now
I believe I did not really know what this was for some time. It was on a Good Friday
- and I cannot say which year[10] - that I noticed this change more particularly. But on

the following Easter Sunday,[11] finding myself in a state quite different from that which I had been accustomed to, I did not receive Communion; about which I spoke the next day to my confessor, Father [Jarry], who scolded me and forbade me ever to take it upon myself to deprive myself of Holy Communion. Since that day I saw clearly the enemies I had to fight.

The first were the violent temptations against the faith - that there was no God, and that all devotion, it seemed to me, was an idle fancy or a mere nothing. My mind was so full of horrible blasphemies, so strongly tormented with these thoughts and imaginings that sometimes I believed myself to be more miserable than the damned. Inexplicable it may seem; but I used to say with bitterness of heart: 'Alas! They[12] believe and know well, to their hurt, that there is a God who punishes them and who will punish them forever, and I, more miserable than they are, do not believe it!' And thereupon, despite all my thoughts, I used to make great acts of faith.

The exercises of devotion were such horrible torments to me that I certainly believe there would not have been any punishment of the rack, torture, the wheel, the gallows, no matter how awful one could imagine it, that I would not have suffered willingly rather than confessing and receiving Communion even once. I was tormented by the cruel thoughts that all my confessions and Communions were sacrilegious. I experienced tremendous doubts and remorse of conscience. The sight alone of my confessor, or even the awareness of his presence in church when I was there, was an unbearable pain to me; and I was in such great terror sometimes on seeing him, if I had seen the earth opening up in front of me, I think I would have thrown myself in. Even when I had asked for him, I needed great determination to approach him, having the desire rather to flee and hide myself so that I would not be seen by him. But our Lord helped me to wait for him with courage and gave me the grace to let him have great power over me; which has been of wonderful help to me. Sometimes I said to him I did not wish to go to Communion any more; and when he was unable to change my mind through reason, he would say to me in the end: 'I wish it, and I command it of you!' He left me on that note. Then, not being able on the one hand to make up my mind to do this for fear of committing a sacrilege, and being pressured on the other hand by the command I had received, I suffered agonies that were much more severe than death itself. Among all the desires that God gave me, that of obeying held the first place. That is why this caused furious battles in my mind. And, sometimes, rising with scarcely an idea of what I was doing, all of a sudden I would go and receive the Holy Host. After this I sometimes felt my heart to be a little released. But other times I was indeed more gravely afflicted, since before receiving I only feared committing a sacrilege, whereas now I feared having committed it. But as if the good desires as well as the bad ones were there in order to torment me, when I was not supposed to receive Communion I had a great and extreme desire for it that was unbelievable. And when I was to receive Communion, I would be seized with terror. I suffered also in this regard to my other devotions.

Deepening

Ardent love throughout the temptations

To these pains was added the temptation of despair. I believed I was too criminal; that God would never pardon me and that I had tried in vain; that there was no Paradise for me! O my God, you permitted the demon to represent to me the enormity of my crimes. So that I would not believe such evil suggestions, you were pleased on your part to let me see how your goodness is infinite; and how, if one has recourse to you in sorrow and with confidence, all the sins one has committed and could ever commit are only like a piece of straw thrown on a great fire, which is consumed in a moment. The fear of Hell and the loss of Paradise were not what gave me pain. I have never envisaged these things except in relation to the will of God who, for his glory, wishes that we avoid the first and that he give us the second. And often, completely transported by love, I used to say to God: 'My God, if you wish that your Hell be eternal and that those who will be there shall have to suffer eternally the rigours of your justice, you had better not put me there, for I would say to them so many things about your goodness and your infinite mercies that they would come around eventually to love you; and by that love, all their torment would be changed into delights. As for me, if ever I shall be at the bottom of that abyss, as my crimes well merit it, I will love you eternally; and nothing will ever tear away your love from my heart. I wish to love you, my God, more than all the demons hate you, and more, if it is possible, than you hate them! I wish to love you with all the love of which they were capable both in time and in eternity, and for every one of the blasphemies they incessantly pour forth against you, I want to give you thousands and thousands of blessings, praises and acts of thanksgiving for all your kindnesses. I wish to love you more than you are loved on earth and in Heaven! My God, it is my joy and my pain in not being able to love as much as you are lovable! It is my joy that you are so lovable that one can never love you enough; and it is my pain, for I would wish to love you as much as you deserve to be loved! I wish, then, to love you with the love with which you love yourself, since it is only you who perfectly fills the extent and force of this love!'

Amid all these temptations, I burned with a most ardent love in which I suffered very much; and often my heart was even full with intense heat and tender warmth.

Once at church I noticed that the devil was perceptibly near me. He threatened me in a most terrifying way and ascertained that despite all my resolutions he would make me fall into sin and return to my bad habits. This caused me more fear than all the torments of Hell. Right from the moment I was touched by God, in the way I have described it, he gave me in his goodness such a horror of my bad habits that since that time I have never distinguished between mortal and venial sin, nor between venial sin and imperfection. This does not mean that there were no bad habits in me. I am saying that I was resolved to suffer all the evils imaginable, to die a thousand times over, even suffer all the evils of Hell, rather than commit one sin. And if it were necessary for me to suffer them forever, or willingly commit a venial sin with a resolute will and composure, I would choose the first in order to avoid the second. This resolution has so pleased you, my God, keeping me inviolate, that, having placed it in the blood of your Son where it gains such force and vigour, I have no knowledge since of having committed any sin deliberately. That it may please you also, my God, through your mercy, to preserve me from those faults of fragility and infirmity of our nature! In order to preserve me from them, make me suffer that which I have to endure as chastisement, ten, nay, a hundred times more!

Now five or six times, having committed a fault, I had a vision of it in which I saw its stain on my soul; but so ugly and deformed that I could not bear myself. I would willingly have run from one extremity of the world to the other in order to escape from myself. O how we know not the enormity of sin! That alone would be sufficient for us to have an extreme horror of it. Sometimes this vision lasted in me for a half-hour; and I suffered the gravest pains because of it, pains I could not describe. After this it pleased God to take the vision from me. If it had lasted any longer for me, I believe I would not have been able to live. Now this vision did not come to me from the devil, but from God who wished by this knowledge to make me develop an aversion to sin.

An attraction for asceticism

I was very much obsessed by thoughts of gluttony. Indeed this brutal temptation caused me great pain and confusion, principally when I had these thoughts on approaching Holy Communion. I compared myself to the miserable Israelites who missed the fatty soups of Egypt and preferred them to the celestial manna they had for food.[13] I did not desire any exquisite things; only those which were free for me to have. And this was not a weak trick of the enemy. For temptation would carry me to that dissoluteness, or to eat at least more often that I had resolved to do, because for long years I had the bad habit of eating at all hours. Sometimes I suffered great hunger, and at other times such weakness that I nearly fainted. But in all this I was resolved to win or die. And from the time I lived alone, often while in that state I would wait until one or two in the afternoon before taking anything, up to when in fact pure necessity compelled me to do so. In this I might well have committed some indiscretion. But I had no other guideline than the interior movement which inclined me to this.[14]

Temptation to vainglory

Vainglory came to mix itself with all this. For it seemed to me that I was good, and that the temptations I had were the temptations of the saints.[15] I was assailed with this three or four times only. The confusion and the stress I suffered in trying to declare these thoughts to my confessor were extreme. Our Lord in his goodness often delivered me from this.

Temptations against modesty

I was indeed attacked by temptations against modesty. At first I could not say what they were, for up to then I had not had any experience of them.[16] That infernal fire was diffused throughout my whole body in an incredible way; for right up to my neck and to the extremities of my fingers I felt sensations of a deep, sensuous kind. Sometimes

I came to that point of misery in which everything I did to quench them only kindled them all the more. Then one day the thought occurred to me to give up all those penances, since they were having such bad effects. I feared even that I might fail in this. But at that very moment our Lord let me know that all this was due only to the works of the devil, and that, without troubling myself, all I had to do was to continue. Fearing also to be mistaken in this, I told it to my confessor, who was then Father [Jarry], and he confirmed me in this.

O how often have I desired, in the extreme harshness of winter, to put myself in water right up to my neck, or other such rigorous things in order to deliver myself from such feelings! There was no corporal punishment I would not have embraced willingly for that purpose. But these things involved too many inconveniences. I did not have the freedom to do these penances as I would have wished, as much because of my confessor as because of the fact that I lived with many people and did not want to let them know of them. So the only thing I could do many times during the day was to draw blood with pins. The pain I felt because of this eased somewhat the internal torment I had as a result of this temptation. In that state my mind was often strongly united to God and very attached to him in thought and will. But when he permitted the demon to seize my imagination, it was then that I was in a pitiable state, such that I cannot describe. Not knowing how to speak about it then to my confessor, I said to him: 'I believe that everything that is of the blackest in Hell is in my mind.' For it seemed to me that I longed and wished for things which, after all, I abhorred more than the eternal tortures.[17] This was the most violent of all my temptations, particularly for the first seven or eight months when it was at its most persistent and I had no respite, except during the times of sleep when I was little disturbed by it.

Elsewhere,[18] I have said how much our Lord in his goodness singularly protected me in this, and also in many other ways which I find it hard to express. I received marvellous help in making the sign of the Cross on my heart and my forehead, pronouncing the words: 'Jesus Nazarenus Rex Judaeorum'.[19] Always since then, whenever the least phantom[20] would come into my mind, not only against purity, but against every other temptation, making the sign of the Cross and pronouncing these words made it vanish as quickly as it appeared. Also, with great affection I used to renew the vow of chastity which I made; and this still gives me great strength. The shame and repugnance I had in admitting this to myself cannot be imagined. But nevertheless, our Lord in his mercy helped me overcome all these difficulties and let me have a great simplicity and candour with my confessors in all things, which, as I have said elsewhere,[21] is a great way of vanquishing anything. But the main thing of all he gave me, was for me to have recourse to him. For at every encounter with him, recognising my weakness, I would often say: 'O my God, it is not necessary for you to use such force and violent temptations in order to beat me down and overwhelm me! One alone would suffice to conquer me, since I am weaker than a broken reed.[22] So I do not pretend to defend myself; but putting myself at present into the arms of your divine Providence and the bosom of your infinite mercy, O my Jesus, I shall remain there no matter what happens to me, without ever moving from there any more than the wound in your sacred side and your loving heart! If I perish, it will be in there, in your arms, that I will perish, since I shall never leave that place!' Acting thus, I imitated what an infant child does who, being frightened by some person, or in some danger, throws itself into the bosom and arms of its mother, and doing nothing else for its safety other than hiding itself there and embracing its mother, lets her have all the care of defending it. I hid myself thus in the wounds of our Lord, embracing them lovingly, sometimes even the foot of the Cross, in order to obtain there the effusion of his sacred blood. And other times I would kiss the feet of the Holy Virgin with an extreme affection, beseeching her as well as my Guardian Angel to help me. In this way I persisted in continual prayer.

Divine generosity

O my God, how unable I am to make known what your kindnesses are and the care you have for those who have recourse to you! For there were formed in me at that time such strong, interior acts of virtue - and of all the virtues: faith, hope, charity, humility, confidence, contrition and others - in opposition to those temptations, that up to the present, I confess, I have not read or heard said anything which surpasses what I experienced and what happened in me! Now I was not only defended by the interior acts, but pushed to exterior ones which made it possible for me to vanquish these difficulties without ever being shaken by them. This I did with great courage. I have often even noticed that these acts happened without my giving any thought to them and that it was then when the temptations were not really strong. It was only then that I gave any attention to them. But you, my God, you who see the most imperceptible of things - you used to take up my defence immediately; for being as I was entirely surrendered into your arms, you wished to preserve me from the slightest surprises of the enemy as well as from his furies. That you may always be blessed for this!

Sometimes it occurred to me to ask our Lord to deliver me from those temptations. But a feeling of pure love of God seizing my heart would gently reprove me, saying to me that I should never ask of him anything other than that his holy will be entirely accomplished in me, and that I offer myself willingly to suffer those pains for the rest of my life and to the end of the world if it is his pleasure and for his glory, asking of him only that I offend him not.[23] This I did, surrendering myself into the hands of God; and have always acted in this way, without any wish, preconditions or reservations whatever. It is true, however, that I have sometimes prayed to him about the temptations against purity, submitting myself entirely, nevertheless, to his will. But what is more strange in this - it was at the height of those temptations that I suffered extreme pains throughout my whole body, for which I was very glad; although this began to tempt me afterwards, making me feel that this could only be an infallible mark of reprobation, since in every other person except myself, with pains so great all sensuality would have without doubt been suffocated and extinguished. So I was tormented in a strange way when these thoughts entered my mind and above all when

I thought I was the object of God's hatred; and this was the greatest punishment of all those I have ever suffered! There is indeed nothing so terrible! So it was the fear of offending him in this that gave me the greatest pain in these temptations. And I would have paid little attention to anyone who would have assured me of not sinning in this! But on the other hand, when a ray of light was communicated to me, which made me see that the goodness of God had not damned me - letting me die at the time of my sins - and had let me live to love him, this gave me affections and feelings of love so excessive that at times it seemed to me they could not be added to.

For about two years, then, I was thus exposed to the fury of the demons who tormented me unceasingly. And it is easy to imagine what state my body and mind must have been in, agitated as they were relentlessly by violent shocks! After this it pleased you, my God, to make these storms cease and give me back the calm of my soul. This did not come about all of a sudden, but little by little; and I cannot tell in which way it did. But these phantoms[24] were finally chased away and I enjoyed a profound peace.

Not that since then have I enjoyed the great delights and sentiments of devotion such as I did previously. And I would not wish for anything in the world to have them; for if I do not accept them with a wonderfully pure intention, nature would nourish itself on them, fomenting the love of self and finding in them its esteem. And even for the little we might savour in them by dwelling upon them, they would be a great hindrance to us in finding God, and all the more dangerous if he is not known. But it pleased you, O my God, to give to my body as much as to my mind a peace, a joy and a tranquillity that were much more purified than all those sentiments of devotion; you gave me such a great light in the truths of the faith and religion that, with this one enlightenment, it pleased you to pour into my soul, imprinting so lovingly on my heart the maxims of the Gospel, that if up to then I had been nourished on the depths of the Barbary coast, and had never heard anyone speak about them,[25] I would have believed them. But it seems to me I would have believed in these truths with so much firmness, that if the whole world had renounced the faith, seeing that it is so evident, I would not have had the slightest doubt about it, being astonished on the contrary that there would be creatures in the world who did not believe it;[26] and I would have conformed my life again to the Gospel and to that of our Lord, which I have seen in an admirable way,[27] and in which consists all our happiness, our present and eternal honour, and all the veritable glory and generosity of the heart.

It also pleased you, my Lord, to rid me of all the thoughts I could have of myself. Because of the experiences I had of your kindnesses, I put my confidence in you so entirely that I have never had hope since in any creature. Your divine Providence arranged things with such sweetness that, no matter what happens to me, or also to others, serves as a means by which I can both detach myself from all creatures and unite myself to you. If I have pain, it is to you, my everything, that I have recourse; for you alone it is who can give me the good and salutary reliefs for this which I would need, or the strength to suffer whatever would be pleasing to you. If anyone assists me, I recognise that it is you who orders it. So all my confidence is in you! I feel myself greatly obliged to the persons who do me good; but thanks be to God, I in no way put my hopes in them! During the most calamitous times,[28] when I saw how much goodwill and charity the people with whom I am staying showed me, and, without asking it of them, the assurances they gave me that they would never forsake me, and that they would share their last morsel with me - all this obliged me to be exceedingly thankful to those people in every possible way; for certainly I am indebted to them. I beseech our Lord with my whole heart to give them ample recompense for this, and to shower them forever with the greatest blessings in Heaven! However, this never makes me think or feel that I should in the least put my trust in creatures, for they are inconstant[29] and subject to perpetual change; and the little one does rely on them, one is exposed to troubles and continual worries.[30] But, myself apart, in these manifestations of goodwill that were shown to me, I say: 'Lord my God, it is you alone that I hope in! Adversity never makes me fear anything, nor prosperity hope for anything. You are always rich, always good, forever all powerful! There is no bad or needy time for you nor for those who hope in you. You will always give them abundantly of everything they need, or the strength to suffer lovingly and with constancy everything it pleases you to send them!' And this last grace, it seems to me, is more advantageous and more desirable than the first. Consequently, when first I made the acquaintance of Madame de   and afterwards went to live in her house, the people who knew me and knew the way I had lived, would say to me: 'This is much better for you, and more honourable!' But I was never able to relish these words; and I would silently respond to them: 'All my better, O my God, and all my best, is to do your will and to be where it pleases you that I be! The dung heap of Job[31] will be my throne of glory if ever you put me there!'

I do not know if this is the general guidance God uses for all rational creatures, or if it is peculiar to me, that provided one hopes in him, the only thing one has to do is not to trouble oneself about anything. For it is more than ten years now that my only concern, either for the body or for the soul, is to do nothing, except put myself into his hands and hope firmly in him. I do not mean to say that it is not necessary to do something to help ourselves in our spiritual and temporal needs, since that would be contrary to his Providence. But that we should await in great peace and submission the means which it pleases him to help us with, and availing ourselves of them freely and with a most pure intention, we never turn our eyes on ourselves for good or for evil. My mind is so strongly removed from the things that are necessary for me, I say even for my life, that if God through some particular Providence were not to provide them for me, I do not believe I would be capable of thinking about them. But, O Lord, who can speak about the care and tenderness you have for those who attach themselves to you and forget themselves in order to think only of you!

A purified spirit

It also pleased you, my Lord, to give me so pure and so clear a spirit that years passed by when, if even the slightest phantom[32] entered my mind, it would vanish as quickly as it was perceived. Regardless of how insignificant they might be, I had an aversion to all things that could hurt in the least way charity and modesty. I have often been astonished, and as if confused in myself to hear preachers shout and fulminate against the conversations people have and the company they keep with one another, not being able to understand what danger there might be, and what difference there is between a man and woman, or to say it better, what malignity is found in them that causes such frightening things as those which one hears spoken of. I even spoke about this once to Father[33] when I went to him; but he responded to me: 'What you are saying is that God has a particular way for directing you and that he gives you a truly special grace. The preachers have reason in saying what they say. Do not judge anyone by your own behaviour; for that ignorance is singular to you.'[34] I avow nevertheless to having felt sensual emotions at times, but, truly, very faintly and rarely. Seeing that they[35] have completely different effects in me, I have also been astonished that they might be, as it is said, an occasion of sin in many, since, recognising my own misery, they are the occasion in me for having recourse to God; making me fear, they humiliate me before God and bring me to mortification and such things. With great insistence, I have often asked him to deliver me from them entirely.[36] I hope in his merciful goodness he will do this for me, and for his glory.

Battle with oneself

It would seen that having passed through these temptations there is nothing more to worry about. But these temptations are not the most dangerous ones we can have, for they come from extraneous causes. The demons - to whom God gives a free hand for a time - are the principal authors of these temptations. And even though the demons execute them with hatred and envy in order to destroy us, nevertheless their power is very little; and when one has recourse to God and fortifies himself with the virtue of the sacraments,[37] they always create more fear than evil. But the temptations which are to be feared most, and which are more capable of destroying us, are our own bad habits - our penchant for sin, the inclination of our miserable nature.[38] This is where we come up against the most arduous thing of all - in so far as it is necessary to arm part of ourselves against ourselves in order to destroy ourselves. Also, O my God, this is where I had great need of your help, being full of so many miseries! You gave it to me with the excesses of your infinite goodness. Lord, that Heaven and earth, angels and men praise you for it, and render you the acts of thanksgiving which this miserable sinner - who never fittingly acknowledges even the least of your favours - can never give you.

To win or die

I was filled, therefore, with a great light that made me see and know my evil inclinations and habits so perfectly that I saw and knew all the malice of my nature, its twists and turns, all its skills and subtleties, down to its least effects. Seeing also the disorders and the sins of my past life, this clarity was accompanied by a generous and strong resolution in me to resist them and to destroy them entirely or to die of them in the struggle. I had this vision for about fourteen months, accompanied with such an acute and extreme pain that I am amazed I did not die because of it. The sight of my offences did not trouble me, however, knowing well that of myself I could not have done anything else, and that if God had not restrained me I would have done even worse. My pain was excessive but tranquil, accompanied with the strong resolution to die a thousand times rather than return to them.[39]

Then I said to my senses, my passions, to my appetites and my evil inclinations: 'You must die! And, as if damned, lose forever the hope of having or of enjoying any pleasure in what is proper and natural to you!' Then, in order to dictate entirely to my passions, our Lord availed himself of what was natural in my proud and ambitious disposition; for a bad tool in the hands of a good worker does not prevent him sometimes from doing good work.[40] So, abandoning therefore all my vain and mad ambitions for the things of the world, I longed to be sovereign mistress of my desires and passions and not to have to suffer the tyranny of them any more. The resolution and its accomplishment were almost one and the same thing.

I deprived my senses, therefore, of all things that could give them satisfaction, regardless of how little, and made them instead take those things which gave them pain. And I had an interior feeling which inclined me so strongly to this that I scarcely found any difficulty in it; and the light I had was so strong that my senses could not deceive me. So, considering the conditions of a dead body that doesn't see, hear or speak any more, and has no feeling for anything on earth, I said to my body: 'Well! this is the state to which I wish to reduce you!'[41]

I closed my eyes, therefore, so as to see nothing but the ground where I had to walk. Many times at church I had been in situations where I could have seen the King, the Queen and the whole Court,[42] having only to lift my eyes to do so. However, I never did this. But, remaining humbly prostrate before the Holy Sacrament, and being grieved at the little respect shown to him on these occasions, I said to him: 'O Jesus Christ, O King of Kings, it is you alone whom I wish to look at and adore, returning to you with all the affection of my soul, all the honours and public praise that are rendered to all the Kings of the earth, due to you all the more incomparably than to them! If I had all their sceptres and crowns, I would throw them at your feet to make homage with them to your sovereign Majesty, rejoicing to see that all those crowned heads are humbled before your sovereign Majesty and that they are great and blessed only in so far as they have the honour of being your servants!'

I was the same with regard to all other things, even those which were conducive to devotion, making more of the mortification of the senses than of the rest. Devotion can undoubtedly be better obtained in this way than in any other way.

To refrain from reading the letters I received was one thing I found a little difficult. Nevertheless, whenever I opened them the feelings of curiosity were entirely extinguished. I believe I kept one of them once for more than five or six days without opening it, because, wishing to do so, I always felt a little bit of curiosity. It was only the necessity of having to respond to it which made me look at it. I avoided with great care hearing anything about the things of the world; and not being by nature a great talker, I hardly ever opened my mouth except to say the things I could not dispense myself from.

On account of poverty, about which I have spoken elsewhere, I was already forced to cut down a great deal on my food. I even refused every little bit of seasoning I could have put on it; and the bread I ate was often nothing more than a sea biscuit.[44] I did this not out of necessity, but by design.

Naturally, I loved company. I used to say that if anyone would have taken it from me they would have taken away a part of my life. Well! I no longer looked for anything but solitude! And when I was in a room of my own, I often passed many days in succession without seeing or speaking to anyone, except for the few little words I was obliged to say out of necessity and decency. With regard to visits, I didn't make any at all; and now that I write this I believe that, apart from going to church, in more than ten years I have not gone out ten times. If it happens that I must go out for other things, always on my return I visit the great and august Sacrament, placing there all my delights and amusements. Whenever people did come to visit me - for there were some who had enough charity for that - I received them with all the welcome and civility that were possible for me; and in order to remain entirely free to be with the Lord, I would pay them back this one visit and no more. And also, what did make me withdraw more particularly from all kinds of other friendships and conversation, was when I saw that people were beginning to have a special regard for me. I do not know why this was, because there was no reason for it. This caused me great confusion; and I made them avoid me as much as I could and discretion permitted.

But although something in me pushed me so powerfully, so sweetly and so lovingly to the mortification of my passions, I was scarcely able to meet with these occasions the way I would have liked to. Whenever some of these people[45] presented themselves to me, I would embrace them with great intensity, and could not thank our Lord enough for them.

Before and after living alone - where I am at present - I lived with a large number of people and with all sorts of temperaments. For whoever lodges on a weekly basis as I did is exposed to this. And I found that for the temperament, those who were hasty-minded and irascible helped me a great deal in mortifying those same defects in myself. And a thought, which God gave me: to look upon everyone as if they were my superior and to submit myself to them, was so strongly imprinted on my mind that, among the children who might come to me as if I were a schoolmistress to ask something of me, there is not one I would not have responded to as promptly as if they had been my superiors. In this way I mortified that rather haughty temperament I had by nature and lived in great peace with everyone, not only for that time, but forever afterwards, never entering into conflict with anyone.

Intense desires

I had such great desires to suffer that, with St Teresa, I could say not only, 'Either to suffer or to die', but also add, 'To suffer is preferable even to Paradise!'[46] These desires and affections I had only in my heart, but they were so violent that I suffered like a martyr because of them; and I would indeed have acted badly if I had practised the precept which requires that we do to others what we would like others to do to us, since I would certainly have wished that they despise me, scoff at me and do all the outrages possible to me. Those thoughts were the only ones I entertained and I conceived of nothing but those longings, but with a fondness of feeling I would be unable to describe. And whenever this happened to me, I was overwhelmed with inexplicable joy. Burdened with insults and shame, I would have wished to be dragged through the streets with all the ignominies possible. Such great desires I had for penance, and to make satisfaction to God for sins I had committed, that considering in myself the things on account of which I offended him, I tore out my hair with violence, twisted my arms, and caused myself thus other pains in my body which I almost wished to pull to pieces. But my confessor prohibited me from following these movements and ordered me to resist them; which I did, having always preferred to obey more than anything else. I greatly desired to live by begging from door to door, or by the door of the church, and to see myself confined to the corner of a street on a piece of straw. It would have been the joy of my soul; but my sins rendered me unworthy of following so closely the poor Jesus.

When my sister and I came to Paris, the Ursuline sisters at [Langres], where I had stayed,[47] had given us many letters of introduction, recommending us with affection to the persons who knew them in Paris. We were known in this way by some people of means and piety who helped us in our needs. It was even arranged that something would be given to us monthly. When my sister was no longer with me, a part of it[48] was continued for me. However, since the time when our Lord touched me so strongly, I was never troubled about having anything secure in this world. Only mindful of taking the things which his divine Providence had provided me with, I regarded this as one of the many means by which Providence wished to help. This is why I went to accept what was given to me. It was customary there to receive us with great civility, on account of the report which had been given them about us,[49] as I believe. But holding on to the honour of rendering myself as conformable as was possible for me to the poor Jesus, I now stayed at the door with the other people, not wishing to enter any more the way I was accustomed to do; and I received willingly the charity that was given to me in the presence of everyone.[50]

When my daily meal was given to me by Monsieur   ,[51] I went sometimes to fetch it myself. It is true that this was not very often, because I was too clumsy to carry it.[52] But frequently I would take back the jug and the dish in which it had been brought to me. I had a certain repugnance for this. But these were things which I had a fondness in doing, more particularly when I felt profoundly some natural revulsion for them, my mind laying claim to such an absolute authority that it never relished being opposed in anything whatsover.

I made my poverty well enough known when I saw that all I received from it was shame and contempt, taking pleasure in swallowing all this in its natural state; but I had only just discovered this when I realised that it was having other effects.

To suffer in secret

I adored with great respect all the designs of divine Providence for me, and I accepted and embraced with feelings of love and gratitude that were very special those designs which succeeded further in destroying nature in me, thus rendering me more conformable to Jesus Christ,[53] who was poor, despised, unknown and suffering. Since then, our Lord in his goodness has always conserved these affections in me. In order to be able to suffer as he did, and to have a human body in which I suffer pains continually for love of him, how often have I thanked him for having created me from human nature instead of that of the angels. However, I complained about it once to our Lord. For seeing that sickness often never shows itself outwardly, nature would indeed prefer a great sickness, and then to have health, than to be the way I am. But inwardly he let me understand that he is more pleased with secret sufferings than with those that are known, something which made me since love my own sufferings for this reason. In this he taught me not to speak about my sufferings. It is by no means a small mortification for nature not to say a word, make a gesture, or utter a sigh in order to complain and have some relief. I ask pardon of you, my God, that often, seduced by self-love, I made known my little pains more than was necessary. Aid me with your grace that, correcting myself of that fault and of all those of my life, I may do and suffer all things in the way that will be more agreeable to you.

Indescribable affection for offenders

With indescribable affections I prayed to God for all those people who had contributed in putting me in this state of poverty and depriving me of all my possessions. Because it is generally accepted that it was M.   [de Richelieu][54] who was the author of the war; and since it was because of this war that I had been ruined, I said many prayers for him. He was already dead when I had those feelings.[55] But I dare say that I have no scruple in believing that if his soul was then in a position to receive relief from prayers for the repose of the dead, I have given some help to him; for my prayers rose out of a great affection. I did the same for the other particular people whose conduct contributed greatly to the ruin of our family. Looking upon all those things, then, with the eyes of the spirit, and seeing them as particular plans of divine Providence for my sanctification, I had feelings so strong and tender for all those people that not even the sentiments of those who would have given their flesh and blood for them would have been comparable to ones I had for them. Our Lord has always granted me the grace to love in this way the persons who offended me, such that if I had a favour to do, or some good to dispose of, I would undoubtedly, in the sentiment and affection with which I feel myself moved, grant it incomparably to those who had offended me rather than to those who had done me a service. I mention the word 'offended', because this is how one speaks ordinarily. But this language is an error, for instead of offending us, as we say, they do us the greatest good of all, they contribute to the destruction of our vices and make us acquire virtue and practise excellently the highest points of perfection. Consequently, they must be extremely dear to us.

To serve without consolation

I used to say often, and almost at every hour: 'O holy poverty and humility, dear companions of my Master,[56] which have kept faithful company with him right from the moment of his birth to the last moment of his death, come that I may embrace you with all the affections of my soul! Let us make an alliance together; be my inseparable companions for the rest of my life! Never leave or abandon me! I put myself under your protection, in order to be governed and guided absolutely by you; and if in truth your direction seems to be harsh and troublesome, to me, however, it will be very agreeable and sweet!' I saw these two virtues one day at Holy Communion to be planted in my heart and to shoot forth such profound roots there that, afterwards, they sent forth their branches not only throughout all the powers of my soul, understanding, memory and will, but also throughout all the members and senses of my body. It appeared to me that all the thoughts, words and actions of my life should be nothing more than one continual exercise of these virtues; something which I desired and ardently asked for from our Lord. 'O my love', I said to him at every encounter, 'O my crucified love, crucify me with yourself! And draw me to that Cross with you!' And because you have said: 'When I shall be elevated above the earth, I will attract all to me',[57] elevate me there, and attach me to it so that I may die there with you! That the world, the flesh, the demon may never have the power of making me descend from it! That there be the bed of our chaste marriage,[58] where I may be able to give birth to and produce all the virtues of which you have given me the example! That I may embrace you all crowned with thorns, covered with wounds, pierced with nails, and pressing you and gripping you lovingly in that state, I may receive the mark of all your pains and participate in them. There is enough time, indeed an entire eternity, O my Saviour, to enjoy your consolations and resemble you in that state of glory! Thus may everything that is left to me of this life be employed at least in transforming me into your sorrows! Ah Lord, because it is so sweet and delicious to look for you here among the pains and thorns, what felicities will there be in possessing you in eternity, in that state of your glory! O, if I could serve you the rest of my days without relish and without consolation,[59] that is in the complete purity of your pain and suffering! But almost every time I had these

affections and made these requests of our Lord, he always made me see in the interior
that it was impossible to serve him without joy, without peace and without tranquillity,
and that these things are inseparable from his service. Consequently, consolations
were the greater the less I desired them.[60]

Noble and kindly poverty

My desires to suffer and to be poor were so great that I think there is no one as greedy
and earnest in amassing wealth as I was in wishing to be completely stripped of it. All
the praises of honour that my heart was capable of I gave to that holy virtue; and
holding conversations with it, I would say to it: 'Noble and kindly poverty,[61] so
despised and rejected in the world, come that I may put you up honourably in my heart!
That I may give you there the most honourable welcome that is possible for me! Only,
making of this heart your throne of glory, enter there completely victorious, and tread
under foot all the wealth and honours of this world!'

I always took great care to mend my worn clothes, feeling that to do otherwise
would be to act contrary to neatness and to lack respect towards those persons with
whom I lived. And even when the clothes had been rent and torn to pieces though my
fault or neligence, I wore them.[62] With the help of the good God's grace and out of
great feelings of respect and love, as if it were the clothes of poor Jesus I was wearing,
I hope to act thus for the rest of my life: holding it to be a great honour to be attired
like him, even in the house of the great and the rich people of the world, wearing them
as much and even more in my heart as on my body, with a sentiment of love, and often
kissing the clothes as a witness of my affection.

Scarcely do I ever hear about the abundance of wealth possessed by these
persons, that I do not thank our Lord with great affection for not having put me in such
a state. Every day I ask him in a particular prayer to grant me the grace both to live and
die in that state of poverty where he has put me, which I hope for from his goodness.
There is only you, my God, who knows how many tears I shed, and with what
bitterness, when they spoke about taking me out of this state; for it seemed to me that
it was a treasure they wished to rob me of! And you weakened all those many desires
you had given me to live by begging; for your divine Providence has always provided
for my life through other means. May this Providence be forever blessed!

A martyr of love

I suffered incessantly on account of the violent desire I had to suffer. Some people who
knew more particularly the state I was in were amazed how I was able to live. I myself
was astonished whey they pitied me so; for as that great desire to suffer burned in my
heart, whatever I was able to endure was nothing but a piece of straw thrown into a
great fire. I longed ardently for martyrdom. But the places and occasions for it not
being found, all I could do was to console myself with the words of St Pachomius[63] to
his religious: 'My brothers, let us not hasten to run where martyrdom is; the life we lead
is indeed as good as it.'[64] I said to myself, that since I cannot suffer martyrdom from

the hands of the executioner, it is necessary that I suffer it from my own! Love will be the author of it. May my life be nothing but one long and continual martyrdom! All the pains which come from the hands of God, such as heat, cold, hunger, thirst, poverty, nakedness, sickness and the rest, I have always accepted with such an open heart and with such affection, that, far from looking for any solace there, I often aggravated them and added to them as best I could. I was sick with a continual fever, rejecting all the little comforts which some charitable people had procured for me.[65] I hardly drank water any more, or just enough to refresh me; and God permitted that whatever water was given me was only to fortify me and not for me to taste. My mind was attentive only to the mortification of my senses and my nature. That is why I took great pleasure in all of this!

To this I added voluntary penances. And this is where nature made her great repugnance known. But all I did was to laugh at it. I had such great strength and vigour of mind that the difficulties I felt with regard to virtue were no obstacle to me in this, but rather a sting which pricked me and urged me on to conquer with more glory. O if I had had the liberty of following and gratifying the vehemence of that affection which turned me to penance, how I would have considered myself as happy! But there were my confessors who - undoubtedly considering more my infirmities and my feeble complexion than the earnestness of those desires - kept me on a very short leash in this regard. It is unbelievable how I suffered because of that restraint. But I was resolved to obey. They gave me permission, nevertheless, to make use of a discipline and of a girdle[66] which, beyond those times which were permitted every week, I was able to use in addition on all the feasts of our Lord and of the Holy Virgin, and of the saints for whom I had a devotion. On the basis of this permission, there was hardly a week in which I did not perform two or three times - and sometimes four - the discipline of two or three Misereres[67] each. Often I wore the girdle twice. And if the days coincided, I did the two together,[68] adding to them a bread and water fast which I did in that manner on all the vigils and feasts of our Lord and of the Holy Virgin. As I have said, my nature felt great repugnance for this; but it seems to me that my interior strength was so great that I would have overcome all obstacles which were preventing me from subduing it [nature] completely and coming to the perfect freedom of the mind to which I aspired.[69]

I did not practise other penances because I was not permitted to do so; although, being as culpable and as criminal as I am, I would have every good reason in doing all the greatest penances that have ever been done. I confess, my God, if I alone had performed all the penances that were ever done, I would not have been able by that to answer for my crimes in the slightest. Being so destitute, then, my God, what shall I do? It is in your infinite goodness, my God, and through the merits of the holy life, death and passion of our Lord Jesus Christ, that I hope for pardon for my sins. This is what I lean upon, and where I put all the hope for my salvation.

My mind desired, sought after, embraced and practised everything which was repugnant to nature, no matter how little, with an ardour and affection that were intense. My mind kept nature so much in subjection that I was unable to make any resistance to what would give me pain, or slacken in any way the accomplishment of the mind's designs. I followed many times a poor person who had an ulcer on his face so that I could kiss the wound; because in looking at it I felt profoundly a certain horror. And in seeing the wounds and the ulcers, I would suck and kiss[70] them with an unparalleled affection and ardour of spirit; and nothing really prevented me from doing it in fact - as I was doing so in mind and out of affection - except for the fear alone of being seen, which would not give a good impression of me. So it was not for lack of willingness or resolution that I did not do it and, it seems to me that it still had the same effect on me of subduing and subjecting nature as if I had done it explicitly.

I pictured to myself the most terrible and unfortunate accidents that could happen in the life of anyone, all the strangest sicknesses to which the human body is subject; and often, by an interior act of the will, I would embrace them, bringing myself to suffer them when it would please God to send them to me. And when it would please you to send them to me I would regard it as a great favour to suffer them, being indebted to your infinite goodness for having put me in that disposition to receive them and endure them not only with peace and patience, but also with joy, love and thanksgiving. Why have I not suffered them?

Total detachment

This love I had for mortification was extended to all things, to the least desires of the heart and movement of the passions as well as to the flesh and the senses. I began therefore to mortify and empty myself entirely of all the affection and natural inclination I had for my homeland and the place of my birth. I renounced all the desires I had retained up to then of returning there, so that I could abandon myself completely to the dispositions of divine Providence, offering myself heartily to the accomplishment of all its designs with regard to my life or my death, such a position or employment, dwelling and the like, and that this Providence would dispose of me as it pleases. I no longer had any desire or will beyond doing in everything and everywhere the will of God.

I was also purged of all purely natural affections and love I had for my relatives, being removed far from everyone, except my sister - who was then working as a servant - whom I saw only rarely, and whom I received kindly only within what reason and charity demanded of me, mortifying all the rest. I did not look upon her any longer with the eyes of flesh and blood, but loved her in God, for God, and for as much as God wishes, and nothing more. Without joy and without sadness I saw her off from Paris to return to our homeland, come back here again, and leave a second time,[71] always having my mind in the same state and disposition, and having no other desire or feeling but that the will of God be done, and that his designs be entirely accomplished in us and through us. The likelihood of never seeing any of those close to me again, and of ending my days in a strange place,[72] does not affect me any more. I have neither the desire nor design of returning to my homeland,[73] nor of staying here either. But abandoning everything into the hands of God so that he dispose of me as it pleases him, all things are the same to me, and cannot be otherwise for the person who seeks only to fulfil the will of God.

There was not the slightest desire one might have in a day, in a season, to do this and not that, one work in preference to another, that was not arranged in me so as to take everything, in general or in particular, from his hand and according to the order of Providence. The least desires and movements of passions were immediately extinguished in me from the moment they were perceived, and completely suffocated before they took form.[74] In fact, it appeared to me that I no longer desired or loved anything according to nature and the senses. And with regard to the delights and sentiments of devotion, I have never desired or looked for them; and in no way did I dwell upon them from any gratification, but attached myself entirely only to God and the accomplishment of his holy will. I had a great love for all the exercises and practices of devotion, but without attachment.

For about the past twelve years since I have been in Paris,[75] I have changed my confessor five times. Divine Providence ordained it so and by this means touched me where I was most sensitive; for every confessor, I assure you, was extremely dear to me, and I have never been able to understand the behaviour of many people who have many confessors and directors. If they hear some knowledgeable or spiritual person spoken of, they go and tell him the whole state of their souls. All the ways of God are good and holy, and I venerate them all with my whole heart. But he has led me in a way so different from that that I have never had any communication with anyone apart from my confessors. To all of them God granted me in his goodness to be most submissive; to have respect for them, a great simplicity in telling them everything they wished to know about me; and also, when I did not see them disposed to this, to be completely unconcerned about saying nothing to them.

In so far as I was able to let him know, there was only one confessor who knew completely the state of my soul;[76] for I had difficulty in explaining myself in many things. But our Lord gave me to this man in a very particular way, such as his heart would have wished. When each time came to change confessors, I was always given by our Lord an extraordinary inclination to request them of him: to beseech him that he himself make the choice; that he give me the kind of confessor that would please him most, so that I would be perfectly directed by someone who would be pleasing to him;[77] and devoting myself to the perfect accomplishment of all he desired, I renounced every satisfaction and self-interest - even with regard to that of perfection - except in so far as he wished it. I asked you then, after the death of one of my confessors,[78] to give me one. It pleased you, O my God, to speak to me, this worthless creature; because she is yours and belongs to you, you have always taken good care of her and directed her so well! It pleased you, I say, my Saviour, to say to me: 'Go to such a Father.' Because of my extreme poverty I feared that I would not have free access to him; and I did not dare approach him. But one day at Holy Communion it pleased you moreover to say to me: 'Do not fear! I will give him a very particular affection for directing you!' Fixing my heart and my mind so much on this, and having been given such a great, interior freedom and facility to speak to my confessor, I myself was often astonished by it all. I won't dwell much on all the knowledge I acquired from this, nor on the other interior words[79] which were spoken to me, except those which are in conformity with the faith. Nevertheless, what followed made me more certain that the indication and direction given me were given me by God. I thank you for it, Lord of all goodness, and I beseech you through your great mercies and the precious blood by which you have ransomed me to give my confessor that interior wish to rid me completely of myself and to attach perfectly my will to your Cross.

When it was necessary to make that change of confessor - which was so painful for me and yet without anxiety of mind, because my confidence was in God - the first thing I did, having asked him, was to renounce my exercises of devotion and way of living, replacing them all entirely in his hands, assuring him that it was purely for his[80] love, his glory and the fulfilment of his designs for me that I had undertaken and embraced them; that I was also as ready to leave them, change them or to take on others completely different; and that the only thing I sought to do was his will. Being so disposed, I was allowed by all my confessors unanimously to follow the same way; for our Lord did not vary his ways of directing me. They arranged my exterior exercises of devotion, like Communion, the time of my prayers, my prayers and the rest; but so far as the direction of my heart and mind were concerned, they only said to me to follow in all simplicity the attractions of God.

Now I have never been drawn very much to exterior works of piety with regard to my neighbour, whether because I had neither the health nor the means, or because of other things of which I am not aware.[81] My attraction, and that to which I applied myself entirely, was more to the mortification of my passions, that is to follow in all things what was contrary to my natural inclinations, and to cut myself off entirely and immediately from all pleasures and recreations which my senses could desire, regardless of how licit and innocent they might appear. I embraced solitude, silence, poverty, disdain, humiliation, prayer, the frequentation of the sacraments, sermons and such things which, if I didn't really have a strong aversion for, I did not at least have any natural disposition towards.

When the thought came to my mind that I would not be able to live in that way, I would coldly say to my body: if you are able to live this way, you will live; if not, you will die! This is something I shall scarcely trouble myself about any more.[82] Refusing absolutely to the senses and to nature what they desired gave me a great rest and tranquillity of mind. I consider it even to be a miserable life that bestows on them one thing and refuses them another; that belongs today to God, tomorrow to oneself; that is enchanted one day with devotion and another with the world. Acting thus, neither the body nor the mind are satisfied and content. But when one gives an entire and generous refusal to all one's desires, in a very short time one enjoys a great interior peace, and one asks for very few things afterwards and desires them so feebly that they are incapable of giving any unrest to the mind.

Infused lights

The transformation of the will

Now such a great, interior light made me see in a very particular way what I must do, when and how, and in the same way what I must not do, the reasons and motives why, that even the least details were made manifest to me. All my actions were revealed to me in such a manner as to make me see their least faults and thus prevent me from falling in this a second time. In this light there was as if a certain ray which made me realise how, in the persuance of each inspiration and the practice of every act of virtue, depended the grace of our eternal predestination. One is not damned because one has failed in the living of some counsel or certain points of perfection; for whoever carries out the commandments will be saved![83] But what I mean is, that I saw how through every act of virtue the bad habit is destroyed, virtue is formed and grace is given to us more abundantly. And as Jesus Christ himself has said, that much will be given to him who will be faithful in little things,[84] in this sense it is true to say that in the practice of every act of virtue depends the grace of our predestination. This light of understanding made me exact in the slightest and most imperceptible of things, but without being troubled or worried in mind.

The mind and decrees of God were also all but shown to me in everything that happened to me. And binding myself tightly to them, there is no sort of punishment or suffering, even that of Hell, I would not have endured willingly in order to fulfil them down to the smallest details. I felt such great desires to do in all things the will of God, and that his will be fulfilled in everything and everywhere, that with a loving sprightliness I often uttered these words: 'O holy and lovable will of God, be done in everything and everywhere, in time and in eternity!' I have seen two or three times this divine will enter into the bosom of my soul, take, eat and devour my own will, transforming it completely into itself while remaining in me to govern, direct and guide me entirely.

It is also true that I do not understand how one can wish, desire or ask on behalf of oneself or others anything other than what God wishes, be it temporal or spiritual, in time or eternity. It has often given me much pain to hear in sermons so many reasons given to people for them to turn to virtue and give up vice, since it appears to me that, in order to persuade them to do so with passion and love, it would be enough to say to them: 'God wishes it.' As for myself, these words alone touch my heart incomparably more than all the threats of Hell or than the hope of all the recompenses of Paradise. Lord my God, your mercies cannot be numbered, and they surpass by far the drops of

113

water in the ocean and the grains of sand on the sea shore! For moreover, it pleased you to diffuse so much clarity into my soul, getting me to see, even while in this world, the beauty, integrity and benefit of virtue, that these lights, so brilliant, made marvellous impressions on my will without any need whatsoever of words or reasonings, since, in effect, the understanding was convinced of these truths at the same time as the will was moved to follow them.

How often have you let me see how miserable is the life of the sinner, how it is the beginning of the Hell into which he must fall if he does not turn away; and how there is incomparably more pain in being damned than in being saved. In fact, the works of virtue are sweetened by your grace; the peace and rest of a good conscience are goods that cannot be estimated, whose delights of mind transport it incomparably more than pleasures of the body and the senses. If the sinner has difficulty in mortifying his inclinations and appetites, he will indeed have much more pain if he follows them and satisfies them! This word 'satisfy' is badly chosen; for this is what never happens, it is not even possible. It seems to me that the passions and the desires one has to gratify the senses are like snarling and famished dogs who take over and torment the miserable soul without ceasing, crying relentlessly to have some pleasure, a morsel of bread or a bone to chew on, but after which they are again as hungry as before. The only thing those who wish to satisfy the senses get from it is to see themselves still more tormented because of it.[85] However, I am astonished to see that everyone in fact experiences this, and prefers to be eaten and chewed by these fierce beasts than to take once the resolution and the trouble to bind them in chains and subject them to reason.

It pleased you once, O Lord, to let me see above all how shameful and infamous it is to live as the slave of the flesh and the senses, and how this sort of life is miserable! This vision remained with me for a very short time, but made such a great impression on my mind nevertheless, that since that time I have always been in that disposition in which I would prefer to die rather than to live even one hour in such a state. And I ask this of you, my God, out of the greatest affection of my heart: that I die rather than ever fall in this! I know well, whether one likes it or not, that it is necessary to concede many things to the body; for need, reason and more, the order of God (which has subjected us to the body), obliges us to do so. But to seek the pure satisfaction of the senses is to act like a beast. I saw therefore, during a great day of light, the pains, the miseries and the ignominy of that sort of beastly life; how the death which follows it is appalling, and the eternity still more terrible. I confess that my mind is astonished at all this, and that I would never understand the madness, or rather the strange passion of people who take pleasure in leading a life so wretched as to render themselves still more miserable for eternity. O, how the vision I had of these truths made me shed tears! Because, seeing the offences which people commit against God and the little care they have for their salvation, I could do nothing but cry for the first years. But our Lord took away from me the vision of these truths, perhaps because I was not able any longer to endure them without them endangering my life.

But if, O Lord, you let me see the punishments and chastisements of vices and of the dissolute life, you certainly also let me know likewise the advantages and recompenses of virtue, as much in this life as in Heaven; and how, seeing that there are no labours and sorrows equal to the grief and bitterness of a culpable conscience, for a relatively short pain (which is always less than that which one suffers because of sin), there is a fulfilled eternity of happiness and repose.

You made me see all these things, Lord, in a way quite different from what I can describe; and in spite of this, Lord, you never guided me by the way of fear or hope, but through the way of pure love. You placed initially, and at the first instant, such a pure and upright intention in my heart that I looked at nothing but you,[86] setting all my happiness in doing your good pleasure in everything. Nevertheless, these visions give untold new strength to the soul, rendering it as though unshakeable in the resolutions it has taken in the service of God; and the soul avails itself of them through an exercise of love, and kindles itself with love, not for the kindnesses which are shown to it, but for the one who gives them. And the soul fears, not the chastisements, but that which causes them, dreading above all the least sin rather than all the torments of Hell, into which it would throw itself without consideration and with joy in order to avoid sin, if it could not be done otherwise, and would never wish to leave Hell, if in coming out from there it would have to commit sin.

Hope in God alone

I had a very evil propensity, a habit of lying. So it happened to me once that I said some words which were not properly speaking a lie, but merely an exaggeration. Now I had a small image of the Holy Virgin and St Anne with the little Jesus; and every day I said a prayer before this image. Then, wanting to perform my devotion, I saw that the little Jesus had tears in his eyes. It is not that I wish to say that he actually cried, but that it appeared to me so. This vision however was only imaginary; and of that sort I have very few. All the visions God gave me were purely intellectual, without form or image.[87] But this time I cannot really say in what way it happened. But, completely surprised by this effect, immediately the remorse of my conscience made me reproach myself of these words because they appeared to be the cause of the tears of the little Jesus. Thus, strained in soul by an acute sorrow, and crying abundantly, I didn't know what to do to appease our Lord; and beholding him, it appeared to me he was looking at me with indignation. I was as if swallowed up in sorrow, suffering an interior torment greater than I am able to express. I was for about one hour in that state, after which our Lord made me see in my mind how the damned will suffer incomparably more at the last judgement by the angered looks of the Judge than by the torments of Hell. This vision remained a long time imprinted on my mind, and there were about two months in particular when I could not look at that image without fear and trembling, dreading always seeing what I had seen. It pleased you in that way, O my Jesus, to purify me and to chastise me for the offences I committed and to correct me of that evil habit I had of lying. I have a singular horror of all sorts of lies, of pretence, double meaning and equivocal words - which I detest in any form more than an obvious lie, because they seem to me to be more evil than a lie where one sees quite well that one has sinned and tries to correct oneself of it. But in such words, one deceives not only one's neighbour but also oneself, thinking that in this way one has covered up well for oneself. But in the presence of God, this is no good; and our Lord has told us that whenever we shall say anything we shall have to say it twice: 'Yes, yes; no, no!'[88] This is to teach us that the mouth and the heart must say one and the same thing.

A person[89] once came to me to say that much was spoken about me at the home of Monsieur .[90] I had only been a very few times in that house, and beyond that I remained completely alone in my room. She added that some people from that house, and others of very great standing, wished to come and see me and that they desired to get to know me. I felt at the start some vain willingness presenting itself to my mind; but turning myself immediately to our Lord, I said to him lovingly: 'O my God, you know that I neither desire nor look for these acquaintances! If they are the means that might please you to avail yourself of in providing for my needs, I pray you then to take my heart and to watch over it well in these encounters; and, if it pleases you, prevent anything from entering there that might displease you.' Lord, who could recount your mercies and the care you have of those who have recourse to you! When I went to that house, everyone made me very welcome with wonderful caresses. But in the midst of all that, I saw my heart to be so firm, a secret and all-powerful virtue rejecting and banishing from myself all these things, farther than from one extreme of the world to the other, that nothing of all this did me any harm. On the contrary really, it united me all the more intimately to our Lord and made me abandon myself entirely to his Providence, hoping only in him alone. With regard to these people, I viewed their virtue with great esteem and had much affection in serving them. I recommended them to God with great earnestness, but so removed in all this from the sentiments of nature that it didn't have any part in it. I thank you that it has pleased you to conserve me [thus] up to the present, my God; and I beseech you through your infinite kindness to conserve me [so] to the end. Amen.

The inestimable knowledge of one's nothingness

Once, on entering the garden,[91] I turned my thoughts to consider the gardener who plants tulip bulbs a great way down in the earth, then covers them with it in order to make them rot, sprout and finally put forth flowers. By this means, then, it pleased you, O Lord, you who use the smallest things to help us discover the greatest things, to enlighten my mind, letting me know that it was thus necessary to hide myself and to cover myself in the knowledge of my misery and my nothingness in order to be able to appear at the spring of eternity. For many days my mind was elevated in prayer on this subject. There is nothing so vile as nothingness, nothing so contemptible, nothing so abominable as sin.[92] But there is no knowledge more profitable to the soul than this. It causes good effects almost infinite in number and inestimable in value. When the soul is well fortified and concealed in this knowledge, the devil has no power over it. For what can he do with nothingness? It is God who out of nothing can make something! And as all his works are perfect, when he finds the soul in this state of perfect nothingness,[93] he makes of it a rare work of art from his hands.[94]

I have seen that all the good that is true and the glory that is real reside in that which men call humiliation and self-abasement, as, on the contrary, all the preferments of this world are nothing but vileness and baseness. On every encounter with our Lord he gave me much enlightenment on this question.[95] And when it pleased him, and still might please him, to communicate these lights of understanding to me, I quit every other activity in order to occupy myself entirely with them. Very few months pass by without my taking this enlightenment as the particular subject of my prayers for many days in succession. And since God is an infinite abyss of all good, I find that we can indeed say that we are an infinite abyss of all evil.[96] I know and understand this truth better every day. But speak, Lord, for your poor servant is listening to you.[97] Inculcate it and imprint it so well in my heart that nothing will ever be able to wipe it out. Renew for me often those lights which you have deigned to give me, since of myself all I have is nothingness and sin. I confess this, and avow to it also in your presence, my God, so that it may please you to preserve me from the faults you sometimes let us fall into in order to make us know that, of ourselves, we have and are capable of nothing else. I declare this before Heaven and earth, angels and men; and saying now that of myself all I have is nothingness and sin, I renounce all esteem, all vain praise that one can give me, and give it back entirely to you, my God, for it is you alone to whom it belongs, and in no way to me. I declare also this truth to the demons - that of myself I am only nothingness and sin - so that these spirits of pride know that I am instructed in this truth; and that they do not come suggesting the contrary to me. I often make this prayer to God. Of all the things I have ever desired to be informed of and to understand, it is this truth.

The Holy Sacrament

The power of grace

Through all those lights and knowledge, and through many others which I cannot describe, together with the interior words[98] which were said to me and which I have quoted elsewhere, our Lord made me resolve to embrace strongly a way of life completely contrary to the one I had followed. But the first means it pleased him to avail of principally for this was the most august Sacrament of the altar. From the start, through his pure kindness and generosity, he gave me such great desires for Communion that, because of the violence of those desires, the evenings[99] of the day on which I was to receive Communion, I entered as into an agony, so much so that this agony was not even relieved by the hope of being able to receive Communion the following day. Often I would go and place myself at the rail for Communion;[100] and seeing Communion being given to others, I would open my mouth as if to receive the sacred host through the mouth of all those who were communicating. Since the time that God touched me, I have never been jealous of anyone, except perhaps of two kinds of persons: namely, priests, because they receive Communion every day; and those who are poorer than I and who suffer more than I do, for whom I had more envy and jealousy than compassion, and from whom if it had been in my power, I would have torn away by force all their pains so as to draw them to myself. And this was a great fault on my part. I did not have enough pity for the pains of others; for which, my God, I ask your pardon. But those desires I had were so great that they prevented me from feeling and seeing the weakness and infirmity of our nature. I remember, in this regard, saying one day to my confessor: 'I really do not know if I am on the path to salvation; but if I am, I do not see what difficulty there is in being saved, for I myself I don't find any!' To which he responded: 'Do not speak any more I like this, for generally there is very great difficulty in this; but say: "My God, what difficulty is there in doing good things when you give us a strong and extraordinary grace to do them, which lifts us over and above all the infirmities and weaknesses of our nature, and because you carry us lovingly in your arms?" For that is the state you are in.' This response has always stayed in my mind. And well I should humiliate myself before you, my God; for if you had let me feel profoundly all the pains and difficulties of virtue I would not have had the heart to endure them.

Holy fervour

Returning to the Holy Sacrament - I say it was our Lord who, through those extraordinary desires, drew me to Communion; he himself who, powerfully and effectually, and out of his infinite goodness, deigned to touch my heart by that divine Sacrament. And approaching it with the fervours and affections of love and confidence, and with the knowledge of my inexplicable misery, I used to say to him: 'O my Lord, from the past I see what I shall be in the future; from what I have done even, what I am capable of still doing, if you have no pity on me according to your great mercies. And so I give you my wicked and evil nature that it may please you to destroy it and win it over completely, knowing well that all my efforts are useless to accomplish this fully. Though I resist its furies, I will not defend myself from its wiles and subtleties: it will disguise itself in so many ways that I will never be able to defend myself from them. But you, O Lord, who are eternal wisdom, you to whom all things are known, pursue this nature to the death, and do not allow that it be satisfied ever again or contented in anything. Plunder now, O my God, all my sins and bad habits. Put them to the edge of the sword, killing them with the spear of your love. Kill utterly that Hydra[101] not only of ten, but of a thousand heads; for such a deed can only come from your all-powerful hand. Do it out of justice and mercy: out of justice, for it is truly fitting that everything which in me has revolted against you die and be completely destroyed; out of mercy, O my sweet Jesus, because you could quite rightly abandon me in my malice and leave me to die in my sin, there being only your infinite goodness compelling you to take me out of it. But, O my sweet Redeemer, break the chains, destroy the links, pull me completely out from under the infamous enslavement to the world, the devil, the flesh and sin. Give me the mark of my eternal slavery to your service. For after all, my God, I am the work of your hands and the price of your blood! Let this blood fall on me in such great abundance that it suffocates and drowns in me every last movement and instinct to sin. With such holy fervour, kindle in my heart that sacred fire which you brought from Heaven to earth; let it burn, down to the marrow of my bones, that which could, no matter how little, displease you in me. In a word, my Lord, I implore you, by your sacred wounds and the abundance of your merits, to make up for my unworthiness, placing me entirely in that state in which, both in body and spirit, it pleases you that I be for your greater glory. Accept from me that service which pleases you most in me. Show me what you can and will do as God and Master when you find a heart and body abandoned to the sovereign power of your love.'[102]

Appearance and reality

Afterwards, whenever I felt the movement of some passions again, or inclinations to my bad habits, having recourse once more to our Lord when I possessed him in that loving Sacrament, I continued to say to him: 'O my Lord, I beseech you to see this passion and look at this evil inclination, for they are only asleep. I desire and ask of you the grace that they die without any remission whatever.[103] Tear away from my memory and from my imagination all foolish things and the recollection of everything that could displease you; tear away, tear away entirely, O my Saviour, the brambles and thorns of all my sins and my bad habits; take away from my understanding all error and ignorance, and from my will all the malice with which it is filled; take away from my eyes all their fickleness, from my taste and my cravings sensuality and gluttony, from my flesh all impurity, and generally all that which in me, no matter how little, is an obstacle to the accomplishment of your good pleasure; fill my memory with holy thoughts, my understanding with the knowledge of your divine and eternal truths; put into my will so much charity and so much love that sin may never be able to enter there again, and into my eyes put simplicity and innocence, into my taste abstinence and mortification, into my flesh a perfect chastity and purity.[104] Finally, my only Lord, make my body and my soul the portrait of a perfect sanctity![105] Do in me,, for your glory, what you do in that divine Sacrament in order to give yourself to me, since you conserve there the accidents but destroy their substance! Leave in me also the appearance of a human creature, but render me completely divine in the interior.[106] Remain in me and I in you, as you have promised,[107] that I may be truly able to say with the Apostle: I live, now not I, but Jesus Christ in me.[108] How dare I invite you, O my sweet Jesus, to make your abode in my heart since it is so full of filth and misery? But, O Lord, you who wished to be born in a poor and vile stable, and who by your august presence rendered it a thousand times more illustrious and more precious than the palaces and Louvres[109] of the Kings; and who, having wished to die on the infamous and ignominious stake of the Cross, rendered it, through your sacred touch, a sign of honour and an instrument of all blessing. In the same way, my Lord, although I am abominable and detestable on account of my sins, you can change me completely by your divine presence. And since you can take more glory from the conversion of a sinner than from the creation of a thousand worlds, glorify yourself in this poor and miserable creature who wishes either to be completely yours or exist no more, to serve you perfectly or to die. Since it pleases you to nourish me with that bread of angels, render me all angelic and fulfil the word you gave - that your servants shall be where you will be,[110] drawing me with yourself into the bosom of your Father so that I may live there with you a life completely celestial and divine, and no longer have any occupation other than contemplating you, praising you and loving you.'

Eucharist, channel of grace

It would be impossible for me to speak about the different attractions by which it pleased our Lord to draw me to that divine Sacrament and to make known even more the abundance of affections he placed in my heart. Consequently, I have no intention to do so; for I desire more to shorten what I have to say than to draw it out at length. But I believe I have to say something about this in order to make his direction of me known all the better; for in this, as in prayer, his was the only guidance I had. I bore inconceivable feelings of envy and jealousy for tabernacles and ciboriums, because these contained and enclosed the sacred body of the Saviour. And when I used to see the tabernacle being shut up after Communion, I would have wished either that my heart be changed into those sacred vessels so as to possess forever the good they contained, or to be able at least, through a loving sentiment, to tear away my heart from my breast and, in a continual exercise of love, to close it up with them. O how often the days on which I was unable to receive him seemed terrible to get through!

While hearing holy Mass, from the time of the consecration up to when the priest has received Communion, or during the time when he distributes it after holy Mass, I never leave church unless I am exceptionally pressed to do so, a sentiment of love and respect in the presence of Jesus Christ stopping me. And moreover, I always hear Mass as much as I can at the high altar, because the Holy Sacrament reposes there.

The heart, blood and wounds of our Lord have been the object of my most tender and loving devotions. I took such strength from them that, in placing there all the resolutions I made to correct myself and to practise the virtues, they never failed to produce their effect. Entering by those doors into the divinity, the soul in the same way remains completely lost and swallowed up there.

Finally, what I can say about this Sacrament, from my experience is this: that unlike all the other exercises of piety and devotion in which our Lord lets his graces flow drop by drop, or rather like streams, he pours them out here in such great abundance that, in order to extinguish and drown our sins and evil habits all at once, in a manner of saying, he lavishes them on us as if in torrents. In the same way as there is greater honour for a captain who wins at arms with his bare hands and, instead of entering in there without finding any resistance, gains ground by fighting generously and giving proof of his courage; so the soul receives in this Sacrament such great strengths (so as to vanquish with greater glory) that afterwards it makes nothing but sport of the greatest difficulties and would almost be distressed if it had found none.

After all, our Lord has his ways with all creatures and different means for their sanctification and of communicating to them the graces which he, in his goodness, wishes to bestow on them. But participation in this august Sacrament has been for me the great channel through which it pleased him to give me his graces.[111] So I was often bound to him in such a way as to be able to put my mouth into his sacred wounds and drink to my satisfaction from those sources of living water.

Hell versus the Eucharist

The devil, who certainly sees the fruit there is to be had at Holy Communion, makes every effort to prevent this. I have been strangely persecuted in this as well as in the rest of my exercises of devotion. I have often been in such great desolation, that it seemed to me I was hanging on by no more than a little thread. Without some hidden virtue holding me there, not perceptible but only manifesting itself in its effects and making me stand firm, I would have given up everything. Now it was not the lack of consolation which put me in that state, but it appeared to me that I was offending God in all of my devotions and not hearing Mass at all. I was so greatly troubled when I went to confession, that all at once I often forgot everything I had to say, remaining so dumbfounded that I was not able to speak. My confessor had need of great patience with me in this. O Lord, you are really just! You arranged with all justification those punishments and chastisements, because of the fact that I had lived almost without faith and without religion.

But during those pains of the spirit, a very peculiar thing happened to me once. It was the feast of St Anthony of Padua.[112] For a long time now I have had a particular devotion to that great Saint.[113] I had planned at that time to make my devotions in some church of his order,[114] as much for the gaining of indulgences as because the Holy Sacrament was also reserved there; which is what especially attracted me. So I attended Mass and afterwards asked the person who had served it if I could receive Communion. He asked if I had been to confession. This question surprised me a little, for I had not been that day. I begged him, then, not to trouble himself, and told him that indeed I would not approach the Sacrament without knowing how to. He said something in a low voice - which I did not hear - to the priest who, on turning towards me, and before everyone present, asked me in a loud voice who I was, which neighbourhood I lived in, and if I had some acquaintance in the house (for it was a house of religious women); and said that one does not give Communion in such a way to unknown people. I answered him in few words; for it was really easy for me to speak to him, being perhaps no more than 200 steps from where he was. But he, without dwelling on what I said to him, left the altar without giving me Communion.

I remained thus on my knees, in the same place, without being troubled or moved in spirit. I then entered into myself to see if I had something particularly on my conscience that prevented me from communicating and why God had permitted that I be refused it. But I found nothing. My soul could indeed have been soiled, perhaps, by many sins while communicating; but I did not see them. And if I were to know that my heart was soiled by a venial sin, I would not be able, it seems to me, to bring myself to receive Communion. So finding nothing, I did not know what to think. But, it seems to me, at that moment I knew clearly that it was the devil who had done this so as to prevent me from going to Communion. 'If it is nothing but that, my God,' I said, 'then it amounts to nothing.' And I left promptly in order to go to another church and receive Communion there, for it was already late. But having received the Holy Host, I don't know how long I was in turning it around in my mouth without being able to swallow it; and my face felt completely on fire, as if someone held me by the throat to prevent me from consuming the Host. Nevertheless, having done so with a great deal of difficulty, it seemed as if I was going to split and burst. I beheld all this, not knowing what it could be; but our Lord let me know that it was an act of the devil, and that, not being able to prevent me from communicating, he, the devil, meant to trouble and disquiet me at least by that.

Transverberation[115]

Once while doing my devotions, I saw flames of fire in my heart, but so beautiful, so pure and so shining that I took pleasure in looking at them. However, I did not feel any heat from them. It was given me to understand that these were the prayers I made without enjoyment and without feeling, and which, having been made out of pure love, are very beautiful and pleasing to God.

Another time, having received Communion with much dryness and aridity, and on returning from there to my room where I was still living completely alone, I was filled with such a great feeling of devotion that, imagining myself to be entirely melting away, I had great difficulty in getting to the place where I dwell. Having arrived there, I sat down immediately, hardly able to support myself any more. And then I saw Heaven and our Lord, who, from the throne of his glory, was putting an arrow or a dart into my heart. And receiving the stab, through a feeling and an affection of love, I threw the arrow or dart back into his heart, in order to provoke it by its return to wound me again more strongly. Our Lord threw again the same arrow, and I again sent it back in the same way. For about a quarter of an hour, or a half-hour (if I am capable of judging the time, considering the state I was in) I received and returned these darts; after which, however, abandoning myself completely to the guidance and sovereign power of love, I remained in a swoon and without strength in body or in spirit.[116]

Effects of the transforming union

Those, more or less, were my desires, my affections and exercises for about four or five years. I strove incessantly towards a continual mortification of body and mind, refused absolutely to nature everything it desired, no matter how little, going against it in every way. This I sometimes did with force and violence when I encountered any resistance. Other times it was done with more gentleness. And, reasoning from the more human side of myself, I used to point out to nature that it was better for it to submit and obey, and that everything that was being done was done for its good. Then it would consent to all my desires, in such a way that the flesh as well as the mind desired to serve God. It subjected itself in a manner and with a promptitude I would have difficulty in describing, to all of God's laws and all the designs of punishment and suffering he had for it. I do not know if our Lord changed my nature, or even how this is done. But well I do know, that on the one hand I loved, looked for, desired and embraced with ardour and love the things I naturally abhorred, and on the other hand rejected, disdained and avoided, as much as was possible for me, all those things I naturally loved.

Knowledge of good and evil

This light I had in knowing my natural inclinations and passions, and the delight I took in battling and destroying them entirely,[117] was present for me always during the time of my temptations. And this had been one of the great means by which God helped me to vanquish them. As to the other desires,[118] they were not strictly speaking entirely taken from me; for good and evil, temptations and good affections were mixed together in my mind. When there was more of the one, there appeared less of the other. However, during the two years of my temptations, this light succoured me a great deal. For me it was a time of extreme suffering. All the feelings of my soul and body were extremely acute. And when I was not suffering the pain and anxiety of interior torments - which were causing me temptations - I was suffering another torment through the intensity of my desires and my love; which torment, although more sweet, was neither less great nor less perceptible. As long as our Lord led me along this road and made me walk by means of his light, I recognised and understood his direction of me. It indeed seemed to me to be good, since it consisted of nothing but a continual self-abnegation; which is so much recommended to us. But, O my God, there has certainly been much change in my life; and I ask you again for your help and the succour of your grace, so that I may be able to speak about that which I do not know, and be able to describe what I see and experience but do not understand. O my God, who have never ordered anyone to do anything without at the same time giving him the grace to accomplish it, since it is your will that I make this declaration, give me the light to do it well. I hope for this, Lord, from your infinite goodness.

The Great Darkness

Dead to the world and to self

Deadening of the senses

I say first of all, then, that I have been in a state [of darkness] for about six years; and I do not know if it has come about all of a sudden or little by little.[119] It was when I was stopping with Monsieur   [120] that I became aware of this state and began to understand it better. But I say that in this state one is not aware of what mortification is. I only knew this virtue by its name; but as regards the practice of it, I was not aware of it at all, or at least so little that it could pass for nothing. For in this state I neither see, hear, taste, touch nor speak any more. Not that I don't perform all these things, or make use of my senses! But it is a seeing without seeing,[121] a tasting without tasting, a speaking without speaking, touching without touching; and so for the rest. The senses no longer desire the things that content them. And when they do come across them, they no longer receive either delectation or pleasure from them. There is in this state, it appears to me, something like a division, a separation of the flesh and the spirit, where the soul is no longer in correspondence with its vain pleasures; and where all visible and perceptible things - be they spiritual or material - are seen to be superficial and dead, because they lack the power to penetrate to the [soul's] interior. In this state one would be very surprised if these external things made any impression of contentment or pain on the spirit. The body has its pains, and sometimes very acutely, the senses have their affliction; but in this state the mind pays no attention to them and does not think about them; for nature would suffer much more. Because, when the taste of the spirit diffuses itself throughout the body, it either lessens the body's pains or gives it a certain strength to suffer them. But when the taste of the spirit is missing in the body, this does not happen. Although the body endures, it is, however, with patience, and the soul takes reasonable care of it, according to its needs, because God wishes it; for the body is necessary to him so that the soul may serve him.

Since I have been in this state I desire nothing and do not distinguish between days, months, times or seasons; and the most perceptible things, it seems to me, are those which make the least impression. Sometimes, with the greatest attention I was capable of, I turned to look at the sky, the sun or whatever objects presented themselves to my eyes. And if someone had asked me, 'What do you see?' I would have answered, 'Nothing!'[122] For whenever I saw anything, it was always with a dead look that made no impression on my soul. What I can say about this sense [of sight],

127

I can also say about the others. There is something which surprises me even in the resolution I took to use all the means I could find in order to mortify myself. I took medicines, swallowing all their bitterness and savouring all the bad taste they could have, even without taking anything afterwards to make the taste pass away. But in this state I don't have that feeling of horror and repugnance which is fairly common in such circumstances. For I can say that I now do these things without being aware of them. Moreover, being amazed at this, I can say that I have put things five or six times into my mouth, things that were capable of causing horror and of making the heart jump just at the mere mention of them, and I had no sensation from them whatever. All I can say is, that it was as if one had placed them into the mouth of a dead person who would feel nothing and would not be aware of them.

During Lent most people, if not all, complain because they find so much difficulty with the fast and the change of food. This is something I have never noticed in myself, even though, through the grace of God, I have always observed Lent to the full, as also all the other days of the year.[123] But in this I don't see or notice any difference in me, except perhaps that I may love the Lenten fast better than others do. But this love was a lot more fervent in me then than it is now.

I was sick about three years ago; and since then, on the advice of the doctors, and indeed more out of consideration for the persons with whom I was living, I drank wine to take away the coarseness of the water. I had difficulty in bringing myself to do this. But my confessors told me to do it and see how I would find it. And I can assure you, that up to the present I have not taken any notice of it. When I drank only water, seeing it beautiful and clear, I had the custom of saying while drinking it: 'Lord, give me a conscience as pure, and throw abundantly on me the pure water of your grace which extinguishes in me all the movements and instinct in me of sin!' And I added to it:[124] 'And intoxicate me with the pure wine of your love.'

I was also counselled to add salt to my food, not having done so for many years. Even though it may seem a little thing, I indeed had great difficulty abstaining from it, there being nothing so insipid than a thing that is not correctly seasoned with salt. But whether it was on account of the long time, or for some other reason, that I had not made any use of it, I no longer experienced this difficulty in refraining from it. I was counselled by a doctor to use salt, because, seeing that a considerable amount of water fell into my stomach, it would dry the water up and be very good for me. For that reason I used it as a remedy; and when I would serve it to myself, I ordinarily rolled these words around in my mind: 'My God, if it pleases you, season me with the salt of your great mercies, and guard me from the corruption of sin.' But as to the satisfaction of taste, I am not aware of having felt any. Now I tell this so as to make known my state, not being able, or not having the means to express myself otherwise.

I have often been astonished by the austerity of the saints' lives and the firmness of their resolve in this. There were many saints who committed themselves to a perpetual solitude, some who could never be persuaded to use wine, others meat, or others still to have conversation with the world; and so forth. If I am able to express it well enough, this for me is a point of great consequence. It is true that, the first four or five years I remained steadfast, there being nothing which could sway me from my resolutions. But since then, having as if lost the feeling of the senses and the discernment the mind makes of them, I have forsaken many things without noticing I had laid them aside and, without knowing it either, availed myself of many others, as those of which I have just spoken.

Furthermore, even though I have left the retreat and solitude I was in for about three years,[125] I still no longer know what it means to be in the world. How much I cried when I had to make that change! I feared that I would let myself be carried away by things which would turn up and destroy in me the little bit of good our Lord in his goodness was able to put there. This is why, full of fear, but confident, and completely in tears, I often said to him: 'My God, I am here for your pleasure, and not for my own; to fulfil your plans, and not for my own interests. Since it is you who put me in this place, Lord, you are obliged to protect me here. Would you have provided well for the necessities of my body in order to expose my soul to the dangers of its ruin? No, Lord, no! It would be a crime to think thus of your infinite goodness. That is why I hope you will conserve me here in purity and innocence. And if it is true what is said, that veins of sweet water run in the midst of the salted waters of the sea without being tainted,[126] so in the same way conserve me in the midst of the world where you have put me, without being sullied by its vanities! Surround me with your powerful protection and separate me from all these things!' Such were the kind of prayers I made then; and in that manner I changed place, dwelling, way of life and food, without being aware however of any change.

It sometimes happened to me that, about to perform my devotions, I saw people the sight of whom gave me pain; and I would indeed have wished to hide myself from their eyes. But retiring into myself, I said: 'O my God, is there any other thing besides you and me in the world? You either wish or you don't wish that I do certain things. If it is the second, well then I must not do them; but if it is the first, must I think of or dwell on anything else but making you content?' And immediately all these creatures disappeared from in front of me.

I would even readily ask: 'Are there really such things as pleasures, riches, honours?' For, of myself, I know nothing about them; and especially since the time God gave me that great vision - which he has since continued doing and so often renewed - all honours, states, grandeurs and so forth, are nothing but a gust of wind, a little smoke and even less. This truth was imprinted on my soul; and I hope it will never be wiped away from it. But I have already spoken elsewhere about this,[127] and about the words which he said to me afterwards: 'I want to take away from you the sight of those things, so that nothing comes between you and me any more.'[128] These words kindled in my heart such great affections for solitude, that I longed incessantly and ardently for it: 'O my God,' I said, 'draw me aside, make me to leave entirely the tumult and perplexity of this world! I now say my last adieu to all creatures and all things of the earth. Lead me so much ahead into that blessed desert that I will not be able to see them any more, nor even hear them spoken of! But this is still not enough! For I desire, O my God, to have neither the slightest thought nor the slightest memory of them! O love that has made all things, unmake them now in so far as I am concerned! Turn upside down and destroy everything,[129] so that remaining alone together with my God,[130] I may be able unceasingly and without interruption to praise him, love him, and bless him!'

Many things of this sort happen in the soul. The effect which this produces is that the soul remains in that solitude it so much desires.

Now when God drew me to this solitude, I beseeched him with great affection to put someone there too; and I was so strongly drawn to this interiorly that it was necessary for me to follow its movements. But I believe that this person had no need of it.[131]

The soul, in this state, rejects absolutely and with an inconceivable promptitude all ideas, images and species[132] whatsoever, regardless of how subtle and fine they might be; for the soul desires only its God. It only wishes to be everything to him, to be completely filled by him, not only in its depths and in the superior part of itself,[133] but also in all its powers and faculties. And because the desires, the species and the images occupy and fill the soul, or at least some of its powers, it rejects them, and, in order to possess its God as fully as is possible, it neither can nor wishes to put up with them. It seems to me that I would suffer an unimaginable torment if anything of the world entered into my soul. I have sometimes experienced a pain greater than I can say when something did enter and occupy a place there. For having understanding and a heart capable of knowing and loving God, it is unlikely I would want their powers filled with hay, straw, wood, stones, limestone, silver, gold and similar things, since these are only goods of this earth - even if a little more polished, trimmed and dressed. Consequently, if ever I happen to give them any consideration, it is only that I may conceive disdain and contempt for them. But to put these things into my heart in company with God, or to give them any thought or value them in any way, is what I have a horror of more than I can tell!

For a few years now this has been one of the effects of Holy Communion. For it is always through this living Sacrament that our Lord grants us the most graces. So, being filled with a generous feeling by the honour of his visit and his divine presence, I have contempt without reserve for everything that is not him. And it seems to me that, in his mercy, he has so strongly closed my heart to all things that they will never have any entry there. And from outside, I sense even that there is some strong virtue that dismisses and rejects them, preventing them from approaching me, and me from feeling any propensity or inclination towards these objects.

Harmony recovered

This, then, is my state as regards visible and perceptible things, and I do not know whether it is better or as good as the one I was in before, where I had the habit of mortifying myself in all things, as much in suffering the painful as in suppressing those which gave me pleasure. For at present, being as if dead to everything, privation does not give me pain nor possession contentment. And so it is that I no longer know, as I have said at the beginning,[134] what mortification is as far as these things are concerned. From the moment I was aware of this change in me, I was astonished and in pain, because I did not see that I would have anything more to do in order to govern my senses and the movements of nature. And someone said to me in my heart: 'There is no more need to put in order what is already ordered!'[135] Yet, these are words which I still have not really understood.

State of annihilation

To be able to say how I see myself since that great vision of my misery and my nothingness which our Lord gave me about seven or eight years ago, is another point of great consequence to me. From that moment I lost the sight and knowledge of my body and my soul, of my being and my substance and remained in that constant awareness of my nothingness and in a continual state of annihilation.[136] It is true that for these past few years, having lost almost all the light that was given me, I have not seen this as much as felt it;[137] and it is not so much by light as by an impression that this truth dwells for me in the soul! And I do not know how to explain this to myself except by this comparison. To teach a child how to read, you give him a book, let him see the letters, syllables, words; but only after he has learned this lesson well do you take away everything that was given to him for this and finally give him what you want him to learn, because once he knows this lesson well, it is no longer necessary for him. It seems to me that now, in the same way, I no longer see my misery and nothingness, but know them; even though, however, our Lord by his goodness, when necessary, often diffuses and renews this light in my soul. Formerly, before being in this state, I saw a number of reasons for the extreme humiliation of our bodies. They are only dust, and will return to dust; they are strictly speaking only sacks of dirt and corruption and are subject to so many miseries that one could not count them. But I do not know how to use these reasons to humble myself, because I do not see that I have a body. I see the body, as I do the rest of visible and perceptible objects, but it does not make any impression on my mind.

At the beginning I received, as I said,[138] an extraordinary light which allowed me to see right down to the least inclinations of my nature. But in no way did I see them at this time, for I did not even see myself as having a nature. And when I hear talk about the depravations and disorders of each and everyone, be they in great or small things, and when one says, 'What our nature induces us to is strange!', this surprises me, because I do not sense the depravation of this nature. And although I follow its movements in many things (which is, however, what I fear more than I can say), perhaps I do not see it!

The riches and pleasures of the senses, which nature prompts in us, are unknown things to me; and that desire for esteem and honour which one says one feels, it is this above all I cannot understand, not being able to imagine that there could be a person who would wish to carry out such a deception and robbery: deception in so far as he might wish to be esteemed completely for other than what he is; and robbery, in so far as he might wish to have honour that is due to God alone. For if some esteem is given to us, it will be for something of good that is in us, which is not ours and does not belong to us. That is why we are indeed evil to desire it and to take praise for it and not refer it entirely to God. Moreover, even if there would be no malice or manifest badness in this, I still see in it such an extravagant madness that for me there is nothing more ridiculous in the world as pleasing oneself with the esteem of mankind! For, after all, people will say some favourable words about a person which the wind carries away and which vanish in the air at the same time. All the praises they could ever give will never add a single degree of goodness to a person, as also all their slanderings will not add a single degree of malice, since one is what one is before God.

Once, on seeing that people were beginning to have a high regard for me, I felt it very acutely and was troubled very much because of it. But now, being as it were dead to all that, when this happens to me I don't think about it; I let it fall to the ground, for it doesn't touch me any more than a stump would.[139]

In a word, I do not know how one sees me and thinks of me, since there is nothing to be seen!

Under the movement of the spirit

I give no forethought to my actions

It remains now to make known that same state as regards virtues and exercises of devotion, and generally the state of my soul as regards all things.

For some years, having already lost the sight of and knowledge for exterior and perceptible things, I only saw with the eyes of the mind. Those same exterior things I saw, not as they appeared to me, but as they were in reality.[140] Moreover, in one great day I saw the mysteries of the faith, the Christian truths, the beauties of virtue, and the uncomeliness and deformity of vice, the recompenses of one and the chastisements of the other; and all these visions embraced the will, the affections proper to these objects.[141]

But, O my God, my soul has been made destitute of its brilliant lights! It has no more feeling! And what I said about the body, I could also say about my soul: it does not see any more; nor does it hear, desire, understand or act any more.

In the first place, I give no forethought to my actions, be they general or particular, spiritual or natural; and nevertheless I am not aware of having omitted even three or four times, for perhaps more than six years, any of the things I had to do. This, then, is my disposition. I say that I do not think about what I have to do. I would not know how to think about it; nor could I foresee it. But at the time, when the occasion arises when I must do something that has to be done, regardless of what kind, a little reminder is given to me, as if someone were to come and say in a low voice in my ear:

'Go and do that!' I say 'in a low voice' because this reminder, unlike the impetuous desires some people have when they have to do something, is given so sweetly that it makes no noise in the soul. But it does the same as far as the effect is concerned, for this is accomplished exactly.

This then is what precedes my actions. When one considers, however, what is needed to facilitate doing an action well, this is a mere trifle, and doesn't take very long. If one comes across some obstacle to one's exercises of devotion, or any other activity which one intends carrying out, one acquiesces sweetly in this and does what comes up then with peace and tranquillity of mind, as if it were the very thing one had intended doing in the first place. Afterwards, one has a sense of liberty and returns to one's exercise. The actions are done and carried out almost in an unconscious way; and passing from one to the other in such an imperceptible way, one is not aware of them. There is neither delectation nor pleasure in the exercise of devotion, and also neither pain nor disgust. But the soul is always in a state of great repose, and such profound tranquillity that it is never disturbed by any movements of passion. The years go by without the soul being even aware of their least attractions: and if it should happen that the soul does feel some passion, it is extinguished in less than no time; for in this state the soul does not know what it is to have passions![142]

I have not had that love and ardent desire I felt in the beginning for the practice of virtue and the exercises of piety. But there is something, I know not what, at the bottom of my heart that is not subject to the senses, that only manifests itself in its effect, but makes me practise those exercises of devotion just the same. In particular, that perceptible desire for Communion! For many years now I have no longer experienced it; nevertheless, I have often remarked that, despite my infirmities which often keep me in bed, there is no difficulty I cannot overcome in order to be able to receive Communion. This desire to communicate makes me leave my bed and gives me the strength to walk and go to church and finally carry out my devotions, after which I have often observed that I felt much better. Nevertheless, this desire is not subject to the senses; it is only seen in its effect.

Briefly, then, I do not know what perceptible devotion or pain and anguish of the spirit are in the state I have been in for more than ten years. I have experienced both one and the other, and to excess, I say. But I am no longer aware of either one. And everything I have heard said about this, and everything I have said, has no impression on my mind so as to make me understand this.

For about three and a half years, two weekly Communions were taken from me. As a just punishment from God, my confessor did not wish to permit me them; for it was I who was the cause of it. To tell the truth, in the beginning this privation was hard on me and made me cry a great deal; but finally, in less than no time, I saw that I was just as content not to receive them as to receive them, placing all this within the hands of God. I did not speak of them any more; and it seems to me that I did not even desire them.

All one requires to approach that divine Sacrament is a great purity of heart, and then a profound respect. For, if the soul were to see itself to be stained by one venial sin, it could never approach the Sacrament until first of all it had been cleansed by the Sacrament of penance. And even though the soul receives there often and ordinarily an abundance of affection, it is not at all with the relish and sentiment of devotion I found there at the beginning; a relish and sentiment the soul does not desire, but, on the contrary, rejects.

Another thing I cannot evaluate is the extreme and intense desires to suffer I had for some years. I no longer feel them any more, nor do I go and seek pain and sorrow everywhere, which I used to do. I no longer suffer pain with the same ardour and affection of mind; I merely accept it and embrace it with a sweet and loving sentiment as a participation in the Cross of Jesus Christ, beseeching him from the bottom of my heart that in this way he might purify it and sanctify it entirely.[143]

I began to seek some relief from my little infirmities which I never did before. It is nevertheless with indifference that I use the medicines, and with complete submission to whatever way it pleases God to dispose of them, be it to leave me in the same pains or to give me relief from them.

Finally, no longer full of desires, my soul has generally neither delectation nor pleasure in any of its exercises. But all this happens, as I have said, in an unconscious way.

No memory

Now, if the soul does not foresee what it must do, and has no feeling for what it does, neither has it any knowledge of what it has done. For, regardless of the kind of actions it performs, corporeal or spiritual, internal or external, it no longer knows nor is aware of anything about them from the moment they are done, in the same way as the vessel which sails and scuds along on the sea leaves no mark or vestige of itself the moment it has passed.

This is the cause of many good things. It prevents one from performing one's actions and exercises out of routine and from custom; for there being no idea or impression in the soul, one does them every day as if completely new, and is not exposed to the distaste which one has from having always to do the same thing. This suppression of knowledge prevents one from being complacent and from appropriating anything to oneself; for one takes nothing and sees nothing.

But also, not to reflect on what one does - be it with regard to good or to evil - is not the way to correct oneself of it! And this is the reason why often, and for more than three or four years now, I am so distressed when making my confession, because I am not aware of my sins nor my actions, any more than if in my whole life I had never committed one single sin. So, if it were not for a ray of light that reveals to me my faults in one moment, I would not be able to recognise them; and, from the moment I confess them, I do not see them any more.[144]

Now, as regards the sins of my past life, although they are enormous and in such great number, a particular light is likewise necessary for me to see them.[145] And from the moment I see my sins or those that are committed in the world, which does not happen to me very often, my soul is penetrated by an extreme pain. But for me, I have often thought that God did not permit me to have this vision ordinarily, because I would not have been able to endure it and live. And he often gives me the grace of contrition without the vision of my sins.

No affection for sin

Another reason why I have found it hard to confess is that, although I see or - to say it better - know that the malice and malignity of my nature[146] is so great and has a foundation of corruption so extreme that I, myself alone, am capable of committing all the sins that have ever been committed and could be committed, and often thank our Lord with great affection for all those sins I have never fallen into and never will, since I am indebted to his goodness alone and to the merits of his blood for this; there is also in the will so much hatred, detestation and horror for sin that I would rather suffer all sorts of martyrdom and death a thousand times over - if the will could endure as much - than commit even one sin. Through experience, I know only too well that one commits many sins that can be attributed to the misery of our condition. But to commit sins cold bloodedly and with affection - this is what I do not understand; or more, to have an affection for sin I understand even less. In this frame of mind, it often seemed to me that the world was going to return to the state of innocence;[147] and many times I even had the thought and the desire to ask of my confessors if it were possible for one to commit sin through malice. For I did not believe that this disposition was peculiar to me, but common to everyone.

A director instinct

This then is the state in which I am. I give no forethought to what I have to do, doing it with I know not what insensibility and conserving no knowledge of it when it is done. They say to me that a blind person does not really let go when a good guide directs them. This, then, is the point which causes me difficulty, because not only for the past six years, as I believe, do I not know where I am and where I am going, but I also don't know who it is who is guiding me and governing me; for what I do is not through light and reason, but by an instinct and movement that directs me.[148] And with regard to that movement, I do not know whence it comes - if it is from God or from nature (which is something I fear more than death!).

And to give some explanation of this state: I say that I have always taken care of the house where I live when they[149] go to the countryside and remain there when the season is fine. Now first, I accept this occupation from the hand of God, as being the disposition of his divine Providence. But afterwards I am led to do these things more from a movement and instinct; and this I do with care and affection, so much so that sometimes it seemed to me that I would have had difficulty in quitting this occupation when those to whom the house belonged - but who had entrusted me with the care of it when they were away - returned. Nevertheless, when they did return, and I had handed back to each and everyone what I had to, I felt so much removed from those responsibilities and in a way lost all thought of them, that it would almost have been impossible for me afterwards to take them up again. And yet, when the occasion presented itself again for me to look after the house, I was almost immediately returned to the initial frame of mind and was ready to forsake this latter feeling. This happened to me for many years and many times in the same year, depending on the circumstances. I do not know what causes such different changes in me.[150]

But there is another thing which will help explain this conduct better; for I would wish, once and for all, that it be understood. For a very short space of time I was going to the confessor of whom I have spoken,[151] and to whom I believe it was our Lord himself who directed me in the manner I have described,[152] when by order of his superiors he changed place and was sent to be superior considerably far from here. O my God, there is only you who knows how acute that blow was to me and what abundance of tears it made me shed; and I myself was very taken aback by this change! This made me realise that it is not time that makes great and close relationships! But it was, however, with much peace and tranquillity of mind that I suffered no distress on account of that removal, and was so entirely in conformity with your divine disposition that, if in saying one word or in giving one hair of my head,[153] which indeed I would have wished to throw to the wind, I would have been able to keep him here, I undoubtedly would not have done so, even though it would have been as much for your glory in making him remain as in seeing him depart. But I desired that your order be carried out as you had given it.

At his departure, he gave me a confessor. But a month later he[154] also came to change house. So I was for about six months without a regular confessor, wandering like a poor vagabond from one place to another. I found some confessors at times who said things to me which suggested that they had some knowledge of my inner life;[155] and when I wished to respond as if to pledge myself to them, I felt my heart tighten and close, as if a hand was put before my mouth to prevent me from speaking. And withdrawing myself, I said, 'Lord, surely you don't wish me there!' And this happened to me many, many times. I had no one whatsoever in my mind, and I did not consider anyone.[156] But stripping myself of all affection, things, interest and satisfaction, and without having regard for anything beyond his greatest glory, I put myself, as much as was in my power, in the hands of God, so that he could place me wherever it would please him. I was like this, I say, for about six months, without pain or anxiety of mind. I performed my exercises of devotion as they had been arranged for me, and waited in peace for whenever it would please God to direct me. But being no longer in a state in which the light of knowledge would lead me, I was urged by a feeling that I had to stay with one confessor, with whom I remained for three years and two months.[157] I had some difficulties, which made me feel like changing; but that same feeling made me stop and remain with him.

Deepening

Time elapsed,[158] and my first confessor[159] was called back here. For more than six months beforehand I was led to expect this. But I do not think, in all that time, I once had the thought: 'When he is back here again, you will return to him!' For my state is such that, when I come to stop some place, I am like a statue which has been set in one place, does not move any more, and would never leave from there if it was not moved by someone else. I was very glad about his return. But all my joy was in seeing God's command fulfilled. For a good three weeks after his return, I think, I continued, as it was my wont, to go to the confessor I then had. But then, all of a sudden, I felt a movement in me to quit this confessor and return to the first. I went to seek him out[160] and spoke to him about the disposition of my spirit. He did not wish to give me an answer about what I should do, but sent me back to ask advice about it from others. I, who have never done this, pointed out to him that I could not do so. But even so, he did not wish to give me an answer. I then had recourse to our Lord through the intervention of the Holy Virgin, beseeching her to obtain for me the grace to know what I should do. 'O my God,' I said, 'I only seek the direction of men so that I may more surely find yours! And if I knew that it was not your will that I should see him, I would tear myself away now, and would not wish to speak to him any more - if I were not able to do it otherwise, and regardless of whatever discomfort this would cause me - than if he were at one extremity of the world and I at the other.' I was many days crying and asking light from God; but I had none. And this urge to go back to him continuing all the time and becoming stronger, I was as if forced to obey. But, as for having supernatural light of human understanding, I had none in all these dealings.

I am like this in all things, great or small, whether I do them or refrain from doing them. And after I have done the things which this urge prompts me to do, I am no longer aware of them. When I had discerned things and accomplished those to which I felt myself drawn, I used to experience a certain jubilation of heart and had some evidence, a perceptible awareness, that I had done the right thing. But by this movement I cannot even know the spirit that governs me. Truly, I have neither pain nor remorse from what I do instinctively through this urge; but I feel and savour no satisfaction from it either, as I used to do. Such a great calm remains in me, that I often had reason to fear it. With regard to the change of confessor, it is also true that, if I had not done it then, I would do it now. I believe that God wanted things from me which I would never have done without this change.[161]

Pure faith

In this state, the soul is not only destitute of the light it had for its own direction but, except for certain small rays that pass by like flashes and do not last in it, is also deprived of that light which it had to see the beauties, usefulness and advantages of virtue, and the hideousness and damage that sin causes. It no longer has that light which used to show so openly the Christian truths and the mysteries of faith. It believes simply and firmly, without curiosity or reasoning: of which it has no need in these matters. But its faith is pure and stripped of light and feeling, except at intervals when it is given some small rays. I notice that the more one advances in this, the more rarely these lights are given; and the smaller and weaker they are. As I have said, the soul does not have the natural light which sees visible, perceptible and exterior things as they appear, but rather the supernatural light which sees them as they actually are.[162] When I speak about seeing and hearing, I mean it in the manner which makes an impression on the mind. In this state the soul neither sees nor hears anything of all that goes on in the world, good or evil, but particularly the evils of pain. It is this which makes the soul impervious to the pains of others! The soul often recommends to God all those who are afflicted, in the interior as much as at the exterior; and it even performs an exercise wholly for that purpose. But it does not see, however, either those miseries or those unfortunate people; and when it prays for them, it is through a special movement.

As regards the good things - those benefits of grace and virtue which God grants to his creatures according to the order of his eternal Providence, both when and how it pleases him, the soul does not see them either, except on the rare occasion when it has some light on this. It seems that the soul is mingled with a drop of that charity which reigns in Paradise, which happens when one rejoices in the goods of one's neighbour as of one's very own,[163] for the soul tastes them and savours them with pleasure, praising and thanking God for his favours, as if it was the soul itself that had received them. The principle of the soul's joy is to see his holy will accomplished in this. But these things pass and do not last very long. Concerning the light (although with regard to that exercise of thanksgiving to God for the benefits - regardless of what kind - he deigns to distribute to his creatures, the soul does it often; and when it is done in that light, it is done in a more effective way than without this light) [. . .][164]

I have truly experienced indeed that the soul as well as the body has its senses; for, in the same way as the body, it sees, tastes, hears, touches and savours the objects that are proper to it.[165] But in the state of which I speak, the soul has no longer the use of its senses; for it has no feelings. The powers of the soul itself no longer have the freedom of their natural way of acting. So I no longer experience in myself any operation of grace or anything that is supernatural! If there is any, I am not aware of it. For I do not see the effects which, for example, the frequentation of the sacraments or the exercises of devotion produce in me, something which I knew of very much in the beginning. I often fear, and with good reason, that, instead of amending and correcting myself, I am becoming worse than I ever was. O Lord my God, ward off from me this dreadful vengeance of punishing my sins with other sins! Throw on me all the other chastisements of your justice so that, provided you never permit me to offend you, I be the butt of all the miseries that can be endured and imagined! That I may suffer all the pains that will please you! Put in the balance of your most rigorous justice all those pains you would wish to make me endure as chastisements for my sins, that I may suffer them in order to be preserved from them, even ten times or a hundred times over; for I do not fear your chastisements, but abhor sin out of sheer respect for your goodness, which I love and which I adore.[166]

Interior deprivation

The soul no longer sees Paradise, the Virgin, the saints, nor the inhabitants of that blessed abode. It prays to them often, however, with great affection, but above all to the Holy Virgin and St Joseph (to whom, out of a special inspiration, the soul has always asked that it might please him to be its guard and its director in the interior and hidden life; for without doubt he has practised this more perfectly than any other saint). The soul honours the saints and invokes them out of affection; but as for having them present in my mind, not at all! The soul no longer sees even the perfections, attributes and excellences of the divinity any more than of the humanity of Jesus Christ.167 In short, it is difficult to imagine how greatly spoliated and deprived of all things, corporeal and spiritual, is the soul.

The soul was not placed in this state all of a sudden, but little by little. At the start I saw that some change was indeed taking place in me, but I could not discern it or say what it was. But finally, seeing sufficiently that I no longer had the same light, the same knowledge and feelings I was accustomed to, I was sometimes made to understand from the interior what was happening to me - that, having desired so much and asked of God to live and die in the practice of perfect charity, this was in fact the perfect poverty of spirit.

I notice, actually, that the soul is indeed poor and stripped of everything in this state, and that it doesn't have the means of attaching itself to or taking delight in anything. He who has left the good things of this world, even though he no longer possesses them in his own right, can in fact enjoy them when he is able to see them, and satisfy all his senses in using them as those who would possess them as their own. But in this state, the soul is deprived of all that.

It was the loss of the spiritual goods that gave me pain; for I would indeed have wished to conserve them and to keep them! And it was said to me in the interior: 'Too covetous is he for whom God does not suffice!'168 Up to then I had never understood well or known the meaning of this, except with regard to temporal things; but I was made to see this also for spiritual things. For there is indeed a great difference between being filled with God and being filled with his gifts! His gifts are only means through which he wishes to draw us to himself. And I have seen how it is possible to be lost with all those gifts, and how it is so dangerous and criminal to dwell on them! But it is necessary that the soul, in order to be secure, is overcome by and loses itself in God,169 and that God also fills it and possesses it fully. He said to me one day, as I was troubling myself over the loss of all those graces and interior lights: 'I wish to put myself in the place of all that!' 'O my God,' I said to him, 'I wish it indeed! It is only you I yearn for and desire!'170 And he imprinted that desire strongly on my heart.

More ardent love

'Come then, O my God', I said! 'Empty me now of all these things, terrestrial and celestial, spiritual and corporeal! And, remaining in a completely pure state of receptivity, may I be able to receive all the communications it will please you to make to me of your divine essence and infinite goodness, neither for my interest nor for my satisfaction, but in order to give you the joy and pleasure you have in communicating yourself and making a lovable profusion of yourself! Be in me, my God, not only in essence, presence and power, as you are in all creatures,[171] but also through grace, love and a particular and special protection! Put an end, O my God, to my evil and miserable life,[172] so that I no longer lead a life of sin! For in fact, if life is not compatible with darkness, what has sin to do with where you live, you who are the source of all purity and essential sanctity? Since you deign to enter so often into my heart, as you enter there truly and really, banish sin from there forever! Put an end also to my human, natural,[173] and even rational life, so that I may live only of your divine life!'

You know, my God, with what feeling I detest and abhor the thought, word, work, action, urge or instinct, be it of body or of soul, which would not be done and accomplished out of the pure movement of your love! O my Jesus, be you the heart of my heart, soul of my soul, life of my life, the principle and end of all my actions![174] Receive them in homage of my servitude and my dependence. That they be accomplished not only for you, but also through you; filled with your incentives and used by you yourself for all that which will be for your greater glory! It is now that I am least aware of your designs for me. But I adore them out of the most profound and sincerest respect of my soul, including all those plans you invented for me in order to destroy me all the more entirely, and through which you will exercise in me a more sovereign and absolute authority. These, my God, I embrace with greater affection and love and with a very particular gratitude! Do not fear, O my God, to wound the liberty you have given me, and so exercise over me an absolute empire; for it appears to me that you will never exact any greater or more sovereign empire than the one I desire! This is where, O my God, I cry out with all my force: 'Even more, even more!'[175] O Holy Virgin, O blessed spirits, if you see my God in that blessed plan for me making use of his sovereign power over me, all say to him in one voice in my favour: 'Still more, O Lord, still more!' O Lord, make this loving promise to my soul; through yourself, I implore it of you: 'I swear to you that I will never permit you to follow and act according to your own wishes and movements. You will do and accomplish always mine. And without caring for your good and your interests, I only wish to have regard for that which will be more for my glory!' And if you do not wish to give me an assurance of this in words, for fear I might die from joy and love, at least let it be accomplished in its effects!

And afterwards, my God, what shall I ask of you as recompense for having served you? For it is in your character to give, you, who are so magnificent and so liberal. Ah, is it not enough recompense, then, to have the honour of serving you? If you had not commanded this, who would dare undertake it? And who are you, and who am I[176] that I dare present you with my respects and my homage? But since your goodness is so great that you deign to receive my respects and promise a recompense for them, I ask you, Lord, that if I have been so happy in serving you in everything, may you grant me the grace to do it still again, and even more perfectly! That the degrees of your sovereignty over me and of my dependence on you may grow as much as the moments of my life, for if I had existed right from the beginning of the world, and were to last right up to the end, I would not wish to use one instant of it except in serving and in loving you!

O saints of Paradise, O blessed spirits, do not be angry with me if I withdraw myself from your company. I say goodbye to the inhabitants of Heaven as well as those of the earth and quit the eternal as much as the temporal things! For what do I desire more than you, O my God, be it in Heaven or on earth? You are my Father, my parents, my goods and my treasure![177] You are my Paradise, my felicity and my sovereign beatitude! My God and my all![178] You are all things to me! Possess me; and that I may possess you! And since you command me to love you, may I satisfy that lovable commandment with all the forces and powers of my soul! But why have you tied up my good and my happiness, my glory and my felicity, be it either temporal or eternal, with loving you and serving you, since whenever you would have commanded it of me - and for that I would have to have been the most miserable of all creatures - I would show you that, when it is a question of your interests and of doing your will, I am little troubled about myself or about anything that concerns me.

O will of God, Paradise of Paradise, how dear you are to me, and how I would prefer to fulfil you even once than all the glory of Heaven! What is there that is lovable and desirable in that blessed abode, O my God, if not that there one will do your will for all eternity, and will burn there unceasingly in the fire of your love! O, kindle it now in my heart with so much ardour - that beautiful fire of your love - that it may never go out! And since you have seraphim on earth as well as in Heaven, make me burn in the flames of this divine charity! If I cannot love you as much as you are lovable, may I love you as much as you are able to be loved! And, O my God, make me who has given you back the love which you desire of me, love you with all that love which so many ungrateful hearts refuse you! Pour it into mine. I offer myself entirely to suffer all the pains and labours which it will be necessary to endure to achieve this end.

I am very glad, and indeed rejoice in all the great plans you have for your creatures and the singular favours you have shown them, and still do every day. But all I ask of you for myself is more love, to love you all the more! Yes, my God, I am avaricious, I covet this love! And as a recompense for loving you, see to it that I love you more ardently and more perfectly, and that I begin right from this world the apprenticeship to that which, through your infinite goodness, I hope to do surpassingly for all eternity.[179]

It is now that I share as far as it is possible for me the feeling of respect, love and abandonment the Holy Virgin had at the moment of the Incarnation, and that I say to you with her: 'Here is your poor and little servant; that it may happen to me according to your word.[180] May your designs be entirely accomplished in me! O my Jesus, since you are the prototype and model, I wish with all my power to enter also into the same

141

affections of love, of respect and dependence which your very great soul and your holy humanity had in letting themselves be guided by your divinity![181] Govern me as my chief, use me as the cause, his instrument! And seeing that at the first moment of your life you offered yourself in order to carry out entirely the wishes of God,[182] I offer myself likewise in imitation of you, and this is in heart and in mind!'

The force of love

These are some of the affections of the soul which I have been obliged to speak about. I have been unable to explain otherwise its sentiments and its dispositions. These are given to the soul in such great abundance that it would be impossible to speak about all of them. But, above all, what cannot be expressed is how they are infused into the soul, and the intimate and loving way in which this happens! O, how many times have I been constrained, through the force of the respect and love I felt in the presence of the majesty of God, to throw myself at full length on the ground, for I would have wished to lose myself in any abyss and vanish utterly, right down to the centre of the world! And in that state, doing nothing but crying and sighing, I would have wished by my tears and my sighs to embrace even more ardently that fire with which I felt myself burning, desiring nothing more than to die in the violence of those passions, beseeching the saints of Paradise to procure for me this happy death, to kindle it with such force that I might be able to burn from it and be consumed by it entirely.

It seems to me that in this state the soul is always empty and always full![183] Always empty in that everything is erased from it, be it the external works it performs or the internal affections it receives, neither retaining nor conserving any idea or memory of them; and always full on account of the loving affections which God pours incessantly into it! Always empty in that it has a simple, sweet, but strong impression of its own nothingness and that of all created things, which empties it of itself and of all creatures. Always full, in that it has a simple impression, sweet, but also strong, of God who fills it, and of all its powers which it gathers together completely! In effect, these powers no longer function naturally. For the imagination, no matter how mad and extravagant it might be, does not rove any more! It is enchained and imprisoned in some port which it leaves no more! Sometimes I thought that I no longer had any imagination, or at least that I no longer had any use for it! Then at other times I heard it said that 'one represents things to oneself and imagines many things'. This surprises me and I cannot understand it; for I have neither image, figure, species or representation, be it corporeal or spiritual, even of the divinity and humanity of our Lord. And when images of them appear and begin to form themselves, something in me rejects and destroys them in a moment, because I desire God, and not his image or a representation of him![184] The memory does not return to the past and does not think about the future. The understanding comes neither from discourse, nor reasoning; or at least so little that it is negligible. And with regard to the will - it is all on fire; and all its powers are in some unknown satiety and repose. The whole soul, in a forgetfulness of self and of all things, is not troubled about itself, its good or its evil, its salvation or its loss. This it doesn't think about! But all its aspirations and desires tend towards and result in carrying out the will of God and in being in the state in which it pleases him. This is what it asks of him incessantly.

Two things I have asked in particular from God. The first, that it might please him to grant me the grace of never seeing, touching or feeling as in any way belonging to me any of his gifts and his graces; but that, returning them to him with the same purity with which it pleased him to give them to me, and not having sullied them by appropriating them to myself, I give them back to him faithfully. The second, that it might please him to grant me also the grace of never seeing, seeking or finding anything in myself; but that, in attaching myself entirely and perfectly to him, I seek nothing but his glory! It pleased him, through his goodness, not to reject my prayers. For truly, there is nothing which humbles me more than the knowledge of his gifts; and, no matter what, I hardly ever think about myself or any creature.

The soul's impression of God surges back and also influences the body, placing its senses in an honourable and modest posture, banishing entirely all frivolity and unseemliness from it, no matter how little.

The soul, it seems to me, simply looks at God, bearing itself in his presence with great respect and great modesty. It does not continue in that exercise of interior acts as it did in the beginning, but looks only at God with that attention and respect. It does not act, or very little, except when those affections of which I have spoken are infused into it, and even then it does not operate through its natural power. The soul is moved, without itself being the agent; it yields itself rather than act on its own.

There is one thing which troubles me and causes me fear. This is when it is a question of forming one's intentions.[185] It is done in this state by a single glance at God, a simple sentiment so sweet and so delicate that often the soul is not even aware of it. Being as swift as it is subtle, this happens in a moment, and no longer or seldom by a formal act. When one thinks of adjusting one's intentions in this way, this troubles the repose and peace of the soul somewhat; and it appears to me that the will is displeased when it is drawn from the place of its repose in order to be employed in those things.[186] I have not been able yet to express myself well in this, so as to know what I must do about it. For I fear more than I can say any thought, word, action or the slightest operation of the body and of the soul that is produced through the movement and instinct of nature, and even of reason itself; because the soul cannot[187] act or operate except through the movement and spirit of God and of Jesus Christ and his love. I have always had a pure intention, together with its sentiment. But for a year now this sentiment has been taken away from me, if not absolutely, at least from day to day. This means that sometimes I know neither where I am, nor why, nor through what movement I do these things. Nevertheless, if I enter into myself and examine my heart, I always find it in the disposition in which I would much prefer to die than do anything that - I do not say offend God, but - would not be in conformity with his will and for its pure accomplishment.

Primacy of love[188]

From the motive of love

The soul in this state hardly functions any more except from the motive of love. If it prays for sinners, for example, it is so that God may not be offended any more. It hardly dwells at all on the advantage of this prayer for those miserable people, if they emerge from such an unhappy state. If it prays for those who devote themselves to the salvation of souls,[189] which it does often and with great affection, it is so that they be able to kindle in all hearts perfect charity, and so that God be known, loved and adored by all. O how many martyrdoms would the soul willingly suffer, even the pains of Hell, in order to do something that would at least help men to be as subject to and dependent on God through love as they are through necessity, for whether they wish it or not, they have to obey and do his will. I have great joy in this! If the soul prays for the just, it is so that God may have the joy and pleasure of communicating his gifts to them and derive from them his divine satisfaction; if for the souls in Purgatory, it is that they may be able to render him all the more praises, love and blessings which he desires of them, and not to think about the deliverance from their torments, and so forth. It is also from a motive of love towards Jesus Christ that the soul prays for them, so that he may have the joy and contentment of applying to them the fruit and merit of his blood, and take from this the effect he intends for himself.

The soul scarcely practises the virtues as virtues any more, but from the motive of love. For example, embracing poverty, the soul no longer practises it as poverty, but remains in this state in order to be able to depend on and to be solely a matter for the Providence of God. And because God holds it as an honour to find someone who wishes to return this honour to him completely intact. And not being able - as indeed it would wish - to subject everyone to him, the soul wishes at least to render him the greatest homage and show him the most complete dependence that is in its power. And if it could know that in doing this it would be the most miserable of creatures - in time and in eternity - and that everyone would come to mock it, to hold it in contempt, and to condemn it as imprudent in wishing to remain and live in this way, the soul itself would not be troubled by this, for provided it is able to honour God, everything else is as nothing to it. Altogether, it seems that the soul would be truly glad of this, having in that case the greater opportunity of further showing God its love.

The soul performs all its actions and exercises with this same motive and sentiment in order to render to God in this the proofs of its servitude and obedience. It is from a motive of love for Jesus Christ and to show him, in embracing poverty, humiliation, suffering, subjection, obedience and so forth, the respect and esteem it has for his doctrines and examples, that the soul renders itself in conformity with him in everything, out of love, and desires nothing more ardently than to be clothed inside and outside in his livery.[190] And if something places itself in the way of this motive, which happens very rarely, this love often reinforces itself; and with strong and vigorous acts dispels all the rest, not ceasing to act until it has made everything disappear and elevated and attached the soul irrevocably to God so as to desire and seek after only the fulfilment of his holy will.

Disinterested love

This love which the soul has for God is unreasoning,[191] without motives and without interests. The soul does not cling on to its favours as belonging to it, because it does not see them - except by small rays of light which, though they awaken in the soul many affections, praises, thanksgivings, humiliation and fear, and others of the sort, pass like flashes.[192] This is without reasoning and without consideration, because against all probability, if the soul had never received any good from God or Jesus Christ, and was never to receive any, but on the contrary was to suffer all sorts of pains both temporal and eternal in serving God and Christ, it would not cease from loving, considering itself to be very happy if only its services and homage be received.[193] It knows that it belongs to God and to our Lord by right of creation, conservation and redemption. For many reasons it rejoices in belonging to God. But the soul belongs to him also through the choice and election of its own free and pure will.[194] It does not desire any other use of its freedom than this alone - to thank him freely and lovingly for being God, its King and its sovereign Lord, whose orders it wishes to carry out without reserve, and so, without any constraint, to serve God as God, because he is what he is. And if it were possible for God to be unaware of something, the soul would not be concerned that he find out, for, to be glad that he knew about this, would indeed seem to it to be giving too much consideration to itself. In short, the soul does not desire even that God know about its love and its services,[195] except in so far as he can have pleasure and contentment from it.

But, O my God, how profound are your judgements and incomprehensible your ways! Who would be able to speak about and recount the pain of the soul in this state? It runs after God, and he withdraws himself! It seeks him, and he hides himself.[196] Incessantly, it asks two things of him with untold affections. First - that it be preserved from all sin and from the least things that could displease him; not from fear of chastisements, because the soul, offering itself to suffer them a hundred times more so as to be preserved from sin, will not have to suffer them in order to be punished. And the second - that he dispose of it absolutely, putting it in a state of soul and body that will please him and, without any regard for what concerns it, will be more for his glory, either for the present life or the life to come, for grace or for glory, for repose or for pain; and that the soul - provided he grants it the grace of never distancing itself from his holy will - accomplish this with all the perfection of the plans he has designed for it, in which all things are sweet and agreeable to it! And in order to obtain the effect of its demands, the soul offers all the merits of the holy life, death and passion of our Lord on which alone it bases all its hopes, without seeing however that its demands are heard, its desires granted, or the merits of our Lord received. And it fears that on account of its sins and infidelities God might punish it with some other sin.[197]

I have heard it said that there are souls in Purgatory who are ignorant of their fate and condition, not knowing if they are condemned or saved. Having desires to see God and to unite themselves to him, which is incomprehensible to our minds, and not knowing what these desires are, the souls in Purgatory suffer more than one could imagine. And in my opinion, I also believe that to be in this incertitude is the greatest of all punishments. This is however the best comparison I can make in order to explain the state of my soul, because I feel, of course, such great desires and affections to serve God and to do his will that it seems to me I would rather die a thousand times than to oppose this in the slightest. But what? In this I am no less ignorant of my condition and my fate! I no longer see the order of his Providence; I do not know his will, and desiring so ardently to do it in all things, I do not see that I am doing it! I walk in such thick darkness[198] that I haven't even one spark of light on this. The more desire grows, the less charity I have; and the more I advance, the less I understand where I am going! It appears to me that I am in no way advancing, apart from the fact that I am forever becoming less aware of where I am and where I am going. It is difficult to say whether this state of such great nakedness and annihilation in which I find myself is good or not, or at least as good as the previous one I was in. In which case, it would be no small evil to fall back instead of advancing! I reject all things in order to find God alone and unite myself to him. But whether in fact I have found him and possess him, I am never too sure, or whether I am guided by him or being led astray.[199]

For more than six years, I think, I have been following this way. I do not know what it is. I have said something about this before now, but certainly not everything; and not as clearly as I have written about it.[200] For I have never had so many graces for this than in writing about it; and this is perhaps one of the reasons why God wished that I be ordered to write about it,[201] so that I would not be misled any longer. I follow this way in simplicity. I know no other road to follow; and I see no other one, because none shows itself to my eyes.[202] I do not see that I am listened to by the Holy Virgin, the saints, the angels and all the blessed spirits, or that the prayers and entreaties I myself make to them to direct me on the road of a solid and true devotion are answered. I remain forever in a state of ignorance, not knowing whether I am doing the will of God or not; for I have no knowledge through feeling or light, nor through any interior words.[203] Nothing of all that!

This ignorance, this state of being deprived of the light of knowledge, gives great pain to the soul, but does not trouble it however - it causes it a hidden torment which cannot be explained very well. Tobit asked, 'What joy can I have, having lost the light of day?'[204] What joy, then, can the soul have, if it has lost all the knowledge it had of walking in the way of God's designs for it? Certainly this pain is greater than one could ever imagine. It is about six years now that I suffer this; and I am ready, O my God, to suffer it the rest of my days, even though they should last until the end of the world! I ask from you only this grace. If you do not wish that I see and know your will and your plans for me, see to it at least that I fulfil your plans while not being aware of your will. For, as long as that may be, this is sufficient for me. And I wish from the goodness of my heart to be deprived of the satisfaction of this knowledge if this pleases you, because my sovereign joy is to do things, and to do them in the way that will please you all the more.

Love and death

To rise from among the dead

To this pain was added the desire to die,[205] which I have had for some years. I am mistaken when I say: 'I have desired to die!' No! But rather, I have desired to live and be freed from the kingdom of death.

For about a year I had a vision almost continually of how this world is the kingdom and empire of death. I saw death everywhere; and everything that presented itself to my eyes had the image of death in it. Death, it seems to me, is nothing but the privation of existence and the separation from all things.[206] Now I saw death, then, to be in all hours, days, weeks, months, years and in all seasons; the beginning of one being the end and the death of the one that went before. In preserving things, I saw death. The goodbyes, the separation which happen at the end - this is death! At table, I saw only death in what one eats; and in part of the food which is taken and changed into us, partly to make us live, I saw only a malignant secretion in us to make us die. Clothes seemed to me to be sheets for burial; the bed and sleep, the tomb and death. The people I saw were as if dead to me; yes indeed, speaking and moving as they do, take a little breath from them only, and they will no longer be able to move themselves or speak. Plaintively, I longed to rise from among that heap of dead bodies and that reign of death.[207] But it seems to me that my spirit especially, retained and imprisoned in my body, suffered something of that punishment which some people were made to endure when they were tied completely alive to a dead body.[208] But the order of God which condemned me to this pain lets me suffer it tranquilly.

So I did not desire to die, then, but to rise from among the dead! And in this frame of mind that I have been in for many years now, it is most probable that I do not know what it means to die! If death is a cessation of existence and a separation from all things, it seems to me, then, that it has no longer any power over me.[209] For so many years now, having no longer anything but the vision and impression of my own nothingness, I have lost all knowledge of my own existence.[210] And so it is no longer up to death to put me into non-existence.[211] I know not if a world exists, or even creatures, goods, honours, riches and pleasures. So death does not separate me from them! O love so strong, stronger than death![212] It is you I have beseeched to separate me from all things, wishing to do all this through the power of love and not from the necessity of death. I have no longer any connection with all that goes on in the world, whether through affection or through knowledge.

But when I say that I have desired to die, and I say that greatly and from the bottom of my heart, I mean to speak in the ordinary way and not according to the sentiments and the disposition of my soul. And regardless of how I look upon death, it appears to me as beautiful, lovable and desirable.

The judgement of God

And in the first place, if I see death in the sentence which God pronounced, I say to all men in the person of Adam: 'You will die.'[213] O Lord, what sentence could you pronounce against me and that I would not desire and take the pleasure of rigorously executing in everything? So, in the execution of this sentence, I desire death.[214]

Satisfaction for divine justice

In the second place, if I regard it as a punishment and a chastisement for sin, I embrace it and desire it with great affection, glad to make this satisfaction to divine justice.

Abandonment with regard to death

In the third place, if I contemplate Jesus Christ dead, I desire also to die. And if God were to give me the choice of entering heaven without dying, I would not want to, because my Saviour died. I wish to die as he did, and to bear that mark of resemblance to him.[215] I have sometimes desired to die forlorn even, and abandoned by all things and all creatures, so as to be more like him. But I do not ask this of him, because I do not know what is necessary for me; so I abandon myself entirely to his disposition.

The circumstances which render death fearful to the majority of people are the very ones that are agreeable to me; for to die without knowing when and how is what gives me joy. I take my whole pleasure from depending on, and being absolutely answerable to, the Providence of God for all the necessities of life! And at death, when my interests are very much at stake, I have indeed more joy in abandoning myself into his hands, so that he may dispose of me as he pleases. Yes, Lord, whether I die in the day or the night, whether my death is slow or violent, abandoned or accompanied; that it may please you! I have only one condition to ask of you - that I die by the death and the manner in which you receive the greater glory from it, and that I be in your grace; and then I am satisfied and content! You are the faithful friend who never forsakes in their need those who put their trust in you. I also hope it will be on that day when, in that last moment, you will let me feel the effects of your greatest mercies, bestowing on me more abundantly the fruit and the merit of your precious blood. Amen.

Adoration of divine justice

When I recall that it is at death that Jesus Christ refutes and makes amends for all the contempt and little esteem shown him, his doctrines, his example and his Gospel, sharing his concern without troubling myself about that which touches me - nor anyone else in the world for that matter - I am indeed glad to see punished and chastised all who are not true to him; and I detest and abhor everything in me which is not in accordance with his spirit, not so much from fear of chastisement as from fear of giving him reason for anger and indignation and pronouncing a sentence contrary to the inclination of his natural goodness. For this vindictive justice is foreign to him and constrained.

I adore often the judgement and definitive sentence which he will give of my eternity - happy or unhappy - at the hour of my death; because I do not know if I shall be in a state and disposition of mind to be able to do it then.[216] I recognise this to be just and holy; and sharing the zeal of his justice, I desire it to be so down to the last detail. There was a time when I used to ask God that I do my Purgatory in this world. But for a long time now I have ceased from making this request of him. I considered it to be pride on my part to aspire to and dare ask for this. For, seeing that one suffers from such grave pains in Purgatory for the slightest faults, would I dare think indeed that, having committed so many crimes as I have, and so enormous, and still commiting such grave faults, I could make satisfaction for all that in this world? No! I stand and render myself entirely subject to divine justice.[217]

For many years I have had a devotion to and particular affection for the gaining of indulgences - plenary or otherwise - and I would be very displeased to pass a day without doing that which was necessary to gain one of them. But I have never intended by this to exempt myself from the punishment due to my sins. My motives for gaining them were in order to glorify God and do in this his holy will, since he wishes that one avails oneself of these indulgences, and to give to Jesus Christ the joy and contentment of bestowing on me the merits of his death and his precious blood and washing me of the blemish of sin, so that there would be nothing in me that might displease him and offend his most pure eyes; and finally, to atone for my sins, but not to avoid pain, so that nothing would delay me and prevent me from uniting myself to him at the hour of death and from going and giving back to him the praises and benedictions which he desires from me for all eternity.

To sin no more

But I have desired to die because, above all, being dead we are no longer subject to sin. O, when I hear it said that the misery of this life is so great that one cannot remain in it without committing sins, even the most just and the most holy! . . .[218] How much have I wept and how much have I desired to leave this life! How often have I desired and envied the conditions of the souls in Purgatory who, although they are suffering, at least do not sin any more! O my God, dare I ask to form this pact and establish this agreement with your sovereign grandeur? Yes, my God, I ask this of you through the merits of our Lord, to whom you must grant in justice and on the truth of his promises, some graces, no matter how great they be, that will be asked of you in his name. The grace I ask of you is, I avow, the greatest you could grant, and the greatest a creature who is still mortal is capable of receiving. But relying on the merits of your Son, and on the truth of his word, I hope you will have pity on me. That is why I will speak to you, my God, of the desire of my heart. I beseech you, then, to see which power or faculty of my soul and of my senses, and which part of my body can still displease and offend you, and to consume it and reduce it to powder! But do not wait, O sweet Saviour, until it has done evil and committed crime! Forestall this evil by ruining entirely this part before it has committed it; for I wish to suffer always in order to be preserved from it rather than to be punished for it.

Supreme dependence

Our Lord, through his mercy, has given me certain visions of sin which have made such great impressions on my soul that I fear and dread nothing more than that. And if I were so wretched as ever to fall into such a state, and live in it for twenty, thirty and forty years, and finally to die in it - a thought which makes me shudder, I say I would prefer right from the first day, I say even from the first hour to die and be damned fifty years and a hundred years rather than to live and commit new sins,[219] if it were even only one! So it is indeed a terrible thing for me to remain in a life that is subject to this misery, during which we are always on the edge of the precipice.

It is true, however, that in this state I feel deeply some joy and tranquil pleasure in seeing that I am answerable to and depend unceasingly on the goodness and the mercy of God. This prevents me from falling into sin.[220] For I prefer to be in evident peril of my salvation, if one must speak in this way, and depend absolutely on God for it, than to be assured of it on my own strength or any other means, if that were possible!

In particular, the passion and death of our Lord have made me realise the abomination of sin. Consequently, I have had all the greater sentiments of affection, love and gratitude towards him for having delivered me from sin than for having freed me from the pains of Hell.

I desired to die with such great longings, it seems to me, that when I offered myself to God in order to be the object of all the miseries, poverties and ignominies, and of all the pains that one can endure in this life for the fulfilment of the plans he has had for me, I showed him but little love and obedience in this; since for a long time I have desired these things more than I have dreaded them. But then I declare my readiness to remain in this world for as much and as long as it will please him, it seems to me I offer him the greatest sacrifice I am capable of. And quite often it happened to me that nowhere did I render him such great obedience than in carrying out the necessary activities for the preservation and maintenance of life!

The desire for death is in my heart as a guide to regulate my whole life. And what I would never wish to do, say or think in dying, neither would I wish in living.

Consuming fire

For all these reasons, and for many years, have I desired to die. But for a year now I have desired this for a new reason, and that is to see God and the sacred humanity of our Lord Jesus Christ.[221] This desire is like a fire kindled in my heart which devours and consumes me in a strange way. This was accompanied by the feeling that I would really die soon. This sentiment gave me much joy, but it also made the intensity of my desire burn more fiercely, which was already so acute that I had neither respite nor repose. I counted the days, the hours and even the quarter-hours, from the time it seemed to me I had to die. My heart and my mind were disposed in a way in which I have never again experienced. The interior acts of virtue were infused in me in a way completely different from how I had experienced and practised them up to then. For the greater part of the time I said my prayers lying on the ground; and when I was in a place where I could do so without being seen, I did this, because my body suffered less in that position. These desires and affections are the life of the soul, and the mind is pleased with them and does what it can so as to conserve them and augment them. But this is the death of the body and the ruin of nature. Not only for a year or so, but for many years it often seemed to me that my body as well as my spirit desired death. For no longer taking any delight in the pleasures that are proper to it, the body has no reason for desiring life;[222] and moreover, it is often called upon to support the ardours of the spirit which unceasingly destroy it and undermine it. Through death, the body will be delivered from its pains.

To speak frankly about this state, I say that in it I have passed through the fire or temptations and through that of exterior and keen mortifications. For that reversal of fortune[223] - which it pleased God to send me - [forced me][224] to leave my homeland and the house of my father,[225] and exposed me to great poverty and suffering! All that, I avow, came from the hand of God and by a Providence that is completely paternal and loving. But I did not know this, and appreciated it even less. But all this is not comparable to the pain these desires cause, and which I believe to be the greatest of all one could suffer in this life, and indeed I could also say in the other as well.

O how I have understood by this, indeed better than through anything I have ever heard said, the torments of the souls in Purgatory! I also saw, on one great day, that regardless of what torments they suffer, these souls would prefer to endure them to the end of the world than to appear before God and enter into Heaven with the least stain of sin. I also felt within myself a severe dread, that, in dying, any sin might delay the fulfilment of my desire to see God and unite myself to him for ever. For it seemed to me, in the intensity of the desires I had, that I would suffer twice as much as others.

This is why my usual practice was to have recourse to the merits of our Lord. And beginning from the moment of his Incarnation, and going on through the mysteries and the actions of his most holy life, and finally the sacrifice of his sorrowful death, I used to say: 'O Eternal Father, I recognise how criminal I am and how unable to pay the debts of your divine justice! Nevertheless I wish now, even at this very moment, to satisfy fully that justice and acquit myself of all my debts in its regard. O Eternal Father, receive then, if it pleases you, the merits of the life and death of your Son and the pouring forth of his blood for the remission of all my offences![226] No matter how great and enormous my offences could be, they are not comparable to the satisfaction which he makes of them to you and which I render you in inflicting them on myself. In this way, my God, I hope not to owe you anything any more; and that, after this satisfaction, you will have nothing to ask of me for all the sins of my life. What is necessary to appease you, my God, in order to pay entirely the debt of my offences? Fastings, tears, prayers, virtues, sorrow and blood? Your Son has done all that! And everything that comes from him is much better and of completely different value than if these actions came only from me. Then, through his merits, give me back my baptismal grace.[227] Put me back in the state of innocence. Make me, through grace, what you are by nature, completely beautiful, completely pure and holy, so that there may be nothing which prevents me from seeing you and rejoicing in you at the hour of my death.[228] O sweet Jesus, be you Jesus to me! [229] And since you are my Saviour before being my Judge, bestow on me effectively one drop of your precious blood, which is the source of all my hopes, and then pronounce against me whatever sentence pleases you!'[230] It was after I had received Communion and at the sacrifice of the Mass that I meditated particularly on such affection, settling my accounts with God and satisfying also his justice. And one day, after Communion, he made me see that it was indeed easy to satisfy him perfectly by this means, because all the merits of our Lord are with us, and the least object drawn out of this treasure, if one can speak thus, where everything is infinite, is of infinite value. I mean, that if only the one which appears least to our eyes were taken out, this would be more than sufficient to atone with plenitude for all our crimes; all the more reason because, if we were to avail ourselves of all his merits - on account of the many benefits he continually gives us and the charity of Jesus Christ[231] who merited them for us - it would be satisfying more his justice than his love. This vision pierced my heart with a dart of love. I desired a new heart and new forms for all my powers in order to love him all the more.

Purgatory of love

Our Lord made me see then, as I say, that with his merits it is indeed easy to acquit us of the debt of our sins; and I did not see, however, that offering them as I did, they would be received and accepted in my favour; nor had I any assurance of this through any feeling or other. Here is the principal point of the state and the disposition of my soul. As I have already said, it is to be in complete ignorance of my fate and my condition; not knowing, in the same way as those poor souls in Purgatory, if I am damned or saved; I mean not knowing what state I am in, if it is the spirit of God or some other spirit that is directing me. I know neither where I am nor where I am going. I know well that I desire to do the will of God in this world and to see and possess him eternally in the next. But I see nothing that might be able to make me hope for the accomplishment of those desires, for I do not see that the merits of our Lord are bestowed on me, nor that any action of mine is united to his which would let me hope for the fulfilment of my desires. I desire without hope, or to say it better, I hope with a hope stripped of all feeling and of every light. In this state the soul suffers a martyrdom that cannot be explained. Not being able to be united to that which one loves, and not seeing any means of reaching that which one desires, is the torment of torments![232]

I reached the stage especially once when, for about fifty days, I continuously desired to die in order to see God and our Lord; and I could well say that my soul was all that time in a purgatory of love. It seems to me that when these desires enter into the heart, they chase out everything, in order to allow themselves to be felt with greater intensity. One is no longer subject to the storm of temptations or agitated by human passions; and the soul is, in some way, outside of the world. The goods and evils of life do not touch it any more than they do a soul in Purgatory. For in fact the soul is not in the world. Nor is it yet in Heaven. It desires to enter there, but the gates are closed to it. And neither is the soul in Hell. There God is not loved; but there the soul burns from his love![233] In Hell one is consumed by a worm of conscience; but here the soul rejoices in a great repose and perfect tranquillity![234] It is a long time indeed that I have been performing the exercise of death, which I do every month.[235] I have thought of myself as dwelling in this world and in my body as in a purgatory, adoring and accepting the sentence of God which has condemned me there and leaves me there. O Lord, how well this thought can make an impression on my soul and how true it is indeed that I am in Purgatory! My salvation will be assured, since all the souls who are in that place will finally see you and enjoy you.

O love, pull me soon from the sad prison of my body, tear asunder my chains and break my bonds! Do not suffer it that anyone else but you deliver my soul from captivity. Separate me entirely from myself in order to be united completely to my God! O divine love, I have completely abandoned myself to your dispositions during my life and will certainly still abandon myself to them all the more at the hour of my death! That I may die, O my God, not only in loving you, but that I may die by dint of loving you! If my sins render me unworthy of dying from this happy death of love, that I may die at least from the regret and the grief of not being able to die from it! And if I do not die from an excess of the sweetness of your love, that I may die from the excess of its sorrow, my heart bursting asunder and being dashed to pieces by an acute contrition of having offended you!

Finish, Lord, what you have begun with such mercy! And since you boast of restoring all your works to perfection,[236] finish your image that you gave me at my creation and which you have restored through the redemption of your Son, our Lord.[237] Finish it, I say, my God, through the light of your glory! That I may leave soon this miserable world where one cannot serve you or adore you except in the medley of the many miseries and imperfections![238] That I may enter into that peace where you are praised, blessed and loved without any impurity, and that I may be able to do so throughout all eternity! Amen.

Appeasement

After the period of about fifty days during which I had those desires to die, that state of my soul was changed in an instant. O Lord, only you can humble and mortify us in the most sensitive of areas, when it pleases you to touch us there! In a moment I lost the feeling that I was about to die. And if the desire itself was not taken away from me, at least it was compressed into the bottom of my heart, acting no longer with the same force. My soul was so desperately sad that it seemed to me I would never again have joy in this world. I began to dread and fear death; and I was astonished at that which I had desired and asked for with such ardour. Ever since that moment - and it is eight months ago now, that I write this - I have only rarely and from time to time felt that desire to die.[239] My God, I accuse myself before you of my misery and confess that I have been indeed glad not to feel those desires any more with such intensity and ardour; for I suffered oddly in this.[240]

This fire[241] is kindling itself again little by little in my heart. For some time now, I have been feeling keenly and more often the attacks I have not had in many months, since the time when these desires ceased for me. I am indeed glad to feel them deeply; but I confess that I dread in them the force and passion in which I have experienced them. Nevertheless, my God, I am in your hands! I offer myself again to you that I may suffer this martyrdom for as much and for as long as it pleases you.

Peace and tranquillity

The disposition of my soul has not been changed, remaining always in that state in which it sees and knows nothing. But the practice of the interior acts was changed. For I was then continually exercising the acts of faith in the hope that I would see soon what I had believed in - the most Holy Trinity, a God in three persons, the Being of beings; the sacred humanity of our Lord; and so for all the other mysteries of faith. As regards these acts of faith and hope, they were almost always without feeling; and instead of the practice of these virtues, I have been more occupied with the virtue of fear (but a sweet fear that does not trouble the soul) of a knowledge of my misery; because, even having recourse unceasingly to our Lord so that it might please him to preserve me from all sin - for which through his mercy he always gives me an extreme horror - I felt even a little the pain and difficulty of virtue (something I did not feel in the other state). And when I speak about sin, I do not mean only mortal sin, but the most insignificant that could be committed. It is a great evil, an evil which causes other evils in the world, to believe that there are such things as small sins, for all sins are great and enormous, considered respectively against the grandeur and majesty of God who is offended by them, and all must be detested with an infinite hatred. Also, I entreat him that it may please him to grant me that grandeur of heart and generosity of courage to follow and imitate perfectly the examples he had given me of poverty, humility and suffering, filling me perfectly with the highest and most noble spirit of the Cross.

This is the subject of the interior affections with which I have been particularly occupied for seven or eight months. Since then I have more often felt an internal aridity and dryness, which I used not to feel before. It is nevertheless always accompanied by peace and tranquillity. For many years trouble and distress have been entirely chased from my mind and, no matter what happens to me, I am always perfectly calm and tranquil. I believe that these states of dryness come the majority of times from the weakness and infirmity of the body. At one time, when I was in a continual exercise of love, my soul was elevated in a marvellous way above all the infirmities of nature; and often when I felt any difficulty from this side of things in doing my exercises, I addressed myself to our Lord and complained lovingly: 'When will it be,' I said, 'my

God, that you will deliver me from this misery and that I will use not only an hour or a day, but a complete eternity without any hindrance or interruption in praising you and loving you?' Immediately my mind received a secret force and vigour; and the soul was no longer hindered by the infirmities of the body. But since that time seven or eight months ago, the soul has suffered from these infirmities all the more. This is what my state has been; and still is now. Moreover, I have a great disgust for myself and for all things.

Conclusion

Guided by a ray of light

When your Reverence had expressed his desire to me to know more fully the things that happened in me, I was very confused about the temptations I had suffered; how our Lord had assisted me in fighting the worst of them (my inclinations and my bad habits); and also, about that state of annihilation in which I have been for so many years, and those desires for death I have experienced. But I saw nothing distinctly and almost did not know where to begin, having nothing ordered in my mind. Yet, resolved simply to obedience, I set about writing; and right from the beginning up to the end, our Lord gave me a ray of light that made me see clearly and distinctly not only the external and perceptible things, but also the internal affections which I have had to write about in many places, having no other ways of describing my sentiments and my disposition, all of which are expressed through the words I use. For I do not think that of all the words used in this writing, even twelve of them are changed (and never with any change in their meaning); and if they are confused, it is as they occurred to me in my mind, and because they occurred in the soul without doubt in this same confusion. One takes little care in arranging what one says, except to say it with respect and love. As I wrote it on the paper, it was accordingly erased from my mind, making no longer any impression; as if what it stood for did not happen to me, or I did not do it. And sometimes when I began writing, I myself would have difficulty in trying to remember things. But, not being able to do anything without the help of that ray, and doing nothing but fatiguing my mind and being unable to stir almost from my place, I was obliged to stop writing. And the other paper which I have already given to your Reverence has been done in the same way.[242]

The grace to communicate with fidelity

This, my dear Father, is what I have been able to say to you concerning that which you have desired of me. I have obeyed in simplicity your desire and the light that was given me in order to describe to you all things in an innocence which will be regarded as ridiculous in many places and circumstances. But I would prefer to err in this than in obedience. The fault against obedience would be criminal; and the other would not. Perhaps our Lord planted in your heart the desire to know the details of my feelings and dispositions, so as to put me back on the right road, because, if I am straying, it is because I am a poor blind person who does not know where to put her foot. Perhaps also, knowing about his guidance of me and his intentions for me, you may procure for me the grace of making me communicate with fidelity in this, because I have need to be taken by the hand, sustained and forced into doing it. But having said so many things to you, there is one thing especially which is the most important of all to me and which it truly vexes me to admit. It is that, after so many graces and mercies granted to me by God, I still haven't got even the first smatterings or impressions of virtue. But I

157

desire to have them and to accept them, even though, feeling deeply this desire every day, I scarcely dare to say that this desire is a true one, for it is not followed by the effect which it should produce. I beseech you therefore, my Reverend Father, to start me henceforth, seriously and truly, in the practice of virtue. And whatever indisposition and resistances you may find in me (for I am filled enough with miseries to be all this and more to you), use the power I have so often asked you to exert over me, in order to make me do what you see God demanding of me.

Great and sublime matters

It remains for me to say how I have been guided by the union with our Lord Jesus Christ, how I was initiated into the mysteries of his life and elevated to the knowledge of his divine attributes[243] and finally all the matters concerning prayer which it has pleased him to communicate to me.[244] But all these matters are great and sublime, and consequently difficult to deal with, particularly for a worthless and ignorant woman like myself, who doesn't even know the terms and words she should use. And if this writing should happen to fall into hands other than those of your Reverence, one could be rightly scandalised that a person like me has written them. Besides, this uses up much of my time I should take to spin and sew, which is an employment that is more suitable to me, more appropriate. So for all these reasons I beseech you, my dear and Reverend Father, to dispense me from it. Nevertheless, I show these writings to you with all the respect and submission possible, and in the complete resolution of obeying you in everything that will please you to enjoin on me. Your will shall always be my sovereign reason, and may it please God that he has indeed put that desire in your heart of using me so freely and absolutely in all things! It will undoubtedly never be in proportion to that which I desire! I would take it as the greatest grace that could happen to me, the greatest testimony of charity I could receive from your Reverence, to which I am entirely[245]

Doxology

Glory to God, to our Lord Jesus Christ, to the most Holy Virgin and to the great St Joseph. Amen.

THIRD ACCOUNT

Light

Supplication

There is only you, all powerful and eternal God, who fathoms the depths of man through your prudence and infinite wisdom. External actions are known to everyone and are quickly explained; but the affections of the heart, and that which takes place in the soul, are not described in so few words. And besides, because you wish that I still continue to bring to the light of day the great mercies you have bestowed on me, it is an act of gratitude, and the first one owes to one's benefactor, to confess and declare the favours one has received from him - this, my Lord, I desire for your glory with all my heart. This is the sentiment with which I wish to make this revelation. Give me therefore, if it pleases you, the light I need for this; for I recognise my powerlessness to do so otherwise. I hope and I believe you will give it to me abundantly, because I desire and lay claim to nothing but the obeying of your divine will.

Decisive light

The principle and most beautiful light it pleased the goodness of God to diffuse into my soul, and which changed me in a moment, was to see the excellence of the end for which I have been created.[1] I saw how far I was from this [end] on account of sin; the abomination of that same sin; and then the unfortunate ending into which sin hurls the miserable soul that is soiled by it. This is Hell. So this horrible eternity appeared to my eyes. Above all, I had a vision of the punishment of the damned,[2] which lasted in me for about fifteen days. To be in the hatred of God for ever; to hate him also eternally and to spew forth incessantly blasphemies against his sovereign goodness! I do not understand how I did not die at the sight of such horrible things; nor how I was able to endure the excessive love that was kindled in my heart at the knowledge I had of how the goodness of God preserved me from falling into those evils and saved me in order to be able to love him. From that very moment I made the resolution to use all the time in my life in that holy exercise, detesting with an extreme horror everything from then on that could distance me from my God.

The book of nature

I was very ignorant about the means and ways that were necessary for me to take in order to arrive at and unite myself to this end [for which I have been created]. But it pleased God to open two books for me, in which I learned everything I needed to know about this. The first book was this visible, this perceptible world; for it was then completely new to me. New eyes were given me in order to look at it and consider it in a completely different manner from the way I had done up to then.[3] The splendour of the sun, the clarity of the stars, the diversity of flowers, and generally everything that is found in nature, and reveals itself to my eyes and to my imagination, were reasons for me to elevate myself and to unite myself to God. I saw his creatures as small participations in his divine perfections, as it were, little flowings from them; and I marvelled at the fact that all these were in perfect submission and obedience to his orders - without failing at all in this for one moment - whereas man, who is more indebted to him than all these creatures put together, runs counter to his laws and his commandments.

The life of Jesus Christ

The second book that was opened for me, and in which I learned by far the most excellent lessons in honouring and serving God, was Jesus Christ and his most holy life.[4] This was put before my eyes and proposed to me as a prototype, a divine model that it was necessary for me to imitate and copy for the rest of my life. Through the grace of my God I had been brought up and nourished in the Catholic religion. And even in our country[5] the Huguenots[6] are not accepted; there it is a crime that is punished by death. But moreover, I had stayed two and a half years - less a few days - in religion,[7] and so I was unable to avoid being instructed in the faith. And nevertheless, I can truly say that up to then [the second book] I was like those people of whom our Lord speaks in the Gospel who, seeing, do not see and hearing, do not understand.[8] There is indeed all the difference in the world between what men teach us and what God teaches us![9] In a manner of speaking, I could indeed say that I have learned the mysteries of faith and religion, and especially the life of our Lord, from him alone. I was then in a state of such great poverty that I didn't have the means of buying any books to instruct myself. But he supplied for this defect through his abundant goodness, and taught me more things in the twinkling of an eye than the most learned and spiritually devoted people could perhaps have taught me in many years.

An observation

Because this is what is particularly desired of me now - to explain how I was guided by union with our Lord and initiated into the mysteries of his life - I cannot describe the order in which these lights were given to me; but I will say how they will be given to me at this moment, throwing also as much clarification as will be possible for me on what I have to say.[10]

Lights on the mysteries of Christ

Terrestrial and glorified life

The Word was made flesh

I saw,[11] therefore, how all men were lost through the sin of Adam; how God could damn[12] us all without any injustice, but that, moved by his goodness alone he had sent his Son to the world in order to save us. I saw the infinite charity in the coming of the Son of God to be our Saviour. The mystery of the Incarnation is attributed in particular to the Holy Spirit, who brought it about in the womb of the Holy Virgin, because, [the Holy Spirit] being the personal love of the Father and the Son, [the Incarnation] is a mystery of complete love that proceeds from infinite love. The wonderful grandeurs of this ineffable mystery presented to my eyes held me in astonishment and adoration. And certainly they could indeed keep me so, because they hold the angels in this way, and will do so for all eternity! A God to be made man! The Creator to become creature! The Eternal to come into time! The Boundless to shut itself up in a little body! The All-Powerful to subject itself to our weaknesses! This great God who is a pure spirit to unite himself to matter! And the Immortal subject to death!

Sometimes, completely carried away and outside of myself with admiration, I say: 'Lord, do you really know who you are and who we are?[13] If all your glory and your felicity were to depend on us, would you do something else other than that which you do in order to compel us to love you? Forgive me, my God, if I dare say to you that it seems to me you might be infatuated[14] with love for your creatures.'

Finally, I saw how this mystery is a mystery of love and of annihilation.[15] For the divinity was as if annihilated, as St Paul says,[16] and did not lose, however, anything of its infinite grandeur. It would be impossible for me to speak about the lights and affections it pleased God to grant me concerning this mystery; particularly, since I only want to write about these things as succinctly as will be possible for me.

Afterwards, I was directed to consider our Lord in his birth. O, how the poverty of that stable and the vileness of that manger touched me appreciably and with such force! It was this vision, it seems to me, which kindled in my heart such an ardent desire for poverty. From then on I adored and embraced the plans God had made for putting me in the condition I was in then. I thanked him with untold affections for giving me those little traits of resemblance with his Son, and desired and asked of him with equal affection to have them for the rest of my life and that he perfect them more and more [in me]. I then threw myself at the feet of our Lord: 'Speak, my dear Master, for your poor servant listens to you![17] Imprint your examples well on my soul, in such a way that I will never forget them!'

With how many insights was my soul filled to [help me] see how poverty is infinitely preferable to riches, and contempt to honour, because God, who has infinite wisdom and cannot be mistaken in his estimation of things, had preferred it so! And is it not infinitely glorious, then, for us to follow the examples of God? I believe that, at the time, if I had had sceptres and crowns and entire worlds to myself, I would have abandoned all in order to embrace poverty for ever,[18] fearing nothing more than seeing myself obliged to have and possess anything for the rest of my life. Several times, transported in mind, I would run throughout the whole world, and tearing away from Princes and Kings their sceptres and their crowns, their kingdoms and all their power, would throw them at the feet of the manger of our Lord in order to do him homage with them by giving them to him as if they had belonged to me!

I was in fact very attentive in considering everything that happened in that stable regarding the mysteries of circumcision and the adoration of the Kings. But these lights were not as great or as abundant as those I had previously. But generally all those I received touched me and made an impression on my soul.

Exile

The knowledge I had of the flight of our Lord into Egypt[19] consoled me greatly. The poverties and inconveniences this sacred family suffered in that foreign place gave me great heart and courage to suffer the same as they did. I rejoiced in seeing myself in a foreign place,[20] being far away from all my relatives and almost from all knowledge of them, in order to honour and imitate in effect the states and mysteries of the life of our Lord. From then on I united the days of exile from my homeland and the separation from worldly goods with the sojourn he wished to make in foreign lands. And because he went there in order to obey divine Providence, and remained there until Providence allowed him to leave, so I desired to remain in exile only with the same submission and obedience he rendered to this sovereign Providence. I was extremely sad not to have had this poverty of intention right from the beginning.

Hidden life

As our Lord gives us his graces to suit the state in which he wishes to put us, [so] he gave me, through his goodness, the grace of a very particular knowledge regarding his hidden life. He let me see how he, who is the light of the world, remained thirty years withdrawn and closed up in a poor room;[21] how he, having come in order to instruct us, remained all that time without appearing or speaking, except once, at the age of 12 years;[22] and - although there was no talk of him; and he himself was content during that time of thirty years to be subject and obedient to his parents - how Heaven and earth were governed nevertheless by his absolute power. He who provides so abundantly for the needs of all creatures, worked with his hands to gain his living. And because he

162

wished to subject himself to this, he did not take any employment that would be greatly esteemed and create a stir in the eyes of the world, but remained in a poor workshop, working with a plane and some worthless pieces of wood! And besides these jobs, which seem so unworthy of his grandeur, he subjected himself moreover to all the miseries of our nature - drinking, eating and sleeping, feeling the cold, the heat and the other inconveniences to which we are subject!

I confess that when I saw these things, I could hardly come to from admiration and astonishment. The things in his life we have less reason for admiring are often the ones that are admired most. For, in effect, to have cured the sick, given back sight to the blind, hearing to the deaf, brought the dead back to life, commanded the sea and the wind - what is there that is admirable in all this? Is not all nature subject to him? Are these actions not proper and natural to him, seeing that he performs all of them through his divinity? But to work, drink, eat and sleep, and all the rest that appertains to life - this is what should fill us with delight.

But why, I'll be asked, seeing that this is not only proper to man, but also necessary for human life? Because he was not simply man; he was man- God. These two natures in him were only one person, having a glorified soul and rejoicing in the vision of the beatific God. The glory of his body was rightly his due from the moment it was united to the divinity;[23] and that he had so set aside temporarily the glory of his soul that his sacred body had no awareness of it (except once - at the transfiguration),[24] and that along with his glorified soul he had a body that was mortal, capable of experiencing pain,[25] and subject to our infirmities, is what one cannot think about without being astonished! I find nothing more admirable in the life of our Lord than this. It is a miracle greater by far than all those he performed to the eyes of men.This is something we don't think enough about.

Imitation of Jesus Christ

Now our Lord, much more by his example than his words,[26] made me know that he did this ²⁷ in order to instruct us to imitate him. Throughout all those visions, I was extremely drawn to the interior and hidden life, to solitude and silence, and considered myself fortunate then to see myself earning my living by the work of my hands in order to follow the example he had given me, evincing nothing any longer but servitude and obedience. I have never been able to understand since how Christians instructed in this learning love to have power over other people and solicit important offices, seeing that the only useful and honourable thing we can have is to be true to Jesus Christ, who rendered himself subject and obedient.

But above all, I could not conceive of nor understand what I heard said only too often, that even religious men and women and ecclesiastical people seek pre-eminence, and love the prime dignities of the Church! I well understand the behaviour of so many saints who flew away from those [dignities] and hid when any were offered to them; for in the way that I see things, unless God gives them, such dignities are oppressive and weighty responsibilities, and I do not know how one would even dare

163

desire them. But in this case Jesus Christ will know indeed how to give what is also necessary to perform these responsibilities worthily. Besides the danger there is in these dignities, in that state one is less like Jesus Christ, who was poor and humble and which is what we must look for principally in this life.

I have always held it as a singular favour and a particular grace from God - for which I thank him very often - that he put me in a state of life that was humble, with poor occupations like sewing, spinning and mending old, worn clothes for the greater part of the time. In this I have every reason for honouring and imitating the lowliness of employment our Lord wanted in the first[28] thirty years of his life; if it is permissible to use these terms, for this is just our way of speaking, because everything he does is infinitely great and admirable. So, doing my job, I have always tried to carry out these occupations like he would, that is to go about them with his intentions and his affections.

I also consider it to be a particular favour that God has not given me those extraordinary graces that sparkle in the eyes of men, for the simple reason that my little exercises of devotion have never been known or recognised by anyone except my confessor, to whom I had to speak about them. For one doesn't think of me, a person of no value. And this is what I desire, considering this grace one of the greatest God could grant me.

Our Lord's passion

I also had some knowledge of his ordinary life, but little compared with the knowledge I had of other things. And this was also not so necessary for me; for although I have been out in the world for six or seven years, I have remained however in solitude, as I have said elsewhere,[29] being scarcely aware of the change.

But finally I was guided to the mysteries of his passion.

Of these mysteries, his prayer in the garden is the one to which I have been particularly drawn. I remember once I suffered many hours in such sadness, dejection, disgust, weariness and grief of heart that I did not know what to do. It seemed to me afterwards that this was a little drop of that torrent of affliction our Lord had when beginning his passion, a slight participation in it. In this mystery I learned about the all-powerful strength of prayer in fortifying our flesh and encouraging it to suffer, because our Lord, after his prayer, approached his enemies generously and gave himself up freely and with courage to the torments of death.

His flagellation was also particularly represented to me, but especially after the barbaric extortion[30] when, the tormentors being more weary in beating him than he was in suffering their strokes, he was abandoned alone to that column, completely rent with wounds and as if drowned in his own blood. This vision pierced my heart with an extreme sorrow and compassion. I was carried away by interior movements and transports of the spirit, as if I had wished to take him away by force and carry him off from his enemies, hide him and put him in my heart; to throw myself at the mercy of the tormentors so that I might receive the strokes, for it was I who was culpable. But crying, and detesting my sins with extreme bitterness - because they were the cause of his wounds - I saw him so covered with wounds that I did not know where to touch him or take him by, for fear of wounding him all the more and renewing his pains. It was this that inflamed me with those ardent desires to suffer and to do penance.

I do not know if there is any greater suffering or more appreciable penance in the world than when, having these visions, and feeling deeply the violence of these desires as I feel them, one cannot and dare not satisfy them. For I have suffered more than I can say in obeying my confessor in this. Very often I have not obeyed him as strictly as I should have, for which I ask pardon of my God.[31] If I had had the spirit to speak to him and to tell him what was happening in my soul, perhaps he would have permitted me to do penance all the more. But I was not able to speak; and I suffered that secret torment, which was extreme.

Crucifixion

It was when I had seen him crowned with thorns and hailed as King through mockery that I felt the greatest affections and sentiments of respect for him; and beseeching him with great insistence to cover me with his clothing, on the exterior as well as in the interior, I recognised him as my King and sovereign Lord. But when I looked at him hearing and receiving his sentence of death: 'O Eternal Father', I said, 'because love equals the lovers, let it be that I die also with your Son! May the sentence that is given against him be carried out also against me! May I carry with you, my dear Saviour, your Cross on Calvary; but not in the manner of Simon of Cyrene who only carried it, and then left it! For I desire to be crucified there and fastened to it with you!'

The soul experiences certain things in this affection, movements that cannot be explained. For it seems to me that the soul crucifies itself and binds all its powers, all its interior and exterior senses, its body and spirit to the Cross of the Saviour; that it expires, in a certain way that cannot be described, dying to itself and to all these things of the world. And as our Lord was nailed to the Cross and fastened to it so strongly that he couldn't move or turn from one side to the other, so the soul - and even the body in some way - does not turn to anything any more, remaining as if dead to all things of this world. One time in particular, considering how our Lord had been outstretched and nailed to the Cross, with all his bones dislocated and put out of place, it seemed to me that the powers of my soul and my exterior and interior senses were torn away from their purely natural operations.

I have always had great devotion to receiving the last breath of Jesus Christ as he died on the Cross, entreating him to expire in my heart and to come and live in me through his spirit, governing me in everything and everywhere.

His holy wounds and his sacred heart were the place of my abode; and I was so strongly drawn there, particularly when I was assailed by temptations (above all, those against purity), that there was little or no possibility of my leaving there. Sometimes I said: 'No matter how impure my heart and mind are, O my dear Saviour, it is necessary that they enter into your loving heart and remain in your sacred wounds, so that they be completely purified in this burning furnace!' And so, from that abode I fought my enemies.[32]

True grandeur

I was drawn primarily to the consideration of the pains and corporal works of our Lord in his passion. This consideration leads naturally to penance - the mortification of the senses and the flesh. Then I was drawn even more to the consideration of his more spiritual virtues, such as his humility, poverty, charity, mildness and others. This is where the soul is stripped and leaves behind the affections of the old man in order to be clothed in those of the new.[33] Jesus is the true bronze serpent.[34] One has only to look upon him elevated on the Cross in order to be healed from all the wounds and evil inclinations one has contracted through sin. I do not understand how one can look upon him attentively in that state and say: 'There is my God, whom I must try and resemble if I wish to be saved!' and still remain after that with the affections and practices of vanity, ostentation[35] and the pomp of the world; in the pleasure of the senses and particularly those which appear to be criminal, no matter how little; in the desire for riches, the esteem and honour of the world, and similar things. I cannot understand, I say, that one could continue to practise and have affection for all this, and say: 'This is my God and my model!' One says this either out of derision or mockery. If these words were truly said from the heart and with full knowledge, one would be pronouncing at the same time the sentence of his own condemnation and death; and a time will come and will not pass, when mockery will be made of those who pronounce these words in making fun of him.

I perceived through an extraordinary light that it is in the imitation and practice of the virtues, which our Lord gave us as an example in his life, and particularly in his death, that constitutes the true grandeur of the courage and generosity of the heart. In effect, if one really wished to examine it, there is indeed more glory in disdaining all things, in throwing away[36] all the goods and riches of this world, and in elevating oneself generously over and above them all, than in falling and burying oneself under these ruins by the excessive esteem one gives to them, and the excessive efforts shown either in amassing them or conserving them. O how those who put their glory, their peace and repose in the riches and goods of this world are blind and mistaken! For I have seen, more clearly than the light of day, that these things are only brambles and thorns that prick you and incessantly stain you with blood; and that man lowers himself and debases himself to the last degree when he esteems them too much and thinks he can get his glory from them. For his glory will consist in keeping them all beneath him, and not in elevating them above himself.

The function of generous hearts

There is indeed a lot more courage and resolution in suffering contempt and in pardoning injuries than in doing the opposite: 'I have too much of a heart to suffer that!' Their lies are shameless in saying that they have a heart. Indeed on the contrary, it shows that they are really cowardly in not being able to suffer a little word and to curb a small movement of passion that dominates them; for often it is nothing more than that. There are even those who sometimes show these resentments for fear only that one might mock them if they were to do the opposite. This is a sign of extreme silliness and weakness of mind, seeing that, in order to avoid a little bantering and to have the approval of some people (who often haven't a jot of judgement), they refuse themselves the esteem of angels and of God himself, and deny themselves the honour of imitating Jesus Christ; in following whom, being what he is, they would undoubtedly have their true glory.

This is so true, for when a virtue is found in people that is a proof against all these currents, it is immediately honoured and respected by everyone; and those same people who laughed at it, afterwards avow that they would really wish to be like those people. Why then don't they do it? Because there is too much pain in acquiring the virtue; and they are too cowardly to be able to vanquish and overcome the difficulties. It is therefore the function of generous and magnanimous hearts to practise a truly Christian virtue.[37]

Resemblance to Jesus Christ

Do we not admire with astonishment those who imitate our Lord in that strength of patience he demonstrated in his passion; in that generous obedience he returned inviolable to his Father, preferring to die, and die that death of the Cross, than to be unfaithful to his wishes in no matter what? What! When you see people, who in all the diverse setbacks that can be suffered in this life - sickness, poverty, the reversal of fortune and the like - remain in peace and in that equilibrium of spirit, always the same and entirely submitted to all the ordinances of Heaven, is there anything better to single out the strength and constancy of a heart and a mind? No, there is none!

This light, which revealed those truths to me, was not a passing one. For some years it had shone continually in my heart, by means of which my understanding was freed from deception and purged of the errors with which it had been filled by the false maxims of the world. The will received the imprint of truth and embraced it ardently, making a firm resolution from then on to follow it, exercising itself in the practice of the Saviour's virtues and trying in everything to take on the features of his perfect resemblance.

The depth of the mystery of the Cross

I was drawn afterwards to the consideration of the attributes of God and the perfections of the divinity of Jesus Christ on the Cross. The depth of this wisdom: its infinite goodness in finding and employing this means to repair the injury done to God and bring about our salvation; its sovereign power in bringing down and destroying our enemies with arms so weak, that through the ignominy of the Cross[38] he subjected himself to everyone - this proves his divinity far more than all the miracles he performed. And this means of showing us is far more effective than is the creation of Heaven and earth! This infinite goodness, wishing to save men, suffered very many pains and labours for their salvation, although he (infinite goodness) could have very justifiably damned[39] them all; for, whether they existed or not, were lost or saved, would not have added to his greatness or his happiness.[40]

Because Jesus Christ has been so severely treated, he who never committed and could not commit any sin, but could only become a surety for sinners in order to be offered up in satisfaction for their sins - this is where I saw how much the justice of God is rigorous and horrifying, and how sin is abominable and must be hated.

In this mystery of the Cross, I discovered in an admirable way the purity and sanctity of God; he is unable to suffer even the slightest trace of sin.

All these visions produce astonishing effects in the soul.

The mystery of the Cross is indeed profound; there are great things to be learned on Calvary!

As one vision was given me, so the other diminished; as when in the case of those more interior and spiritual virtues of our Lord, I saw less his bodily pains, so when I was elevated to the knowledge of his divine attributes, I saw less his virtues.[41]

Apprenticeship to eternity

Our Lord, in his goodness, has made me see very often some examples of the ravishing beauty and splendour of his sacred humanity after his glorious resurrection; and, since these visions, everything I have seen or have heard spoken of, in this world, to be beautiful to our eyes and admirable to my ears, seemed deformed and defective in comparison; which is indeed the case.[42]

The knowledge the soul has of the glorified life of our Lord elevates it in an astonishing way. The soul feels itself to be endowed, in advance, with the dowries[43] of glory, and it appears to it that the body itself in some way has become completely spiritual, because it [also] has no longer any feeling or affection for the things of this world. No more does one want any employment or occupation here other than that which one hopes to have for a whole eternity, that is to praise and love God.[44] In order to unite itself to God, to repose in him alone, the soul is pulled away, delivered so vigorously from, and elevated over and above everything that concerns it - pleasure, profit, spiritual or temporal interests, and even all the gifts of God - that it neither dwells nor reflects in any way upon all of this.

My spirit was so strongly immersed in the life of our Lord, in the things he made for us and in the examples he gave us, that through a particular mercy of God my mind was filled with it at all times and on every occasion. Up to the point even, that it often happened to me when Madame took me on a visit with her,[45] I felt myself drawn to prayer in an extraordinary way from the moment I mounted the carriage; and comparing the fine clothes and pomp of the world[46] with the life of our Lord, would feel astonished at how the Christians who recognise him for their God and who make profession of his law - that tends only to renounce and have contempt for all riches and vanities - take glory in riches instead of blushing with shame in having them and in possessing them, seeing that this makes us unlike him, and because all our glory consists in following his examples and in observing his laws. Yet, from some strange turning of the mind, one is ashamed however to be like him and holds it as an honourable thing to be the opposite! In my heart I bitterly deplored that evil and that blindness; and moved to a true glory by the feeling to imitate our Lord, I conceived for all goods, honours and pleasures of this world such a great contempt, that I only looked at them so as to despise them.

I was extremely stirred by the motive of glory, and moved to follow the examples of our Lord; for having naturally an ambitious spirit, and drawn to great things, and having been freed from the error in which I had lived up to then - of thinking that honour was in having temporal things - I felt myself honoured, and considered it as a great glory to see myself stripped and in a state of life that had something in common with the one he led on earth. For the highest point of honour, of true honour that one can aspire to is to be like him; all other honours are only fantastical and imaginary.

With this knowledge, I saw the goods and pleasures of the world to be filled only with thorns and bitterness. I mean that I saw nothing but the pains involved in amassing riches, and the grief and sadness of spirit they cause in losing them; nothing but the bitterness and disgust of the pleasures of life; in short, that those who have the greatest honours and who seem to be elevated by their dignity over and above the rest of men, are in effect the most complete and utter slaves of all. And that this is so, the proof of it is evident: if they wish just to leave their house, do they not depend on their footmen, their coaches and their horses? Thinking themselves to be independent, they depend, I assure you, on as many persons as they have domestics. O, how this great show, this ostentation has strange constraints and is a pitiful slavery! How sweet and free is the poor and humble life in comparison![47]

But also, when I looked at the rarest goods of this world, the most dignified honours and exquisitely refined pleasures available to escape boredom, and compared them to the eternal pleasures that are prepared for us (which were easily perceptible to my mind and more present to me than those I saw with my eyes and touched with my hands); and most especially to the possession of God for an eternity, for which we are destined in his goodness, I said: 'O eyes of mine, close and look no more at anything that appears on the earth, for no matter how beautiful and admirable it might seem, it is unworthy of your smallest glance!'[48] I conceived such great contempt for all visible and transitory things that I could not understand how it is possible to desire them, or to value them in any way.

Unlimited topics

These were the feelings it pleased God to grant me for many years, and which occupied my mind whenever, in the midst of the world, the occasion presented itself to me to converse with anyone or pay them a visit. They indeed made me realise that there is nothing to fear when it is God who commits us to anything; for he knows how to make everything succeed for the good for those who put their trust in him.[49]

Looking at him,[50] sometimes in solitude, now praying, working, conversing, drinking, eating, suffering and observing his behaviour in everything so as to imitate it and to make myself completely like him, I was almost constantly about the sacred person of our Lord.[51] All this I did with so much ease that often all I had to do was to take whatever was given to me and show some concern in taking care of it.[52]

The Holy Virgin, our Lord, and the endless things our Lord has done for us are unlimited topics with which to occupy our minds, instead of using our minds [as we do] on so many whims and frivolities, which is indeed unfortunate for us. Occasionally it seemed to me that these topics are proposed to us as an admirable spectacle to satisfy all sorts of people and their affections. For those who are pleased with seeing things in their simplicity and innocence will indeed find a great deal to content themselves with in the mysteries of our Lord's infancy. Those who prefer the sad and outrageous things, will equally find what will satisfy them in his sorrowful death and passion. And for those who desire things full of pomp, glory and majesty, his resurrection, his ascension, all those wonderful apparitions he performed, and the many great miracles he did throughout his mortal life - all are considerations that will satisfy any desire to the full.

There is so much matter in the life of Jesus Christ to entertain us, that to think about it as little as we do, and to be even subject to so many distractions and extravagances of the mind during the little time we give to God in prayer, is a proof that our misery and our ingratitude are extreme. As I see it, I believe we fall into this evil because we go to prayer without due preparation, and without proposing to ourselves any subjects to occupy our minds with.

The coming of the Holy Spirit
The mystery of all mysteries by which he brought to a completion all he had accomplished for us, was to send his Holy Spirit to the world. I recognised that the principal end for which the Holy Spirit was given to us and came, was to render us a testimony of Jesus Christ;[53] that producing nothing within himself, the Holy Spirit came to form Jesus Christ in our hearts,[54] to give us understanding of the truths Jesus Christ had taught us,[55] and to imprint his law of love on our hearts. Beseeching him to bring about in me the effects of his coming into the world, I could not describe the things that happened in me in this regard. But my sins and ingratitude prevent me and destroy the effects of his goodness.

The Eucharist

The Mass and the real presence
What shall I say about the light and understanding it pleased God to give me about the great means he established in order to communicate to us his graces and bestow on us

abundantly the fruit and the merits of his life and passion, I mean the holy sacrifice of the Mass and the most august Sacrament of the altar? I have spoken in many places of the attractions it pleased him in his goodness to give me to approach it. I would still have many more things to say! But I have scarcely spoken of the lights I have had on the truth[56] of this mystery. Yet, there is none I have known so clearly. When I say that I have seen a hundred and a hundred times over, and again a hundred and a hundred times over, that after the consecration by the priest the substance of the bread was entirely destroyed, nothing remaining there other than the accidents alone; and that the body, the soul and the divinity of Jesus Christ were hidden under there, I would not be believing too much in it in saying this, nor would I be exaggerating in any way.

It is not that I have ever seen anything with the eyes of the body; but that, with those of the soul, I have such a great certitude and light of the real and veritable[57] presence of our Lord at the most Holy Sacrament, that I have often said: 'My God, in this mystery it is no longer faith I have!' For faith consists in believing in that which one does not see! And I perceive so clearly and evidently your true presence in this Sacrament, that everything I see, hear, and touch, indeed all the things I can be certain of through the senses, seem weak fables[58] to me, lies in comparison to the certitude I have of this truth![59] And in fact they are just that.

This does not happen in the soul by way of an image or representation,[60] but through a light that is infused into the soul, more brilliant than that of the sun to our eyes, and which fills it in a moment with so much splendour and clarity to make it see this truth openly, so not the slightest doubt lingers in the soul. This has happened to me often. But I do not have this light except at the sight of the host the priest has consecrated and the one I myself receive. But many times it pleased God also to give this light to me for all the Communions I saw,[61] which were in very great number for this happened to me sometimes on the days of great devotion.[62]

I declare that I saw in a wonderful light how Jesus Christ is in all things and in all parts of the host with the same glory and majesty he possesses in Heaven; how the most Holy Trinity in its entirety is there, with all its perfections and attributes, and that, although the Father and the Holy Spirit are there only in attendance,[63] having only one and the same nature, divinity and substance, they are indivisible.

Our Lord, still acting out of the greatest mercy, did not give me this light [only][64] during the holy sacrifice of the Mass; but for a very long time it has been almost constantly with me. Listening to the sermons[65] that were given on this subject, I saw more clearly all the wonders and verities that are spoken of concerning this adorable Sacrament; that it was not the objects[66] that were presented to my eyes I saw, when I looked at them with more attention. Even my own understanding was often a lot greater than the one I heard preached.

These lights imparted themselves to me so abundantly that I could not believe there was a person in the world who did not know of these truths, seeing that they were manifest and visible, if I dare speak thus, to one like myself. This I said to my confessor, who responded to me that it was not as common as I thought, and that this was a particular grace from God I had received from his goodness.

These lights caused a profound and marvellous respect to spring up in my soul, of the sort that when I entered the church, I sometimes fell all of a sudden into a profound state of annihilation[67] before his Majesty that is hidden and as if destroyed utterly in that Sacrament. At other times, in looking at him I was overtaken by a trembling throughout the whole body, which originated in a loving respect.[68]

Certainly, we do well to know that we lack faith when, in the churches, we let ourselves be carried away by so many irreverences and impieties; for in church we should have no less respect and love than the angels and saints in Heaven have, because in church we are in the presence of the same God as they are, and adore him as they do. If it were indeed possible, we should adore him more than they, seeing that Jesus Christ does more for us in some way than he does for them. He gives them the light of glory, through which he elevates them to himself so that they can see and contemplate him; but in that Sacrament, he hides the glory of his Majesty and covers it entirely in order to descend and unite himself to us. The more he lowers himself and humbles himself on our account, all the more should we owe him reverence, honour and love.

There are those who say that the excessive readiness with which people approach Communion diminishes respect for it.[69] This is what I do not understand; because there is no thought or reflection that causes more fervour and kindles in me such affections of love, than to behold this great kindness of our Lord and his readiness to give himself to us.

Regarding the treatise *De la fréquente communion*

It was only about two years or so that our Lord in his mercy had touched me[71] and drawn me more particularly to the frequentation of that august Sacrament, when the whole commotion against frequent Communion began to explode more and more violently.[72]

I have never read any of the books that treat of this subject, nor have I been present at any sermons of those of that party;[73] because, distrusting myself, and having neither science nor doctrine,[74] I feared exposing myself to error. I wasn't even curious to hear this subject spoken of. And nonetheless, because these discourses were so common that there was hardly a person who did not implicate himself by expressing his feelings on the subject[75] only too often was there a reason why I heard it spoken of.

For a time then, perhaps three weeks or a month, I had great light and understanding on this subject. This light caused me terror; because it seemed to me that I had nothing to do with all of this, and that a worthless young woman like me should not be part of this knowledge. Nevertheless, I spoke to my confessor about it,[76] and he reassured me; but not so much that some fear did not remain, because I was still not accustomed to seeing things the way these were shown to me; for it was a light diffused in my soul, which in an instant brings out some truth. I cannot describe this and make it better understood than in comparing it to when, unexpectedly, and without thinking about someone, you see that person before your very eyes.

This way of seeing from the interior has since become almost second nature and normal to me. But in the beginning it frightened me; and of itself, what I saw caused me then some disquiet. These clear insights followed me everywhere. I was like someone who, no matter where he turns, and regardless of where his eyes bring him, always sees the same person transported before him. For I saw these things whether I was at prayer or at work; but more particularly at Communion.

That this doctrine[77] was the foulest and most evil Hell has vomited up on the earth was all the more malign and perverse that it was masked in the appearance of piety and perfection. Jesus Christ has not remained among us in the Holy Sacrament of the altar to be simply adored, to be revered there and to listen to our prayers. For he would indeed have received all this in Heaven. But he has remained among us to communicate himself to us in that admirable way, to be received in Communion, and to be eaten. It is not respect and humility towards God to refuse his gifts. In fact, we can never render him a greater honour and reverence than in accepting them with thanksgiving and recognition of our unworthiness, faithfully availing ourselves of them in accordance with his purpose. It is pride and not humility to do otherwise.

To think that we must have burning desires for Communion and feel them deeply when approaching to receive it![78] The desire for Communion comes in communicating! For that bread of angels excites the appetite in eating it. It is not necessary then to wait to communicate. Moreover, such ardent desires and affections for Communion are undeserved favours, particular graces God grants when he wishes, as he wishes and to whom he wishes. When he gives them, they should be accepted with thanks and carefully preserved. When he does not give them, it is good to desire and to ask for them with humility. But to lay claim to them and to want them absolutely to begin with, is an arrogance greater by far than that which any subject of a king would commit who does not wish to obey the King's orders and carry out his wishes except on the condition that he see him, speak to him, and enter into his chamber and his study whenever he likes; in a word, that he have all sorts of liberty and familiarity with his [the King's] royal person. Who does not see that his would be a show of indignation rather than a testimony of respect and obedience, seeing that these privileges are accorded to very few people whom he regards as good and faithful subjects? Possibly those who will never have seen the King, but who will have faithfully obeyed his wishes, will perhaps by this give him reason for keeping them close to his person and endow them with his most singular favours. If it is that he doesn't grant them this, he will never leave off loving them and giving every consideration to them. But for the honour and good of the King, it is fitting that he has faithful and affectionate servants far away as well as near to his person.

This is the comparison I keep in mind to help me understand the way in which we should approach this Sacrament; because there are souls to whom God will perhaps never communicate these ardent desires, whom he will love however and cherish a great deal, and who will consequently render him no less service remaining in the ordinary ways and as it were distant from his Majesty than those who in approaching him have all those desires. True humility never lays claim to anything extraordinary. Everyone must serve God according to the grace he communicates to him, and must use it well; for to do otherwise is to specify conditions and prescribe them for God. I will receive Communion if he gives me a great desire for it! And perhaps he won't give me any beyond a very mediocre one, and often none at all! This is very true; and as he gives them, he also takes them away; at one time we will be all fire, and soon afterwards all ice. And yet there is no one who understands the practice of true devotion who would ever say that we should dwell on such changing [feelings].

Jansenist exigencies

With regard to such an excellent disposition and this purity of heart which is demanded for Communion - it would indeed be good to hope that we all had it! We are unable, far from it, to have a disposition such as the dignity of the Sacrament requires. But it is the Sacrament's proper effect to bring it about and to produce it in the soul, as it is the peculiar effect of fire to warm those who approach it. In one Communion alone the passions will be more mortified and vices and bad habits destroyed; in it more graces and more strengths will be received for the practice of virtue than in any other exercise of devotion we would perform, even for long periods.

Even if it would only be once in their whole lifetime, it is difficult to understand that those who do not wish to permit Communion except in this disposition dare receive it. For, is it possible to believe and to persuade oneself that one has this disposition without vanity?

I remember once, when I had hardly made any preparation for Communion - beyond perhaps recognising my misery and the great need I had of having recourse to our Lord, he said to me after I had received it: 'This is the best disposition for approaching me!' So it is through the knowledge of our poverty and the experience of our extreme misery that we must approach Communion, and go there as to the sovereign remedy of all our ills and the source that can fill us to the brim with all goods.

But let us see more particularly what effects this doctrine,[79] so beautiful in appearance, will produce. Undoubtedly, it is true that the more frequent Communion is, the more the disposition must be perfect; that this disposition must be altogether different in a person who receives Communion three or four times a week than in a person who only receives it every month or every fifteen days. Likewise, this disposition must also be greater in those who receive Communion every day than in those who do so less often. Consequently, this disposition must be far stronger in priests than in all other people, because they not only communicate every day, but also offer the sacrifice of the Mass; and by their character, they are bound to a greater perfection than lay people. In spite of that, it is only too true that very few priests are in that blessed state. They should not say Mass, then![80] For at the very least they must not communicate with a disposition less than that which one would desire in a lay person! To say otherwise is to go against all reason and fairness! And this being true, under the pretext of a greater reverence towards the Holy Sacrament, we destroy the holy sacrifice of the Mass, and consequently the Christian religion; because sacrifice is its soul and spirit.[81] Any religion without sacrifice would not be a religion.[82]

Excellence of the Mass

Some people, zealous for that party,[83] and who approve of this doctrine, sometimes say: 'O! if only one Mass in the world were said at a certain time or in some particular place, it would be more majestic by far and would beget much more respect!'[84] This reasoning may seem pious; but in fact it is pernicious and malicious! This one will realise, considering the reasons for which our Lord has come into the world and the motives behind all he did. Was it not chiefly to glorify God, to render him all the honour due to his sovereign grandeur, and which all creatures together could never have rendered him; to repair the injury that had been done to him in transgressing his commandment; and then afterwards, to bring about our salvation, which follows necessarily this reparation and atonement he accomplished for our offences?

So the first and principal motive of the Incarnation, death, passion and of all the actions of Jesus Christ, was the glory of God. He himself says so in precise words: 'I do not seek my glory, but that of my Father.'[85] He could not have chosen any other end, for all his works are perfect, and this the most excellent. Also, has God not been more glorified by our Lord than by all creatures put together? And even today, on account of the sacrifice Jesus Christ makes to him[86] of himself, does God not receive more honour and glory from one Mass - even though it be said by an evil and abominable priest - than from all the praises, adorations and homages which all the angels and men of all time and eternity could render him?[87] Who are we to wish to deprive God of that great and infinite honour he receives from it, in order to excite in ourselves some respect for the holy sacrifice of the Mass? What honour could we render to God that would take the place of Christ's sacrifice?

But also, what reason could there be in thinking, that if we were to hear only one Mass, and if we were to receive Communion only once in the whole of our life or even once a year, we would have reverence and admiration? Undoubtedly, it would have to be the rarity of it, and not its grandeur and its excellence! If our respect for Communion comes from the latter, it does not mean that it is any the less for receiving it every day rather than seldom. Since every sacrifice of the Mass is always equally great, the large number of them that are said does not diminish in any way their price and excellence. On the contrary! The goodness, liberality and infinite charity of Jesus Christ are all the more apparent, in making us participate so often, and so free from restraint, in this august mystery. This is what must transport us with love, and bind us with a greater gratitude.

That is how, under a beautiful pretext of rendering him more honour, they [by this doctrine] wish to take from God the one person who alone is worthy of his sovereign majesty and grandeur!

For us, if we do not value it [Mass] and benefit from it as we should, because of the fact that it is readily available to us and that we can enjoy this favour every day,

175

this would come from our malice and ingratitude. For we must never for that reason deprive God of that infinite glory he receives from it; because the glory of God is to be considered more than all the rest.

Fruits and dispositions

We should always consider whether or not it is better for us, and to our advantage, to participate often in those sacred mysteries, seeing that it is for the greater glory of God that they are celebrated often. Yes, without doubt!

Our Lord in his mercy has sometimes given me very great lights in order to make me see how the things he did for us were not only infinite in value, on account of the divine agent,[88] but also infinite in number, seeing that he yielded up for our salvation the thoughts, words and actions of his whole life, all the sufferings of his passion and death poured out to the last drop of his blood, one of which alone would have been more than sufficient to ransom a thousand worlds.

But afterwards, I also saw that, without the holy sacrifice of the Mass and the Holy Sacrament of that altar, only very little, it could almost be said, would have been done for us! Not that the things he did for us would not have in themselves much value and merit, but I mean that we would have hardly drawn any profit from them. The Mass is the great means he established to bestow on us this fruit and his infinite merits. Although there are very few people already saved,[89] there would be far fewer still again; and of the hundred who will find salvation, there wouldn't be perhaps ten.[90] This is so evident and so manifest, that everything that is recognised to be of true virtue and piety among Christians is to be found in those who approach and participate in those divine mysteries; and almost all saints whom he has wished to endow with an eminent sanctity, he has drawn to those mysteries in a particular way.[91]

It is not that I wish to say that we cannot have true virtues without participating frequently in this mystery! That can happen; but it is rare! And it is always to be feared that such virtues are neither as strong nor as solid as when one eats that bread of angels which is the nourishment of our soul. Ordinarily, those persons will be more subject to falling than the persons who will draw their force from the virtue of the Sacrament.

For a long time now two thoughts have been in my mind. First: that when the devil tempted our Lord in the desert, presenting him with stones to be turned into bread, our Lord overcame the temptation, saying to the devil that man does not live on bread alone, but on all the words that proceed from the mouth of God.[92] By this he wished to show us that the Holy Sacrament of the altar, containing truly and actually[93] the substantial Word of God, which expresses all his grandeur and which he gave us to eat, nourishes us deliciously and makes us live a life that is completely celestial. With this divine Word we can shatter the violence of all temptations. Second: that it is the holy sacrifice of the Mass that makes the world last, as much on account of the sovereign honour God receives from it as because our Lord, being offered for the remission of our sins and immolated on the altar, diverts from above us all the strokes of God's justice, and asks the grace for our pardon, as he did for his enemies, on the

Cross.[94] By our malice, let not his merits and his prayers be rendered to no effect in us; but let us try to reap from them the practical worth he envisages.

This is more or less the knowledge I had at the beginning, and then again afterwards, intermittently, when the greatest outcry was heard against frequent Communion. It caused me great pain. For I felt I had no need to know all this. Nevertheless, perhaps our Lord in his goodness wished to give this knowledge to me so that I would not falter in a point of such great importance. This imprinted on my mind an aversion for the whole of this doctrine. Consequently, it has never given me any pain personally, although sometimes I have been acutely touched by it on account of the harm it could cause.

It is not that we should not prepare for Communion, with great care! Woe be to those who approach it unworthily![95] But to render things so difficult is to make us lose heart and to despair instead of bringing us to perfection.

The only disposition necessary is not to be soiled by sin, to avoid the next occasion of falling into sin again, and to have a right will along with this.[96] After which, our Lord will have pity on us. That sacrifice and that Sacrament are the memorial of his passion. Through this memorial he bestows his merits more abundantly on us, in order to deliver us from all our sins. The sacrifice [of the Mass] is also the memorial of the most illustrious virtues of which our Lord has given us the example throughout his life and which he renews here every day. Through this memorial he also imprints these virtues more strongly on our hearts, and by this means we will be able to arrive at that purity and eminent sanctity.[97] But to wait in order to approach Communion is an abuse.

This is something we know more clearly from the first Communion the Apostles made, which our Lord gave to them from his own hand; although they still had very notable defects and would still fall afterwards into greater ones, at least some of them - something our Lord was indeed aware of. And nevertheless, their Communion was very good. And this could be attributed with just as much piety as reason to the grace some of them received not to lose the faith, and that which they all received to come together in meditation and finally convert themselves, there being only the unfortunate Judas who crowned his malice in approaching Communion unworthily and was therefore lost forever.

It is not that those who communicate once and twice a week, or for some reason more often, require no other disposition than to be exempt from mortal sin and distance themselves from the proximate occasion of falling into sin; for to avoid only this sort of sin is the mark of slaves, who only act out of fear and impetuously, as it is the mark of children to avoid and detest the lesser and more trivial faults.[98] For it is enough [to know] that these [sins] would displease God in order to oblige us to avoid them, since it is in this Sacrament where he shows us more tenderness and love. And for our part we must show him the same in return, in approaching it with great purity; for it is an established fact that for a person who is in the habit of venial sin and has no desire or resolution to correct himself of it, although his Communion is not criminal to the point of being a sacrilege, the effect of the Sacrament is nevertheless harmed, which is not brought about fully except in pure souls. But there are certain sins that are as if tied to the misery of our nature, or that God leaves sometimes even in the souls that are dearest to him, in order to give them scope for battling all their lives and to keep them in continual humiliation. But this must not stop us from approaching the Sacrament; for, having the intention of ridding ourselves of them, it is here we receive the strength to be able to do so.

As regards myself, it seems to me that I have never overcome any sin, or destroyed any bad habit, or developed any inclination for the good, except through the grace of the Sacrament. This is why, my Saviour, I will always approach you as often as is possible for me, because you are my whole strength and the sovereign remedy for all my miseries and poverty. You are all my delights in this august Sacrament. And, until I have the good fortune of seeing you face to face in your celestial abode, through your infinite goodness and in virtue of your merits, I shall pass as much as I can of my life at the foundations of your tabernacles, serving an apprenticeship to that which I hope to do eternally, which is to praise you and to love you.[99]

Lights on the mysteries of God

The order of Providence

With all these lights our Lord gave me, the one on his Providence brought about astonishing effects in my soul. In one great day of illuminations, I saw then how it is this Providence that arranges everything - in general and in particular - for the great as well as the small things, nothing happening fortuitously or by chance, but everything being well planned and organised in the counsel of divine wisdom; which [Providence] governs with care the little grub on the earth as much as the highest intelligence in Heaven, being applied to creatures one and all, but without disquiet or labour. There are those who have implied that God does not involve himself in little things, thinking that it does harm to his grandeur to attribute the government of them to him.[100] In this they are mistaken. It is in this even that his sovereign power and infinite wisdom appear all the more.

This knowledge raised me up and put me, almost in a moment, above all the setbacks of fortune and the regrettable accidents that can happen to and touch the life of anyone. For what could I fear any more, being well informed about and persuaded of this truth: that everything happens through the order and arrangement of God, who sends to each and everyone that which is fitting for them, with a love greater than that of a father and mother for their infant? Thus, considering my own life in particular in this divine arrangement of things, I loved the condition of poverty and suffering in which I found myself; and there was no kind of pain and labour I would not have suffered willingly in order to accomplish all God's plans for me.

Since then, and up to the present (which is about eight or nine years), the two passions of desire and fear have been as if destroyed in me. Being unable to fear anything that comes from the hand of God, and desiring nothing but what I receive from it, either in nature or in grace, or in the interest of the glory I expect from it through the goodness and merits of Jesus Christ, I am more content and satisfied with all things, and accept them in the order of his Providence, as if they were of my own choice. However, abandoning myself without reserve to this divine Providence and throwing myself into its bosom, I dwelt there as in my centre, the place of my repose, no longer troubling myself about anything that affects me. And I took so much pleasure in depending on Providence and relying on it from moment to moment that many times, having taken the midday meal, and having nothing for the evening one, I preferred to have it so, to be unsure of it, so as to depend on Providence more completely and have reason for hoping in it. Moreover, since that time, it has never failed me.

Though all the kings and potentates of the earth would have given me their word and guaranteed me all their goods in order to provide for all my needs, and if I were assured of this no matter how little, it seems to me I would die of poverty and need. But being confident, and putting my hope entirely and firmly in divine Providence, I swim in great waters, like the fish in the sea. Also, beholding often the abundance of goods that are on the earth, I said: 'O my soul, everything you see, and many other things you do not see, belong to your God by his own right. Those creatures who possess them hold them from him only on a loan; and he will always dispose of them as it pleases him. Do you fear that he will leave you to lack anything, you who need so little to live on, seeing that he gives his goods with profusion to so many Turks[101] and infidels? To you,[102] to whom he has given the lights of faith and to whom he has granted so many graces and mercies, will he refuse those things of little value, if you put all your confidence in him? No, no, do not fear it! Hope in him faithfully and he will take care of you!'

Thus strenghtening myself to put all my waiting[103] in God without leaning even a little on any creature, I was all the more confirmed in this the more I consciously felt the effects of it. Because, in truth, having put myself as if in a state of forgetfulness in order to render myself only attentive to serving God and accomplishing in everything his holy will, I no longer gave any thought to myself; he took such a particular care of me that it is almost incredible. Sometimes he assisted me through the goodness of his creatures, exciting in them such strong affections for helping me, without my asking anything of them or making my need known to them; so much so that, when I had nothing at all [to eat], many people worried about me and showed charitable concern for me. At other times he catered for my needs himself, without the intervention of anyone.[104] And it happened in this way. When I found myself stripped of everything, I used to say: 'O my God, I adore your designs! I thank you for having arranged these for me, and I heartily offer myself to fulfil them all my life. I am quite ready to beg for my bread. You know sufficiently well that it is not out of shame that I do not expose my need, but only to suffer all the more in this state!' I uttered such words - similar to the ones I spoke elsewhere[105] - with great love and submission to God's commands. And immediately, having been filled with such abundant consolation that even the body [too] was filled with it and satisfied, I felt myself drawn into him by some powerful attraction and did not desire any other food.

For about a year or fifteen months our Lord provided for my needs more in this way than in any other way. Moreover, I used often say within myself: 'O my God, it is not always necessary for you to supply bread and meat for the nourishment of people: when it pleases you, you do it just as well in another, more excellent and more loving way!' But, on the whole, he provided for me by means of his creatures. That he be always praised and blessed for all his directions!

Conformity to the divine will

Beyond the confidence and total abandonment this vision of divine Providence produced in me, our Lord in his goodness instructed me how to praise and bless him for all things that happen in the world, whether ordinary or exceptional things; in such a way that, whether I saw rain or beautiful weather, felt heat or cold, I would bless him for all this, rejoicing in that in this his will was accomplished. If I heard the misfortune of some people spoken of, considering this to be the order and disposition [of his Providence], painful things in general or in particular, and especially if I saw that these were eminent people and of dignified position, having great pleasure in seeing the powers of the earth humiliated under his powerful hand, I would immediately adore God's orders, submitting myself to them and performing acts of conformity to his will as if it had been to me that these things happened. With regard to propitious and agreeable things, I would bless and thank him for them as if they had been given to me. It was the love I felt for my neighbour and the desire for his good that made me esteem and savour this as something done to me. For some years this has been my more common and particular exercise, as long as I saw what was happening on the earth, and as long as it made some impression on my soul.[106]

Providence in temptation

Our Lord, by a most equitable justice, permitted that I be tormented by temptations that were connected with the sins I had committed, and which, as I have already remarked in some place,[107] he made me know in order to chastise me and punish me for them. And out of a most ineffable kindness, he granted me also graces corresponding greatly to the temptations I had suffered. One of the most vexatious I endured was against the faith - that there was no God. Then, afterwards, he gave me such clear understanding of the mysteries of faith and the Christian truths that I could see and know them in my mind in a more sensible and palpable way than I could through the senses. But above all, he gave me so many insights into his divine being and his divine perfections that I find myself indeed at a loss to say anything about them or the effects they bring about in me. However, in order not to fail in obedience, I will say what I can about them.

The Being of beings

So a light, great and extraordinary, was infused into my soul, which made me see how God is the Being of beings, necessary and eternal, and necessarily eternal, infinite, incomprehensible, and of himself blessed and independent of all creatures; for, all created things have no being and substance except through him, and if against all probability it were possible for creatures to destroy him, they themselves would be destroyed at the same time. But the reverse is the case - he would be able to make them all return to their first nothingness while he would suffer no alteration of any kind.

Finally I saw in an ineffable way the truth of that word which God spoke to Moses: 'I am who I am',[108] and perceived also through the same light the truth in what Isaiah said, that all the things of the world are in his presence only like a small drop of water left in a bucket after the bucket has been well cleaned;[109] or, to say it in another way, it is as if all these things never were.

I understand in plain language what the dignities, goods and social positions of this world, which men make so much of, are before God. In his presence they are mere wind, smoke, a veritable nothing. There was imprinted on my soul a great respect for the majesty of kings, because they are the visible images of the power of God. But the nothingness and vanity of all that exterior pomp which surrounds them was so obvious to me that I could never be moved with the slightest esteem for it.

Those wonderful lights produce amazing effects in the soul. The will is filled with affections for God in his divine perfections, affections of joy, of love, benevolence, esteem and others of the like. It is filled with so much contempt for all the things of this world that it has no more regard for them than for the mud on the street. And ordinarily, having the visions of that sovereign and superior Being, when I observed people coming and going, they appeared to me as tiny grains of dust the wind plays with, or as tiny particles [one sees] elevated in the air through the rays of the sun.

It was here also that God made me know how one act of virtue alone and the slightest degree of grace are worth incomparably more than all the visible and perceptible world. Moreover, I thanked him with much greater affections of gratitude for the inclinations and will he gave me to say even one Ave Maria than if he had given me the empire of the world. Of course he grants us more graces than this; and we are infinitely more indebted to him for them. O, why don't we see these truths correctly? Why aren't they imprinted well on our hearts beforehand? We would indeed be very different from what we are!

Effects of the knowledge of the divine attributes

He also gave me a clear understanding of his infinite wisdom that sees all, knows all, and cannot ignore anything, and which, as the sage says, governs all by number, weight and measure.[110]

This knowledge was not given to me in a purely speculative sense; for it always brings about astonishing effects in the soul. Consequently I did not acquire it through learning and study; but it was directly infused by God into the soul. That is why this knowledge penetrates right to the depths of the heart.

He gave me an understanding of his sovereign power that elevated me in a certain fashion which I would have great difficulty in explaining entirely; because, though I was poor and stripped of all goods, raised up by God and united to him as it were in his sovereign power, I felt and saw all things to be underneath me, as if I myself had been lady and mistress of the universe. In giving himself to me, God gave everything with himself; and in uniting myself to him, I seemed through that union to be reigning with him, in such a way that I feared nothing, either for the body or for the soul, sustained as I was and supported by this supreme power.

God brings about prodigious things in his creatures when it pleases him, which things the lack of words and the state of darkness in which I am at present (which takes away in part from the knowledge I have of this) obliges me to leave in secret and remain silent about; for I wish to say nothing other than that which I shall know clearly.[111]

Finally I was given an understanding of the immutability of God. But it was in a different way from the one in which I understood the other perfections and attributes. For I understood this perfection through the very state in which my soul was placed, whereas the others I understood through infused light. So I felt deeply in myself this state of the immutability of God who works all things and remains unceasingly in perfect repose;[112] who changes his orders without changing his counsels; who gives movement to all things and remains perfectly immobile. For my soul was placed in great tranquillity and perfect repose; not being agitated any more by the movement of the passions,[113] it became like an image of eternity where visible things have no longer the power of impressing the soul in the ordinary way. I was no longer aware of any change in myself, because I carried out all my actions with such joy, peace and tranquillity of spirit that I felt no agitation from them. Not only did I attach myself to the will of God and the pursuance of his orders in everything, but I was also as if immutable in this through the rectitude of my intention. In attaching myself to God alone, I saw all things to move and turn, and I myself as immobile in the midst of all.

Finally, Lord, continuing in your ineffable mercies towards me - although I was the most unworthy of all your creatures - it pleased you to make me see how you are present in every place and in all things by your divine essence, filling everything by your immensity. So I saw God present in every place and in all things. I was as if forbidden and deprived of the use of my exterior senses, so that I might not be kept or diverted by them from that divine object. Not that I see myself, hear, speak - and so forth - as I have described elsewhere![114] But that all this is wrought in a death-like manner, which makes no impression on my soul.

I united myself to God in the way that all creatures do. Walking on the earth, I felt him to be carrying me, sustaining me; taking air, I breathed only through him; and often even, in the meat I took for food I saw and tasted only him, taking it in order to receive him in this and to unite myself to him, not however with that union which takes place at the Holy Sacrament of the altar: there we unite ourselves particularly to Jesus Christ who comes to make us one and the same thing with himself by applying his merits to us and transforming us entirely; but here the soul is united to God, for Jesus Christ is not present.[115] This union is intimate and loving and brings great benefits to the soul.

Whether I was in the country or in the city, I was not aware of changing place or position, because I looked and could see nothing but God everywhere; and finding him equally in every spot, my heart was always full and content. I would often admire the happiness of a soul that loves and desires only God, because it can possess him and rejoice in him at all times and in every place. In company the soul cannot be prevented from conversing with God; and in solitude the soul finds him present there, in its innermost recesses. This presence of God so strongly effaced all the other objects of my soul that I did not notice if I was in a dungeon or a golden palace, because I did not reflect upon places, that is, upon visible objects; for my soul was completely absorbed in its God.

Not being able to understand why one is not always content and satisfied, I was greatly astonished to see people pleased in some places and displeased in others, since God alone is our joy and our beatitude and is found equally everywhere. But, above all, I was even more astonished about this with regard to religious people who, having left everything for his service, are more fond of one house or a cloister than another, for they find in one and in the other the object of their love.[116]

I was equally astonished by people who appear and speak in public, be they preachers or orators, whether they speak about spiritual matters or science: for I saw that their vigorous preparation to achieve success[117] stemmed from I know not what fear and apprehension of the multitude of people and of the quality of the persons there,[118] that they would reproach themselves heartily if they were to commit the slightest fault.[119] I could not understand how this would give trouble to and worry a Christian, since the Christian should only consider God. It appeared to me to be an even greater madness and weakness than if some sage or learned person who had to deal with a king, were not to consider principally the esteem and approbation of the prince, but was only concerned about pleasing some villagers who, by chance, happened to find themselves at his harangue.[120] I mean by this, that nothing should astonish us so much and spur us on to do things well other than the respect for God which we have with us all the time.

But I was completely bewildered by another blindness that reigns among men. Those who hide themselves[121] from one another in order to commit their crimes: they would be ashamed to have witnesses to their actions yet they haven't any shame in doing so before God who sees them and who observes them everywhere.

The knowledge of this presence of God caused me to be everywhere in the same state, disposition and composition of body and mind, walking in his presence with great simplicity, beholding only him alone, as if there were only he and myself in the world,[122] and fearing only his eye,[123] which shows me a light everywhere.

Hidden life in God

For a very long time, then, God continually gave this light to my soul, to see him and to feel him thus present in every place and in all things. These truths were not manifest to me at intervals and as though in flashes, but rather as a sun that shines and warms unceasingly. For these lights were continuous in me, and not only for months, but for entire years. Not always, admittedly, with the same force and splendour! For nature itself would not have been able to endure them.

Afterwards, I felt the presence of God in another way; for I saw all things [to be] in him and that he contained them all with greater amplitude than Heaven would contain and envelop the shell of a nut. I perceived then that St Paul had indeed good reason to say that we live and move in him,[124] because by his fullness he includes everything. I had desires and cravings to lose myself in this immensity of God. The fish in the midst of the sea would not be as much in the water, nor the bird in the air, as I found myself in him. O my God, you are the pleasant and delicious abode of a soul when it is lost in you! The soul is in the plenitude of joy and repose: nothing troubles it and nothing can give it pain any longer.[125]

I hid myself in and imbued myself with God, making of him an unsurmountable tower around me in order to cover me and to defend me from the persecutions of the demons and of the attacks of sin; for, O my God, I said, sin cannot approach you nor is it compatible with your purity and sanctity.

Finally, having God thus present, and being entirely in him, this has guaranteed me against all the natural fears that are very common with those of my sex. It is true that I was not fearful to the extent that certain people are! Nevertheless I was afraid. But having God present, I have no more fear of spirits[126] or of demons; and I remain completely alone without fear, not only in rooms, but in whole houses.[127]

The Trinity

One day, on the vigil or the feast of the Holy Trinity, I unexpectedly had a great and extraordinary light. And in order to show that the visits of God are not restricted to a particular time or place, but that they depend on his good pleasure, I remember quite well that I was at table and in company[128] when I was enlightened by this truth: that God is a pure act[129] that cannot be augmented or diminished, and that it is impossible for there to be a God who is not in a Trinity of persons. Because, contemplating himself, he knows himself perfectly; and this knowledge is what we call his Word, his Son, who receives and contains all the nature, perfections and attributes of God.

I perceived more particularly that which seems to set minds even more ablaze: that the Son is as great and as eternal as his Father. For, if God for a few instants was ever without knowing himself, or that this knowledge [of the Son] did not contain the whole nature and perfection of God, there would be a defect in God; which is impossible. He [the Son] is therefore equal to his Father in everything, because the Father gives him and necessarily communicates to him his divine nature and his infinite perfections.

From this knowledge that God has of himself, of that mutual regard which the Father has for the Son and the Son for the Father, is produced the Holy Spirit. The Holy Spirit is the personal and infinite love that God has for himself; and because this Holy Spirit receives and contains likewise all the substance and perfections of the divine nature, is equal in everything to the Father and to the Son, but is equal to the Father through the way of love, as the Son is equal through the way of knowledge.

This is what distinguishes the three persons of the Holy Trinity, for the Father is not the Son, nor the Son the Holy Spirit. They are three distinct persons, but not separated; for they are one and the same God through unity of essence, power, wisdom, goodness and all the perfections that are proper and essential to the nature of God. The Holy Spirit is the termination of the Holy Trinity, because God can only know and love himself.[130]

Contemplating the life of the Trinity

For about two years after that I had almost a continual vision of that adorable mystery. My soul was always in the presence of the most Holy Trinity, seeing incessantly how the Father engenders the Son, and the Father and the Son produce together the Holy Spirit - this being the continual and eternal occupation of God: to know himself and to love himself.

This produced amazing effects in my soul. In imitation of him, I desired to be unceasingly occupied in that same work of knowing and loving him. I have had a particular devotion for this exalted and profound mystery; and during the same time that those things were more present in my mind, I did a little writing on this mystery[131] and the effects it brought about in me. I desired to send it to the same person who asked me to write all this;[132] but, on the advice of the confessor I had at the time, I didn't do so; and so I burned it.

The resplendent grandeur of God

After all those lights, God gave me a light on his sovereign Majesty and grandeur.

O Lord, help me with your grace, for it is here I have indeed need of it so as to be able to say something about that which cannot be explained. Some place else I have already spoken about this; but there are so many things to say on this subject, that everything I shall be able to say about it will be indeed much less than all that which will remain for me to say.

It was therefore in the presence of that sovereign Majesty and grandeur that I lost absolutely the sight of all creatures, visible or invisible, of men or of angels. In the same way as in the presence of the sun one no longer sees the light of the moon or of the stars, for the sun wipes out by its rays all the light that those had; so this vision of the grandeur of God annihilated all things [in me], and subsequently I began to see them and to know them in a manner completely different from the way I had done up to then.

In the first place, I was no longer able to elevate myself and unite myself to him by means of his creatures, because be they spiritual or corporeal, they were all annihilated as far as I was concerned. Being as if dead to all things visible and perceptible, and further, with my exterior senses no longer functioning in the ordinary way, even the powers of my soul were elevated above their natural operation. I was so annihilated by the presence of that supreme Majesty of God that I didn't see myself as having either being or substance.

I was aware therefore of a presence of God and of his divine perfections in himself and through himself; and the least knowledge one has of him through a means without a means[133] is incomparably greater than all the knowledge one could have through the means and mediation of creatures, as also the [state of] love that is kindled in the soul is of a completely different intensity and order than all the other states of love in which one could be.

I was not able to understand the error we make in thinking that we merit many praises and great recompense when we serve God. Indeed we should rather admire the excess of the goodness and love of God, who, being what he is, is willing to accept our services. For who is he? And who are we[134] that we dare approach him and present him with anything? When we serve him, he certainly owes us nothing. But we owe him much thanks and praise when he deigns to avail himself of us in anything.

That is why the final grace, the grace of perseverance, is always gratuitous; and in this grace, like all the other ones he gives, God is not obliged to us in any way;[135] but it is because of his words and promises, which are infallible and true, that he follows in this the inclination of his love and of his natural goodness, which brings him immediately to do good.

It is here I saw how it is such a great honour for us to serve him, and how it is in this alone in which our joy consists. If, against all probability, it were possible for some touch of honour or drop of consolation to fall into Hell,[136] the souls that are there, and who have rendered him any service, would have some honour and joy from it.[137] But on the contrary, in that place of horror they [the souls] do not receive anything from it except infamy and despair; for they have left the service of such a great and formidable God in order to serve the devil, and commit sin.

It was here also I perceived, in a most particular way, the malice of sin and the justice of Hell for a mortal offence. And no matter how grave the torments might be, I perceived also that there is still a ray of mercy in all his punishments, God being able with great justice to render them greater.

I felt deeply such great horrors for sin that I had joy and satisfaction in hearing spoken of the severe chastisements with which God punishes it, having great pleasure in seeing him revenged on his enemies. With regard to myself in particular, I desired justice rather than mercy, for I wished that everything that would henceforth have offended him in me be punished and chastised. With unequalled affections, and in order to be preserved from sin, I asked of him this grace, to make me suffer through mercy what it would be necessary for me to endure in order to satisfy his justice after having committed sin. Placing my confidence in the goodness and merits of our Lord that he will hearken to me and preserve me from falling into sin, I have continued to make these prayers to him and will continue to make them to him all my life.

Engrossing contemplation on the attributes of God

That is what I can say about the knowledge it pleased God to give me of his divine perfections (together with what I have already said about it elsewhere,[138] and which I do not intend to repeat) and the effects this knowledge brought about in me. It was not a passing knowledge, that is at intervals, but continuous and lasting, not however always with equal force, because nature would not be able to endure it. For sometimes, not being able to take it any more, I threw myself on the ground and cried out to God to withdraw himself from me and not to approach any further, because I felt myself melting away and fainting.[139]

I have been about three years or three years and a half continually elevated by and absorbed in this knowledge of the divinity, at all times and in all places, because, not being able any more even to apply myself to the mysteries of the life and passion of our Lord, for which I felt some pain, my mind was incapable of thinking about or seeing anything else, and I feared there might be some evil in this. I told this to my confessor, who was very well versed in spiritual matters, and he said to me that this way was very good, and that as long as it would please God to lead me by this way I had only to follow it with simplicity,[140] for Jesus Christ only came to the world to make God and his divinity known. This wise reponse put my mind in perfect repose and allowed me to follow with freedom and confidence the attraction of God, which is a point of great consequence, both for those who direct souls, and for those who are directed. For I think there is scarcely any greater pain than if God wishes to lead a soul in one way and the confessor in another. He has not allowed me to experience this,[141] having always put me, by his goodness, in the hands of people who have always known well his direction of me and who have done nothing but allowed me to follow this. That he be blessed for it forever!

Application as if through affections alone

After this period of about three and a half years, I felt myself again most particularly drawn towards and attached to the sacred person of our Lord.[142] But it was in a different way from that which I had experienced him up to then. In the beginning, I saw him almost always in one or other of the mysteries of his life or of his death and passion, and I was devoted to him in that mystery through the affections that were in accordance with it. These mysteries were shown to me, not on the strength of discourse or imagination, but by affections that presented themselves to my mind; and ordinarily it happened from within myself, in such a way that I had only to close myself within and enjoy to my ease the good that was presented to me.

But now I almost never had a representation of any mystery. I was intimately consecrated to our Lord as if through the affections alone of respect and love, with the ardent desires of seeing him in order to praise him and to love him for all eternity and to be no longer interrupted in that holy exercise by the miseries of this life. In such a way that, often when I would see the holy host elevated at the holy sacrifice of the Mass, I used to cry out in the interior in a plaintive and loving voice: 'When will the hour and moment come, my Lord, that I will see you no longer veiled and hidden by the species and accidents of bread, but that I will see you openly in the splendour of your glory?'[143]

All the light and knowledge I had right from the beginning - how honourable it was, and useful in helping me to imitate and follow Jesus Christ - was taken from me in this state; and I did not desire to imitate and follow him except through the movement of love, in such a way that whoever would have asked me, 'Why do you prefer poverty to riches, affliction to pleasures and contempt to the honour of the world?' I would have answered: 'It is the love of Jesus Christ that makes me act thus, in order to render myself in this, as in all other things, as much as it will be possible for me, like unto him.' 'But what intention have you in this, and what good can he return to you from it?' 'I don't know! I have no reflection or thought on that. I do not desire or pretend anything more than to show him by this the esteem and respect I have for his doctrine and his examples; that I am[144] through pure love. If, in good time, some advantage redounds to me from it, is something I do not think about, and something I do not look for.' This is [practically] the whole understanding I have of my behaviour, and the only reason I would have been able to give for it.

Effects and value of the divine action

Contempt

That is what I can say about the knowledge it pleased God to give me of his sacred humanity as well as of the perfections of his divinity. For more than eight years without interruption, I believe, he held my spirit so attached to himself and engulfed that I did not understand how one could see, look for or desire anything other than God and our Lord Jesus Christ.

The first years I was elevated thus [to God] through the means of visible and perceptible creatures, and then by the marvellous works he wrought and accomplished for our salvation.

For at least four years, I think, I was not united to God and raised up through these means. It was through lights infused immediately by him into the substance of my soul. Moreover, although I was almost continually sick and with great pains in my head, this did not prevent me from the exercises of the mind and of prayer, because this took place independently of the organs of the senses and of the body. My confessors said to me that indeed this state was extraordinary and special. I listened to what they said to me with the greatest submission of spirit that was possible for me; but I could not understand it, because, as it seemed to me that one could not be otherwise and that this state was natural and common to everyone, I could not think that there was anything extraordinary in me except evil and sin.

I now recognise indeed that my mind was in error. And this was not for a short time; but this error occupied my mind for at least four or five years; and I would still not be purged of it, if it were not for what happened to me later, of which I shall speak shortly.

But in order to make my state more clear, for example, it was with me as though a person in the body of the sun and greatly penetrated in all parts of his body and soul with the sun's lights, was enveloped also from the outside by all its rays. Because it is an established fact that this person would not be able to see the darkness while he is in this state. Now, it was the same for me. For I was so greatly swallowed up and drowned in God, illumined with such splendour of the mysteries of faith and of the Christian truths - which are as opposed to human reason and above the senses as poverty is infinitely preferable to riches, contempt to honour, pain and suffering to all the pleasures and delights of life - that all the glory of the world was as nothing to me, a little puff of smoke or wind; that the esteem of men, which is valued highly, was the most vain thing one could feed on, because all this makes us neither better nor worse, and is of no use to us before God; in short, that the value of the least degree of grace

191

and the smallest act of virtue is incomparably greater than the control of the whole world.

I was so penetrated and enveloped by these illuminations that I did not see or understand things according to nature and the senses, for the light of truth had dissipated their illuminations, which are only false and deceitful, and represent things to us other than they are. But I just did not believe that one could see and behold these things in a way that was different from myself and how they were manifested to me.

At the time, one day my confessor asked me: 'Have you always been like this? 'I don't know', I said to him, 'I cannot give any reason for it, for I have no longer any knowledge of how I have been, nor any foresight as to what I shall be. I am in a state in which I can think of nothing but God; I praise him, love him, and am astonished by the folly of those who don't do so!' Because, to tell the truth, this being so easy for me, it would have been necessary for me to do great violence to myself in order to detach my mind from it.

I thought that everyone was like that. And this error has been the cause of my not appreciating this grace as I should, or rendering to the goodness of God the praises and acts of thanksgiving I ought to have. Lord, have pity on me according to your great mercies;[145] pardon me that sin through the precious blood of your Son, and all those sins of my life; you know that it comes more from ignorance than from malice. I beseech you to receive all the praises and blessings which have been rendered to you and will be rendered to you throughout all eternity by all the saints and blessed spirits and above all those the Holy Virgin and the sacred humanity of our Lord have given and forever will give to you, which I offer to you in reparation and as a supplement for my ingratitude and inability in praising you for your favours. Amen!

In the flesh without the flesh

All these things brought about marvellous effects in me, in the soul as much as in the body.

In the first place, in order to speak about them according to the lights I have had lately of this state, I can say that I was stripped of all the sentiments of nature. It happens in this way. God draws the soul by his powerful attractions, which the soul follows with all its force, in such a way that God holds it so united to himself and engulfed in him that it has no longer any correspondence with the sentiments of nature, which [nature] remains deprived of all delectations and pleasures in all its operations. For example, the eye looks at some delectable and pleasant objects, and yet receives from them neither pleasure nor delectation. It is the same for the other senses of the body: hearing, touching, tasting and so forth; because the body is as if dead to all pleasures that are proper and natural to it. It is, moreover, the same for all things which would honour nature or give it pain, things which the body does not experience any more; because from all quarters the body's feelings are destroyed and bound in such a way that it is not moved by anything.

It is not that [in this state] one does not carry out all of one's natural operations;

for with regard to one's exterior activity, there is no difference in this from other people. But it is no longer through the movement of nature that these operations are done, nor with the feelings that are proper to it; for everything is done through the movement of grace and out of a supernatural motive, and also in the heart and mind of Jesus Christ whom it takes for its model in all things. This is because God wishes it so and has subjected us to it.

Once, I remember, I was thinking how God performs marvellous things in many of his saints, in allowing some of them to live without food. He let me understand at the same time that he had done greater things in me. This has always stayed in my mind, although, as I believe, it has been more than five years since it was given to me to understand this in the interior. And I was not aware of such great things God had done in me, except that recently he let me see them.

Certainly, greater grace is needed in order to annihilate all the sentiments of nature in all its actions, than [is needed] to make it live and subsist without its ordinary food. I even believe that in some things this grace is [considered to be] better and more excellent, in so far as it is more interior and hidden, and therefore less subject to vanity. And hence, this destroys all the more [in us] love of self and nature, which are glad indeed that the gifts of God are [made] known, still finding now and then [in this grace] little satisfactions.

Strictly speaking, in this state, one lives in the flesh without the flesh; one is in the midst of the world, and does not know it, because the soul is so much lost in God that it neither sees nor turns to anything else. It is certain that if the soul is in harmony with the feelings of the body, and if the body were in the midst of objects the most charming and the most capable of giving it contentment, the soul would not receive any of them! An extremely great grace is necessary for this. When God gives this grace to us, we are as if exempt from all sin; for it is the bodily and sensual pleasures that are sin's sources. It is after this pleasure that we run; and it is this which carries us away in disorder and dissoluteness.

This then is more or less where I stood with regard to the body and the senses.

It remains for me to speak about things that are more spiritual, but which nevertheless depend on the material.

Nature subject to the mind

I was also entirely stripped of all purely natural sentiments and of earthly love towards my relatives, my homeland and other human things. I did not love them except in God, for God and out of a well-ordered charity in my mind that gave to each the rank and place they should hold there. With regard to where honour, goods and the esteem of the world were concerned, things to which nature is much inclined and attaches itself so strongly that it seems that there is nothing capable of making it abandon them, I was almost as in an instant without any feeling for them at all. In the affections and esteem which many people of quality have shown to have for me, I have no knowledge of having had the slightest movement of joy and pleasure, nor the confidence in those people to depend on them even in the slightest. For all my natural sentiments were so extinguished that I didn't feel even one, but remained in the midst of all this as if dead and insensible.

I was particularly drawn by God to live an extremely poor life, and to abandon myself so much to his direction and Providence that I depended on him not only from day to day, but from moment to moment, not seeking any assurances for my daily needs.

In this state, nature was so much subdued and [content][146] with this type of life that it seemed even to be itself that desired it. With regard to whatever the spirit desired, nature made no resistance to it at all. It seems right for the body to become spiritual, having the same sentiments and marching in step with the spirit.

In a word, after God in his mercy had delivered me from the temptations I suffered in the beginning, he also delivered me from the most evil and terrible of my enemies, which was my body, making me live almost according to the spirit alone. I was so strongly detached and distant from all the affections and pleasures of nature, that I did not understand how one could experience it in this way. So much so, that when I heard it said: it is pleasant, and it is indeed agreeable to live well, to go for a walk, to have great goods, to hold beautiful positions, a great reputation and esteem in the world, and the like, my spirit would remain completely confused in myself, understanding nothing of these discourses; for my sentiments and my inclinations were entirely contrary and opposed to them. And thus, all the hindrances of nature (which are the most troublesome and most difficult to vanquish) towards devotion and the exercise of devotion having been taken from me, I followed without determination and without resistance the attractions of our Lord, living a blessed life as much as one can have it in this world, rejoicing in a peace and tranquillity of body and soul that did not admit of any change.

I was more than six years without interruption in that blessed state. But [during that time] my mind was in great error, for I did not perceive or understand that one could be otherwise. It seemed to me that everyone was like that. I knew [then] very well how I was, but not as clearly as I do now. For my error was in not perceiving the value of the great graces and mercies which God was incessantly granting me; and consequently I did not appreciate them as I should have done. My God, have pity on me, for the ignorance and error are mine! And whenever you grant graces, if at the same time you give lights in order to recognise them, undoubtedly we will be able to see them.

Facility and promptitude

Your loving kindness, my God, did not stop there. You gave me still greater gifts than all those. Because it is your wish that I declare all the mercies you granted me in secret,[147] I will do so, my Lord, so that by this you be praised and blessed.

So I say, that in the exercises of devotion and the practice of virtue, there is encountered a certain delectation and pleasure that is to be greatly feared, because self-love can enter in there. All foods are proper to self-love; it nourishes itself on spiritual as well as on corporeal things, for there is a spiritual sensuality as there is a corporeal one.[148] Very often this is what renders devotions so disordered and little in keeping with people's [real] condition and that which God truly asks of them, because finding therein a pleasure, they abandon themselves to it too much.[149]

And very often this is the [real] reason for the complaints that are made concerning devotion. And if we were to look for the true cause of our complaints, we would see that we only complain because we have lost the pleasure and perceptible taste we felt in devotion. I do not regard it as a small grace for God to deprive us of them, and early on at that.[150]

I do not recall ever having had these consolations so perceptibly, except for the first six months after God had touched me.[151] Since then, out of a great mercy he took them from me. But he gives the soul [in turn] a great facility and promptitude in all the exercises of devotion and practice of virtue, with a very great peace, joy and tranquillity. The body is so subject to the soul, and the soul to God, that there is no longer trouble or rebellion. Self-love and one's own will were so much destroyed in me, that I could not conceive that one could think of, desire, look for and love anything other than that God's will be done; because, in my soul or in my body, I had no other affection or sentiment. And the soul is so strongly drawn out of itself through the force of love, that we no longer have any thoughts or reflections on all that which touches our lives, as if we did not exist.

Thus the soul leads a blessed life. I believe that in this state one feels something of the blessedness of Paradise; for the soul, raised up over and above all the miseries and infirmities of nature, does nothing except love and engulf itself in its God. And it rejects everything that is not him and for him; in such a way that it destroys by its affections Heaven, earth, Paradise, Hell, men, angels, all creatures visible and invisible, its body, its soul, its life and all its interests, annihiliting itself entirely before God, that he might do with it according to his good pleasure. And raising itself up over and above all its gifts, on which it does not dwell, it wishes only him alone, and to find in possessing him all its goods and all its repose.

It seems to me that I am entangling myself, rather than making myself clear, when I speak of this state, because I don't have the words to make known what I have experienced.[152] Also, in truth I have experienced a great repugnance in writing this. But it is better for me to fail in everything else but obedience, desiring from all my heart to make an entire sacrifice to our Lord of my judgement, my will and my whole life.

Stability

I have been six or seven years directly in this transport of spirit and love, almost without any interruption; and having hardly any change in my soul, but being in this as in a permanent and stable condition, I feel none of the inconstancies of human life. Here are the faults and errors I had in my mind. I said, so many times: 'I have my mind in darkness!' And it was indeed true, but I did not know in what darkness! Only lately have I had knowledge of it; and yet I perceived my errors only little by little.[153]

First error

The first error I committed was that it seemed to me that my state was ordinary, that is, common to everyone; I did not conceive how one could be otherwise. Say to a person entirely plunged in pleasures that there are incredible sweetnesses in weaning oneself away entirely from them, and he will not believe you; and will understand this even less. He cannot imagine that he might be able to do otherwise. I was completely the same. Because of those great and ardent desires I had to suffer poverty, humiliation, scorn; that facility for all exercises of devotion; the loving embraces of God for the soul and the soul for God in prayer and Communion; those desires to die in order to see him and to enjoy an eternity with him - all such things that were taking place, burning incessantly in my soul, had so much restored to me an unknown state that I did not think that one could be otherwise.

Cessation of another error

My second error was that I did not know the value or excellence of this state; and consequently, I neither had the opinion of it I should have had, nor thanked our Lord for it as I should have done.

I saw indeed that when I spoke to my confessors about it, they made a great case of it and valued it very much, saying to me that this state was supernatural, which God gives when he wishes, to whom he wishes and how he wishes; that all the human forces cannot reach it, and that this depends absolutely on his liberality and his goodness. I was astonished by their words. But I had no more lights at that time to see the truth of what they were saying to me, because this destruction of all things - if it is necessary to speak thus - that happened to me, was wrought in me not through any intellectual consideration or the light of understanding, but only through the affections of the infused love of God in my soul. He separated my soul from all things in order to draw it to himself and to empty it of everything, so that he himself alone be present in it, and that, there being nothing more there that would hinder it, the soul might love him with all its strength. And God, finding it empty, fills it with a greater love. The soul, drawn by this love, distances itself even more from all things; it dies and expires in this love entirely. It does not wish that death separate it from anything, but that love itself, which is stronger by far than death,[154] accomplish in the soul what it must do: abandon out of a good heart and a good will that which it would have to leave just as well out of necessity. It is not that after this one does not make use of the necessary things for life; but this is done no longer with the sentiments of nature, for nature is as if dead. I followed his attractions, but blindly, not perceiving the value of the good that was given to me, nor how this way was sublime and exalted; because this guidance is from pure love.

I think that I would have always been in this erroneous way of thinking - which I well recognise now - were it not on account of what happened to me about a year ago; and about which I am going to speak in order to show to him[155] who wishes to know - right down to the slightest folds of my soul - its secrets, and to whom I must tell them. O Lord, how your judgements are profound and how we have all the reasons to fear and to humble ourselves before you! For if in the least you were to take away your hand from us, no matter what graces you had granted us, and regardless of what high state you would have raised us up to, we would fall at once into the depths of misery. I have indeed experienced this truth. Nevertheless, my God, up till now you have always held me, in order not to let me fall down into the extreme misery of sin; and I hope in your loving goodness, and through the merits of our Lord Jesus Christ, that you will hold me so strongly that you will never let me be hurled into this misery. But you wished that I feel profoundly how much a propensity I have for and inclination to evil and an incapacity for the good, if you do not help me with your abundant grace.

Gentle awakening of my natural existence

For about a year or thirteen months, then, changes began to take place in my soul. I have at times, felt little stirrings of the passions: anger, sadness and a disgust for the things of devotion.

All this passed very lightly in my mind. Nevertheless these things were indeed extraordinary to me; for years went by when I did not have the slightest attack of them.

And I saw that, when something happened against my desire, I suffered pain from it. I know that only a spark of fire is needed in order to set a house on fire, even a complete city. So I began to fear greatly that these movements would give way to sin in my soul. Our Lord, through his mercy, since the time he touched me, has always given me an extreme horror of sin, not for fear of his chastisements, or the loss or hurt he could cause me, but out of love for him.

Thus I had recourse to him with many tears, beseeching him to have pity on me and not to punish my sins by permitting me to fall into new ones: the vengeance of God, the most terrible sin of all, which I fear and dread most of all. I have been assured on your part, my God, that you would never punish me in that way; which gives a great consolation to my soul. In effect, he assisted me according to his great mercy.

Nevertheless, he did not give me his grace so abundantly as to extinguish in me all the movements of nature or the inclination to evil. I have not had much readiness to do good; nor did I feel that love of poverty and contempt,[156] when the occasion for them presented itself; I felt some sort of repugnance for them. I felt I know not what turning in on myself. I was somewhat concerned about the things I had need of; and, remaining no longer in such a great abandonment within the arms of Providence, which I had done for so many years, I felt some aversion for my state and my condition, with I know not what propensity and inclination to return to my homeland and to be with my relatives. The exercises of devotion were tiresome to me; I desired to find short Masses; an hour of time at prayer seemed so long to me that I had great difficulty indeed in remaining there. In entertaining such dislikes, I was sometimes in a state in which it seemed to me that if I had not undertaken to do the exercises of devotion, I would never have done them.

Moreover, I desired not to let my confessor know of my state, and even to distance myself from him; because I feared that having great knowledge of the direction God held over me, he would use the power he had over me and oblige me to do that which it seemed to me I could not do any more. On the other hand, if he had not done this, it would have affected me greatly; so much so that I saw nothing but difficulty for myself.

All these diverse movements that agitated me opened the eyes of my mind and made me realise that when our Lord leaves us in the weaknesses of our nature, we are indeed in a different state than when he raises us up through his grace. Now it is not that all these things happened all at once in my soul, but now one thing and then another; nor that all these movements [of the passions] were even really that strong, but it was in the same way as the smallest grain of dust or the slightest dirt that hurts the eye would not be felt were it on any other part of the body, because the other part of the body would neither be as delicate nor as sensitive. And as nothing made me feel so much all these little stirrings of the passions, which at that time were rising up in me, as [the recollection of] that great calm in which I had been (not having then the least attack from any of these things), I feared sin greatly in all of this. I cried often with much bitterness before our Lord, so that he would have pity on me. For what I found worst of all in that state was that I did not have interior vigour to combat and suffocate these diverse movements which rose up in my heart; so much so that I did not know of any other way to overcome them than to run to God, confess my extreme misery and hope in his mercy.

One day he gave me a light that let me know how it was he who made me feel nature's inclinations and the propensity it has for the things of the earth. Nevertheless, it was only in things of little consequence, for I did not desire riches, but only the necessitites of life. Sometimes I would have desired these necessities to be a little more beautiful and in greater number. I did not have great fears even in encountering humiliations and sufferings! But I did not desire or look for them, as I had done previously. In short, I felt deeply the difficulties nature has in exercises of devotion and mortification and yet I did not refrain from doing them. What I can say about this state is that I felt profoundly the inclinations of nature in those things which I have indicated. However, it was only at intervals.

But where I really felt human infirmity was above all with regard to prayer. The soul works naturally only with the body and through its organs, which means that when the body is sick and dejected, the soul cannot act as well as when the body is well disposed. Now I did not perceive this any more [I think] than the rest of humanity did; because being always sick and especially subject to great pains in my head, this did not hinder in me the exercise of the mind. Because, for more than eight years now our Lord in his goodness has granted me a manner of infused prayer that does not depend on the body and its organs; and consequently the body's infirmities do not hinder the soul. But being left here in my natural existence, I saw that the only other thing I could do was to remain before God as a statue, offering him my pains and languors as a sacrifice of praise, seeing that I could not give him any other, sometimes and often saying to him: 'My Lord, you have said, "Do not trouble yourself so much about speaking when you pray! Your Father in heaven knows your needs before you say them to him.''[157] You know mine, my Lord; and weighed down with my misery, I do not know how to utter them to you. But have pity on me according to your great mercies.'[158] Other times I desired to enter into the communion of the saints, to be as much with those who are in heaven as with those who are on the earth, and also the suffering souls in Purgatory, to praise him with them and bless him as they do. And then I remained, in that way, without doing anything else.

This, then, was the manner of my prayer when [it pleased] our Lord not to draw me to it in the ordinary way. I was at times three or four days in this state. And then, having pity on me, he would raise me up in a moment high above all the weaknesses of my nature, which he sometimes continued [to do] for many days in succession; and then I was as before, so I was now eight or fifteen days more or less in one state, and then in the other. It is true that, since perhaps about two months or so, I have been almost always like this with regard to prayer, except sometimes on days when it was not so noticeable.

Discernment of the effects of nature and grace

Now all these changes made me recognise those great graces and mercies which God granted me, for without such changes I would not have known them. And one thing I saw in particular: that the whole direction he held over me was internal and hidden; something my confessors knew well. But the value of the graces he granted me and the excellence of the state in which he had put me, was hidden more to me than to any other person. For I knew nothing of it at all; but now from time to time, he sheds certain rays of light which reveal them to me, not all at once, but little by little, and still not in their entirety.

This knowledge excites great affections of love and gratitude in me, and humbles me in an extraordinary way, because I have great reason for being confused, seeing that after this I have still so much propensity to evil and incapacity for the good. Our Lord had given me this light in particular in order to make known to me my nothingness and my misery, as one will be able to see scattered throughout my writings.[159] But I saw this nothingness and did not feel it. At present, through the different movements by which I am agitated, I feel it indeed. Sometimes our Lord draws a good effect from a bad cause. For feeling my misery through experience, I was humbled all the more. The knowledge of these graces fills me with I know not what dread and makes me shiver with fear in case I do not use them well, and if through my fault they do not produce in me the effects of virtue and sanctity for which they are given to me.

Thanks to these lights, I begin to discern the effects of nature and of grace. Nevertheless, this knowledge is still not perfect in my mind, because the lights I receive on this subject do not make a strong impression as yet on my mind. But little by little, however, I am emerging from the ignorance in which I was - not knowing the operations of grace and the value and excellence of the gifts of God has been the greatest ignorance of my mind.

I was especially in a state in which I did not feel the mortifications of the body and the senses. Being deprived of all that which satisfies the senses did not give me any pain; nor did I feel any contradiction in getting them to do the things they abhorred naturally, but on the contrary they seemed to take pleasure and delight in this.[160] This is why, it seems to me, I did not know that virtue [of mortification] any more except in name only.

But there are certain mortifications of the spirit in which our Lord has tested me for the past seven or eight years, and of which I do not know if there are any greater. I had great desires for perfection[161] and wished to do all things in order to fulfil the will of God, without any turning in on myself for no matter what, either for good or for evil, present or future, temporal or eternal. These desires and affections burned and consumed my heart entirely; and nevertheless I do not see my progress. I am like a person who works always without seeing the result of his efforts. I carry out my exercises of devotion every day, in all months and years; and I do not see in any way what I do. In all the prayers [and vows] that I made to God in order to consecrate myself entirely to his service, and to beseech him, even to compel him if it were possible, to exercise over me a sovereign and absolute authority, disposing of me entirely according to his good pleasure (for my sentiments and feelings tell me that he will never dispose of me as entirely and absolutely as I desire) I have not had any knowledge for the past seven or eight years that he hears my prayers and hearkens to my desires.

For example, if a person were to offer some present to a prince, or a great lord, or to any other person one might imagine, the greatest pleasure this person could have is if this lord received his present, showing him that he was very pleased with it; whereas, on the contrary, his greatest displeasure would be to see himself rejected if the lord were to refuse what the person was giving to him willingly and with a good heart, or indeed would pretend not to listen to him. So, the more this person would offer the lord his service and everything that it was in his power to give, the less he would know that it was accepted. This is now the state in which it has pleased God to keep me for the past six or seven years, for the more I desire to be his, that is the more I make prayers and entreaties to him to dispose of me according to his will and good pleasure, the less I know if he hears them. Truthfully, I do not see myself rejected in my prayers, but neither do I see that he has heard them, remaining as I do in complete ignorance as to whether he has accepted them, or all that which I present to him.

O my God, do you fear that you would make me die from joy, or from love, if you were to let me know that you will accomplish so completely and sovereignly your will in me; that you will never spare me in any way, either in body or in soul, when it is a question of your interests and of all that which will be for your greater glory? Make this promise to my soul, O my God, and then it will be content and satisfied; for this is all that it desires. If sometimes you find resistance there, do not abandon me to my malice or to my evil inclination, but constrain me to carry out all your wishes as absolutely as much as lovingly.

I have been making all these demands to God for a long time now without knowing in any way if he hears them. But my soul is, however, in great peace and tranquillity in this state, taking this as God's guidance of me, submitting myself entirely to it, and taking this blindness in patience.

The greatest pain in this life

Moreover, for many years now the desire to die burns in my heart. I have spoken elsewhere of its causes and motives.[162] And even though I went for some months without feeling it at all, I now feel very often its force and ardour. Only those who have experienced this martyrdom know the greatness of it. I do not think that anyone can suffer a greater pain in this life. None of the corporeal pains are comparable to it. Just as the greatest pain of the damned is in being separated from God,[163] the greatest pain of the souls in Purgatory is in being deprived of God for a period. It is also the greatest torment of a soul, when God makes it feel its exile and banishment and gives to it the desire to see him and enjoy him.

That which has served me greatly in renewing those affections in my heart has been the different movements of passion with which I have been agitated. For seeing and believing myself to be so often in danger of offending God, I do not mean mortally, for that would be horrible to contemplate (and it seems to me that this would be capable of making me die from dread and horror), but to commit some venial sin would greatly make me desire death so as to be no longer subject to falling into sin!

It is not that I have felt any affection for sin, or inclination towards it since God touched me about twelve years ago. Our Lord has not given me rein to that extent, as one says; but only some feeling and inclination for things that could make me offend God more easily. Although they were of little consequence in themselves, they were very great on account of the light he had given me and of the state into which he had put me.

I longed with great affection to pray for those who are tempted and find difficulty in virtue, so that it might please God to give them the strength and courage to vanquish and overcome generously all those obstacles. And also for the souls whom he calls to a higher and more eminent perfection so that it might please him to protect them particularly and that they might be able always to walk this way with firm steps, without ever turning back. I had for a long time an attachment to recommending these persons to God. The feeling and experience of my weakness has made me do this even with more care and affection.

Finally, I experienced that we always have a sufficient grace[164] that preserves us from evil and makes us do good, if we wish to avail ourselves of it as we should. That is, that we are always able to pray and have recourse to God, beseeching him to have pity on us. If we cannot do anything else, we can always do this, by means of his grace, which is never lacking to us for this. I know from real experience, not only once or twice, but too often to count, that we never have recourse to God (recognising our misery in his presence, asking of him with confidence his protection) that he does not make temptations cease, or give us the strength to fight them. It is true that his help is indeed more swift and more obvious at some times than others. We must believe in the ordinances of his providence and revere them for our greater good. But I say, that when in this last year I felt myself attacked by the attachments of nature, when I had recourse to our Lord, he extinguished them, and I did not feel them any more; or else he gave me the strength to vanquish and destroy them by performing contrary acts of virtue, interior as well as exterior. Prayer is thus an all-powerful remedy for our infirmities and miseries.

That is what I can say about the lights it pleased our Lord to give me of the mysteries of his holy life and of the perfections of his divine essence. If there is anything contrary to the faith in this, I disown it, because I only believe in that which the Church believes, and I believe it firmly. But I have not learned the truths which are contained in my writings through human means, nor through the mediation of any creature. Our Lord, through his infinite goodness, has himself taught them to me.[165] That he may be forever blessed for it!

FOURTH ACCOUNT

On Prayer

Three stages of prayer

Time of intimacy

It would not be necessary, it seems to me, to say anything at present about prayer, since prayer is nothing but an elevation of the mind and heart to God; because my soul is elevated to God with marvellous affections and is transported to him through all those lights I have indicated, and is in him. I point to this, however, as the state in which my soul dwells at all times, on every occasion, in every place, occupation, encounter and event. But there are other things far more intimate and special that happen between the soul and God when it withdraws itself and sets aside a time destined only for that holy exercise.[1]

'O my God, because this is where I have experienced more singularly your infinite kindnesses, assist me now with your grace, for I confess that I have exceptional need of it in order to tell what can indeed be felt and experienced - but not explained - of your infinite sweetness. However, because you, my Saviour, desire this testimony of me, I hope you will give me the light and words to make it known for your glory, to which I submit it all.'

Infused prayer

I do not pretend to speak about prayer done through reflection, that is through reasoning and the understanding in order to move the affections of the will and afterwards form resolutions to regulate one's life. Although very good, this manner of prayer is one I have scarcely ever practised, except in my youth maybe, when I was in religion[2] (but such a long time ago now that I have hardly any recollection of it) and again, perhaps, for a year or two of the first years I was in Paris (though often our Lord would raise me up [in prayer] in a way I would not be able to describe).

But it pleased our Lord to grant me an infused prayer for about the past nine or ten years, when months (I could say years) went by that he did not deny me this grace. Moreover, thinking all this to be a quite common and ordinary experience, and that it was as easy for everyone as it was for me (who did nothing but place myself before God, and then I was filled and agitated[3] according as it pleased his infinite goodness), I was also mistaken on this point, as I was with regard to the other things I mentioned.

This infused prayer is given by God, is received by the soul in diverse ways, and consists of many different degrees. I do not know how to name these. The person who asks me to write this down will judge this better than I can.

Preparation for prayer

I believe it is necessary before all else to declare in what way I put myself in the presence of God and make my preparation for prayer.

For some years, in keeping with the subject I had taken for prayer, I placed myself in the presence of God by representing him to myself in various ways according to his divinity and his humanity. In this manner the imagination has still some part to play in prayer, more or less according to whether the subjects are more spiritual or perceptible. But for the past seven or eight years I have not practised this any more; or so rarely indeed that I would regard it as something very exceptional for me.

Since then this is how I have set about prayer. I begin by an act of faith in the presence of God, without a representation or image; because the imagination has nothing to do here: it is bound and tied down in such a way that it doesn't move, for fear that, by its runs and whimsicalities, it might hinder the soul. Afterwards I adore God with a profound respect. I then enter through a loving sentiment into the communion of all the just who are on the earth, of all the saints who are in Heaven, and even, if I remember it, all the suffering souls in Purgatory, in order to honour and glorify God with all of them. But I desire above all to unite myself to the Holy Virgin and our Lord Jesus Christ, entering as much as it is possible for me into their heart and mind in order to praise, bless and love God, even uniting myself to the selfsame in order to do this as he does,[4] so as to render him all the honour and love which is due to his sovereign grandeur. And then, I offer him my prayers for some particular end, according to the need or present occasion.

I recommend myself to the Holy Virgin, to the great St Joseph, to my Guardian Angel, and to my holy protectors, and others, according to my subjects[5] and how I feel myself drawn, beseeching them to intercede for me. Then I address myself particularly to our Lord Jesus Christ, making him an entire homage of my body and soul, entreating him to take complete possession of them and to dispose of them as things of his own, things which belong really to him. I entreat him to do with me and in me whatever will please him: making me part of the purity of his intentions and perfect care, so that it might please him to unite my worthless prayers to his (which are completely perfect and divine) and to apply them himself to whatever will be for his greater glory and the fulfilment of his designs for all creatures. And abandoning myself entirely to him, and to the movement of his spirit and his love, I remain empty of all things and in a completely pure readiness for receiving all the communications his goodness would wish to bring about in me.

That is the way by which I put myself in the presence of God, and is also my disposition and preparation for prayer. I have forgotten to mention that, before all this I always say the Veni Creator in order to invoke the Holy Spirit, and the Ave Maria to the Holy Virgin, disowning, moreover, entirely and absolutely, all the aberrations or apathy of mind that could befall me during prayer.

Subject without representation

Every evening I never miss reading twice my subject for the morrow, or simply setting one before my mind depending on my disposition. There are those who would say that the best method for prayer is not to propose any subject to oneself, but to go to prayer and accept what God will give. His directions are varied. He leads some in one way, and others in another. But with regard to myself, I would not wish to do it thus, because it seems to me that this would expose myself to many extravagances. I read a subject, therefore, but do not arrange in advance its considerations, reflections, affections and so forth; for my way is more simple.

With regard to the representation or fabrication of place,[6] for some years all this happened in me in the normal way. However, for many years now, I have no representation or fabrication of place, be it for the mysteries of the life and death of our Lord, or for any other topic. Nonetheless, I believe firmly and simply in the mystery or theme which I must consider; for faith has taken the place of all images and representations, and the imagination has no part in this type of prayer. All this takes place very briefly, and almost always in the same way. The soul, being thus prepared, remains as if annihilated before God through a profound respect.

God, sole master of prayer

For a longer or shorter period of time afterwards, the soul remains in a state of humility and respect in the presence of God. If God leaves the soul in this state, without giving it anything else for itself, the soul will not desire or lay claim to any other thing beyond rendering God all the greatest honour of which it is capable. It looks and longs not for the gifts and caresses of God, but for him alone. This purity of intention is extremely necessary. God often gives the soul greater graces; and the soul enjoys a greater repose on account of them, because all things are the same to it. The soul neither dwells on nor reflects on consolation or desolation. It is equally content with one as with the other, and gains its contentment in doing what God wishes and in being in that state in which it will give him more glory; the soul is so indifferent to all the rest that it doesn't think of it.

What does God do in a soul that seeks him so purely [in prayer]? He showers it with a magnificent kindness. I say, he fills its understanding with lights and its will with wonderful affections, which are ordinarily in keeping with the topic [chosen for prayer]. I say ordinarily, but not always; because often he draws the soul into prayer, revealing to it truths and mysteries it has in no way foreseen or thought of. The soul must always, here as in everything, but particularly at this point, follow freely and simply the attractions of God.

The difficulty [here] is to describe clearly how those lights and affections are communicated to the soul. It seems to me that they are infused all of a sudden into the understanding, which remains convinced in an instant and persuaded of the truth that is manifested to it, without there being any need of reflecting or reasoning for this. If one were to discourse or reason about it, it would be out of admiration and astonishment, and not in order to look for and discover the truth, because the truth appears clearly.[7]

For example, God bestows this light on the soul: that it has of itself but nothingness and sin - an incapacity for good and an inclination to evil; that all the things of the world, of which men make such fuss: nobility, riches, dignities, the beauty of the body and the like, are nothing but a puff of smoke and wind, and even less than that; that mortal sin is such a horrible and detestable thing, because it makes us the object of God's hatred; that an entire eternity of the pains of Hell would be better than to be for one moment the object of his hatred and in his disfavour; that venial sin, of which most people have a poor opinion, is such a great evil that it would be better for Heaven and earth to perish and all angelic and human nature to be annihilated than to commit even one of them.

These truths and other similar ones, which God lets the soul see by means of these infused lights, are so evident and manifest that without any reasoning the soul is persuaded and convinced of them in one moment.

Affections

That is what concerns the understanding. Now the will. I say that it is filled all of a sudden with affections, in conformity with the lights it has received. It enters into a veritable defiance and disdain of self, appropriating nothing of the gifts of God, but referring everything to his glory; and having contempt for all visible and transitory things, regardless of how beautiful and excellent they might appear, it looks upon them as nothing more than dust, smoke that serves only in doing harm to the eyes when it happens to touch us there. The will detests sin with sentiments and affections of horror that cannot be explained; but not from fear of chastisement. For, if there were as many as a thousand hells, compared with the grandeur of God who is offended, the soul would throw itself into them rather than commit even one, I don't say mortal but venial sin: the smallest and slightest that one could imagine - if there are any small ones, which I don't believe there are.

Ordinarily the soul does not receive many lights all at the same time, but one after the other. Moreover, one light suffices to fill it and occupy it entirely. Often, from one truth to the next, which he shows to it, the soul even says to God: 'Speak, my Lord, for your poor servant is listening to you![8] Imprint and engrave so profoundly these truths on my soul that nothing will ever be able to erase them from it.'

Now, although God communicates to the soul these truths at other times as well as at prayer, it seems to me that they are usually greater at prayer time; or it is that, the soul being entirely occupied in looking at them and disposed to receive from them their benign influences, these truths bring about at this time the strongest and sweetest impressions.

Every light will produce a great variety of affections in the soul so that the soul will be imbued with them and thereby fortified in the known truth and thus draw from these affections conclusions to regulate the rest of its life, which conclusions it will put into practice afterwards all the more easily that it will have been more fully convinced of the truth.

God often gave to me only one such light for entire weeks and months on end, and at times with a greater abundance of affections; and he would repeat all this many times.

This disposes the soul in a wonderful way. And afterwards it hardly hesitates any more about the affections it has thus tasted and savoured, which were imprinted in the depth of its heart.

The soul is as if drawn out of itself

I have said how God reveals the Christian truths to the soul. Likewise, he shows it the mysteries of faith and religion, making it see through lights more resplendent than those of the sun, how there is one God; how this God is necessarily in three persons, who are all equal in goodness, wisdom and power and in all the perfections which are essential to God, because, although being three distinct persons, they have all only one and the same essence, and are one God through unity of essence and nature; how the second person of this adorable Trinity clothed himself in our flesh in the bosom of a virgin, and was born in a poor stable. He reveals to the soul the mysteries he accomplished by his life and his death; what he did and said, and for what end - namely, that he himself serve the soul as an example, pointing out to it what it must do and what it must not do.

It is here that the soul, seeing the excessive kindnesses of its God, is as if drawn out of itself and completely transported in love; it feels profoundly such burning affections from these kindnesses that at times it seems that it should die of them.

There are it seems three ways of making a portrait and a representation of a person. The first and the most difficult is through sculpture, in which it is necessary to hew, to chisel and to use up much time and pain; and in which, afterwards, one does not often succeed. The second is through painting. And the third - the easiest and most certain of them all - is to cast a mould. Through these three means we can also make ourselves three portraits of Jesus Christ, our prototype and model.

The first and the most difficult, through a continual mortification, cuts, slices and takes away incessantly that which makes us unlike him. What pain and labour there is in that exercise! How much time and work is needed in order to accomplish so little! Because our nature has a depth of extreme corruption in it, we see and experience that it shoots forth incessantly more bad weeds than we are able to pull up. This is indeed why we have difficulty in doing that which we intend.

The second means of achieving this is painting. This is through the exercise of devotion and the practice of all the virtues, which, as in the case of beautiful colours, we use for all the world like strokes of a paintbrush to make ourselves perfect copies of the great original. All this takes a long time and much pain; and often we do not succeed in it.

But through the exercise of prayer and love, the soul is thrown all of a sudden into Jesus Christ so as to take from him and retain all the traits of a perfect resemblance. It loves in the same way as he loves, and loves only him. The affections and esteem it has for things are entirely in conformity with his. It hates what he hated, disdains what he had contempt for, loves what he loved (because all its affections tend towards a perfect imitation of that which it sees him doing) and practises his counsels and his law on all occasions and in all encounters, there being no need, then, to make any particular resolution to practise such and such a thing. The soul continues to imitate him in everything, through the strong impression it has received of him; for it is filled with the love of the virtues which it contemplates in the Saviour.

These affections are infused into the soul in great abundance and variety. In this the soul observes neither order nor rule to provide them: it all happens in a loving confusion and well-ordered disorder. And the soul is occupied so much in loving its God and in abandoning itself completely to him, that it neither knows what it does nor what happens to it; for it gives no thought to all of this nor to itself. Nevertheless, sometimes God lets the soul know this through a particular light; or indeed - in order to dispose the soul well and to ground it in the knowledge of the truth or of the mystery he makes it see - lets it become aware of it through the length of time, for often he will visit the soul in the same way many days in succession, even many weeks and many months. This he does so as to engrave virtue solidly in the soul.

These lights, which the soul has, are not received through image or representation; they are purely spiritual and intellectual, particularly at the end, as I am going to tell.

This was the first way of infused prayer, its first degree to which I am unable to give a name, and which it usually pleased God to give me almost every day for some years. In this prayer there are lights in the understanding and affections in the will, coming to the soul from the goodness and liberality of God; for indeed the soul senses that they are given and do not come from itself. The visions and understanding the soul has of God and of his divine perfections, of goods and of eternal punishment, are infused into it in the same way. From the moment these lights enlighten the understanding they strike the heart straightaway and fill it immediately with the interior affections of the virtues, which it exercises with great vigour and ease, because God brings them about. The soul does nothing on its part but consents and abandons itself fully to him, that he may accomplish in it, through it, and with it all that which will be for his good pleasure. That is what I can say about this first manner of prayer which God communicates to the soul.

Ignorance of the vocabulary of the spiritual masters

As regards the second way of prayer, or the second degree, it is not so easy to explain. My God, help me; for without your special help I cannot proceed! However, because you wish that the most interior and secret things, which have happened between your divine Majesty and me, your poor and unworthy creature, be brought to light, grant me the grace of being able to explain it. You know well, my God, that I have said much about my being only a worthless young woman without knowledge or understanding; that I neither understood nor knew the proper words for treating this subject matter! This is true; for I did not say this as an excuse. And nevertheless, I have been requested to do this work. It is necessary, then, my sovereign Lord, that your grace supply for my insufficiency. He who started me in this[9] indeed believed without doubt that you would not deny me the grace for this work. I commit myself to it entirely.[10]

Second degree of infused prayer

In this degree of prayer, then, I see that there are no lights in the understanding, nor do I see any from where prayer itself is concerned. All the lights with which prayer had been enlightened regarding the mysteries of faith, religion and the truths of Christianity, are extinguished entirely in this second degree of prayer, except at times when God, according to the need the soul finds itself in, causes some flashes of them to shine forth in it. But this fire - these lights in themselves - makes the soul see more clearly and more certainly the mysteries of the holy life, death and passion of our Lord, than it would have with its own bodily eyes: how indeed he is truly and really [present] in the Holy Sacrament of the altar, true God and true man, and how in so far as he is God, he is everywhere by essence, presence and power, and so forth. Now, I say that the soul no longer has as it used to have - though very slightly and seldom - those lights which, either at prayer or any other time, reveal and manifest these mysteries to it; for [in this second degree of prayer] there remains of them in the soul only a small recollection of having seen them; and it seems to me that this recollection even diminishes almost every day.

The soul only sees those lights through faith.[11] And since the time I lost those lovely lights our Lord used to give me so abundantly of his mysteries, and particularly of the Holy Sacrament, when I am in his presence and ready to receive him, I often say: 'My God, the less I have of lights and knowledge in order to see you now in this adorable Sacrament, so much the more firmly I believe you to be there. For it is not because I have had particular lights to see you there so often and so certainly that I believe you to be there, but because you have said so and your word is true.'[12] This then is how the soul remains in the obscurities of the faith, without having more definite lights to reveal its truths to it. But because everything that faith declares is infallible and true, and because in everything else there can only be illusion and error, the soul remains in great peace in this obscurity, looking for no other certitude and knowledge than that of faith.

But it is to be remarked that there is certainly a great difference between having faith and having the lights of faith. In the first state of prayer, the soul has very great lights for all sorts of things, and has them abundantly; but in this state, stripped of its lights, the soul has faith that is completely pure. This is why there is no longer any image or representation in the soul, be it of spiritual or corporeal things. So when the soul is at prayer, it is without the operations of the understanding, be they natural or supernatural; or if it has them at all, they are so imperceptible that the soul is not aware of them.

Nonetheless, since it is said that knowledge always precedes love and that the will is only moved by the link the understanding has with it, I say that this is true; but not always however, and particularly in this matter.[13] For the soul is filled with affections and does not see in itself any actual light that might be the cause of them.[14] But what I can say and point out is, that there remains in the soul a ground of certitude with regard to truths it has known (which it itself does not know, because it does not reflect upon them); and the least recollection the soul has of these truths it embraces with affection, without it being necessary on that account that it sees them clearly and distinctly.[15] For example, one may be accustomed to seeing a certain person in a certain place or employment. Then this person absents himself and is no longer to be found there. Those who loved him and were accustomed to being there in his company, being themselves in the same place and employment will remember him forthwith. And although they do not see him and do not particularly represent to themselves the qualities that made them love him, at the mere recollection of his person and his name, they feel themselves moved and filled with affection. It is the same in this case, because the soul coming to prayer is completely transported with love at the mere recollection of God, though it has, however, no actual light - at least as far as it knows - of his grandeurs and perfections or favours it has received from him. The light of knowledge it had of all this is taken from it. And yet, in this recollection there remains some notion or other, some impression of God - there being no need of anyone else - that embraces it and makes it love ardently. In the same way the soul, at the mere recollection of sin, without having light that might reveal to it the sin's horror and deformity - the goods of which it deprives us, and the evils into which it hurls us, or even how much it is injurious to God and how he abhors it (which makes the soul detest sin all the more) - without the soul having, I say, any of this knowledge, at the mere recollection of sin it feels itself moved with horror right down to the depths of its bosom and detests it in a way that cannot be explained. It is that there is a secret impression on the soul, which the knowledge of the truth has made there, and which moves the affections according to the objects that are present to the soul. I say the same for all the rest.

Infused affections reduced to love and annihilation

That is the second way of prayer, where the understanding does nothing but furnish the soul with a little reminder of the truths it knew; and where the will is filled with the greatest affections.

Indeed I go on much farther and say that [in this prayer] one enters a certain state in which the understanding has no activity, and nevertheless is occupied and filled with all the powers of the soul in a way that is unknown to me. These powers, not running from one side to another, are calm and are at rest; have a certain satiety and plenitude of peace, so that the soul desires nothing but the good it possesses. God does things by means that are in accordance with the order of his ordinary Providence; but when it pleases him he also acts directly. Moreover, in the matter of prayer, he ordinarily gives lights before affections, which he uses as a means of moving the affections. But when it pleases him, without these lights, he infuses these affections into the substance and the most intimate part of the soul. It seems to me I have experienced this and certainly noticed it very much in myself. And in this case the soul has not such a great variety of affections as it had during the preceding times, when it exercised the affections of all the virtues in diverse ways. But here, in fact, the affections are almost all reduced to two, namely annihilation and love.

Firstly, the soul annihilates itself; and entering into the profound abyss of its own nothingness in the presence of this supreme Majesty, it says to him: 'O God, because it is proper to you and belongs only to your sovereign power to make something out of nothing, make now of this nothingness something good for your glory and your service; make it a perfect and complete copy of your Son.'[16] The soul reduces to nothing in itself all visible and invisible creatures, Heaven and earth, men and angels, so as to remain alone with the well-beloved of its heart;[17] and so that none of these things should stop it or deter it from the exercise of its love. The soul annihilates Paradise and Hell so as to look at no one but him alone in all the services it desires to render him without hope of recompense or fear of chastisement. And although all this does not allow one to live or be as before, it is not just with regard to the soul, which, by its affections, has likewise annihilated them; for in fact the affections are to the soul as if they did not exist.

And love separates the soul so entirely from these things (not, however, with regard to their use, because they are still necessary for contact with life; but indeed with regard to the pleasure, comfort and recreation the soul could receive from them), that I fail to see what more death could accomplish in the soul. Moreover, the soul desires to do all things and renounce all things through the force of love and not through the violence of death.

And this God causes to take effect in the soul, without the soul knowing what he is doing; because the understanding (where knowledge resides) is not employed in this work. The soul follows and consents to all these movements, without knowing what it does or where it is being lead.

God grants to the soul in a special way the affections of final love and esteem; for it is to him that the soul returns all things with such great purity of intention that it never turns in upon itself, either for good or for evil, temporal or eternal. Its only care is to do his good pleasure; for it has such a great esteem for everything that concerns his service, that it sacrifices entirely to his interests body, soul, goods, health and life itself; and a hundred thousand bodies, a hundred thousand lives, and millions of worlds, if it could have as many of them to give, rather than fail in this in even one point. It would rather wish to lose them all and destroy them utterly, than to do the slightest thing which might displease him.

That is what I can say about prayer which is done without the lights of the understanding, natural or supernatural. As regards the first [natural lights], for a long time now they are extinguished and are of no service to my soul, for all the world like the brightness of a candle which is of no use in the presence of the sun. Moreover, the soul had so many and such great supernatural lights for its direction in all things that it had nothing to do with those of human reason for this. So, indeed far from wishing to avail myself of them, I rejected them. Not that they are not good and that it is not necessary to follow them; but when one has greater ones and better ones, it is those which one must follow. Consequently, the soul did not intend to live any longer simply as a rational creature, but instead as a Christian, and thus to be ruled by the lights of faith and the truths of Christianity, and no longer by the sole lights of reason.[19]

Sancta Sanctorum

It is now that it behoves me to enter into the *Sancta Sanctorum*[20] and to speak about that which is called the most intimate and secret between God and the soul. Finish, Lord, your work, you who pride yourself in having rendered all your works perfect![21] Direct my pen right to the end, and grant me the grace to say something about that which you made me feel concerning your ineffable goodness, so that Heaven and earth may bless you for it.

The soul being so disposed, and empty of all things, is drawn to certain loving embraces that I cannot explain except by the comparison of two persons who love one another ardently, meet each other unawares and, without one word being said, throw themselves into each other's arms, and do nothing but embrace, hug and squeeze the heart of each other; and then begin again to embrace and caress anew. The soul is suddenly drawn, pulled and elevated to those loving embraces of its God; which happen in different ways, now with God, then with Jesus Christ. Sometimes the soul feels that God embraces it and caresses it tenderly; and it embraces him also with a distracted love, but with so much respect and reverence however, that in the transports of its love it never forgets the respect it owes to his grandeur. Sometimes it seems that the soul even draws back and does not dare enjoy his familiarities. But it is raised up as if by force into the arms of its God, and when it finds itself there, it stretches and opens its own arms, distending its heart in order to receive him and embrace him. It remains more or less in this state according as it pleases him to keep it there. (It seems to me, however, if one can judge and measure the length of time in this state, that it does not continue more than a quarter of an hour.) Then afterwards, the soul looks only at its God; for it seems to me that it does nothing but that: at that moment love gathers together all its powers; and the soul hasn't the freedom to speak about the affections of its heart, except by means of some sighs and some interrupted words, after which it enters anew into those loving embraces, doing nothing but hugging and pressing tightly to its heart its God. It keeps him thus embraced and can indeed say with the spouse, as she says it: 'My beloved is mine, and I am completely his.'[22] The soul melts away through love as wax does in the physical fire.

A certain union is established here, or rather a transformation of God into the soul and the soul into God who penetrates the soul and all its powers completely - and the body also - right through to the marrow of the bone. I cannot explain any better this infusion which God makes of himself into the soul; for it is so intimate and penetrating that the soul feels itself completely filled with God. In order to be filled with God, the soul no longer desires or wants either his gifts or his graces, but he himself so as to be filled and gratified. It abandons itself totally to him in an inexplicable manner, that he might effect in it all the communications of his goodness that will please him. In this state the soul enjoys a certain delectation, an amplitude of heart, with a most pure openness [to his goodness] it would wish to render infinite, if it were able, in order to give him the chance of contenting and satisfying fully in it the desires he has of communicating himself to his creatures.

Satisfy, O my God, your loving inclinations, and for your glory follow the loving movements of your natural goodness, bringing about in me all the communications of your divine essence that will please you; for I do not intend any other thing by this. Spare neither my body, my soul, my health nor my life: I consecrate all this to you and wish, if need be, that it all perish under the weight of your loving operations.

The soul does nothing, on its part, but thus abandon itself fully, entirely and lovingly to all the designs of its God, doing nothing more than suffering and accepting that which it pleases him to accomplish in it. That is what I can say of this communication which God gives of himself to the soul. From its side, the soul is drawn into and submerged in God in such a fashion that it remains happily lost there. It has certain yearnings to bury itself there and to be lost all the more; but not being able to do so sufficiently by itself, it beseeches God himself to absorb it and draw it entirely into himself; which he does. And the soul soars up with a loving vigour, like a person who throws himself with strength and impetuousness into the sea, and who, through the force and tenacity with which he hurls himself there, always goes to the bottom and no longer appears on the surface of the water or comes to the shore. The soul thus throwing itself into God, is drowned and sinks ever further. And as this person who has thus thrown himself into the water would not see or feel anything but the water, so the soul sees only God; in him and through him it touches or feels only him, and in the same manner [as in the water] and no longer by means of creatures as it used to beforehand, sees his perfections and attributes in the divine essence; for it has no longer any knowledge of them through means of his creatures and his works. The soul remains in God as in a tower, in a place of security, making of him a high wall and a rampart that it puts before its enemies in order to secure itself against their attacks and persecutions. And nothing enters into the soul any more, it seems to me, I mean into its powers and faculties, without passing into God who surrounds it so entirely before reaching the soul; because the soul is more in him through the affections of love than the infant is in the womb of its mother. As regards the heart and the depths of the soul, no one but God alone enters there, for he is their Lord and absolute Master; for the soul could not suffer any other thing to be there apart from him. This lasts not only during the time of prayer, but also afterwards; for the soul remains always thus in God, even though it does not feel it as much as when it is completely engrossed in prayer.

That is what I can say about how in prayer God communicates himself to the soul. The soul throws itself into God and is lost completely as it is penetrated by him from the inside, all around and from outside. And the soul wishes to see and hear nothing else but him, and the mutual embraces of one and the other. This manner of prayer was very common with me for some years. In his kindness, God granted it to me often.

However, for the past six or seven years, he gives it to me in another way; or to put it better: he took away from my prayer something which was only there for my contentment and my particular pleasure. I am going to say what this other way is.

The soul at prayer has certain swift and extraordinary feelings of the presence of God. Yet, however, it does not see him. A blind person can indeed be in the company of a Prince and be assured of his presence without seeing him. In the same way the soul, when it no longer has that light which makes him visible and perceptible to it, if one must speak thus, cannot be in doubt about the presence of God. Its understanding is darkened, but its heart is filled with such a great love that it feels itself wholly consumed. At times it is resolved to hold back its tears and sighs and not give solace to its heart in case it might come to melt through this excess of love. Other times the soul wishes to redouble those tears and sighs, as the wind kindles the furnace and with a little drop of water afterwards renders the fire more inflamed, so that they might help it embrace him all the more and thus enable it to die in that excess of love. The soul is greatly agitated by these affections and loving movements and does not know how they are given to it. It seems to the soul that it is completely alone in this exercise, for God does not give to it any sign of his presence. The soul embraces him and grips him firmly with love and respect, but it seems that God is so cold as to give the impression of not seeing it. In actual fact, he permits the soul to approach him, to touch him and to present its homage to him, but he does not give it any indication that he finds them acceptable. The soul is impassioned with and as if transported by the desire to please its God, imploring him, in all the ways that respect and love can suggest to it, to dispose of it freely (and of all that which concerns it) according to his good pleasure, and that he permit it never to follow in anything its own inclinations, but to do in everything his holy will. And God does not respond to it; he gives it no knowledge that he hears it, and that its desires are acceptable to him. To the soul this is an exercise in mortification, patience and resignation, of which I do not believe one could have any greater or more real. One has to experience this in order to know it. I believe it has been more than seven years now that God keeps me thus in his presence. During this time this manner of prayer is the most usual kind for me; feeling deeply the affections of love and the desires to please him, that anything I could say would be nothing in comparison to what is the reality. And I have no knowledge that he deigns accept them.

I have given you everything, my God, for I have given you all that I could possess of the goods of the world. And not only that: I have given you the whole world and the empire of Heaven in so far as they were mine. I would give them up for your love and

I would restore them to you as their absolute lord. With the help of your grace and mercy I have given you my body by the vow of chastity and consecrated it to you right from the age of 12 or 13.[23] I have given you my liberty and all the actions of my life. Offering them to you as a sacrifice, I renew with all the affections of my heart the vows of my baptism and those which I have made also in order to give myself more particularly to you. I know well, my God, that all these gifts are unworthy of your sovereign grandeur; for who am I to dare present anything to you and to be able to offer you what might be worthy of you? However, permit me to say to you, my God, that I am the work of your hands and the price of the blood of your Son,[24] and that in this respect I can indeed present myself to your august Majesty. Deign to accept then, if it pleases you, my sacrifice, since it is from a good heart, and from a good and open will that I offer and present it to you; which sacrifice you hold in great esteem. Finally, my Lord, although I am unable to know that you deign accept this sacrifice, I have confidence however in your divine goodness that you do not reject it. I shall leave all things at your feet as something that belongs to you, and as for myself, I no longer have nor wish to have the right or power to use them. If these things I have given you are worthy of your using them for your service, recognise them at least as yours, my God, so that they remain in your power.

So that is how the soul in this sort of prayer does not see God. It only feels him and touches him. He does not let it know if its services are acceptable to him; and it seems that the soul is completely alone in loving, that it is not loved or at least that it receives no sign of his love. Thus it remains deprived of the knowledge that could give it greater satisfaction. However, as it could not have any greater satisfaction than being in the state in which God wishes to place it, putting its sovereign contentment in doing in everything his holy will, the soul is not troubled; and, having this confidence that God has not abandoned it on that account, it suffers this privation in great peace and resignation. And even this serves it as a goad which prods it and presses it incessantly to serve God purely and perfectly, so that it can recover and enjoy again the manifestations of his love.

Familiarity of Jesus Christ with the soul

To speak through obedience

What can I say now about the loving intimacies and familiarities of Jesus Christ with the soul and the soul with him? I would pass over them willingly and in silence, because they can not be fittingly explained. However, seeing that obedience wishes that I speak,[25] I entreat you, my dear Saviour - you who have loved obedience so much; and which you have preferred to your very own life - to grant me the grace to be able to accomplish this now, and to render me in effect and in practice such as you desire me to be. You have made me know sufficiently well your desire in this matter, because you have imprinted this on my heart: 'I wish you to be obedient.' I desire to be so, O my Lord, in imitation of you,[26] having henceforth no greater pleasure than to submit myself in all things for the remainder of my days.

The ways in which the soul sees Jesus Christ

Our Lord, then, makes himself visible to the soul so often and in so many different ways that there is scarcely a moment when it doesn't enjoy his divine presence and receive signs of his love. Take note that I say: 'He makes himself visible to the soul';[27] for as regards corporeal and perceptible visions, and which are seen with the eyes of the body - I never had any of that nature. The visions of which I speak are purely intellectual.[28] Sometimes the soul sees him accomplishing in human form the mysteries of his holy life, death and passion, or, to put it better, representing them to the soul. At other times, and often, it sees him in the majesty of his glory, being made to see a ray of his ravishing beauty,[29] which makes the soul cry out: 'O my Lord, you have ravished my heart, and pierced it with a dart of your love by the look of your eyes.[30] Alas! How shall I be able any more to live and dwell on the earth?'

He caresses the soul with so much tenderness and love that, with a force and loving sweetness, he draws it into his sacred wounds and right down into his loving heart, so that he might make of his heart the habitual place of the soul's dwelling. The soul is so distracted and confused that, coming from the knowledge of its unworthiness, it makes I know not what resistance, yet is drawn with greater force and love. And as he said to St Peter: 'If I do not wash you, you will have no part with me!' which made this Apostle answer: 'Lord, wash not only my feet, but also my head,'[31] in the same way the soul - like a piece of iron, which of itself is hard, black, ugly and rusty, when thrown into the furnace loses all those things so as to receive and take instead all the qualities and properties of the fire - yields with fear and confidence to all those loving furies and throws itself into the sacred wounds of his sacred heart; for it enters into the heart of Jesus, and wishes to remain there as in a furnace of love in order to be purified in it of all its stains, and to receive and get there his divine qualities and properties.

At other times he opens and presents his heart to the soul, so that the soul may receive from it all the graces and virtues it will need; nor does he cease afterwards from communicating to it the power to put the acts of virtue into practice, until the habit of virtue be formed in the soul. As these acts, however, are brought about by God with marvellous force and vigour, and the soul gives its consent to all that which it pleases him to do, the habit of sin is destroyed in the soul in less than no time, and that of virtue formed in its place.

He takes the soul lovingly in his arms; and in the same way as the infant taken in those of its mother (or its wet nurse; who gives it only milk) is beheld, pressed and hidden lovingly in her bosom, so the soul now and then experiences those same tendernesses. It drinks from his sacred wounds, and is inebriated from such an excess of love that, following this, it no longer returns to its ordinary ways.

Finally, our Lord shows so much love to the soul and caresses it in so many ways that, seeing itself to be incapable of perfectly tallying with him in this, the soul at least wishes to use what it has of strength and vigour in his service and consummate its life by dint of loving him.

It is particularly at Holy Communion that the soul receives from its Saviour the greatest testimonies of his love; and it is at this time it forces itself, on its part, to give itself more fully to him.

O my Saviour, you are the great priest according to the order of Melchizedek![32] You yourself, then, consecrate me in your service. Make my soul your temple! With absolute power chase from it, and place outside it, everything that could profane it![33] My Lord, may my heart serve you as a tabernacle; and do not permit that sin ever enter into a place you have honoured with your divine presence! What! My God, that sin even enter my heart after you have deigned to enter there so many, many times! No! I hope you will show me that loving kindness by making me the target of all sorts of misery, rather than suffering my soul to be soiled ever again by any sin. Do not permit ever that the brambles and thorns of this world's goods enter my soul, but let them remain there among the flowers and the roses of a true contempt for myself and for all decayed and perishable things. You who are the spouse of chaste and pure souls, embellish me both in body and in soul with the lily of a perfect purity, and, as you have promised, make of them the place of your delights. If it pleases you to dwell in my heart, resigning my judgement and will entirely to you, I shall offer you there a continual sacrifice of obedience, make you a perfect sacrifice of all the actions of my life, and, in doing and obeying all your holy wishes, submit myself to you in everything and everywhere.

It seems to me that our Lord empties the soul so much of all things to such a degree that nothing remains in it but he himself, who completely fills it and equally all its powers. And as the rack draws the lover, a certain attractive virtue in our Lord draws the soul so strongly that the soul throws itself and all its powers - together with the body and all its senses - into him; in such a way, it seems to me, that the soul in this state can indeed say with St Paul: 'I, myself, no longer live, but Jesus Christ lives in me!'[34] And then again: 'Who will separate me from the love of Jesus Christ?[35] Will it be goods, riches, pleasures or the pains and afflictions of this life? No more of that: on the contrary, it is he who serves me as a rampart and shield and who separates me entirely from all those things.' Now the soul enters into its Saviour, and passes from his sacred humanity to his divinity, and from his divinity returns to his humanity, thus making itself in this a continual and gracious homecoming, which overwhelms it with delights.

That manner of prayer was the first the soul had with its Saviour, which it pleased him to make me part of for many years, and in which the soul sees him and looks at him. He caresses the soul and gives it testimonies of his love. The soul, on its part, receives them with great respect and gratitude; and God and the soul are - both - in an exercise of mutual and reciprocal love.

Martyrdom of love

But in short, the state of the soul is changed. It no longer has lights to see - as it had been accustomed to - its Saviour, nor the mysteries of his life and his death. Some small memory of them does remain with it, which, too, begins to wear away day by day. But in place of all this, however, the soul has a simple and firm faith that allows it to believe in these mysteries and that which the Church teaches about him.[36] It doesn't trouble itself about anything else. If its lights have been taken away from it, its love has not. But on the contrary, in fact, for it seems that, having nothing more to see, the soul does nothing else but love. This love strengthens the soul, becoming so active that it burns the soul and consumes it in a strange way. The soul, nevertheless, remains completely alone in these affections of love, not seeing them any more in its Saviour.

'What then, O my Jesus! Have you not desired my heart with so much ardour that you have come from Heaven to earth to have possession of it? And not content with all that, have you not bought it with the price of your blood? And now that I give you the sovereign and absolute domain of it, do you not wish to take it? Do not refuse, Lord, that which you have desired so much and have bought so dearly with a precious price!'[37]

But no matter what the soul does, and regardless of the favours it deeply feels, it has no knowledge that our Lord is pleased with it, nor that he deigns accept that which the soul presents to him. This makes the soul weep and sigh, fearing that its sins might be the cause of it. Nevertheless, this does not trouble it in any way: its sorrow is peaceful and tranquil. Yes indeed, it seems to me that one could really call this a martyrdom of love.

Now the soul at prayer does not speak and deal only with God and all the three divine persons, and with Jesus Christ, but also with the Holy Virgin, the angels, and all the saints in Paradise. When my soul had lights, it conversed familiarly with them and saw that they were very swift in aiding and succouring it. In this state, however, it no longer has the knowledge of their protection and goodwill towards it. Yet, it says to them: 'O inhabitants of the celestial Jerusalem, you who rejoice already in the presence of the Beloved of my heart, say to him that I languish and am consumed with love:[38] show him the violent fervours of my affections so that he may throw me a glance with his eyes.'[39] But the poor soul has no solace from any side, and no one responds to its complaints or to its loving languors. Nevertheless, remembering that which our Lord said: 'Seek and you shall find, ask and it will be given to you, knock and it will be opened to you,'[40] the soul perseveres constantly, hoping that in the end its yearnings will be heard. I have been in this state of prayer for about the past seven years.

Love alone

There is still another sort of prayer; and it is done in this way. The soul feels itself composed in all its powers from a profound and extraordinary respect for God, and does nothing else but remain thus in his presence. And in this state, such a great calm is created in the soul, the body, all the passions and appetites, that the soul feels nothing but a sentiment of peace filling it so abundantly that it seems it might begin to melt from these excesses. But this never lasts more than a quarter of an hour, and often even less.

These are the different ways of prayer it pleased God to give me for the past nine or ten years. This last one, of which I have just spoken, I have had only rarely. As regards the others, they were all equally common to me. And whenever our Lord does not give them to me, making a prayer of patience, I suffer in patience either the pains of the body or the languors of the spirit that hinder these prayers in me, and not being able to glorify God through the affections of devotion, I do so through suffering.

In all these types of prayer there is no work for the mind, because in them the understanding is not taxed by any sort of consideration that would tire the mind by force of reasoning; for one does not reason in these prayers, or so little (and so rarely even) that it could pass for nothing. Here one only loves; and love banishes pain and exercises the acts of all the virtues. In these prayers one takes no notice of either point or rule; everything is done in a well-regulated and ordered confusion, because it is God and love that give order to them. The soul is so transported in this and drawn out of itself, that it knows neither what it has done, or what happens in it. And when it has some light which lets it see this, it is completely astonished at what is taking place in itself; because often there are things the soul had neither foreseen nor thought of.

It is greatly recommended to those who practise prayer to make a small review of it at the end, and to take note of some of the points that touched one most, in order to recall them during the day. I practised prayer in this way at the beginning, remembering moreover the resolutions I made then so as to carry them out with care. But in the sorts of prayers of which I now speak, this is impossible for me; for at the very time the prayer is finished, it is effaced from my mind, in such a way that I no longer have any knowledge of it and can say nothing about it if God does not give me some particular recollection of it; which he did at the times and on the occasions in which it was necessary, renewing for me all those ways of prayer in order to be better able to write about them.

For I have no knowledge of this matter, and only speak about it through experience. This is why it is not written in the terms and with the words I would have couched it in if I had studied this topic and had some particular knowledge of it. Consequently, I have not put myself to great trouble in this beyond saying simply and naïvely what has happened in me; for I do not intend, really, to be eloquent, but to become, through means of the grace of my God, truly obedient.[41]

It still remains for me to say something about the different ways in which God speaks to the soul and the effects his words, and these types of prayer of which I have spoken, have on the soul; the things I have recognised and experienced to dispose one marvellously to prayer; the degrees of obedience in which the soul is exercised, and some practice in this.

How God speaks to the soul

The ways in which God speaks to the soul and governs it
One of the ways in which God speaks to the soul is with clearly pronounced and intelligible words at the bottom of the heart, which are spoken to the soul and are understood by it in the same way as we ourselves understand and speak.[42] Now, in order to know if it is God who speaks to us, seeing that we are indeed capable of speaking to ourselves and persuading ourselves that it is God, I see there are four kinds of spirit which can urge us and speak to us: the spirit of God; the spirit of the angel; of the demon; or of the human spirit, that is, our very own spirit.

Now when God speaks, he speaks suddenly. His words surprise at the beginning, but forthwith they bring peace to the soul. They bring about infallibly what they mean, for they are efficacious words that change the heart in a moment. The effects they carry out in the soul are not transient; they last forever. Sometimes he speaks to instruct the soul. At other times, with stern, loving words, he reproves it for its failures; after which the soul does not fall in this again. At other times he speaks only words of pure love to the soul, which embrace it and are capable of melting its heart. God says a thing but once; when he speaks in this way, it is not necessary for him to repeat it many times, because from the very beginning it has its effect. His words remain imprinted in the soul and are never forgotten. The soul conserves them with care and repeats them often to itself - according to its needs - so as to encourage itself to guard them. The soul renders them a swift and punctual obedience.

Another way by which God speaks to the soul is with light, making the soul know what pleases him and displeases him and what he desires of it without, however, giving it any specific command; in the same way as a superior will make known his intentions to his subject, leaving him nevertheless the choice of whether to follow them or not to follow them! For example, he makes the soul see the excellence of the sufferings of this life: how poverty, contempt,[43] humiliations are pleasing to him and are of an inestimable price in his presence; how one's own will displeases him and the sin it produces is horrible and abominable; and so forth, for I only say this to explain myself. And in these lights God gives to the soul, he shows it the truth about things and allows it the use of its freedom to act or not to act upon it. However, there is something powerful and efficacious that moves the soul unfailingly to stand forth with ardour to embrace that which it sees to be acceptable to him and reject with horror that which displeases him. The soul obeys his intentions without having been given any particular command to do so.

God speaks to the soul in a third way, that is by sentiment and desire. For many years it pleased him in his infinite goodness to tell me and show me his plans and wishes by the two ways I have just spoken of. But this was during the time I had lights in the understanding. However, because he has taken them from me, I no longer feel myself to be guided by these means. And in order to make the state in which I am better understood, and how I am governed in it, I say that I no longer have those particular lights that made me see and discover, sometimes the perfections and attributes of God, then at other times the mysteries of the life of our Lord, and so on; but instead, a lively faith remains in the soul, a great desire, that is, to follow these mysteries and imitate them. Now, although I have lost the lights that made me see the beauties of virtue and the deformities of sin, and so forth, I love virtue nevertheless. I profoundly feel a great love for the good and an extreme hatred for evil. Whether it is that the lights I have had made these impressions on the soul, or whether it has come about in the way I am now going to speak of, is not clear to me. For this is a knowledge in which I have not been well confirmed, not knowing whether it is really true. If I were indeed certain of this knowledge, it would be a great source of consolation to me. This is why I would be very glad to clarify it for myself.

This then is what I was made to know on this subject. In this dark state, God has taken an entire possession of the body and of the soul of his creature. Being its Master and absolute Lord, he shapes this creature and makes it conform to what pleases him and seems good to him, so that, availing himself of the full and entire consent the soul gave him so many times to do with it completely as it would please him, he considers the soul as an instrument that he plies and turns manually, as it seems good to him, in such a way that the soul does what it does (and does not do what it does not do) without reason or explanation, and cannot say or give any reason for its behaviour, except that it feels moved and pushed from the interior to all of these things, and that there is something absolute in it that governs it so. The soul is being exercised here in blind obedience; because it no longer acts out of reason or judgement, but only from an interior movement that incites it and applies it to everything, which makes it practise good and avoid evil, and it does this much more rigorously that when it foresaw things for itself or reflected deeply on what it had to do or avoid.

It seems to me that, in these first ways of God speaking to the soul, it is so much like a mother who says to her child, 'My Son, do such a thing, go to such and such a place!' and, taking him by the hand, she actually does this very thing with him, although the child walks and works as much as it has the strength to do, its mother helping him and consoling him much. But in this third way, it is like when the mother who takes her child in her arms, her very bosom, and without saying anything to him, carries him everywhere she wishes and gets him to do what she wants, and the child, for his part, doing nothing but gripping on to his mother, abandons himself to all her movements. Strictly speaking, this is more a question of acts than of words. Moreover, the operations of God in this state are much more secret and unknown to the soul than in any other state, because God does not make known to the soul where he is leading it, nor to what end his work leads.[44] For many years this has been my state.

O God, would I dare have this thought of being thus directed and governed by you? If this consideration enters my mind, it is because I believe you love to grant more graces to those who are the most unworthy of them, in order to make your infinite goodness and mercy shine with greater brilliance. If, my Lord, through the merits of your precious blood, you have granted me this favour, I beseech and entreat you, by that same sacred blood and your holy wounds, to continue it in me for the rest of my days. Take from day to day and from moment to moment a more entire possession of my body and my soul, both of which I do not wish henceforth to call mine but yours, seeing that you have indeed bought them; and which, besides, I have given totally to you. Exercise in them and over them more than ever your sovereign and absolute dominion. For my part, I disown and renounce with all my power all the movements and inclinations of nature, not wishing to follow them in any way. I speak even for all those that come from purely human reason, because I do not wish any more to be guided and governed except by the pure motion of your love and of your Holy Spirit dwelling and living in me. And it seems to me that you will never wish to rule me as absolutely as I desire, so great is the longing I have for it; so I accept for that reason all humiliations, privations, interior and exterior mortifications and all temptations. Briefly, I am ready to do everything and to suffer everything so that your authority in me and over me be sovereign and absolute.

I wish to be yours, and to serve you in the condition of those slaves whose body and life are in the absolute power of their lord, and have no means nor hope of ever getting out of their state of servitude and slavery. I do not wish on that account to serve you through force and constraint, because I desire all those conditions freely, ask them of you with all the affections of my heart, and accept them with a thousand and a thousand more acts of thanksgiving, praise and gratitude. And the more you would wish to possess me in this way, all the more I shall hold it to be of the greatest obligation, imploring you that if ever I was so unfortunate as to wish to retract in this, make me feel profoundly the effects of your most rigorous justice in order to keep me to my duty.

I ask this of you absolutely, my God. Do not leave me any more in that unfortunate state of freedom to withdraw myself from you no matter how little, or to be able to do anything that could displease you; keep me for ever in that entire submission, dependence and perfect obedience to all your guidance and wishes. Grant all the other graces and favours (which you have been accustomed to grant to those who honour you and serve you) to whomsoever it pleases you. I have no desire for them and do not ask them of you. But to be removed from you no matter how little; that others love you more than I do and are more submitted than I am, this I can neither suffer nor think of without pain!

These are the more intimate and special ways by which God speaks to the soul and governs it, and the sentiments and affections with which the soul wishes to serve him and obey him. I do not speak of all the other ways by which he speaks to it, as sometimes by the reading of a good book, for instance, or at other times by the voice of a preacher, and by so many other means, for there is scarcely a creature in the universe he doesn't make use of, when it pleases him, in order to speak to us and touch our hearts. I do not speak at all about this, because God has hardly ever availed himself of it in my case. But I speak only of what he says and of what he himself does in the soul without using secondary causes.

There remains for me to speak about the things I have experienced that dispose one greatly to prayer, and the effects which they have on the soul as well as on the body.

What disposes to prayer

Fast and abstinence
Moderate fast and abstinence are a very good disposition for prayer. The reason for this is natural; because, not having the brain so full with the vapours of food, the mind is indeed more free for all the spiritual exercises.

Mortification and the purity of intention
The mortification of the senses is absolutely necessary. Prayer and mortification are full sisters and walk with the same stride. One has as much of prayer as one has mortification. One must deprive oneself of sensual pleasures in order to enjoy the spiritual. How could God, who is pure in spirit, communicate himself to a soul completely carnal and sensual? In order to arrive at the supreme degree of prayer, it is even necessary not to seek the favours and sentiments of devotion, nor to dwell on them or delight in them when God gives them, but to avail oneself of them as a means of finding him, elevating oneself over and above all this and desiring nothing but him alone. It is a great error, indeed folly, to wish to savour God through the senses, he who is pure spirit! Consequently, when his operations in the soul are perfect, they are no longer perceptible to the senses. However, he gives us all those delights and sentiments on account of our extreme weakness and because our nature is so sick and seeks so much itself that it will never quit the terrestrial things and the pleasures of the senses if God does not sever it from them, showering it with desires of devotion. So at the beginning, he gives them to the soul with greater abundance. Blessed are the souls from whom he takes these desires away so that they may serve him out of the motive of pure love. This purity of intention serves greatly in receiving greater graces.

Solitude and recollection
Solitude and retreat serve even more greatly; but indeed solitude of the heart a lot more than of the body. For what help would it be to us to be alone in a room if our spirit is among people and in the confusion of the century?[45] One should not go to the trouble to inform oneself out of curiosity about that which has nothing to do with one: the mind fills itself so much with all this, that God cannot enter nor find a place there.

Silence
I have experienced especially that silence is the guardian angel of devotion. And a person who is not obliged[46] by his ministry and a special vocation to speak a great deal

will scarcely ever have sentiments of devotion if he does not bridle his tongue strongly, even though he would speak of spiritual matters. For the tongue would not cease, eventually, from dissipating the mind. With regard to those who are obliged to speak a great deal on account of their responsibilities, may they not fear that evil effect: for God will even avail himself of this evil to make them more perfectly recollected. But silence brings us great benefits and delivers us from many evils, and St James has reason to say that he who does not sin with the tongue is perfect.[47]

Total oblation

Beyond all the means that dispose us to prayer, rendering it marvellously easy for us, for reaching its supreme degree, as also that of the highest perfection, is the means without a means.[48] This is that one offers and abandons oneself totally into the hands of God unreservedly and without condition, refusing nothing and asking for nothing, giving oneself only to him so that he do or undo in the soul such as it will please him and he will find appropriate. I call this a 'means without a means', because the soul does nothing and yet does everything. O, how happy we would be if we knew how to practise this well, because we would have nothing to do but to let God act and take from his hand everything that would happen to us, making all things serve to our sanctification. For all things would be the same to us. Sometimes we say this to God: that he may do with us according to his good pleasure. But when he wishes to do it, we are so miserable that we take back our word; we don't wish it any more. For if a sickness happens, a setback, a humiliation, an interior desolation, some temptation or anguish of mind, suddenly we complain and we no longer wish that God does with us, or to us, that which pleases him. We were thinking, perhaps, that he would treat us very differently. O, let us not mistake this: it is thus that he is accustomed to treating those who place themselves in his hands in order to heal their wounds. It is necessary to cut the bad member in order to give health to the rest of the body; it is necessary to suffer the rack and the fire in order to be delivered from some dangerous malady. Thus God avails himself of those things in order to purify us of our imperfections. This is why, let us not draw back; let us say constantly to him and always in the same fashion: 'That your will be done!'[49]

This does not serve only in order to dispose us to prayer and to make us acquire it, but it will also give us marvellous repose for our whole life. For we are so often at a loss as to what exercises are the best for us, through which we shall be able to serve God more. There is nothing better than to take everything from his hand! We can never serve him better than acquiescing in his wishes! He does not trouble himself about our exterior work! Let us not trouble ourselves as to whether our work is worthless or excellent, but let us try to do it with a love equal to that of the cherubim and seraphim; and if we do this, God will undoubtedly make us part of his more particular favours and bring about in us afterwards the most ineffable communications of his goodness he has been accustomed to make felt in those who thus abandon themselves to him unconditionally.

These are the things that to me seem to serve especially as great dispositions to prayer. The more we shall practise them, the better we shall pray, seeing that, when things are well prepared, carrying them out is easier. With regard to a more immediate preparation for prayer, I do nothing other than that of which I have already spoken:[50] to read a topic twice in a row, or to propose one to myself in my mind. After which I think no more about it. If by morning God opens my heart on this, as usually happens to me, I take what he gives me. If I feel myself drawn to other things, I follow freely and simply that attraction.

There only remains for me now to speak about the effects prayer produces in the soul and the body.

Effects of prayer

Aversion to sin

It seems to me that the first effect that this divine prayer works in the soul is to develop a hatred of and an extreme aversion to sin; I don't say mortal sin, for the soul cannot think of this without trembling with horror, but venial sin; I mean even the slightest of sins. When this prayer is from God, it necessarily and infallibly produces this effect. I say when it is from God, for the devil sometimes transforms himself into an angel of light. May all the directors who have under their guidance souls who have this infused prayer take notice of this effect. If the soul does not have this aversion to sin, they should regard this infused prayer as false or very suspect. The reason for this is evident, because through prayer God unites the soul to himself and transforms it; and through this union and transformation, the soul loves what he loves, hates what he hates, holds in contempt what he disdains. And as he brings to sin an infinite hatred, it is a necessary consequence that the soul hates it also; and moreover, that it has a hatred and a horror of it that cannot be explained.[51]

Filial and loving fear

The second effect. The soul is filled with fear, not servile, but filial and loving; and does not rely on itself against falling into any occasion whatever of doing what could displease him by thinking that it would have sufficient strength in order to resist; but the slightest appearance of this it discovers in itself, it withdraws from more quickly than if it had encountered a basilisk[52] or a poisonous beast; because it distrusts itself and is afraid of giving God a reason in this for granting it free rein and making it know its extreme weakness by its fall. If he puts the soul in any condition or occasion in which it sees everything to be full of dangers, it fears nothing in this, but instead recommends itself to God, places all its confidence in him, and then remains in great peace and repose. Here, moreover, he protects the soul so powerfully, and holds it and guards it so carefully that there is no longer any danger to it. Often it is at this moment even that he grants the soul the most graces.

Annihilation of the soul

The third effect. This prayer humbles the soul to the point of annihilation. And indeed far from having any vainglory or complacency because of the favours God grants it, it is even humbled and confounded all the more by this, being so transported with astonishment that God should deign to preserve and entertain it so familiarly, and not only permit it, but command the soul to love him and to serve him.[53] O Lord, because of your infinite grandeur and our baseness and vileness, if you had not given us this commandment, who would dare undertake it? That is why, in the exercises of devotion and the practice of the virtues, the soul always finds in this something with which to humble itself and so guard justice strictly by giving to God that which belongs to him, which is everything that is good, and to itself contempt and confusion, seeing that it can do nothing but evil.

Plenitude

The fourth effect. This prayer fills the soul with a great knowledge of God and of itself. These two perceptions are equal: at the same rate as we empty ourselves, God fills us with himself. We shall be as much filled with God as we shall be emptied of ourselves and of all things. It is the same with grace as it is with nature: it does not suffer a void. The soul knows this; so it rejects and destroys absolutely all things in itself in order to be filled in all its powers with God alone. It can tolerate nothing any more but God alone. And by his divine communications, he has so inspired the soul with a magnanimity of heart and a generosity of courage so great, that it can only dwell on him and be content with him alone. Moreover, the soul is equally so entirely his that it neither thinks, desires, nor acts outside of pleasing him, giving no thought to itself or to any creature.

Simplicity

The fifth effect. The soul is rendered extremely simple in its words and actions, and generally in all its behaviours,[54] because the spirit of God does not know what deceit or fraud means. In particular, in this effect one enjoys a marvellous facility in explaining oneself to those who direct one. And after having told them frankly all about one's dispositions of mind and what one thinks, one does not go back over them any more, as if these things were never said, because one speaks with the same simplicity and innocence as a child of 1 year would do, who at that age is not capable of those reflections and repetitions, and who, moreover, has neither the spirit nor the malice to say anything other than that which it has in the mind. That is why it is said that their testimony is true.[55]

Suppleness

The sixth effect. It renders us extremely supple and pliable with regard to the wishes of those who direct and govern us. It is in the nature of the mind of God to lead us to obedience, even to give us a great compliance in our [relationships] with our equals and our inferiors, that is, in everything in which there is no sin. For [in this effect] one desires neither to elevate oneself nor be preferred to anyone; but on the contrary, judging oneself to be the least of all, yields easily to everyone. The spirit of God suffers neither contention nor dispute.[56]

Peace

The seventh effect. This prayer puts peace in the soul. And in so far as the soul is perfect, this peace is greater. Peace calms the tempest of the passions, which strictly speaking, in this effect are more dead than mortified; because the years pass by when one feels no movements of them, I mean even those early passions and those that are in no way in our power to control.[57] This effect uproots and tears away from us the least sentiments of covetousness, concupiscence and pride, which are, as St John says, the three masters and roots from which spring and abound all the sins of the world. For many years I had none of these sentiments and did not understand how anyone could have them. God kept me in such a state that I was astonished when I would hear it said that it was necessary to leave the world in order to serve him, and that in the world one could not attain one's salvation; for, nothing being any hindrance to me, I went my straight way without turning to the right or to the left; and feeling nothing withdrawing me from God (because I had tied down and extinguished all the feelings of nature and everything else that could be of hindrance to me), I even thought that everyone was like that. However, for a year now, God permitting that I feel profoundly the movements of nature, I have indeed realised that this was a state of grace. It is true that, in his great mercy, these stirrings of nature had been so far for me an occasion for the exercise of virtue rather than of sin. I have noticed that God permits this from time to time, so that the soul may be awakened (for it could fall perhaps into some dangerous numbness) and begin all over again the exercise of virtue; for this is a needle that prods the soul and brings it to this awareness.

Forgetfulness of self and of all things

The eighth effect. The soul, through this prayer, arrives at a complete forgetfulness of self and of all things, as much as one can have it in this life. It remains as if in a sweet sleep between the arms of God,[58] longing incessantly to see him fully and manifestly, and awaiting with great desire, but with patience and resignation too, the last moment of its life,[59] which will be the end of its exile and the first moment that will place it in the full and perfect enjoyment of its God for ever (for it hopes for this from God's goodness and the merits of Jesus Christ).

The body, for its part, remains as if dead. It has no longer any desires, sentiment or pleasure for the objects that are proper and natural to it. It is adaptable, and complies with everything that the soul desires of it, giving it no longer any pain or opposition. It is content with less rather than more, and suffers all the treatments the soul wishes to give it without complaint or murmur. This prayer subdues the body more powerfully than all the penances and austerities could do, because the soul, being drawn by God and following his attraction with a great force and vigour, draws accordingly all the spirits[60] to itself in such a way that the body remains as if dead and has no longer strength to perform its ordinary operations. Sometimes I do not know how the body can exist and live, for it is in a state entirely contrary to its natural one.[61]

These are what seem to me to be the principal effects that this prayer brings about in the soul and in the body, for to wish to speak of them all would be difficult. In a word, prayer fills the soul with blessings that are all the more great in that they are neither changeable nor transitory. They are perfected more and more, because they are the effects of this divine cause that subsists and lasts forever in the soul, right from the moment prayer has brought them about.

Excellence of the divine communications

True sanctity

I have often thought to myself that, in writing about the lives of saints, people write about everything but what makes saints saints. For they write about the saints' vigils, fasting, prayers, penances, austerities, exercises of external devotion and suchlike; and this is not what makes them saints, being nothing more than the means to arrive at sanctity. For sanctity in no way consists in these things, because they can be practised by people who are very evil, and often with a greater appearance of devotion than by the people who are truly virtuous. That which makes saints saints is the communications of God with the soul and the soul with God; for it is that which purifies, sanctifies, deifies, unites and transforms the soul into God, in which consists our perfection and our sanctity. We are sanctified in so far as we are united and transformed into God. And these things cannot be talked about; or not very much. But one is right not to describe them, because no one is able to speak worthily of the intimate and loving way in which this happens. I may not know enough forceful and significant words for this [work].

I have no difficulty and no trouble in believing in the great familiarities and intimacies we are told God our Lord has shown to some saints; for, finding souls so well prepared and well disposed, what could he have otherwise done, seeing that I myself, who am filled with so many miseries and so many sins, and in whom he has found such great obstacles (and it is recommended that I tell everything in order to show the kindnesses and ineffable mercies of my God), have tasted or experienced almost more than any I have read about or heard spoken of? Nevertheless, this has always happened in me in the interior, for, no one being found there but him and me, his guidance of me has been wholly interior and peculiar to me, as indeed my confessors rather than myself have remarked.

The Eucharist, supreme favour

But when I reflect on what a complete and ineffable communication he makes of himself in that most august Sacrament of the altar, neither myself nor anyone else should have any trouble in giving credence to all of the communications, for they will always fall short of this one. For myself, I would not wish to change even one Communion, nor the communications God gave me of himself there, for all the fortuitous glory of the angels and the saints in the beatitude of Paradise.

One esteems so much the favours the Apostles had in drinking, eating, conversing and dwelling with him; and one has good reason to admire and value them, for these favours are great and incomparable. But I would not wish to change one Communion for all of them, for I possess the same Lord the Apostles have seen, and in a wholly other way than they did during his mortal life.

How happy Magdalene must have been in being at his feet always, listening to his divine words! - we are much happier in holding him in our hearts, where he makes himself much more familiar[62] to us.

The favour given to St Francis to carry the sacred and painful stigmata of the wounds of the Saviour in his body cannot be admired enough. But I would not wish to exchange one Communion for it; because in Communion [the Saviour] gives us, not the mere resemblance of his wounds, but the wounds themselves, his glorious body being marked with them; and [in Communion] comes to apply their fruit and merit to us, even though he does not perceptibly imprint them in our hearts or on our bodies.

The grace our Lord granted St Catherine of Siena is also admirable. He gave her his heart in exchange for hers. In this adorable Sacrament, he gives not only his heart, but also his soul, his divinity and all his merits. And if [in this adorable Sacrament] he does not change our heart for his, taking it in return for his material and perceptible heart, he changes the soul of our heart, which is our will, uniting it and transforming it to his will. He puts his will in place of ours so that we do his will forever. This is something much greater than changing a heart of flesh.

What love did he show to St Teresa[63] when he said to her: 'If I had not made Heaven and earth, angels and men, I would make them out of love for you.' He shows much more love to us in coming every day a thousand and more times from Heaven on earth, in order to give himself to us in that divine Sacrament, than he does in creating Heaven and earth, angels and men for our purpose.

Finally, the greatest of all the graces God has ever granted to a pure creature, is that which he gave to the Holy Virgin, being incarnated by taking flesh in her virginal womb. The Fathers of the Church call the Eucharist the extension of the mystery of the Incarnation,[64] so much so that, receiving truly and really[65] the same God and man whom the Holy Virgin conceived and gave birth to, we are made participants by this in the greatest and most incomprehensible grace she has had.

And after this, we dare say what is sometimes said: 'If I had received from God the same favours as such saints have, I would be holy likewise!' He has given to all of us without reservation the greatest and most excellent favour he could ever give. All we have to do is to receive it! It is the most efficacious means his wisdom and his love have invented, whereby, communicating himself to us, he unites and transforms us into himself. In this consists our sovereign perfection and beatitude.

Inflamed desires

O my God, how little gratitude men have and how little profit they make of your benefits! For these benefits are not that rare! No matter how great these benefits are, men take no account of them! And how little they know you, refusing to approach you! Grant me the tears, but tears of blood, to weep for that blindness, which is the source of all their miseries and all their unhappiness.

Put me at the gates of Hell till the end of the world, in order to keep it closed and prevent the demons from coming on earth and placing such unfortunate persuasions in the mind of people,[66] that it is always a torment and a troublesome thing to pray and to approach you! Alas! What is more honourable and sweet for us to do than to speak to you? If I could remain there too, my God, in order to prevent these same people from falling in, through the greatness of the torments I could suffer there I might help them somewhat to love you, know you, and depend on you not out of necessity, but through love.

If only I could put the fire of your love ablaze in the four corners of the earth, and at its centre, so that all would burn from it![67] If all hearts were in my power, they would never burn from anything else but that divine and sacred fire. If all their bodies and all their souls were at my disposition, they would never be used in anything but serving and loving you. But, alas! I am only a worthless and miserable young woman! Desires and tears in this regard are only useless. However, I cannot prevent myself from speaking to you about those desires and shedding my tears in your presence.

So, my Lord, seeing that I can do nothing for the salvation of men, I pray you to give your Holy Spirit and an ardent zeal for your glory to the head of the Church and to all the cardinals, archbishops, bishops, prelates and ecclesiastical people, so that they may perform their duties worthily. That you may be known and loved by all! I ask the same of you for all confessors, preachers of your holy Gospel, for all superiors of religious houses, and generally for all those men and women who are employed in the direction and conversion of souls, that it may please you to bless their work, so that they may have an abundant harvest and that the glory of your name be brought to the whole earth.[68]

I recommend to you particularly him[69] in whose hands you have put me for my guidance, beseeching you to change his heart into an ardent furnace, so that all his words and actions be inflamed coals of fire burning with your love the hearts of those who will approach him. Make him know in a singular way your plans, your guidance of me, so that he may be to me a visible angel who will make me fulfil these plans strictly and in every detail. If there is still something earthly and human in him, destroy it entirely, consuming him in the fire of your love, and rendering him completely divine [70] by a perfect transformation of him in you. So be it!

The problem of intentions

The soul does not pray for people when they wish or for what they wish. Moreover, I do not like promising this to those who recommend themselves to my prayers, because that does not depend on me. Ordinarily I say some vocal prayers for them to discharge myself of the duty. But there are things and people to whom the soul feels drawn in prayer, that it seems that it struggles body to body with the good God, like another Jacob, saying to him: 'I will not leave you until you have blessed me;[71] I shall not leave you until you have given me what I ask of you.'

For a time, because of these attractions, I knew the outcome of things. But since God has taken all lights from me, I no longer know what effects my prayers have, neither for my soul nor for other people.

Necessary discretion

In conclusion, this prayer is not subject to distractions. It is very rare that one has any in it; and, like a fly moving before the eyes, they are only things that pass lightly in the mind, provided I myself am not the cause of them. All that which happens around me does not distract me. It is only sometimes that the soul experiences some slight obtrusiveness from things! But it is very little, and only rarely. Nevertheless, I have always been glad to have a particular place to pray in, as much for avoiding distractions as because the movements of the mind prompt one sometimes to do things that one would not wish to be seen by anyone, such as throwing oneself on the ground, lying there at full length, and shedding many tears. For, although I may be very hardened in this, there having been more than ten years now in which I have not wept more than four times, regardless of what might happen to me, nevertheless, right from the moment God gave it[72] to me in prayer, I have always shed many tears in great abundance, often with great sighs, according to the affections with which the soul is filled. Thus one performs many other things that would [normally] trouble people if they were made known. So God, in his paternal Providence, has given me a place where I can perform my devotions privately and freely.

The body and prayer

Finally, when it is in its perfection, this prayer is not hindered by the infirmities of the body. I have often noticed that when my body was more emaciated and pining, it was then that my mind was more elevated in a loftier prayer; because prayer does not depend on the body nor on its organs, being infused by God immediately into the soul; not always, however, to the same degree. And although prayer ordinarily subdues the body and weakens it, however, sometimes it gives the body relief according to its needs. God manages thus the forces of its creature, in order to be able to bring his work to completion.

General conclusion

Submission to the Church

That is all I can say about it.[73] I would never have undertaken to make one stroke of the pen on this subject, nor on all that which is contained in this present writing, if it had not been so enjoined on me, because all this is infinitely beyond my capacity. And if there is anything contrary to the faith and the good and holy doctrine of the Church found in this writing, I disown it entirely, completely ready to disavow and to retract it, because, through the mercy of God, I am a daughter of the Church and hope to live and die therein. Amen.[74]

Nunc dimittis[75]

My God, this then is the completed word of your servant; you who indeed said to me that I would not die before this work was completed.[76] Bring likewise to a completion, then, if it pleases you, the desires of my heart: pull me out of this miserable world! It seems to me now that I have nothing more to do on the earth, having declared to him[77] your mercies to me, just as he has desired to know them. You know how much this desire to see you prods my heart incessantly, which causes me a martyrdom as continual as it is secret and unknown to everyone else but you. I am nevertheless entirely submitted to the dispositions of your adorable providence and united to the merits and blood of your Son, accepting the pain and length of my banishment for the complete satisfaction of my offences, so that, being wholly acquitted of them, nothing will hinder me or keep me back, at the hour of my death, from enjoying you and entering into an exercise of love and of praise that will no longer be interrupted, but will be perfect and will last for ever.[78]

'I have rendered my soul visible to your eyes'

It is now, my dear and Reverend Father, that I can truly say that I have put my heart into your hands and rendered my soul visible to your eyes, having satisfied the desire you had to know fully and in detail God's guidance of me throughout the course of my life. It is not that other things, too, do not happen in the soul, and many! But it seemed impossible to me to be able to describe them all.[79] These nevertheless are the principal ones.

These are sufficient, it seems to me, to let you know his plans for me. Your Reverence is the only person in the world who can help me fulfil them, everything else being, as far as I am concerned, as if it did not exist. Right from the first time our Lord sent me to that person,[80] and the second time when he himself brought me to him,[81] I deeply felt much fear in seeking from him the care and pain that were necessary to have with me, knowing well that I did not merit them. But in these perplexities of mind, an interior voice said to me: 'Look at yourself in the blood of Jesus Christ and you will see what you are worth!'[82] So, looking at myself therein, I said: 'Certainly I am well worth the cares and pains of someone, because the Son of God has preferred my soul to his blood and his own life!'[83] I throw myself, then, anew at your feet, beseeching you that, in this consideration, it may please you once again to take care of me.[84]

I have told you so many things, that I should not have much difficulty in saying one more to you. I always feel in my heart a certain desire for virtue and perfection,[85] which I renew every day. Our Lord has placed in your person so many advantageous things for me and powerful enough to make me arrive at virtue and perfection, that I have been sometimes astonished by the effects you bring about in my mind.

These writings are a good proof of this, for I do not know if there has been anything more difficult for me than that,[86] having no aptitude for it, and moreover having lost my memory for all things. I had no idea or representation of this work in my mind, not knowing how to go about writing. I have always worked in all of this blindly and gropingly, as one might say, not seeing before me or behind me; I mean, not having had a great and penetrating light that would reveal to me many things at once, as the light of day makes us see the quantity and variety of objects; but a ray of clarity that guided me little by little, and which helped me to reflect not on the things written, the recollection of which I immediately lost, but only on those things that were in my mind [at that moment], and which [beforehand] were to me myself unknown and hidden, as they are now, for all in the world as if they had not passed through my mind.

It is your word that makes a sweet and strong impression on my soul, without making me feel profoundly any pain because of it. It is true that I have had some little pain recently, because my feelings were not obedient enough. Nevertheless, your word never fails to have its effect. I beseech you, then, my Reverend Father, seeing that our Lord gives you so much power over me, to help me vigorously to correct myself of my faults and render myself faithful to his guidance.

Glory be to God, to our Lord
Jesus Christ,
to the Holy Virgin and to St Joseph.
Amen.

240

Notes

Introduction

1 In 1959, Father Jean Guennou, then the archivist of La Société des Missions Etrangères in Paris, wrote a book entitled *La Couturière mystique de Paris* (Paris: Editions du Cerf, 1959). In it he gives a detailed account of his research carried out on a manuscript dating from the end of the seventeenth century, entitled 'Notes spirituelles par une Demoiselle, datées du 17ᵉ siècle', in which he shows how the results of his research proved that this manuscript 1409 was the spiritual testimony of a young woman named Claudine Moine. Using well chosen, illustrative excerpts from the text, Guennou presents a portrait of Claudine Moine and her spiritual journey, preceded by a description of his historical research and followed by a brief synthesis of Claudine Moine's spirituality. Many reactions to this book, from all sides, were so positive (all attesting to the exceptional quality of this spiritual portrait, but all equally regretting the fact that the full text was not available to the public) that Guennou undertook the editing and publishing of the complete text. Among the positive reactions was the feeling that there was much yet to be said about this soul: discovery about her was only just beginning. For one thing was certain: Claudine was bringing us a message; see L.H. Parias, writing in *La France Catholique*, Paris, 22 January 1960. The same source will speak about Claudine being a mystic of the Eucharist. Another reviewer will say that what attracted him most about the mystical life of Claudine Moine, to which our contemporaries will be sensitive, is her total involvement in the life of manual labour (see Father Jean Perrin, writing in the *Bulletin de Société des Missions Etrangères de Paris*, Hong Kong, 1960, p. 218). Of course, the reference here is to the fact that Claudine earned her living by being a dressmaker, and that this was no hindrance to the summits of spiritual perfection she arrived at. But by far the longest and most profound study from among the critics interested in the text itself was undertaken by Jean Orcibal in *La Vie spirituelle* (Paris, May 1960), pp. 533-9. The scholarly director of the Ecole Supérieure des Hautes Etudes in Paris gives himself over to a detailed examination of possible sources for Claudine, concentrating particularly on an analysis of the images used in her writing.

But as yet these critics had only known the chosen excerpts! And indeed the exceptional quality of the text made some reviewers wonder about its complete authenticity. The simple reading of the entire text would be the better response to all the difficulties arising from the obvious perfect quality of some pages written by Claudine, which are particularly well written and of a deep quality, both spiritually and theologically. So, finally, in 1968, Guennou edited and published, with introduction and editorial notes, the entire French text of the writings of Claudine Moine, under the title *Ma Vie secrète* (Paris: Desclée et Cie, 1968). The same book was reprinted in 1982, under the new title *La Couturière mystique de Paris* (Paris: Téqui, 1982). In this, my Introduction to the first English translation of this text, I will incorporate a considerable amount of the material used by Guennou in his Introduction to the French edition, but will integrate it in a way that is suitable to an English-speaking audience and adaptable to my own translation. My Notes to this first English translation will also include Guennou's editorial notes to the French edition; but essentially my Notes constitute in themselves my own commentary on the text. Consequently, throughout the course of this Introduction, and in my Notes, there will be no direct reference to Guennou's work. For this I refer the reader to the respective works cited above. In short, the book introduced here, *You Looked at Me: the Spiritual Testimony of Claudine Moine*, is the English translation of Jean Guennou's edited French text, with Introduction and Notes by the translator as his own personal commentary.

2 Evagrius of Pontus (346-99), speaking about prayer, admirably sums up this two-fold quality, this happy combination of a theologian's ideas and a writer's skill, the blend of the visionary and the intellectual, when he claims that the theologian is the person who has seen God, for if he has not seen God, he cannot speak about him: cf. *Century 5:26*, in Patrologia Orientalis 28, ed. R. Graffin and F. Nau (Paris, 1903), pp. 186-7. Patrologia Orientalis is referred to subsequently in these Notes as PO. The same idea is expressed again by Evagrius in his treatise on prayer: 'If you are a theologian, you will truly pray, and if you pray, you are a theologian' (cf. *De Oratione, 60*, in Patrologia Graeca 79, ed. J.P. Migne (Paris, 1856-66), col. 1179; cited in Paul Evdokimov, *L'Orthodoxie* (Paris: Delachaux et Neistle, 1965), pp. 50-1). Patrologia Graeca is referred to subsequently in these Notes as PG. Also, cf. Irenée Hausherr, SJ, *Les leçons d'un contemplatif: Traité de l'Oraison d'Evagre le Pontique* (Paris: Beauchesne, 1960), p. 85. For not only do we have in Claudine's work a fascinating account of her own spiritual experience, but also a series of reflections on that experience. I quote these sayings of Evagrius as a way of introducing us early on to the exceptional spiritual and theological quality of the work translated in this book; for here is perhaps a suitable place to point out to the reader from the start its dual characteristic. Theology is comprised of a doctrinal element, the objective teaching of the Church, its Catechism; but more profoundly, in its sap, it listens to the saints and nourishes itself from their spiritual experience of the Word (cf. Evdokimov, pp. 49-50); and this is the theology of the mystery that can only be known and savoured through revelation and a real participation in the mystery of God. The author of these writings takes hold of the words of God from the inside, from her own experience, that is from the side of beauty more than from truth, relishing the intimate manifestations of God, thus indicating that the divine transcendence teaches us that you can only go to God by coming from him and finding yourself to be already in him. This explains the author's own words: 'with those eyes of infinite and extraordinary mercy, you looked at me', in describing her conversion, and is my reason for using them in the title to this book. In presenting this unknown text and unknown author to the English-speaking world, it will be a help, I hope, and not a hindrance to the reader to have some initial key to the understanding and greater appreciation of the work translated in this book, which undoubtedly merits a place in the great spiritual classics of the French Church.

3 Cf. Gregory of Nyssa, *La Vie de Moïse* (Sources Chrétiennes 1, ed. H. de Lubac and J. Daniélou, Paris, 1955), pp. 108-9. For *Life of Moses* by Gregory of Nyssa, see also *De Vita Moysis*, in PG 44, col. 327A-430D. All further references to this text will be taken from Sources Chrétiennes. The other works of Gregory of Nyssa referred to will be taken from PG.

4 Stemming as they do from an age when French mysticism was in full bloom, these writings of Claudine Moine can only reveal their splendour and their charm, their deep spiritual and theological value to anyone who reads them. In the twelve volumes of his *Histoire littéraire du sentiment religieux en France* (Paris: Bloud et Gay, 1926-32), Henri Bremond undertook to reconstruct for us the mystical face of France in the seventeenth century. His monumental work is a joy and an enchantment for many readers. The highest and most delicate, the most enlightened and affectionate souls are presented to us in this work. However, many spiritual people escaped the investigation of this indefatigable pioneer. He limited himself in his research to the printed material from that century, but did not venture into that rich, unexplored world of the manuscripts. So Claudine Moine does not appear on any page of Bremond's gigantic work on the literary history of religious sentiment in seventeenth-century France. He knew nothing about her.

5 The archives of the Missions Etrangères were classified, between 1884 and 1894, by Father Launay, a tireless worker who published more than fifty volumes on the history of the Missions. He was obviously too absorbed in his subject to attach much importance to a manuscript that was protected by cardboard covered in buckskin, upon which he put two labels, one of them carrying a

title: 'Notes spirituelles', the other carrying a number: 1409. It consisted of sixteen notebooks of sixteen pages each, held together by ribbons of green silk. The text is set out in paragraphs that are generally long, on account of the thirty lines or so per page. The writing, beautiful and regular, dates back to the last quarter of the seventeenth century. In the analysis catalogue arranged by the same archivist, this manuscript was given a more explicit title: 'Notes spirituelles par une Demoiselle, datées du 17e siècle'. It was sufficient to peruse through the first few pages of the manuscript to determine that the author was a young woman and that she was born in the seventeenth century.

6 Her writings evoke many warm memories of the Marais quarter of the city, the conditions of the existence she led there and the religious world of seventeenth-century France that centred around the Jesuits and their church of St Louis. Within a very small room, in this Marais section, this secret life was lived. Somewhere between the Place des Vosges and the church of St Louis, Claudine occupied a small room where she remained for a good part of her life in Paris, except for short periods when she took care of her benefactors' house, until she went to live with them permanently. Claudine worked as a dressmaker. She regarded herself as in exile in Paris, in a strange city, in a foreign land. Her sole contact, when she first arrived, was with the convent of the Annonciades célestes (see below, Note 12) which she continued to frequent right from the beginning of her time in Paris. This convent occupied then the place where the Lycée of Victor Hugo now stands, on the present-day Rue Sévigné. The Rue Sévigné leads into the Rue Saint Antoine at right angles, and directly opposite, on entering that street, is the baroque church of St Louis.

7 Father Guennou saw that the manuscript was from the end of the seventeenth century and that it belonged to the celebrated Abbé de Choisy. By itself, this did not bring Father Guennou very far, because the manuscript was only a copy that was unsigned and from which all proper and place names (except Paris, Dijon, Annonciade and Ursulines) were eliminated. But Father Guennou re-established almost all of them; and from his research he has been able to show that the manuscript consists of four separate written accounts addressed between 1654 and 1655 to her confessor, Father Castillon, SJ, by Claudine Moine, born in 1618 in Scey-sur-Saône, in Franche-Comté.

8 The war in question here was the Thirty Years War, which began in 1618. In 1635, France, in her turn, entered it. Uniting herself with Sweden and the Protestant state of Germany, she fought against the coalition of the Catholic states: Austria and Spain. Franche-Comté, then attached to the Spanish crown but historically part of France, was unable to avoid being involved in the conflict, despite the accords of neutrality it had concluded with the neighbouring provinces. So, the armies of the two camps confronted one another, starting in 1636. This war creates the setting for the historical background which occasioned the events that led up to Claudine Moine having to leave her homeland, Franche-Comté, and ending up in Paris as a refugee in exile. For a full account of the Thirty Years War, see C.V. Wedgwood, *The Thirty Years War*, first published in 1938. The references here are taken from the Jonathan Cape paperback edition (London, 1964).

9 Cf. C.V. Wedgwood, *The Thirty Years War*, Jonathan Cape paperback, p. 11.

10 Cf. ibid., p. 12.

11 For evidence that Vesoul is the city in question, see for greater details: Louis Monnier, *Histoire de la ville de Vesoul* (Vesoul, 1909); Abbès Coudriet de Châtelet, *Histoire de la Seigneurie de Jonville* (Besançon, 1864); *Histoire de Jussey* (Besançon, 1876). The author of these writings considered herself to be in exile in Paris; she had come there in 1642 to get away from the war in her own country, which had benefited previously from a status of neutrality. The Protestant reform was not tolerated in Franche-Comté, whereas in France the Edict of Nantes, signed by Henry IV in 1598, had restored religious peace. Also the city of Dijon is mentioned in the text itself in terms that make it clear that it was not the town in question. From this convergence of details, one recognises that the homeland of the author must be Franche-Comté, which had been given as a dowry by Mary of Burgundy at the time of her marriage to Maximillian I in 1477 to the house of Austria, and was later given back to Spain by Charles V in 1546. Conquered by Louis XIV in 1608, this province was definitively reattached to France in 1678.

12 Among the proper names mentioned in the text, Claudine refers at various stages to the convent of the Annonciades. She used to go there often, she says, to fill her bottle with water; and she states that the sisters at the door (*tourières*), seeing her distressful situation, would help her in whatever way they could. For the period which interests us here, it is important to know that there were four houses of this order of nuns in Paris: see *Dictionnaire historique et géographique ecclésiastique*, vol. 3 (Paris, 1924), col. 403-12. Three of these convents pertained to the order founded by St Jeanne de France (1465-1505) in 1500, subsequently affiliated to the order of the Franciscans in 1514. That it was not one of these three to which Claudine is referring here is clear from an episode she relates in the text. On the feast of St Antony of Padua, Claudine wished to be present at Mass in a convent of the Franciscan order, to which, of course, St Antony had belonged. She went to a chapel of religious sisters where the celebrant refused her Communion on the pretext that she was not known by the sisters in the convent there. Thus, the Annonciades whom Claudine frequented were not those of the Franciscans, for she would not have had to change from her usual habits if they had been. There remains, then, the fourth convent, that of the Annonciades célestes, known in France by the name of the *filles bleues*. Founded in Genoa, in 1602, by the blessed Victor Fornari, with the aid of a Jesuit, Father Bernardin Zénon, the Annonciades célestes remained in direct relationship with the Fathers of the Company of Jesus. They had established themselves in Paris in 1622, in a suburban residence. Four years later, the Marquise de Verneuil acquired for them a property in the middle of the Marais quarter of Paris, situated in the Rue Couture-Sainte-Catherine (today Rue Sévigné, named after Madame de Sévigné who lived in the area). The Rue Couture-Sainte-Catherine was the street that led to the fields which belonged to the convent of St Catherine. It would seem that this is the convent Claudine is referring to, and, as we shall see later, the one which played such an important role in her spiritual life. The act of acquisition of this property for the Annonciades mentions the fountain which was situated in the outside court, at a time when only thirteen fountains were to be found in all of Paris: see F. and L. Lazare, *Dictionnaire administratif et historique des rues et monuments de Paris* (Paris, 1855). As stated above, it was to this fountain that Claudine came to fetch water. All these facts fit in with Claudine's own account, and there are still other pieces of information which help to complete the picture that Claudine Moine is the person whose spiritual life these writings attest to. The Annonciades célestes had taken in as lodgers religious of their own order who had come as refugees from the war-stricken area of Franche-Comté. The Duke of Longueville, at the head of a contingent of the French army, took possession on 29 August 1638 of a town in Franche-Comté called Champlitte, and from there he evacuated twenty-four Annonciade sisters to a place in France called Humes, not far from Langres. The Bishop of Langres, Monseigneur Zamet, believing that he was not able to guarantee their security and the wherewithal to live, managed to get them to Paris, where these refugees from a country at war with France were housed very cordially in the house of their own order. In order to pay for their keep they devoted themselves to sewing and dressmaking, and the chapel collection was reserved to pay them for their work: see the manuscript from the archives of the Annonciade of Langres, 'Annales du premier monastère de l'Annonciade Céleste de Paris', vol. I, p. 30. It was to these Annonciades célestes of Champlitte, then, that Claudine alludes in her writings as sisters from their own country, when she speaks about herself and her sister looking for work.

13 The church today carries the name of St Paul St Louis, because the parish church of St Paul was destroyed in 1792. See E. de Menorval, *Les Jésuites de la Rue Saint Antoine, l'église Saint-Paul-Saint-Louis et le Lycée Charlemagne* (Paris, 1892); L. Plond, *La Maison professe des Jésuites de la Rue Saint Antoine* (Paris, 1956). The church of St Louis stands on the side of Rue Saint Antoine, which, in the sixteenth century, was at the heart of Parisian life. Cardinal Charles de Bourbon, the uncle of the future Henry IV, was very favourable to the Jesuits, only recently founded. They wanted to found in Paris a *maison professe* (that is, a house for those who had already pronounced their vows), and he bought for them in 1580 a house in Rue Saint Antoine. It was in fact a very large establishment that he gave to the Jesuits, on the express condition that they would build a church or a chapel there in honour of his ancestor St Louis, whose name no church in Paris carried. After a few abortive attempts

to build a church, and their expulsion from Paris in 1595, the Jesuits were eventually reinstated in the same place in 1606; and from 1618 to 1629, with the help of the King, they acquired many houses in the area for the construction of a church. In 1626, Louis XIII himself, in great solemnity, laid the first stone. Work progressed rapidly, and in 1629 Cardinal Richelieu (1585-1642), who was interested personally in the whole affair, demolished at his own expense houses that were blocking the way to this edifice so that the great façade could be built. The Cardinal himself laid the first stone of the façade in 1634. The church was finished, and on Ascension Day 1641, Richelieu celebrated the first Mass there in the presence of the King, the Court and fifteen or so bishops. Thanks to Claudine's writings, we have precise information concerning the spirituality which was prevalent in the middle of the seventeenth century in the house of profession of the Jesuits and the church of St Louis.

14 Father Alexandre Jarry (1586-1645).

15 See D. de Hansy, *Notice historique sur la paroisse royale Saint-Paul-Saint-Louis* (Paris, 1842), pp. 50ff; V. Dufour, *Le Charnier de l'ancien cimetière Saint Paul* (Paris, 1866), pp. 30-41; F. de Guilhermy, *Inscriptions de la France du 5ᵉ au 18ᵉ Siècle*, vol. I (Paris, 1873), pp. 519ff.

16 1588-1648.

17 See Wedgwood, *The Thirty Years War*, p. 17.

18 See ibid., pp. 17-19.

19 See ibid., p. 19.

20 On the question of the religious and intellectual crisis of the seventeenth century, see Hugh R. Trevor-Roper, *The Crisis of the Seventeenth Century: Religion, the Reformation and Social Change* (New York: Harper & Row, 1968), pp. 1, 34-50. He says that early in the seventeenth century there is a deep crisis which affects most of Europe; and that the years 1620-60 mark the great distorting gap in the otherwise orderly advance and could be described, in short, as the period of revolution (ibid., p.1). According to Trevor-Roper it was a revolution of the laity against an overclericalised Roman Church: a revolution which gave rise in the Roman Church to a reaction in the way of a Counter-Reformation; and this, it seems to Trevor-Roper, succeeded in creating what he refers to as a Counter-Reformation state with the priests as the ruling class (ibid., pp. 34-40). However true this thesis may be (and indeed it could be argued against), we can at least agree with Trevor-Roper that the middle of the seventeenth century, the time when Claudine was writing, saw an irreparable break with the past; and that, intellectually, politically, morally, we are in a new age, a new climate. In short, the crisis of the mid-seventeenth century - in the way of summing up Trevor-Roper's analysis of this period in Western history - happened to bring about the break down of the medieval synthesis which both Reformation and Counter-Reformation had artificially prolonged (cf. Hugh R. Trevor-Roper, *The European Witch-Craze of the 16th and 17th centuries*, Pelican Books, 1969; reissued in Peregrine, 1978, pp. 108-117). Whether one agrees or disagrees with Trevor-Roper's understanding of the crisis, we have got to say that Claudine's writings are bound to manifest, intellectually and spiritually, many of the theological aspects of this crisis. An example of this is seen later on in her treatment of Jansenism.

21 See O. Lefèvre d'Ormesson, *Journal*, vol. I (Paris, 1860), p. 373.

22 See above, Note 13.

23 See above, Note 13. The following is what Wedgwood says about the importance of the Jesuits in the Counter-Reformation: 'Only with the foundation of the Society of Jesus in 1543 did the Counter-Reformation truly begin. It was in a sense the last of the military orders and the greatest; in its ultimate development a hierarchy of highly trained men bound by an oath of unquestioning obedience to their superiors and controlled by the General, its organization was essentially that of an army. When the Catholic Church arose at length from the Council of Trent armed for conflict, it had a fighting force in the Jesuits who were prepared to carry the faith by any means and at any personal cost into any land of the globe. Under their influence the Inquisition, native in Spain, had been re-established at Rome as the effective instrument for the discovery and extirpation of heresy.' (ibid., p. 21). We must not forget that Claudine's confessors were all Jesuits; and it is only natural that much of the Jesuits' spirituality would have influenced her.

24 Cornelius Jansen (1585-1638), Bishop of Ypres, was father of the religious revival known as Jansenism, the religious principles of which he laid down in his work, *Augustinus*. This was simply a summary of the teaching of St Augustine; Jansen wrote this book with a special eye to the needs of the seventeenth century. It became a controversial text, and it inevitably brought Jansen into conflict with the Jesuits.

25 One of the interesting features of Claudine's text is that it grew out of the historical background of seventeenth-century French theological controversy, a characteristic which makes Claudine's writings important as a theological source as well as a spiritual source. For one will notice that Claudine had as a director of conscience Father de Sesmaisons, author of 'Question s'il est meilleur de communier souvent que rarement'. This text has been conserved by Arnauld in his treatise entitled *De la fréquente communion*, in which Arnauld refutes the thesis of de Sesmaisons that it is better to receive Communion often. Now, Father de Sesmaisons directed Claudine from 1645 to 1648, during which years he was the direct target of Antoine Arnauld on the question of frequent communion. With regard to Father Castillon, the addressee of Claudine's writings, he has left us two works on the Eucharist: *Desseins de Jésus-Christ dans l'institution de S. Sacrement de l'Autel*, Paris, 1669; *Les Merveilles de l'amour de Jésus-Christ dans le Saint Sacrement de l'Autel*, Paris, 1669. Accordingly, this goes to explain the unexpected mention of this controversy in Claudine's text and her very judicious treatment of it.

26 See Corneille, *Poleucte*, Act I, scene I, line 45.

27 See Jean Guennou, *La Couturière mystique de Paris* (Paris: Les Editions du Cerf, 1959), XXIV, pp. 64-6.

28 See Clement of Alexandria, *The Stromata*, Book I, chap. I, in *The Ante-Nicene Fathers*, American reprint of the Edinburgh Edition (Grand Rapids/Michigan: Wm B. Eerdmans Company, 1983), vol. 2, p. 299.

29 See *The Life of St. Teresa of Avila*, translated by E. Allison Peers (London: Sheed & Ward, 1944 and 1979, reprint 1984), p.9.

30 See St Teresa of Avila, *Interior Castle*, translated and edited by E. Allison Peers (New York: Image Books edition, 1961), p.22.

31 ibid., p. 235.

32 This comes from the Latin verb *transverberare* (to pierce through), and it is normally used to indicate the 'wound of love' in the mystic's loving union with God: cf. *The Life of St. Teresa*, p. 191.

33 *Le Cid*, written in 1636, probably very rapidly, was presented for the first time at an unknown date (November or December 1636, or January 1637), in the Théâtre Marais.

34 See St François de Sales, *Oeuvres* (Paris: Bibliothèque de la Pléiade, Editions Gallimard, 1969), p. 24.

35 See 'De la Retraite spirituelle', *Introduction à la vie dévote*, chap. XII, ibid., pp. 96-8.

36 This is the great name that dominated the mystical scene current in the Company of Jesus in France of that time: see Louis Cognet, 'La Spiritualité moderne: I. L'Essor, 1500-1650', *Histoire de la Spiritualité Chrétienne* (Paris: Editions Aubier-Montaigne, 1966), vol. 3, p. 425. The central period of his influence would have been between autumn of 1628 and autumn of 1631 when, at Rouen, he was instructor of the third year, or tertiary, as it is called, for the Jesuits. During that time he had among his disciples great names of the company who became famous later, and among whom Castillon must have featured: see J. Jimenez, 'Précisions biographiques sur le P. L.L.', *Archivum Historicum Societatis Jesu*, XXXIII (1964), pp. 318-20. Lallement was not a writer. We only possess documents on the instruction he gave at Rouen to the Jesuit fathers of this third year. The greater part of these documents are collected in a volume entitled *Doctrine spirituelle*, published in Paris in 1694 by Father Pierre Champion (1633-1701): see *Doctrine spirituelle*, edited by A. Pottier (Paris, 1936); and *Doctrine spirituelle*, edited by F. Courel (Paris, 1959). It is from this second edition I quote here. The contents of *Doctrine spirituelle* are made up for the most part of notes taken during the conferences of Lallement at Rouen by his disciple, Jean Rigoleuc (1595-1658), and came into the hands of Pierre

Notes

Champion through the agency of a friend of Rigoleuc, Father Vincent Huby (1608-93), who had been the inheritor of his papers (see Louis Cognet, p. 426). This does not resolve in any way the question of the sources of Claudine Moine; but, on the basis that Castillon had been a disciple of Lallement and the spiritual director and confessor of Claudine, it is more than acceptable to believe that the spirituality of Lallement furnished at least its essential indications. Lallement regarded the third year ordinarily as a time of second conversion in which one renounces once and for all one's own interests and satisfactions, and which he describes as 'taking a leap' (see *Doctrine spirituelle*, p. 90). It would be profitable to see how this notion influenced the life of Claudine. Secondly, although a Jesuit and therefore given to a more activist and humanist approach to spirituality, Lallement was also in the line of the greater part of French spiritual people of the seventeenth century who were influenced strongly by the Flemish-Rhineland mystics with their strong emphasis on renunciation of everything. But Lallement gave his own personal nuance to this. Again it would be profitable to see how Claudine's spirituality was an expression of this Nordic influence with its emphasis on the apophatic (*via negativa*) while maintaining the Christocentric balance in her thinking. This, however, may also account for Jean Orcibal's belief that it is to the Rhineland mystics that we owe most of the images used by Claudine Moine in her writings, and above all with regard to the Eucharist: see Orcibal, *La Vie spirituelle*, p. 537.

37 For a treatment of the abstract school of spirituality, see Louis Cognet, pp. 233-73. Essentially this spirituality was a voluntary extinction of every notional activity in order to attain to the divine essence directly, bypassing every created intermediary, even the humanity of Christ.

38 An exact contemporary of Lallement, Jean-Baptiste de St Jure (1588-1657) comes closer to having a more direct influence on the writings of Claudine Moine. He would have known Lallement at La Flèche in 1616 and 1617. It was only in 1634 that he began his career as a writer with the publication of his celebrated and voluminous work: *De la connaissance et de l'amour du Fils de Dieu, Notre Seigneur Jesus-Christ*. He had a great knowledge of the northern mystics, something which is astonishing for a person who was immersed in the profane writers and the historians of antiquity. The examples of the great mystics held his whole attention, and he cited them often, in particular St Catherine of Genoa and Angela of Foligno. But what makes him particularly useful in the present context is that he also showed an interest in the mystics of his own day who were still alive. A case in point was the Baron of Renty, whose spiritual director he became and whose life he wrote and published in 1651, after the Baron's death in 1649. In that work he used and inserted a number of very fine letters of his penitent (cf. Cognet, pp. 446-7). De Saint-Jure used this material in a wonderful way, integrating it into his own work so as to create a spiritual work of the highest order. This is what interests us here; for it is quite possible that he used some information about Claudine Moine in his book *L'Homme spirituel* - the one which we shall consider presently as a possible source for Claudine's own writings - and which is considered to be his great work, and the most characteristic of his spirituality. In it we see that both the Ignatian and Flemish-Rhineland sources are more apparent than in his *De la connaissance et de l'amour* and possibly explains the striking parallels between it and the writings of Claudine Moine. The work of de Saint-Jure certainly presents a certain parallelism with that of Lallement; however, it is clearly distinct from his and does not depend on it. Both works stand alone, and are characteristic of a wider current that embraces them both at the interior of the Company of Jesus: that of a mystical tradition of an Ignatian inspiration, but in which we also experience the confluence of Nordic elements (cf. Cognet, p. 452).

39 Cf. de Saint-Jure, *L'Homme spirituel*, 1646 edition, p. 123.

40 Cf. ibid., p. 317.

41 Cf. ibid., p. 160.

42 Cf. ibid., p. 91.

43 Cf. ibid., pp. 73-4, 81, 86-8, 91.

44 Cf. ibid., pp. 92, 129.

45 ibid., p. 144.

46 See text, p. 147.

47 See de Saint-Jure, *L'Homme spirituel*, p. 201.

48 See text, p. 181. Apart from *L'Homme spirituel*, Claudine could have read other treatises by the same author. In *Le Livre des Eluz, Jésus Christ en Croix* (Paris, 1643), she could easily have found the image of the Cross becoming the nuptial bed of the mystical marriage. Other works of de Saint-Jure, such as *Les trois filles de Job* (Paris, 1646), the *Méditations sur les plus grandes et les plus importantes vérités de la Foy* (Paris, 1643), the *Maître Jésus Christ enseignant les hommes* (Paris, 1649) contain some expressions which one finds also under the pen of Claudine; but generally the resemblance is insufficient to establish a definitive influence.

49 1447-1510. She is generally known by her works, *Purgation and Purgatory, The Spiritual Dialogue* and also by her *Life*. The quotations and references that follow are from the 1627 edition of *La Vie et les oeuvres spirituelles de Sainte Catherine Adorny de Gennes*. It was only in 1551, more than forty years after the death of the Saint, that there appeared in Genoa, *Libro de la vita mirabile e dottrina santa de la beata Catarinetta da Genoa* (the only known copy of this edition belongs to the Capuchins of Genoa); a second edition, slightly touched up, appeared in Florence in 1568. In 1597 the above French translation appeared, published by the Carthusians of Bourg-Fontaine. This translation was often re-edited. A point to mention here, which is significant when compared with Claudine's writings, is that Catherine wrote none of her own works: they were written for her by those who knew her very well and were fully aware of her spiritual experience. We know that this work, *Libro de vita mirabile e dottrina santa*, giving an account of the Saint's words, had been put together by her disciples, among whom a priest, named Cattaneo Marabotto, was principally responsible. Editor, as it were, of the *Life* and the *Treatise on Purgatory* that followed it, Marabotto uses the everyday language, whose simplicity comes across as even more accentuated by the French translators. Writing in the same style that is removed from all pretension, Claudine would naturally use the same terms to describe the facts of the same spiritual experience. However, as will be made more clear later on, one cannot avoid thinking that Claudine is impregnated with Catherine's work, to the point of using unconsciously expressions which appear to be reminiscences from her readings. On the life and doctrine of Catherine, one must consider the following work of F. von Hügel as of capital importance: *The Mystical Element of Religion as Studied in Saint Catherine of Genoa and her Friends*, London, 1909, two volumes. Also, for a most recent English translation of her works, see *Catherine of Genoa: Purgation and Purgatory, The Spiritual Dialogue*, translation and notes by Serge Hughes, introduction by Benedict J. Groeschel, OFM, CAP, in The Classics of Western Spirituality (New York: Paulist Press, 1979).

50 Orcibal also sees many similarities between Catherine and Claudine: see Orcibal, *La Vie spirituelle*, p. 534. Even the use of the word 'Purgatory' in Claudine's text recalls the celebrated work where Catherine of Genoa describes the incomparable contentment which accompanies the extreme pains of the souls who are plunged there without taking from them any touch of pain. Very rare, of course, is the Eucharistic character of the spirituality of Claudine. But even here there is some contact with Catherine of Genoa: see, for example, *La Vie*, chaps. 3 and 47. According to Orcibal, in many cases Catherine of Genoa (see *La Vie*, chaps. 22 and 35) was able to serve as intermediary and has certainly inspired Claudine (see *La Vie*, chap. 31) with an understanding of the infused 'little souvenir' which permitted the emptied soul to rise out of the abstraction (see above, Note 37). In other words, Claudine's apophatic tendencies (see above, Note 36) were only transitory: she did not remain in the abstract school of spirituality. And she also owes to Catherine (see *La Vie*, chaps. 3 and 22) that fruitful union produced by the Eucharist, a union that renders faith superfluous.

51 See *La Vie*, chap. XXII, p. 153.

52 See text, p. 213.

53 See above, Note 28.

54 See Gregory of Nyssa, *La Vie de Moïse*, Sources Chrétiennes 1, pp. 108-9.

55 See above, Note 2.

Notes

56 See Jean Daniélou, *Platonisme et Théologie Mystique: Doctrine Spirituelle de Saint Grégoire de Nysse* (Paris: Aubier/Editions Montaigne, 1944). I shall refer copiously to this book throughout the course of my Notes and commentary on Claudine's text. This remarkable work by Daniélou provides us not only with a very comprehensive analysis of the works of Gregory of Nyssa, but also with an astonishing key to the understanding of Christian spirituality. Accordingly, we have an in-depth study of the classical three ways of spiritual perfection as Daniélou sees them portrayed in the writings of Gregory of Nyssa. Particularly helpful is the fundamental role of baptism in every spiritual awakening; and it is this emphasis by Gregory of Nyssa which makes us sensitive to the extraordinary quality of Claudine's text, beginning even with her opening words: 'I was born, or baptised in any case'. In unravelling the great traits of the spiritual doctrine of Gregory of Nyssa, Daniélou points out that it centres around the mystery of death and resurrection with Christ. The whole spiritual life is thus conceived as a prolongation of baptism, following through with a stripping of the old man according to the culpable passions right up to the passive purifications of the mystical life, and at the same time putting on Christ and being transformed into him (see Daniélou, *Platonisme*, p. 309). Consequently, Daniélou's book has helped me to appreciate the two revelatory aspects of Claudine's text: first, the authenticity of her spiritual experience; and secondly, her extraordinary ability to put it into words. It is this dual characteristic of seeing and bearing testimony (see text, p. 13) which characterises the exceptional quality of Claudine's text both spiritually and theologically. In a sense, and as I shall explain later, spiritually she becomes her own parent and her own theologian.

57 Cf. Daniélou, *Platonisme*, pp. 48-60, 85, 210-22.

58 We know how ancient Christianity and pagan antiquity were at one in their classifications of the different stages of spiritual ascent. Origen, in his Commentary on the Song of Songs, deserves our attention in this regard for the influence he had on Gregory of Nyssa and on subsequent spirituality. For Origen, philosophy comprised three stages - ethics, physics and theory (contemplation): the first is perfect purity and charity through the observance of the commandments; the second is the good use of all things through means of a religious consideration of the world and the persuasion of the vanity of the visible world; and the third has for its object the contemplation of the divine (cf. Andrew Louth, *The Origins of the Christian Mystical Tradition*, p. 58). Origen relates these three ways to the three books of Solomon, Proverbs, Ecclesiastes and the Song of Songs (see Origen, *The Prologue to the Commentary of The Song of Songs*, translation and introduction by Rowan A. Greer, The Classics of Western Spirituality (New York: Paulist Press, 1979), p. 232). Gregory of Nyssa takes Origen's division of the three books of Solomon according to the three stages of the spiritual life: Proverbs is infancy; Ecclesiastes is youth; the Song of Songs is maturity. The first consists above all in showing the price of spiritual goods in order to excite desire for them; the second in order to see the vanity of the world; and the third, when the soul is purified of every attachment to the perceptible, introduces the soul into the divine sanctuaries where a union takes place between the human soul and the divinity. The three stages of spiritual experience outlined in this description of the three ways are not necessarily the best and only way of understanding the spiritual experience of Claudine Moine, because every spiritual experience is very individual and personal and easily transcends analysis of this kind; but the long tradition behind such a description of the spiritual life does help to throw some light on the notion of spiritual progress and the virtuous life that is found in most Christian experiences of God. So Claudine is no exception in this. I can say the same with regard to the notions of *apatheia*, *parresia* and *epectasis* which I use as analytical tools later on in my commentary on Claudine's text.

59 Cf. Orcibal, *La Vie spirituelle*, pp. 537-8.

60 An intellectual awakening is not sufficient: one needs grace in order to know God. To know God means that God gives himself to us; the intellectual awakening makes one the recipient of grace, ready for grace. 'You looked at me' is grace; and this grace leads to vision: in the ultimate analysis, it is a question of the rationality of love. In knowing God we are not assenting to a proposition, but accepting a person: cf. Andrew Louth, *The Origins of the Christian Mystical Tradition: From Plato to Denys* (Oxford: Clarendon Press, 1981), p. 1. It denotes her real experience of God in contrast to the more

intellectual awakenings of other forms of spirituality: 'How beautiful are you, my Beloved,/ and how delightful!/ Your eyes are doves' (S. of S. 1:15).

61 Cf. text, pp. 31-3.

62 Cf. above, Note 28.

63 Cf. Gregory of Nyssa, *La Vie de Moïse*, Sources Chrétiennes 1, p. 327.

64 Cf. ibid., p. 103; Deut. 34:6-7.

65 Gregory of Nyssa uses this passage from St Paul, with particular emphasis on the Greek verb ἐπέκτείνω (to strive ahead), to show the meaning of spiritual progress; hence the word *epectasis*. For a full treatment of this, see Daniélou, *Platonisme*, pp. 291-307.

66 Cf. *The Cloud of Unknowing and Other Works*, translated by Clifton Wolters (London: Penguin Classics, 1961), p. 66. Here the cloud of forgetting is discussed as the only way forward in contemplation, the point being that we must forget the past, burying it under a cloud of forgetting.

67 See the simile of the cave in Plato's *Republic*, Book 7, 515C, for this notion of a complete about turn as the only authentic conversion.

68 Christ referred to himself as the way, the truth and the life: cf. John 14:4-6.

69 See Gregory of Nyssa, *La Vie de Moïse*, Sources Chrétiennes 1, p. 327.

70 Cf. Andrew Louth, *The Origins of the Christian Mystical Tradition*, p. 84. These two concepts (*apatheia* and *parresia*) will be dealt with in greater detail in my commentary on Claudine's text. For a full treatment of these two concepts, see Daniélou, *Platonisme*, pp. 92-115.

71 Again, this is an illustration of the three ways; and they seem to have some real correspondence to the normal progress in the spiritual life.

72 See Gerard Manley Hopkins's poem, 'That Nature is a Heraclitean Fire and of the Comfort of the Resurrection' (*Poems and Prose of Gerard Manley Hopkins*, selected with an introduction and notes by W.H. Gardner, Penguin Books, 1953, 1963, p.66). According to Heraclitus, the Greek philosopher (c. 540-c. 480 BC), the most important thing for man was the understanding of the *logos* (Word), the universal formula of things in accordance with which all natural events occur and which all men should be able to assimilate, an important manifestation of which was the underlying connection of opposites. It is the *logos* that gives order and meaning to all things, through which we apprehend the formal unity of the world; and at the heart of this world order is an ever-living fire. Being all at once what Christ is, the *logos*, or Word made flesh, we not only know God but experience the very fire of his love. All this comes about through the resurrection of Christ.

73 See Gregory of Nyssa, *De Beatitudinibus* (On the Beatitudes), PG 44, col. 1272C; also Daniélou, *Platonisme*, p. 98.

74 Throughout her text, Claudine constantly uses the French verb *anéantir* (to annihilate). It is used with a very definite reference to a movement in French spirituality known as *anéantissement* (annihilation), which in fact points to a spiritual state equivalent to the *kenosis*, or emptying of Christ referred to in Phil. 2:6-7. So, this state of emptying oneself as Christ did is what Claudine has in mind when she uses the verb *anéantir*. This does present problems with its translation into English.

75 Cf. Gregory of Nyssa, *In Cantica Canticorum* (On the Song of Songs), PG 44, col. 1096B; also Daniélou, *Platonisme*, p. 98.

76 See Gregory of Nyssa, *In Cantica Canticorum* (On the Song of Songs), PG 44, col. 824C; also Daniélou, *Platonisme*, p. 99.

77 See Gregory of Nyssa, *In Cantica Canticorum* (On the Song of Songs), PG 44, col. 824B-C; also Daniélou, *Platonisme*, p. 100.

78 Among the favours which formed part of the patrimony of the first Adam, and which the grace of Christ restored to man, one must give a very special place to this reality which Gregory of Nyssa calls in Greek the *parresia*. It is a difficult word to translate into English. We know that it was the term through which, in classical Greek, was designated the freedom to speak at the assembly of the people, a freedom that was the privilege of the free citizen as opposed to the slave. In Christian language it refers to the confidence that man has in his relationships with God resulting from his capacity as a son

Notes

of God. Thanks to it, in effect, man can speak to God with a certain equality - and not as a slave addresses his master: cf. Daniélou, *Platonisme*, pp. 103-4.

79 The *parresia* is the crowning, the blossoming of the *apatheia*. The soul, purified by the *apatheia*, discovers the liberty of its relationships with God; it dares again to present itself before him, it enters into his familiarity. The appearance of the *parresia* marks thus the end of the Purgative Way, the restoration of the soul into the Paradise of divine friendship: cf. Daniélou, *Platonisme*, p. 104.

80 Cf. ibid., p. 104.

81 Cf. ibid., p. 105.

82 Cf. Gregory of Nyssa, *La Vie de Moïse*, Sources Chrétiennes 1, p. 103.

83 See Origen, *An Exhortation to Martyrdom*, translation and introduction by Rowan A. Greer, The Classics of Western Spirituality (New York: Paulist Press, 1979), p. 43.

84 See Philo, *On Abraham*, XIV, 62, translated by F.H. Colson, Loeb Classical Library (Cambridge, Massachusetts: Harvard University Press, 1935), p. 35.

85 See John Moschus, *Le Pré Spirituel*, introduction and translation by M.-J. Rouet de Journel, SJ, Sources Chrétiennes 12, p. 55.

86 See St Athanasius, *Life of Antony*, in The Nicene and Post-Nicene Fathers (Grand Rapids/ Michigan: Wm B. Eerdmans Company, reprinted 1980), vol. 4, p. 195. For a more recent English translation, cf. *The Life of Antony*, translation and introduction by Robert C. Gregg, in *Athanasius: The Life of Antony and the Letter to Marcellinus*, The Classics of Western Spirituality (New York: Paulist Press, 1980), p. 30.

87 See Evelyn Underhill, *The Essentials of Mysticism* (London: J.M. Dent & Sons Ltd, 1920; New York: AMS Press Inc., 1976), p. 132 (1976 edition).

88 Ibid. p. 43, Note 31.

89 See Pascal, *Pensées*, fragment 277 (New York: Dutton paperback, introduction by T.S. Eliot, 1958), p. 78.

Autobiography

1 Father Castillon.

2 These opening words evoke in us something of the author's own intuition and convey to us from the start that she witnessed a new birth in herself. There is an historical and simple explanation for them. In the seventeenth century of Claudine Moine only the baptismal registers existed as a certification of birth; and often, but not always, children were baptised on the day they were born. As Claudine goes on to indicate, she was sure of 17 January 1618; but knowing that the date of her baptism did not correspond necessarily to that of her natural birth, she points out in these words that she was uncertain whether this date was the day of her natural birth or the day of her baptism, or both.

This uncertainty is to be taken less for its historical veracity than for its spiritual significance and how it relates to the text translated in this book. As an example of her perspicacity, the antithetical opposition she sets up in these words between 'born' and 'baptised' attests to the acute mental vision she had of entering into the spiritual life. Consequently, it is not her natural birth she is going to write about here; with these words she is announcing the first of four accounts, or spiritual reflections, which will tell the story of her soul's rebirth. So I regard them as containing in embryo the spiritual and theological characteristics of this text.

In my understanding of this text, I have been helped enormously by my own studies of the spiritual literature of seventeenth-century France, but I have also drawn on the scriptural and patristic heritage of the Church to aid me in analysing more accurately its many spiritual features and historical significance. Among its features, first I would like to bring to the reader's notice that the reference to baptism at the beginning of this text is more than a mere coincidence; its mystical significance permeates every line of this spiritual testimony. Secondly, we shall see that Claudine's testimony springs as a direct result of this initial grace of baptism, bringing us through the traditional ways of spiritual progress: the breaking off with vice and error (Purgative Way); the purgation of the spiritual senses in the Great Darkness (Illuminative Way); and finally unity with God through love (Unitive Way). Here the works of Gregory of Nyssa have inspired me a great deal in my treatment of Claudine's text. I shall quote periodically from Daniélou's excellent study on these works: Jean Daniélou, *Platonisme et Théologie Mystique* (Paris: Aubier/Editions Montaigne, 1944). Finally, a third feature of this text is its two-fold characteristic - a unique blend of spiritual vision and theological understanding. For - as the opening words obliquely suggest - Claudine will be treating us to a continuous theological reflection on her previous life in the light of her present knowledge, her rebirth. I say 'theological' in St John's sense of bearing testimony to what she has seen (1 John 1:2). The recollection of the past will not be an historical description of the past, but its spiritual memorial in the light of the present reality of self-knowledge - Claudine awakes spiritually to the truth that her real birth is in baptism.

3 Cf. Ps. 44:20-1 - 'Had we forgotten the name of our God / and stretched out our hands to a foreign one, / would not God have found this out, / he who knows the secrets of the heart.' This translation is taken from the Jerusalem Bible; as are most biblical quotations in these Notes.

4 Cf. Ps. 123:2 - 'Like the eyes of a slave girl / fixed on the hand of her mistress, / so our eyes are fixed on Yahweh our God / for him to take pity on us.' Also, cf. Ps. 25:16 - 'Turn to me, take pity on me, / alone and wretched as I am.' As these psalms testify, in her desire for God to look at her in pity and to have mercy on her, Claudine is echoing and witnessing to that spiritual awakening which is found in every genuine religious experience. In this prayer or supplication of Claudine resides much of the spiritual and theological significance of her thinking. It is the weak and human eye turning towards the hidden truth: see Werner Jaeger, *The Theology of the Early Greek Philosophers* (Oxford University Press, 1960), p. 96. We shall see indeed later on that this is the language she will use to describe her conversion: 'you looked at me'. She is in fact, in this prayer, reflecting the classical language of seventeenth-century France: 'Dieu regarde en pitié son peuple malhereux' (Racine, *Esther*, Act III, Scene 4).

5 See above, Note 4. The stark realisation that the beginning of her life would have been smitten with irredeemable wounds if it were not for the fact that God had pity on her is typical of that spiritual awakening that prepares the soul for the gratuitous gift of his grace - a spiritual awareness of the horrors of one's life without God. This is the first fruit of the grace of baptism. But I would like to point out that this effect of baptism must be seen as the result of one's spiritual rebirth, which is to be understood as a free choice to follow Christ. Hence, the spiritual life can be seen as a constant renewal of baptism. And Claudine's moment of conversion was when she became aware of that truth in herself; and, constantly aware of this as she writes, we see her here reflecting on that moment before she even reaches it in her narrative: see below (Note 22), 'you looked at me'. This is the whole purpose of her writing; and the main feature characterising the entire text.

6 It was probably in January 1630.

7 The reference here is to 'goodness' and 'virtue' of the previous sentence.

8 From January 1630 to July 1632.

9 Towards January 1631.

10 From about July to October 1632.

11 Claudine probably had recourse to an intermediary, perhaps to an aunt; and her father's answer was transmitted to her in the same way.

12 The meaning here, of course, is that if she was not allowed to go back to the convent she was at least going to continue a form of religious life at home, wearing the simplest of clothes.

13 This is a difficult sentence to translate into English without succumbing to the temptation of injecting my own interpretation into the French. So the reader will have to appreciate the irony in the statement. She means, it would seem, that she only needed to look elsewhere for some more companionship, in addition to that of her father's, in order to topple the delicate balance of her

spiritual life and thereby fall back into the world; which she explains, really, in the following sentence.

14 Reference to the time she spent at the convent in Langres.

15 From 1632 to 1639.

16 May 19 1635. The war mentioned here is the Thirty Years War. See the Introduction for a fuller treatment of this.

17 Franche-Comté had concluded an agreement of neutrality with the neighbouring provinces. See the references in A. Garnier, 'Les misères de la ville de Langres et de la campagne langroise: 1610-40', *Les Cahiers Haut-Marnais* (Chaumont, 1948), p. 109, n. 22.

18 7 May 1636.

19 There is a blank in the text here. This identification, which is only probable, rests on the circumstances of her return journey. Dole was too far.

20 In 1639.

21 It is probably a question here only of those who were travelling.

22 In answer to her prayer, 'Look at me, my God, in pity, and have mercy on me' (see above, Note 5), we see Claudine here at the threshold of the first signs of spiritual birth, conversion. For when the weak, human eye turns towards the hidden truth, life itself becomes transfigured. Ps. 130:5-6 reads: 'I wait for Yahweh, my soul waits for him, / I rely on his promise, / my soul relies on the Lord / more than a watchman on the coming of dawn.' Claudine is experiencing here her first spiritual awakening to the contemplation of the divine mysteries with the eye of the soul (cf. Daniélou, *Platonisme*, p. 37). Remember that she had made a general confession a few days previously. And as all manuals of spirituality will say, no one should dare undertake becoming a contemplative before they have cleansed their conscience of all past sins, according to the ordinary rules of the Church (cf. *The Cloud of Unknowing*, translation by Clifton Wolters, London: Penguin Classics, 1961, p. 95). Accordingly, her deep desire for God to look at her and take pity on her is rewarded with the purification of the soul's eye which makes it possible for her to see God. This spiritual awakening, foreshadowed in Claudine's opening words - 'I was born, or baptised in any case', is for Claudine the first real step in contemplation.

23 Cf. Matt. 4:6, citing Ps. 91:11-12 - 'He will put you in his angels' charge, / and they will support you on their hands / in case you hurt your foot against a stone.' The same idea is expressed in Ps. 121:3-4, where the psalmist is speaking about the guardian of Israel: 'No letting our footsteps slip! / This guard of yours, he does not doze! / The guardian of Israel / does not doze or sleep.' So the spiritual awakening in Claudine is not a mere intellectual awakening to a knowledge that holds on to God, but rather to a knowledge that is upheld by God: it is not an awakening that is merely intellectual - a platonic intellectualism, but one that is thoroughly rooted in the biblical and Christian experience of God. God is not an idea; God is a person, and like the guardian of Israel, he is always awake taking care of her. It is in furthering this distinction throughout the course of this commentary that I hope to present the authentic Christian quality of Claudine Moine's spirituality. She could truly make her own the following words from S. of S. 5:2, 'I sleep, but my heart is awake. / I hear my Beloved knocking.'

24 Cf. Luke 23:46, citing Ps. 30:6 - 'Father, into your hands I commit my spirit.' This text is used for Compline (night prayer) in the office of the Church. A rather strange and amusing coincidence! Was Claudine speaking to the soldier or to God? Typical of her spiritual consciousness, we shall see the same ambiguity expressed in the way she refers to her confessor, the one to whom she addressed her writings. For example, is the 'you' in the final pages of her writings the 'you' of the Preliminary Oblation of her work to the 'Reverend Father', or is the 'you' in question now addressed to God? I mention this here in order to alert the reader to this feature of the text. And indeed, throughout the text as a whole the addressee of the many prayers Claudine composes as an integral part of the narrative itself is one moment 'God' and the next moment 'Our Lord'. The same is true with regard to the soul: one moment she is speaking about the soul, in the third person; and the next moment that very soul she has been speaking about is herself, in the first person. In my translation I have left everything the way Claudine wrote it; for I believe this is a very fundamental characteristic of this text and a strongly

revealing feature of Claudine's spiritual consciousness.

25 Ambiguous not only in language, but also in meaning, this sentence reveals nevertheless the spiritual expectations of Claudine, and foreshadows much of her later use of language that dwells a great deal on light, vision, the Lord looking at her, etc., and clearly puts Claudine in the more intellectual school of spirituality.

26 In bringing together all the given facts of the text, one obtains the following diagram of Claudine's return journey: 1) one league, the first evening; 2) the night rest; 3) morning, an indeterminate distance on horseback; 4) the accident; 5) two leagues in the arms of the soldier; 6) two hours of rest - the great halt; 7) seven leagues on foot. The distance between Besançon and Scey-sur-Saône being 13½ leagues, one can establish the fact that the accident happened in the morning time, during the course of the fourth league. [N.B. A league is a distance of approximately three miles.]

27 By St Francis de Sales.

28 14 September.

29 More than likely it was some form of malaria, which causes very painful shivering.

30 For further information about this, see Introduction. See also, Louis Monnier, *Histoire de la ville de Vesoul* (Vesoul, 1902); Abbès Coudriet de Châtelet, *Histoire de la Seigneurie de Jonville* and *Histoire de Jussey* (Besançon, 1876).

31 There is an underlying sense here, an understanding that Claudine and her sister were considered to be refugees and that they could hide, as it were, there in the convent.

32 Claudine and her sister, coming from Franche-Comté, which was Spanish territory, and Spain being at war with France (see Introduction for discussion of the Thirty Years War), could easily have been taken in Langres for spies, since Langres was considered part of France.

33 Claudine says earlier that it was her schoolmistress who wrote to her. Obviously the schoolmistress was speaking for all the sisters.

34 According to the indications about distance given above (Note 26), this village could be Fayl-Billot, the first locality in French territory, 24 kilometres from Langres.

35 As in the case with other proper names, this is left blank in the text.

36 One could only enter the town of Langres by the gates. And there were guards there controlling those who entered and those who left.

37 See above (p. 45) for previous reference to this, when Claudine was leaving the convent school to return home to her father.

38 20 April 1642.

39 This incident happened about halfway on the journey, that is, somewhere near Troyes.

40 Therefore, the Wednesday after Easter Sunday.

41 The Annonciades de Champlitte, a group of sisters (nuns) from Franche-Comté, had taken refuge in the convent in the Rue Couture-Sainte-Catherine, Paris, since 17 December 1638. This was a convent of sisters of their own congregation: the Annonciades célestes (see Introduction for further information about this order of nuns). Champlitte had been taken by the Duke of Longueville on 29 August of the same year.

42 From 1642 to 1644.

43 From the summer of 1642.

44 Jesuit (1586-1645). He became Claudine's first confessor in Paris. He entered the Company of Jesus in 1608. In 1642, he had already spent eleven years as procurator of the Jesuit novitiate house which was established in Rue Saint Antoine, next door to the church of St Louis which had just been completed in 1642. Claudine attended daily Mass in this church. All of Claudine's confessors were Jesuits from this community. For further information about this church - which belonged to the Jesuits - and the Jesuit priests who were Claudine's confessors, see Introduction.

45 Later on Claudine says nine or ten months; and then this period of time is reduced to 'the greater part of the first year'. This final estimation, a good semester or so, seems to be the more correct: see Jean Guennou, *La Couturière mystique de Paris* (Paris: Editions du Cerf, 1959), p. 66.

Notes

46 These words are the source and inspiration behind the opening words of this text (see text, p. 43, Note 2) and the spiritual testimony they evoke. What does one say about this most gentle, yet most real of contemplative experiences? Its simplicity says everything. A real experience of God - and not just an intellectual awakening - is the way I would like to describe this moment of conversion in the life of Claudine Moine. For indeed many spiritual truths are contained in this one moment alone: everything of significance, in fact, in her life and writing can be reduced to that one moment when, as she puts it, 'you looked at me'. We are immediately reminded of Ps. 13:3 - 'Look and answer me, Yahweh my God! / Give my eyes light, or I shall sleep in death.' 'Turn to me, take pity on me,' says Ps. 25:16, 'alone and wretched as I am!' (see above, Notes 4, 5). Also Ps. 119:123 - 'Turn to me, please, pity me, / as you should those who love your name.' In S. of S. 2:9, we read: 'My Beloved is like a gazelle, / like a young stag. / See where he stands / behind our wall. / He looks in at the window, / he peers through the lattice.' And also in S. of S. 2:16 - 'My Beloved is mine and I am his.' As these texts clearly indicate, so do Claudine's words - 'you looked at me' - testify to having seen God, and they are in the direct line of Christian spirituality. This will be made more abundantly clear to us throughout the subsequent reflections she makes on this moment in her life. Attesting to this authentic, Christian experience, she will write later on: 'What do I desire, O my God! in Heaven and on earth, if not you? And what do I want from you, if not you yourself? I did not say to you: "Give me humility in order to prevent me from being proud, and poverty that might make me have contempt for the things of this world"; and so forth. But, O my God! give me yourself, and put yourself between me and vanity, between me and all the things of this world, between me and sin! Submerge me in yourself, sink me in yourself; that there I may be happily lost to all those things.' If her testimony is true, then, we must believe that God really looked at Claudine, touched her and changed her whole life. Spiritually speaking, we can regard this vision of God as first of all a return of the soul to itself: the abandonment of the multiplicity - which is the exterior - for the spiritual unity. Daniélou points out that, in virtue of the principle that only like knows like, this unification is a condition for the knowledge of God or, as he uses the language of Plato, the One (cf. Daniélou, *Platonisme*, pp. 38-9). It is the person with many eyes who is spiritually blind; for only the person with the one eye of the soul looks upon the only God whose regard is truly penetrating (cf. ibid., p. 38). So the soul that has found the unity of sight - the one eye of the soul - can contemplate the One (cf. ibid., p. 39). Despite the obvious use of Plato in his study of Gregory of Nyssa, Daniélou's analysis here can be applied with equal effect to Claudine by showing that her spiritual awakening as indicated in 'you looked at me' was a genuine example of her contemplation of the one, true God. Moreover, Claudine's words are not just an intellectual awakening to a mere contemplation of the One; because, for Claudine, the One has eyes, and looked at her. This sudden vision of God reported by Claudine can be likened to Dante's experience of the Trinity and how it inspired him for the writing of the entire Divine Comedy. He describes it in the last Canto of the *Paradiso*, Canto XXXIII, lines 80-1: 'I united my gaze with the Infinite Goodness' (cf. Dante Alighieri, *The Divine Comedy, Paradiso: 1, Italian Text and Translation*, Bollingen Series LXXX, translated, with a commentary, by Charles S. Singleton, Princeton/New Jersey: Princeton University Press, 1975, second printing, with corrections, 1977, pp. 376-7). In commenting on this, Singleton writes: 'God is thus named "the infinite Worth" as the journey in gazing attains to Him through the light of glory by which he sees Himself' (cf. Dante Alighieri, *The Divine Comedy, Paradiso: 2, Commentary*, ibid., p. 575). In a single moment (line 93), this is such a supreme revelation to any mortal eye, continues Singleton, 'that the poet, in the very affirmation of his glimpses of it, feels a glow of contentment which seems to confirm that his report is correct' (cf. Singleton, ibid., p. 579). In fact it was after this experience that Dante began to write *The Divine Comedy,* the complete story of his 'journey in gazing' that brought him to see himself in God, for his whole identity and destiny were revealed to him in a single moment. Similarly with Claudine: in this sudden vision she sees herself in a new light and begins to write for her confessor, Father Castillon, a report of the great graces God had given her. In the same way as the ray of light (*Paradiso* XXXIII, 77) which led Dante in that upward movement to its goal in the 'Infinite Goodness' (81) inspired him in the writing of *The Divine*

255

Comedy, so Claudine will be guided by a ray of light (see text, p. 159) to put her heart into our hands and render her soul visible to our eyes (see text, p. 239). And her testimony, too, seems to be true, for suddenly, as she goes on to say, 'I felt a great desire for virtue and perfection.'

47 This sudden desire for virtue and perfection is a clear example that every real and authentic spiritual experience must bring about a change in the life of the person. 'I will instruct you, and teach you the way to go;' we read in Ps. 32:8, 'I will watch over you and be your adviser.' With his eye on her, God is going to give counsel to Claudine and lead her through the various stages of virtue and perfection until she is ultimately one with him. But she must respond freely to this grace, and be prepared to put her past life behind her. The first few lines of Gregory of Nyssa's life of Moses prefigure this first stage of spiritual progress in the putting to death of the daughters of the Hebrews (Exod. 1:15-22), symbolising as it were separation from the sensual life (cf. *La Vie de Moïse*, Sources Chrétiennes 1, p. 108). It is a free choice; for he says: 'Spiritual birth is the result of free choice and we are thus in a sense our own parents, creating ourselves such as we wish to be and moulding ourselves through our will according to the model we choose.' It could be argued that here Gregory of Nyssa places too much importance on the will in its capacity to achieve this end and not enough on grace as the cause of conversion. But Daniélou says that this is not the case, and points out that for Gregory the action of freedom is only possible because first of all the Word of God is united to humanity and has defied it (cf. Daniélou, *Platonisme,* p. 24). Grace, then, is anterior to freedom; and the role of freedom is in giving oneself to this grace (ibid.). So, no more than we can regard Claudine's vision of God in 'you looked at me' as the end result of the pure activity of her mind, neither should we consider her sudden desire for virtue and perfection as coming purely from the activity of her will - that would be voluntarism. 'Because,' as St Paul says, 'God by calling you has joined you to his Son, Jesus Christ; and God is faithful' (1 Cor. 1:9). So Claudine must be seen as responding to this grace shown to her by God. Yahweh said to Moses: 'I know you by name and you have won my favour' (Exod. 33:13). And remember how Claudine's whole reason for writing is to recount to her confessor all the favours God had shown her (see text, Preliminary Oblation).

48 The French word here is *dam.* It refers to separation from God as distinct from the suffering of the senses.

49 This makes us recall a similar sentiment expressed in the life of St Catherine of Genoa. 'She was also made to understand the extent of her ingratitude and mirrored herself in her sins; and she was overcome with such despair and self-loathing that she was tempted to confess publicly her sins. And Catherine's soul cried out, "O Lord, no more world, no more sins!"' Cf. 'The Spiritual Dialogue', in *Catherine of Genoa: Purgation and Purgatory, The Spiritual Dialogue* (The Classics of Western Spirituality), translation and notes by Serge Hughes, introduction by Benedict J. Groeschel, OFM, CAP (New York: Paulist Press, 1979), p. 109. The same sentiments are expressed in the life of Angela of Foligno: see *L'Esperienza di Dio Amore: il libro di Angela da Foligno*, translation, introduction and notes by Salvatore Alliquó, Città Nuova Editrice (Rome, 1973), p. 286.

50 Allusion to John 8:29.

51 Cf. Ps. 40:5 - 'I want to proclaim them, again and again, / but they are more than I can count.'

52 This first report was given to her first confessor, Father Jarry; and it is not to be confused with the report given to Father Castillon. She was accustomed to giving a written report to every new confessor, indicating the state of her soul. But the report given to Father Castillon is the one that developed into this text (see Introduction for a full treatment of the history of the text). We have seen how Claudine regarded her writings as an act of obedience to God, as represented in the person of her confessor (see Preliminary Oblation). She verifies this in so many words near the end of her text, when she writes: 'It is now, my dear and Reverend Father, that I can truly say that I have put my heart into your hands and rendered my soul visible to your eyes.' Such language speaks for itself: it highlights not only the spiritual beauty and accuracy of the author's thought, but also her deep theological sense. Letting her confessor know through her writings the state of her soul turns out to be one endless, theological reflection on the nature of the spiritual life. As she becomes her own parent spiritually,

theologically we can also say that she becomes her own theologian. This is what makes this text exceptionally important in the history of spirituality: it is not just the story of a soul, but a complete theological meditation, as it were, on the soul's spiritual experience. It is the highest form of spiritual autobiography, of the kind we normally associate with the *Confessions* of St Augustine. And one last point of significance to be mentioned here is the fact that Claudine wrote her own text; which was not the case for some of the well-known mystics, such as Catherine of Siena, Catherine of Genoa, and Angela of Foligno.

53 The reference here is to the time she was a boarder in the convent school at Langres. Remember (see above, p. 44) that her schoolmistress introduced her to this exercise.

54 The French word used here is *privautés*. The meaning to be derived from it is that of taking liberties with someone, or being familiar with someone. But Claudine is already introducing us here to a very central aspect of the spiritual life, namely that of becoming the friend of God. We can recall how Abraham was tested with many trials before becoming the friend of God (see Judith 8:25-7). We hear about Yahweh speaking to Moses as a man speaks with a friend (see Exod. 33:11). The state of serenity and boldness (cf. Andrew Louth, *The Origins of the Christian Mystical Tradition: From Plato to Denys*, Oxford: Clarendon Press, 1981, p. 84) in which the soul finds itself before God is the goal of the first way, or Purgative Way (cf. Daniélou, *Platonisme*, p. 104), and prepares the soul to be ready to approach God. Two Greek words, *apatheia* and *parresia*, are used by spiritual writers to convey these two concepts of serenity and boldness as they apply to the spiritual life, in particular the Purgative Way. For a full treatment of them, see Daniélou, *Platonisme*, pp. 92-115. See my Notes to this translation for a more detailed discussion of these two concepts and how they relate to Claudine's text. 'To be known by God and to become His friend' is the way Gregory of Nyssa describes the goal of the virtuous life (Gregory of Nyssa, *La Vie de Moïse*, Sources Chrétiennes 1, p. 327). While describing her conversion Claudine states that all of a sudden she felt a great desire for virtue and perfection (see text, p. 51, Note 47). So, as we move through the reading of this text, we shall be helped by the notions of *apatheia* and *parresia* in our understanding of the spiritual progress Claudine makes in her desire for the life of virtue and perfection.

55 Country (in French *pays*) has here the sense of locality - homeland. But Franche-Comté being then under Spanish rule, Claudine would have considered it as a separate country from France. She in fact regarded herself to be in exile in Paris.

56 This is typical of the way Claudine refers to her true identity: her humanity is something taken out on lease, an accident and not the substance of who she really is. This becomes more evident throughout her writings; but this must not be seen in the negative sense as a rejection of the human in her spiritual understanding - for it would be no longer Christian then, but as her way of explaining how much she belonged to God. Her sister's scolding of her refers to her as being 'toute bête'. I have translated this as 'silly'. But perhaps Claudine had in mind the literal meaning of the word *bête* (beast) when she was referring to 'their' condition, intending by this to indicate the difference between the animal and angelic condition of our human nature.

57 After two years' sojourn in Paris, in about 1644.

58 The sisterhood of the Dames de la Charité, whose function it was to take care of the sick in this way, had been established in the parish of St Louis from 1634.

59 Hospital in French is usually referred to in the seventeenth century as the *Hôtel Dieu*.

60 Her confessor.

61 Claudine and her sister Nicole. This is a good example of Claudine's narrative, how she treats of events in her writings. Nicole, her sister, has already left; yet Claudine is here reflecting on another incident in their lives before their separation. This is typical of Claudine's methodology. Events are not seen as part of the literal, historical presentation alone: they are now lived again with a new spiritual insight. Remember (see text, pp. 51-2), in the follow-up to the account of her conversion, how she says she would gladly go through all the afflictions of her life again with the new knowledge she has gained.

62 The district where the church was situated was outside the city walls.

63 The change which is described here happened on Good Friday, more than likely that of 1643, which fell on 3 April that year (see text, p. 93). This again is another example of Claudine's flicking back and forward in her reflection on events in her life, recalling past events in the light of her present knowledge. This accounts for the epistemology peculiar to her writings.

64 Through voluntary mortifications Claudine wished to prove before God that she was really disposed to die rather than sin. She explains her attitude later (text, p. 58).

65 This is an interesting piece of information that should be noted. The idea of distributing Holy Communion immediately after Mass, or outside the hours of Mass, is a practice that existed in the Catholic Church even up to the Second Vatican Council.

66 This passage clearly shows Claudine to be well established in the grace of baptism. The supreme effect of baptismal grace is seen in the mystery of the death and resurrection of Christ, in dying and rising with him. After the soul has broken off from its attachment to sin, says Gregory of Nyssa, 'it desires through the sacramental kiss to bring its mouth to the source of the light and through water find itself enveloped by light and washed of the darkness of ignorance' (Gregory of Nyssa, *In Cantica Canticorum*, PG 44, col. 1001B). The sacramental kiss is a direct allusion here to baptism. Baptism in particular is the beginning and unique source of all illumination and every virtue. So baptism is to be considered above all as a renunciation of error; it is the sacrament of regeneration. And Claudine's sudden 'desire for virtue and perfection' (see text, p. 51) must be seen in this light, as the first fruits of baptismal grace. The vividness of her description here can only bespeak the deep, incarnational dimension to her spirituality.

67 Because of the union between herself and Christ - the Incarnate Word - Claudine states specifically that she was given the courage and strength to see all Hell under her feet. As an effect of baptismal grace, the soul is given mystical illumination through union with the Word. Every doctrine of mystical illumination is a supernatural reality inherent in the grace of baptism (cf. Daniélou, *Platonisme*, p. 35). In his *On the Song of Songs 1*, St Bernard will emphasise the same idea of union in showing how the kiss signifies the union of the Word with humanity - the Incarnation; and accordingly we can state that the union of every individual soul with the Word is the union of the Word with human nature (Bernard of Clairvaux, *On the Song of Songs 1*, Sermon 1-20, Kalamazoo/ Michigan: Cistercian Publications, Inc., 1981, p. 10).

68 This meal was usually taken around midday.

69 Her confessor, Father Jarry.

70 To the watchword of St Teresa of Avila (1515-82), 'Either to suffer or to die', responds that attributed to St Mary Magdalene of Pazzi (1566-1608): 'To suffer and not to die.' During the course of her final and last ecstasy, on 24 June 1604, the Florentine Carmelite said in effect the following: 'In Paradise, we will not be able any more, as in this life, to suffer for the love of God; so I do not desire to die' (cf. M. Vaussard, *Sainte Marie Madalene de Pazzi*, 3rd edition, Paris, 1925, p. 165). Here Claudine takes up the declaration of Mary Magdalene of Pazzi, who had been beatified since 1626. Later on, Claudine will transcribe the two celebrated watchwords one after the other, word for word. All the time she was writing, Claudine thought that she had not collaborated sufficiently with the redemptive work of Christ. The day will come - as we shall see in the General Conclusion to her work - when she will manifest above all her nostalgia for Heaven.

71 Undoubtedly, this was in October 1648 and October 1652 (see Introduction).

72 Obviously the result of the sacrament of penance, this healing presence is saying something about the true way of Christian salvation. As a result of her union with Christ, and as a clear indication of her continuation in the grace of baptism - that is, of course, the continued effect of her spiritual awakening to this grace in her life - Claudine can say with St Paul that she has forgotten the past and is striving to what lies ahead: 'I can assure you, my Brothers, I am far from thinking that I have already won. All I can say is that I forget the past and I strain ahead for what is still to come; I am racing for the finish, for the prize to which God calls us upwards to receive in Christ Jesus' (Phil. 3:13-14).

Notes

United with Christ, then, Claudine is conscious that she is no longer trying for perfection by her own efforts. Since the time when God touched her ('you looked at me'), Claudine has never looked back, but has continued to progress spiritually. This notion of spiritual progress refers to the various stages of the spiritual life which correspond to the soul's desire for God. It is this notion of striving ahead (ἐπέκτασις), the stretching out or the reaching forth, which Gregory of Nyssa takes from St Paul as the central idea of perfection in his study of the life of Moses: cf. Gregory of Nyssa, *La Vie de Moïse*, Sources Chrétiennes 1, p. 263. For Gregory of Nyssa, perfection resides in progress itself, in the endless movement of the soul towards God. For a full treatment of *epectasis*, see Daniélou, *Platonisme*, pp. 291-307. Claudine's simple acknowledgement of the fact that she no longer had any knowledge of her sins after confessing them is a concrete proof that the grace of God was working in her and that she was well on the way of perfection; in other words, she was definitely at the end of the Purgative Way and probably well established in the Illuminative. Daniélou sums up the goal of this first way in two Greek words, *apatheia* and *parresia*, serenity and boldness (ibid., pp. 92-115). In this way the soul is prepared to approach God (cf. Louth, *The Origins of the Christian Mystical Tradition*, p. 84). These two words are discussed below in relation to Claudine.

73 On the fountain which was in the courtyard of the Annonciade, see F. Bournon, *Rectifications et additions à l'histoire de la ville de Paris de Lebeuf* (Paris, 1890), p. 358.

74 It is probably the Fontaine de Biraque, situated in front of the façade of the church of St Louis that is referred to; otherwise the nearest fountain was that of Place Royale. See F. and L. Lazare (eds.), *Dictionnaire administratif et historique des rues et monuments de Paris* (Paris, 1855), p. 109, col. 2.

75 The room she was staying in.

76 See text, p. 64.

77 In her room.

78 One recognises here the Franciscan watchword.

79 See Introduction for more information on Catherine of Genoa's influence on Claudine, and in particular Claudine's use of Catherine's language in the way she addressed the body.

80 This image of God as nurse definitely comes from the Jesuit influence in Claudine's spirituality. Cf. de Saint-Jure, *L'Homme spirituel*, Paris, 1646, pp. 323, 343. For more information about de Saint-Jure's *L'Homme spirituel* and its influence on Claudine, see Introduction.

81 He died on 2 November 1645.

82 Claudine here is referring back to the time when Father Jarry had given help to her sister and herself when they had just arrived in Paris.

83 1642-45.

84 Father Jarry.

85 It is Father Jarry's illness and death that are being referred to here.

86 This time it is Father de Sesmaisons who is referred to.

87 One extra communion every week.

88 This time it is the death of Father de Sesmaisons she is referring to; it happened on 3 October 1648.

89 See text, p. 60.

90 Allusion to Luke 22:35-6.

91 Partnership here must mean that she wished to have someone working with her at dressmaking.

92 Allusion to the Pauline doctrine which one finds, for example, in Gal. 5:17.

93 The young lady mentioned here is not the lady of the house, but more than likely a daughter or young woman staying there. There are all sorts of speculation as to who Claudine's benefactors were. Guennou has not succeeded in finding out. They were definitely a well-known family living in the area. It is extremely tempting to think that the young woman in question might have been the future Madame de Sévigné: cf. Guennou, *La Couturière*, LXXXII, pp. 266-7. There are many elements pointing in that direction, but they are perhaps dangerous, for no conclusive evidence is forthcoming.

94 It has not been possible, up to now, to identify this 'very significant house'. The name Philippe de Coulanges, given by Guennou, in *La Couturière*, LXXXII, p. 266, is a mere hypothesis.

95 The work mentioned here is also in connection with Claudine as a dressmaker.

96 The French text says 'une fille'. Its position in the sentence is ambiguous, and so it is not clear whether this young woman went to the country with Madame, or stayed in the house with Claudine when Madame was away. See above also, Note 92, for the ambiguity surrounding the identity of this 'fille' - is she the daughter of Madame or a young woman who was also living in that house?

97 3 October 1648.

98 Here is the first mention of her confessor to whom her writings are addressed.

99 Her benefactors.

100 Although Claudine does not mention the word 'passions' here, it is clear from what she says that her soul has already entered that state of serenity we normally refer to as *apatheia* (see above, Note 72). When she speaks about the natural sentiments of the soul, she is referring obviously to the emotions of the soul that are carried away by nature instead of being subject to God. In classical antiquity the passions were the 'emotions', in other words, the movements of the soul which cause sensations of pleasure or pain. In early Christian writings these passions were considered in a negative sense to be the disordered impulses of the appetitive aspects of the soul which needed to be controlled by the intelligent aspect. These impulses led to sin and gave the demons control over the soul. So this is why we regard the struggle against the passions (by means of *ascesis*) as *apatheia*, a stripping away of the passions so that the soul - liberated from the covetousness of life which enslaves the soul to the passions - can come to direct knowledge of God. But there are dangers in this for Christian spirituality. Festugière holds that *apatheia* is the characteristic trait of that spirituality developed on the margin of the Gospel, not authentically Christian, whose representatives would be Clement of Alexandria, Origen, Gregory of Nyssa, Evagrius of Pontus and Denis the Areopagite (A.J. Festugière, *L'Enfant d'Agrigente*, Paris, 1942, p. 146). But in defence of Gregory of Nyssa against this accusation, Daniélou points out that *apatheia* for Gregory is essentially a question of the soul stripping itself of the old man and clothing itself in the new man, that is Christ himself (Daniélou, *Platonisme*, p. 103). It is not to be understood in the negative, ascetical sense, that is in the Platonic sense of doing away with human passions in order to see God, but in the positive Christian sense of our passions being transformed into the image of God in us. *Apatheia*, then, is essentially the way of finding again the image of God in us which was lost through sin (the Fall). This 'finding again' begins with baptism, with the divesting of the sordid tunic of the life of vice and dressing ourselves in the white robe of virtue. Claudine can definitely not be accused of *apatheia* in the negative sense - as the following sentences in the text will verify - but in the full Christian sense of transformation into Christ. She is here attesting to the fact that all her soul's natural sentiments (passions or emotions) were not taken away but rather taken over completely by God.

101 Every form of nourishment necessary to sustain life.

102 It is fair to say that Claudine's *apatheia* as expressed in all of this paragraph is not the result of a gnostic stupor, but the effect of a true union with the divinity of Christ's humanity, manifested in every simple event that happened to her; as she herself goes on to explain. Of course, it is important to mention here that one of the more serious aberrations of the negative aspect of *apatheia* was seen in seventeenth-century France in the movement known as 'Quietism'. This movement held that the road to perfection is when we suppress our own direct action and leave all to God. And the names we normally associate with this movement, or I should say with the controversy over it (for it was condemned by the Church), are Archbishop Fénelon and Madame Guyon. I also doubt if Claudine could be accused of this either; the life of prayer and penance she led is proof enough that she played a very active part in the living out of her spiritual life.

103 Many spiritual people have developed the theme of solitude with God (see Plotinus, 'The flight of the alone to the alone', *Enneads*, 4, vii). The origin of this is biblical: 'I will betroth you to myself for ever, / betroth you with integrity and justice, / with tenderness and love; I will betroth you to myself with faithfulness, / and you will come to know Yahweh' (Hos. 2:19-20). As in the case of a negative *apatheia*, we could see in this notion of solitude with God another danger for Christian spirituality,

whose essential tenets are summed up in the love of God and the love of one's neighbour. Could it be that Claudine fails in this fundamental Christian virtue? Not really: as the next few lines will verify, her heightened sensitivity to the plight of the poor and her own identification with them in living the vow of poverty herself, her own work as a dressmaker together with the obvious popularity she had (as the text shows) among those who had the privilege of knowing her - all these things are ample proof that Claudine's solitude with God did not prevent her from the Christian realism of charity, but on the contrary enhanced it and inspired her to it. We must not forget, either, that Claudine prayed continually for the universal Church (see text, for example p. 86); and many more instances throughout the rest of her writing. As in the case of *apatheia*, where her soul's passions were not taken away but taken over by Christ, and thereby were freed to grow spiritually, so her solitude with God should strengthen her all the more to be a sacrament of God's love to all people. It seems to me that a more accurate interpretation of Claudine's words, 'there was only the two of us in the world', could be sought in the notion of spiritual progress we discussed above (Note 72), where the striving ahead (*epectasis*) will never leave the soul content until it is fully united with its loved one: 'On my bed, at night, I sought him / whom my heart loves. / I sought him but did not find him' (S. of S. 3:1). The simple lesson of Luke 9:62 sums it all up: 'Jesus said to him, "Once the hand is laid on the plough, no one who looks back is fit for the Kingdom of God."'

104 Claudine has thus come to the end of the autobiographical section of her work - 'a brief summary of how God, from the interior and exterior, watched over me.' From now on we shall see her move from this more literal and historical presentation of her life to a more spiritual interpretation of everything that happened to her. From here she begins to be her own theologian, as it were, going beyond narrative, beyond language, beyond self, in order to render her soul visible to our eyes.

105 See Job 2:8.

106 Compare this with the prayer of St Francis de Sales, exposed as he was to the temptation of despair: 'Ah! Whatever may happen, Lord, if I am not able to love you in the afterlife, since in Hell no one praises you, at least that I may make the most of loving you all the moments of my short existence.' (See Aug. de Sales, *Histoire du B. François de Sales*, Lyon, 1634, p. 12).

107 This prayer takes up that of St Francis-Xavier, known in Europe through a letter of P. de Quadros of 1555: 'Lord, enough, enough!' (cf. A. Brou, *Saint François-Xavier*, Paris, 1912, vol. 2, pp. 278, 282). The episode is narrated in *Les Fleurs des vies des Saints* (A. Ribadeneira and A. du Val), vol. 2 (Rouen, 1645), p. 732, col. 2.

108 Claudine, attending the church of St Louis, which was next door to the Jesuit house of profession in Paris at that time, and having the Jesuits of that house for her confessors and spiritual directors, could not have been but strongly influenced by the Exercises of St Ignatius Loyola. This phrase and what follows recalls immediately the opening words of the *Spiritual Exercises*: 'Man is created to praise, reverence, and serve God our Lord, and by this means to save his soul. The other things on the face of the earth are created for man to help him in attaining the end for which he is created. Hence, man is to make use of them in as far as they help him in the attainment of his end, and he must rid himself of them in as far as they prove a hindrance to him' (*The Spiritual Exercises of Saint Ignatius Loyola*, Louis J. Puhl, SJ, Chicago: Loyola University Press, 1951, p.12).

109 See St Augustine: 'What are you to me? Have pity on me, so that I may speak! What am I myself to you, that you command one to love you?' (*The Confessions of St. Augustine*, Book 1, chap. 5, translation, with introduction and notes by John K. Ryan, New York: Image Books, 1960, p. 45). Cf. also, A. Ribadeneira and A. du Val, *Les Fleurs des vies des Saints*, vol. 1 (Rouen, 1646), p. 655: the words of our Lord to St Catherine of Siena - 'Do you know who I am, my daughter, and who you are?'

110 The sentiment expressed here fits in spiritually with an episode described in Gregory of Nyssa's life of Moses. In response to Moses's request to see God's face, Moses is placed in a cleft in the rock and sees God's back as he passes by: cf. Exod. 33:18-23; Gregory of Nyssa, *La Vie de Moïse*, Sources Chrétiennes 1, pp. 279-83. The spiritual meaning Gregory wished to give to this episode is that the spiritual journey to the vision of God is through darkness; and that, allegorically, for the Christian this

means following Christ wherever he goes - Christ leads us through the darkness into the light. Christ, then, is the face of God for us, and it is our calling to perfection to follow him; even in darkness and not seeing our way, we must follow Christ step by step. This is the only way to the vision of God for us. Claudine's words firmly establish her spiritually in this Christian tradition; for, as she goes on to explain in the lines that follow, her sole wish is to follow Christ step by step.

111 A possible source for this emphasis on 'Nothing' in Claudine's thinking could be found in the 'apophatic' school of spirituality - the name given to the theology based on the *via negativa*, which is the way of God through negation (a commonplace of all mysticism, whether Eastern or Western), that is, where no predicates are attached to God and no words may be legitimately used to describe him. The converse of this is the *via affirmativa*, which is an approach to God through positive assertion about his attributes, and this way is commonly referred to as the 'cataphatic' school of spirituality. A book very much read in the seventeenth century, *La Règle de Perfection* by the Capuchin Benoît de Canfield (Paris, 1609) could have influenced Claudine a great deal in this respect, especially in his treatment of the notion of 'annihilation', which Claudine herself refers to often throughout the course of her writings. For full reference to this notion of annihilation, see Jean Orcibal's recent publication of the full text of Canfield: *Benoît de Canfield: La Règle de Perfection / The Rule of Perfection*, Bibliothèque de l'Ecole des Hautes Etudes, vol. LXXXIII (Paris: Presses Universitaires de France, 1982), pp. 384-421. Another possible source for this notion in Claudine could have been Jean de Saint-Samson, who in the seventeenth century was well known for this kind of spirituality. Brother Jean de Saint-Samson, who was blind, belonged to the old observance of the Carmelite reform. His works, profound but without art, were edited in 1651, 1654 and, above all, in 1658. Before beginning to write, Claudine, who would have been guided in her readings by Father Castillon (see Introduction), could only have known the first collection of Jean de Saint-Samson's works: cf. Donatien de Saint-Nicolas, *La Vie, les maximes et partie des oeuvres du vénérable Jean de Saint-Samson*, Paris, 1651. In this work the mystic is described as being 'completely dead and lost in the infinite sea of God, which submerges him totally in obscurities and darknesses, without he knowing where he is, nor what he does, waiting for God Himself to pull him out by admirable ways, so that he may bypass all things in total ignorance, without doing anything but to follow, suffering the loving dart of God, and totally unknown to him' (ibid., p. 60). Certainly, the experience of the person described here is of the same order as that witnessed to by Claudine. For full information on Jean de Saint-Samson, see Suzanne-Marie Bouchereaux's excellent study on him: *La Réforme des Carmes en France et Jean de Saint-Samson*, Etudes de Théologie et d'Histoire de la Spiritualité, vol. XII (Paris: Librairie Philosophique J. Vrin, 1950).

112 Admittedly Claudine's use of such terminology does obfuscate periodically the more simple and spiritually satisfying flow of her thought and narrative. The only possible sources for this must be the sermons she attended at the church of St Louis or else Father Castillon himself.

113 Claudine redeems herself here and is undoubtedly at her best in this wonderful ability to combine a profound theological idea with a beautiful and simple use of language. Notice also that here she is deeply Christological in her thinking.

114 The intuition which Claudine displays here is remarkable. The 'sting in the flesh' which St Paul speaks of in 2 Cor. 12:7 has been commonly interpreted as the sting of concupiscence. But Claudine did not understand it in that way; and indeed contemporary exegesis generally rejects this interpretation, unknown in the Church before the sixth century. It was merely a matter of some infirmity of the body.

115 Even despite her Jesuit spirituality, we can detect nevertheless in Claudine's thinking here a certain pessimistic, or Augustinian, understanding of nature and grace. The Jesuit understanding would have been more humanist in outlook; that is, it would see some positive value in nature itself while at the same time not denying the need for grace. It is, of course, the perennial problem of grace and free will which is central to this question; and it suffices to recall the controversy of the time on this issue between Pascal (representing the Jansenist, or Augustinian approach) and the Jesuits. See

Notes

Pascal, *Lettres Ecrites à un provincial*, chronology and introduction by Antoine Adam, Garnier-Flammarion edition (Paris, 1967), pp. 37-61. Pascal writes about the opinion of the Jansenists, which is that 'grace is efficacious, and that it determines our will in doing good': cf. Garnier-Flammarion edition, p. 37. But we shall see later on - when dealing with the question of Antoine Arnauld's *De la fréquente communion* and its Jansenist teaching - that Claudine firmly establishes herself on the side of the Jesuits on this whole issue.

116 Again, this countenances a Lutheran/Augustinian understanding of nature and the Fall.

117 The allusion here is to Phil. 2:5-8.

118 We can safely say that St Paul (Phil. 2) is the source for this passage. In this whole section, Claudine has carried out a sort of exegetical commentary on passages from this chapter in St Paul's Epistle to the Philippians.

119 Claudine arrived in Paris on 23 April 1642. This page was written, then, around the end of July 1653.

120 Claudine outlines here in a very forthright but simple way the classical and commonly accepted three stages of the spiritual journey - the Purgative, Illuminative and Unitive Ways. It would be helpful to point out here that the first appearance of this tripartite way of perfection to be found in Christian literature is in Origen (c. 185-253/4), in his Prologue to his Commentary on the Song of Songs, in which he applies this distinction in the way of perfection to the three proto-canonical books of wisdom ascribed to Solomon - Proverbs, Ecclesiastes and the Song of Songs: see Origen, *The Prologue to the Commentary of the Song of Songs*, translation and introduction by Rowan A. Greer, The Classics of Western Spirituality (New York: Paulist Press, 1979), p. 232. But for a few, slight variations of interpretation from that of Origen, the way of the soul is also divided into three stages by Evagrius of Pontus (346-99). But it was with Gregory of Nyssa (c. 335-94), commonly accepted as the father of mystical theology, that we find the fully developed idea of the three ways in the form they have influenced Western spirituality. Daniélou's masterly study on Gregory of Nyssa, *Platonisme et Théologie Mystique* (which I have used extensively in these Notes), gives a wonderful analysis of this: see pp. 18-23. In fact Daniélou's book is itself divided into three parts; and they correspond respectively to each of the three ways of the soul. For information on the above three authors - Origen, Evagrius of Pontus and Gregory of Nyssa - and how they understand the three ways of the soul: cf. Andrew Louth, *The Origins of the Christian Mystical Tradition*, pp. 57-60, 81-97, 103-4.

121 Perhaps the accusation of complicity in a theft, recounted in text, p. 55.

122 A person from Franche-Comté, during the mid-seventeenth century, would have considered France as a foreign country.

123 Considering herself to be an exile in Paris, Claudine could easily look upon herself as a type of those strangers and voyagers on the earth which the ancient monks, abandoning their fatherland and family, were conscious of becoming in their search for their heavenly home. It is the theme of the pilgrim - which Claudine goes on to explain - who follows in the footsteps of Abraham, a theme which Origen, influenced by Philo, had strongly developed. 'Of old it was said by God to Abraham', writes Origen, '"Come out of your land"' (Gen. 12:1). 'But to us in a short while it will perhaps be said, "Come out from the whole earth." It is good to obey Him, so that He may presently show us the heavens in which exist what is called the kingdom of heaven. Now we can see that life is filled with contests for many virtues, and we can see the contestants.' (Origen, *An Exhortation to Martyrdom*, op.cit., p. 43). Philo writes: 'Under the force of an oracle which bade him leave his country and kinsfolk and seek a new home, thinking that quickness in executing the command was as good as full accomplishment, he [Abraham] hastened eagerly to obey, not as though he were leaving home for a strange land but rather as returning from amid strangers to his home' (Philo, *On Abraham*, XIV, 62, translated by F.H. Colson, Loeb Classical Library, Cambridge, Massachusetts: Harvard University Press, 1935, p. 35). 'No matter where you shall be', writes John Moschus (died c. 619) in *The Spiritual Meadow*, 'always say, "I am a stranger"' (cf. Jean Moschus, *Le Pré Spirituel*, introduction and translation by M.-J. Rouet de Journel, SJ, Sources Chrétiennes 12, p. 55). Indeed Claudine goes on

to mention that she considered herself as a pilgrim on the earth, and to point out that if one wishes to be at home with God one must be a stranger everywhere else. See Introduction, pp. 37-8.

124 Cf. John Moschus, ibid., p. 55.

125 See text, p. 75: 'Poor creature! Is not the whole world a strange land to you?'

126 Perhaps her sister, Nicole, who returned for a time to her native region (see text, p. 109). More probably, however, it is Father Castillon, who was named for a new position at Orléans around the end of 1648.

127 This idea of this life being only an apprenticeship to eternal life comes up again later on in Claudine's writings.

128 Claudine's vocation to the hidden life she vowed in a special way to the apostolate of prayer. Her ardour redoubled during Advent and Lent, times which, of course, were marked in the seventeenth century - as in the centuries that followed - with numerous sermons. While we might be tempted today, especially with our sense of Church since the Second Vatican Council, to criticise Claudine's individual spirituality - her aloofness and detachment from the world as not what the true message of Christianity demands - it might be of help to recall here how the hidden, contemplative life of St Teresa of Lisieux captured the missionary spirit of the Church during the first half of this century. Like Teresa, Claudine prayed constantly for the missionary endeavours of the Church (see above, Note 103).

129 Mention has already been made about the darkness and obscurity surrounding our journey to God (see above, Note 110). This notion of knowledge through darkness - or dark night of the soul - is well established in Western spirituality. Suffice it to recall the whole spirituality of St John of the Cross. The meaning is that as there is a purgation of the physical senses in the spiritual life, so there is a purgation of the spiritual senses; and this later state comes about through a darkening of the understanding, it is as the title of the great classic of the fifteenth century indicates, 'The Cloud of Unknowing' (*The Cloud of Unknowing and Other Works*, translated into modern English with an introduction by Clifton Wolters (Penguin Books, 1961; reprinted with *The Epistle of Privy Councel*, *Dionysius' Mystical Teaching*, and *The Epistle of Prayer*, 1978)). Claudine's second state she refers to above would seem to be an example of this, and curiously enough corresponds to the Illuminative Way. But even as one enters the Unitive Way this very darkness becomes even more intense. Although Claudine speaks about a third stage, or state, here, it is probably a little premature to say that this third stage of hers corresponds exactly to what we normally refer to as the Unitive Way. After all, this third stage is not within the domain of language to describe. It was with Gregory of Nyssa that the journey of the soul to God as through the dark night was firmly established in the history of Christian spirituality: cf. Daniélou, *Platonisme*, pp. 190-208. For Gregory the whole idea of the progress of the soul consisted in this (cf. Daniélou, p. 232). Indeed the following pages will show that Claudine seems to be well established in this spiritual tradition.

130 Claudine develops this further in the following account, 'Deepening', where she treats of the Great Darkness (see text, pp. 127-55). But notice here the strength of language she uses to drive home her point: hurling her actions to the bottom of the sea. The same ultimacy in her thinking we have already come across when she was describing the immediate effects of her conversion (see text, pp. 51-2). Spiritually, we are led to think of the all-or-nothingness of a spiritual conversion: there are no half measures where commitment to Christ is concerned.

131 See *apatheia* above, Note 100.

132 This reveals more than any other statement of hers that she was experiencing the darkness that goes with true knowledge of God. See Pseudo-Dionysius's prayer to the Trinity: 'see that you rise up with me in this grace - though we do not know how it can be - so as to be united with him who is above all being and knowledge' (*De Mystica Theologica*, in PG 3, col. 997-1064; 'The Mystical Theology', in *Pseudo-Dionysius: The Complete Works*, translation by Colm Luibheid, The Classics of Western Spirituality, New York: Paulist Press, 1987, p. 135). Here we have the identification of the mystical contemplation with the images of entering into the cloud, or the darkness. Indeed, the same *theologia mystica* (col. 1000A-1001A) is an echo of the same idea expressed in Gregory of Nyssa's life of Moses

(see above, Note 110): 'It is now that Moses with his especial love is separated from the priests already mentioned, and enters by himself into the darkness of unknowing, a darkness which is indeed hidden, one in which he forgoes all knowledge capable of being known' (the translation of these two passages from Pseudo-Dionysius is taken from *Dionysius' Mystical Teaching*; cf. *The Cloud of Unknowing and Other Works*, pp. 209, 211-12). Claudine's understanding of the darkness is further explained when she moves, in the following lines, into a critique of Ecclesiastes. And recall from above, Note 120, that the book of Ecclesiastes was taken by Origen to correspond to the second stage in the ways of the soul, the Illuminative Way.

133 Cf. Eccles. 1:6.

134 Victims of a certain magic, bewitched. The meaning here is - how much drugging does it take?

135 Cf. Eccles. 1:2.

136 The operative word here is 'knowledge'. By saying that the knowledge of spiritual things was taken from her, Claudine is implying that the spiritual life can not be reduced to mere contemplation, an intellectual understanding of spiritual things. As in the case of many mystics, here she is touching upon a deep theological question that has separated the West and the East spiritually. The question centres around the problem of a real union between God and us. The West has found difficulty in expressing this reality on account of its notional approach to the problem; in the East, the real experience of God being the basis of their theology, this union can be explained only through love. Love of God in this sense is not a concept; it is not a faculty, as many scholastic theologians of the West have understood it to be. God is love (St John); love is God - that is the reality. Generally in Western thinking, love is synonymous with the will; it is a faculty. But love is more than a faculty, it is a reality, an ontological sharing in the very being and life of God. For example, if I am sick and have lost my health, no discussion about sickness or health is what I want; I simply wish to be healthy again. In the case of Claudine, then, it was a true love of God, union with Mary and the saints that she desired; not just a pleasant image, form or representation of this. Her thinking is made abundantly clear in the following paragraph.

137 At this stage in the spiritual life of Claudine - following upon the interior word reported in text, p. 78: 'I want to take all these things from your vision . . .' - the soul is pushed, through an interior motion ('an instinct from within me', p. 77), to seek God without an intermediary.

138 Notice here that union with God is seen to be real, not just a concept.

139 Notice here the use of the oxymoron: empty/full; the soul is empty, but it is also full. On the use of the oxymoron in the writings of Gregory of Nyssa, see Daniélou, *Platonisme*, pp. 274-84. The idea is that the oxymoron - full/empty; sleep/awake; sober/drunk - is a more truthful description of the way we experience God. Of course, we are already in the language of the mystics by this stage. Claudine's union with the divinity could be seen here as stemming from the fact that she was asleep to the world and all things around her while she was totally awake to God; for experiencing God as neither present nor absent, neither completely in the world nor outside of the world, immanent or transcendent, is closer to the nature of our relationship with the infinite God. Recall in Exod. 33:18-23 (see above, Note 109) how Moses was not allowed to see the face of God, only his back.

140 See above, Note 127.

141 The reference here is obviously to Antoine Arnauld's *De la fréquente communion* (1643). Claudine in fact comes back to this very point at a later stage and discusses this work (see the third account, 'Light'). Being directed by the Jesuits, she would have found herself opposing the spirituality of the Jansenists, of whom Antoine Arnauld was one of the great upholders.

142 The allusion here is to St Paul, 1 Cor. 11:27 - 'and so anyone who eats the bread and drinks the cup of the Lord unworthily will be behaving unworthily towards the body and blood of the Lord'.

143 For previous mention of this, see text, p. 61, Note 80. This image which could shock us today was common in the spiritual literature of seventeenth-century France: cf. de Saint-Jure, *L'Homme spirituel*, pp. 323, 343. For St Francis de Sales: cf. the reference in H. Lemaire, *Les Images chez Saint François de Paris* (Paris, 1962), pp. 288, 321.

144 This vivid imagery clearly acquits Claudine of whatever intellectualism she could have been accused of a few pages earlier (see text, p. 78) where she stated that only rarely has she ever an image of the humanity or divinity of God our Lord; and that, if she does, she would reject it immediately, desiring, as she says, the original and not the image or representation of God. Despite the exaggerated imagery used here, Claudine's use of language in this whole paragraph strongly places her spirituality firmly on a Christological basis.

145 While receiving Holy Communion.

146 There is already a hint here of the sexual dimension of the mystical experience, the most famous description being, of course, that of St Teresa of Avila: see *The Life of Saint Teresa of Avila*, translated by E. Allison Peers (first published in The Complete Works of St. Teresa of Jesus, London: Sheed & Ward, 1944; this independent edition published 1979, reprinted 1984), chap. XXIX, p. 191. Later on Claudine will describe her mystical experience (see text, p. 123, under the heading 'Transverberation') in almost a word-for-word repetition of Teresa's description. The whole of this section leaves no doubt in our minds as to the real and authentic Christian aspect of Claudine's spiritual experience. Her spirituality, despite its obvious intellectual quality, was deeply set in the real, and was not the disembodied spirituality of the angels.

147 These same ideas are developed later in the fourth account, 'On Prayer'.

148 This is the way North Africa was referred to in the seventeenth century.

149 Here there is a blank in the text.

150 Her benefactors.

151 Her benefactors.

152 The Angelus.

153 Her benefactors.

154 The sermons given in the church of St Louis - which Claudine always attended - were evidently one of her sources.

155 The feast of the Immaculate Conception (8 December) was celebrated on a Monday in 1653. This page was probably written, then, prior to the feast (cf. text, p. 75, Note 119). Thus, right from the month of January, Claudine consecrated to the Immaculate Virgin the day of the week which corresponded to 8 December of that year.

156 The story of the six bourgeois from Calais, in 1347, who had to present themselves to Edward III of England in their night attire with the cord round their necks was known by everyone.

157 Her benefactors.

158 She will always refer back to that moment of her conversion, 'you looked at me', as the moment when God touched her and changed her whole life.

159 From the time she found herself again under the direction of Father Castillon.

160 Cf. text, p. 64.

161 In the following account, 'Deepening', she will give more details of this.

162 It is important to be aware here of the substitution that has begun to take place in her own mind of God for her confessor: there is a transference of roles. The 'you' (addressee of her writings) is no longer Father Castillon, but God.

163 In all probability, this is where the signature of the author was in the original manuscript.

Deepening

1 Her confessor.

2 The notions of desolation and consolation have been broached by all the spiritual authors since the patristic period. However, the vocabulary was not fixed until the seventeenth century: cf. Louis Poullier, 'Consolation spirituelle', *Dictionnaire de Spiritualité*, edited by M. Villier (Paris, 1932-), vol. 2, col. 1617-34.

Notes

3 A confusing interpolation here; yet a reminder to us that Claudine is writing from a constant state of the present.

4 From the time she had left the convent school. Claudine is referring to the two years she spent with the nuns at Langres.

5 The French word *malheur* is always very difficult to translate. No English word exactly conveys the meaning. *Malheur* contains in itself a certain sense of inevitability or doom. I feel that 'misery' is the nearest equivalent in the context in which Claudine uses the word.

6 From 1639 to 1642: these were the years just before she arrived in Paris.

7 Cf. text, p. 46, Note 22. It is important to be aware here of the nature of her narrative: it is a constant reflection on past moments in her life, seeing them now as it were more clearly in the light of her present knowledge. Here she is recalling her journey back from Besançon, just before her accident (text, p. 46).

8 Text, p. 51.

9 Father Castillon. Cf. Guennou, *La Couturière mystique de Paris* (Paris: Editions du Cerf, 1959), LXXIV, pp. 248-55.

10 1643, apparently. If one were to opt for 1644, the time spent in Paris before the moment when God 'looked at' her would have lasted more than a year and a half, which does not tally with the previously given facts: see text, p. 51, Note 45.

11 5 April 1643. In 1644, Easter Sunday fell on 27 March.

12 The damned.

13 Cf. Num. 11:5.

14 See text, p. 58. After that, Claudine understood that her mortifications, in all circumstances, had to be submitted to the control of her confessor.

15 It is possible she had in mind St Catherine of Siena or Angela of Foligno, both of whom are recorded to have had similar temptations of vainglory in the course of their spiritual lives.

16 A significant avowal, especially in view of the fact that she mentioned earlier that she had led a worldly, mundane life: see text, p. 45.

17 The French here is 'gênes éternelles', which could be an indirect reference to 'Géhenne' (Gehenna, Hell): cf. for example Matt. 5:22; 29-30, etc.

18 See text, pp. 56-7.

19 Cf. John 19:19.

20 Fancy: the flights of imagination.

21 See text, p. 56.

22 Allusion to Matt. 1:20, citing Isa. 42:3.

23 Claudine has already entered into friendship with God, and the fear of offending him was the result of love and the desire not to lose his divine friendship. To be known by God and to become his friend is the way Gregory of Nyssa describes the goal of the virtuous life: see *La Vie de Moïse*, Sources Chrétiennes 1, p. 327. See also, Exod. 33:11. However, here there is no mention specifically of the word 'friendship'; but a certain familiarity with God is to be understood. Having gone through the state of *apatheia* (cf. text, p. 64, Note 100), or purification of the senses and the passions, Claudine now felt bold enough in the presence of God (p. 60, Note 72). Daniélou refers to this state of familiarity with God as the *parresia* (Daniélou, *Platonisme et Théologie Mystique*, Paris: Aubier/Editions Montaigne, 1944, p. 111). 'What proof more worthy of faith have we,' writes Gregory of Nyssa in his commentary on the Song of Songs, 'that Moses has succeeded in coming to perfection than the fact that he was called the friend of God . . . For truly, there is perfection: not to abandon the sinful life through fear of punishment, in the way of servants, but to fear only one thing, the loss of His divine friendship and to value only one thing, to become the friend of God, which is the perfection of life': PG 44, col. 430B-C.

24 Fancy: the flights of imagination.

25 Maxims of the Gospel.

26 The 'it' is referring to the content of the faith.

27 The certitude which Claudine depicts here is not an intellectual awakening to the truths of faith, the result of the pure activity of the mind, but rather the result of having thrown her conscious self upon the mercy of the powers of God in complete self-surrender; it must be regarded as having been the vital turning point in her religious experience: 'you looked at me'. Her faith stems indeed from a rationality of love.

28 During the Fronde: cf. F. Vincent, *Histoire des famines à Paris* (Paris, 1946), pp. 65-7.

29 Cf. Thomas à Kempis, 'Of the love of Jesus beyond all', *The Imitation of Christ*, Book 2, chap. 7, translated into modern English by Edgar Daplyn, FRSL (London: Sheed & Ward, 1952), p. 60.

30 Claudine sees the action of God exercising itself in the world through the intermediary of creatures. However, she shows herself very grateful to her benefactor: see text, pp. 85 and 86.

31 Cf. Job 2:8. For the same sentiments expressed, see text, p. 67, Note 105; p. 69, Note 109.

32 Fancy. Immodesty is understood.

33 Perhaps Father Castillon. It seems that this episode took place after 1648. It was only after that date that Claudine would have found herself in any real way in the frequent company of men, and this obviously would have been in the house of her benefactors. Also, the reference here to preachers is definitely in connection with the many sermons she listened to in the church of St Louis, renowned for its tradition of famous preachers.

34 The ignorance here is in reference to Claudine's own ignorance, or lack of experience of being in the company of men.

35 Sensual feelings.

36 Is Claudine asking to be delivered from all passions, or simply that they be transformed? Could it be argued here that Claudine, in desiring to be delivered 'entirely' from her sensual passions, was succumbing somewhat to the dangers in *apatheia* (see text, p. 64, Notes 100 and 102). If so, in what way then, we may further ask, is Claudine's spirituality influenced by the right or wrong understanding of *apatheia*? For we must concede that there is a certain Christian tradition which is not exempt from all contamination of the Neoplatonic *apatheia*, that is from the complete elimination of all desires as the only way to perfection and the knowledge of God. In the Christian sense, *apatheia* is understood to be the suppression of 'bad' passions as the way to virtue. In Neoplatonism it is not only a question of uprooting the evil passions, but of suppressing all desires, no matter what; the state of *apatheia* only comes about from the radical extirpation of all affective sentiment and passion of human nature. *Apatheia*, in the Christian understanding of the word, is what designates the supernatural life, that is the participation of the soul in the divine life (habitual grace), and in no way consists of the entire elimination of the passions in the physical sense of the word (cf. Daniélou, *Platonisme*, p. 94). In considering, then, her desire to be delivered 'entirely' from the passions of sensuality, it would be more in keeping with Claudine's spirituality to see her state of *apatheia* as the result of her having been purified by the touch of God, a state of spiritual quiet in which all her passions are centred on the one who 'looked at' her (see text, p. 51) and changed her whole life.

37 Rooted in the sacramental life of the Church, Claudine's spirituality will be safeguarded against the dangers of Neoplatonism (see above, Note 36) and the wrong understanding of *apatheia*. We shall see later how her spiritual experience is firmly established in her personal encounter with Jesus Christ.

38 Here again we have a confirmation of the fact that Claudine's *apatheia* is not the elimination of the passions and feelings, but a bringing of them into line with Christ, healed, in other words, by the grace of God.

39 See 'offences' of the previous sentence.

40 Cf. text, p. 64, Note 100. This whole sentence places Claudine quite clearly on the positive road of the *apatheia*: she is by no means influenced by Neoplatonism in her notion, but strongly anchored in the Christian tradition.

41 The imagery is strong here, and would seem to call into question what I said earlier about Claudine and *apatheia*. But we can only understand this language in the context of her complete

involvement in Christ. The radicalism of the *apatheia* here is still not due to the Neoplatonic tradition in spirituality, which would normally be seen as the achievement of the pure activity of one's own mind, but is rather the result of her total commitment to Christ. It is important to see it in this light, as she herself will go on to justify in the next paragraph when she says, 'O Jesus Christ, O King of Kings, it is you alone I wish to look at and adore . . .'

42 The church of St Louis had been built in honour of King Louis, the Saint; and the whole court - King and Queen included - used to come there twice a year for this reason.

43 This is the word Claudine uses, but it is unlikely that it is meant to be taken literally.

44 Cf. text, pp. 64. In French the 'biscuit de mer' was the light cracker sailors would eat at sea which had very little substance.

45 She has just been speaking about the great confusion she had in meeting people who were beginning to have a special regard for her.

46 Cf. text, p. 59, Note 70. The fact that Claudine refers to St Teresa of Avila twice in her writing makes it more than probable that St Teresa is a definite source for Claudine. For further comments on this, see Introduction.

47 She is either referring to the time she herself spent at the convent school at Langres (see text, p. 44) or the time she and her sister were at Langres on their way to Paris (see text, p. 48).

48 The monthly money.

49 The 'us' here is obviously in reference to the original report about Claudine and her sister that had been given to those people in the letters of introduction they brought with them from Langres to Paris.

50 Cf. text, p. 60.

51 Her benefactor.

52 This could be in reference to the fact that Claudine suffered from some infirmity or other: see text, p. 63.

53 Allusion to Rom. 8:29.

54 Notice here Claudine's strong mind, not afraid to have deep convictions even when they involved severe and open criticism of well-known prelates of the Church. The person she has in mind is Cardinal de Richelieu, and the war in question is the Thirty Years War: cf. text, p. 46, Notes 16, 17, 18.

55 Cardinal Richelieu died on 4 December 1642, the year Claudine arrived in Paris.

56 In the tradition of St Francis of Assisi, Claudine dialogues with poverty: cf. text, p. 107 Following her vocation to the hidden life, she joins humility to this.

57 John 12:32.

58 The French word is 'ménage', which means household, family or married couple. The English word 'marriage' best translates the intended meaning, which could also be referring to spiritual marriage, or the Unitive Way.

59 Cf. text, p. 91, Note 2.

60 She is referring here to a definite period in her spiritual journey.

61 Cf. text, p. 106.

62 This sentence must not be separated from the preceding one. Claudine mends her own clothes before wearing them.

63 St Pachomius (287-346) is one of the greatest figures in the history of the Church, because he founded coenobitic monasticism, which was to develop greatly and have a profound influence on the spirituality of the West. In contrast to the anchorite, who was one who withdrew or secluded himself from the world (that is a recluse or a hermit), the coenobite was a member of a religious order living in a community. Hence 'coenobitic' is of the nature of a monastic community; and it was this type of monasticism which influenced St Benedict and monasticism in the West.

64 It is difficult to trace the source of this quotation. Not being an expert by any means in the Fathers of the Church, Claudine had to have heard of Pachomius from elsewhere. Is she quoting here from

some sermon she attended in the church of St Louis? Guennou extends his gratitude to M. Aubineau, SJ, for having had the goodness of communicating to him an erudite note on the probable source for this saying of Pachomius and the role that Surius (1522-78) had in its transmission (see *Ma Vie secréte: Claudine Moine*, edited by Jean Guennou with introduction, Paris: Desclée et Cie, 1968, p. 204, n. 1; *La Couturière mystique*, p. 204, n. 1). Provided thus with all the necessary indications, it is possible to establish the fact that this maxim was found almost word for word in : E. Binet, SJ, *Abrégé des vies des principaux fondateurs des religions de l'Eglise* (Anvers, 1634), p. 64; S. Martin, *Les Fleurs de la solitude* (Paris, 1652), vol. 1, p. 459. Also, the saying is underlined by A. Ribadeneira and A. du Val, *Les Fleurs des vies des Saints*, vol. 1 (Rouen, 1646), p. 734, col. 1. Lawrence Surius was a Carthusian spiritual writer of the sixteenth century and is known for his monumental work on the lives of the saints: *De Probatis Sanctorum historis* (Cologne, 1570-5). Many editions of this work followed, and it is not improbable that Claudine knew about it in the seventeenth century. But it is highly unlikely that her knowledge of this work or of the life of Pachomius was in any way gained from her own erudition. It is more likely that Claudine would have known of this maxim through her confessor, Father Castillon.

65 Cf. text, p. 55.

66 Cf. text, p. 89, Note 156.

67 While flagellating themselves as an act of discipline, the religious used to recite the Miserere (Ps. 51).

68 Wearing the girdle and flagellation.

69 An important sentence, and not to be forgotten when later Claudine will assure us that she took pleasure in mortification: cf. text, p. 199.

70 To kiss the leper was a common feature of the hagiography of the Middle Ages, and this had made an impression on Claudine; but without taking her to the accomplishment of the act itself, which would have been incompatible with her vocation to the hidden life in God.

71 Did Nicole, Claudine's sister, return for good to Franche-Comté? The following sentence would seem to indicate that she did.

72 Claudine would have regarded Paris to be a foreign land to her, and would have felt that she herself was in exile there. Cf. text, p. 75, Note 123.

73 Franche-Comté, then under Spanish rule.

74 Cf. text, p. 62.

75 This was written, therefore, sometime around 23 April 1654.

76 Father Castillon, the addressee of her writings.

77 'Tel qu'il lui plairait . . . par celui qu'il plairait.' This repetition in the French emphasises the total dependence of Claudine with regard to the will of God.

78 Father de Sesmaisons.

79 Cf. text, p. 119, Note 98; 146, Note 203. Claudine, it would seem in this rather curious sentence, is countenancing here a certain private revelation that is not in conformity with the normal formulation of the faith of the Christian Church. But she is only voicing the well-known problem of those who find it difficult at times to see where their deep spiritual experience fits into the formulated doctrine of the Church; for there always has been a clear distinction in the Church between the experience of charisms, that is direct private revelations, and the experience of the hierarchically organised life of the Church. It is the perennial question of the inner Church and the outer Church - are they opposing Churches or are they two sides of the Christian mystery working itself out in history? I think the second, if it is not the case, should be the case. Claudine is merely expressing the sentiments of many great saints in history who effected spiritual renewal in the Church, and who found themselves at times in conflict with the external mechanism of the Church. But we must not forget that formulated doctrine can never adequately put words on deep spiritual feelings; so even there we see a healthy struggle between language and the reality it is trying to express. Is not Claudine herself doing just that, trying to communicate her deep spiritual experience: an experience that defies almost any language?

Notes

80 So absolute is Claudine's obedience to her confessor as the will of God that it makes easy the reciprocal exchange between God and her confessor in her mind.

81 That is, for reasons known only to God alone.

82 This sentence is also addressed perhaps to her body. The punctuation in the manuscript, translated and reproduced here exactly, does not permit us to break up the conversation between Claudine and her body.

83 Cf. Matt. 5:19.

84 Cf. Matt. 25:23.

85 Here again we have Claudine's treatment of the passions, and she likens them to animals, dogs hungry for a piece of bread. In Gregory of Nyssa's life of Moses we come across the same description of the passions when he writes, 'For who does not know that the Egyptian army - those horses, chariots and drivers, archers, slingers, heavily armed soldiers, and the rest of the crowd in the enemies' line of battle - are the various passions of the soul by which man is enslaved? For the undisciplined intellectual drives and the sensual impulses to pleasure, sorrow, and covetousness are indistinguishable from the aforementioned army. Reviling is a stone straight from the sling and the spirited impulse is the quivering spear point. The passion for pleasures is to be seen in the horses who themselves with irresistible drive pull the chariot' (cf. *De Vita Moysis*, PG 44, col. 361C-D) (this translation is taken from *Gregory of Nyssa: The Life of Moses*, The Classics of Western Spirituality, translation, introduction and notes by Abraham J. Malherbe and Everett Ferguson, New York: Paulist Press, 1978, p. 83). There are two kinds of passions represented here, one by the chariots and the other by the horses. In so far as they are the functions of the soul, the passions are likened to the drivers; and in so far as they are bad passions, they are seen to be the horses. The horses are the unruly, unbridled passions, while the drivers stand for the rational side of the soul whose duty it is to control these passions. In the same text, Gregory goes on to say: 'In the chariot there are three drivers whom the history [he means the first part of his book which deals with the historical, or literal side of the Life of Moses] calls "viziers". Since you were previously instructed in the mystery of the side posts and upper doorpost, you will perceive these three, who are completely carried along by the chariot, the appetitive division of the soul, meaning the rational, the appetitive, and the spirited.' So the understanding is that the soul, in order to arrive at the state of *apatheia*, must fight against the unruly passions. And for Gregory, the passions are above all represented by animal life and the different kinds of beasts (cf. Daniélou, *Platonisme*, p. 73). Curiously enough, Claudine in this whole section seems to fit in admirably with this way of thinking, and goes on to display a very balanced view of this spiritually when she says below, 'But to seek the pure satisfaction of the senses, is to act like a beast.' We have already come across an early reference in Claudine to this state of *apatheia* as one of being freed from the unruly passions, or, as she implies, their condition [of the animal]: see text, p. 54, Note 56.

86 It is helpful to recall here the use of the same language in the description of her conversion, 'you looked at me': see text, p. 51, Note 46.

87 See text, p. 78, Note 137.

88 Cf. Matt. 5:37.

89 One of the sisters at the Annonciade who attended the door. See text, p. 63.

90 Her future benefactor.

91 The garden in question would be the garden of her benefactor, in whose house she was eventually to reside.

92 Perhaps this construction is not the same as that of the preceding proposition; perhaps it is necessary to understand: 'excepting sin'. In this case, it would be necessary to add a comma after 'abominable', and the full sentence would read: 'There is nothing so vile as nothingness, nothing so contemptible, nothing so abominable, excepting sin.'

93 Cf. text, p. 70, Note 111. The French is 'dans un parfait anéantissement'. And I have translated it as 'state of perfect nothingness'.

94 In these pages Claudine is repeating the same ideas she has already expressed elsewhere: cf. text, p. 71, Note 113; see also p. 153 Note 237.

95 All Claudine's knowledge, then, is not the result of a gnostic stupor, the result of the pure activity of her mind, but the gratuitous effect of her encounter with Christ. This is a clear indication of how authentically Christian her spiritual experience is.

96 What she means here does not come across clearly. She would seem to be referring to the tension that rises from the presence of God's love and the existence of sin. While it is right to say that God is 'an infinite abyss of all good', it is an exaggeration to say that we are 'an infinite abyss of all evil'. This dualism in her thinking would seem to indicate that Claudine gives a substantive value to evil, thereby placing her outside the main-line Christian teaching on redemption, which is that fallen nature is restored to the image of God in us. This sentence can only be understood in the context of the paragraph as a whole, in which Claudine is desperately trying to say that all good in us comes from God, and that we have nothing of ourselves; that does not mean, of course, that we are evil to the core of our very existence. Although Claudine's exaggerated language is chafing dangerously here against the main tenets of Catholic doctrine, I feel she must be taken in this context as trying to preserve in her mind the allness of God which she has experienced mystically.

97 Cf. 1 Sam. 3:10.

98 By 'interior words' she must mean those spoken to her by God, the result of internal visions and not the intellectual awareness she had of God's truths in those lights: cf. text, pp. 53, 57, 75, 78, 81-2, 105, 111.

99 She means the vigils, or the evenings before the days on which she was to receive Communion.

100 At the first row of those receiving Communion.

101 The fabulous many-headed snake in Greek mythology whose heads grew again as fast as they were cut off. This snake was eventually killed by Hercules.

102 This long prayer - typical of her narrative - answers the questions we raised above concerning the dualism in Claudine's thought: cf. above, Note 96. In this prayer she is firmly rooted in the Christian tradition. 'For', as she says, 'after all, my God, I am the work of your hands and the price of your blood.' She speaks about her heart and body being abandoned to the sovereign power of God's love; so the sense of her own nothingness (cf. text, p. 116) and seeing herself as the 'infinite abyss of all evil' (text, p. 117), is not a denial of the human in herself, but a testimony to the fact that everything in her that is human has been transformed totally into Christ, and that if anything of herself were to remain, it is to be regarded as a nothingness and an evil.

103 If remission is to be understood here as forgiveness, it is difficult to see the meaning behind this statement. Perhaps Claudine wishes to put across the idea that forgiveness might still keep this passion and evil inclination alive; whereas her use of the word 'remission' here would seem to indicate that she wanted them eradicated from her life; to be completely dead in her, with no chance of ever becoming alive again. But the understanding is that this can only come about through the grace of God. Here, as in this prayer as a whole, the inspiration seems to be Pauline; and the allusion is to Col. 3:5 - 'That is why you must kill everything in you that belongs only to earthly life: fornication, impurity, guilty passion'.

104 St Paul continues to be the source here - the stripping oneself of the old man, of one's evil passions, and clothing oneself with the new man, Jesus Christ: cf. Col. 3:9-11. It is not an uprooting of the passions, but a transformation of them into the likeness of Christ. We are reminded here of the words of Gregory of Nyssa: 'All those according to Saint Paul have stripped the old man as the sordid vestment with its works and covetousness and dressed themselves again with the purity of life, the luminous vestments of the Lord, such as they are shown to us in the Transfiguration on the mountain; or better, those who put on our Lord Jesus Christ himself with the charity which is his robe, and who have been transformed into the image of his *apatheia* and his divinity, can listen to the Song of Songs' (cf. Gregory of Nyssa, *In Cantica Canticorum* (On the Song of Songs), PG 44, col. 746D; the translation is mine). This is made abundantly clear by Claudine in the following sentence, where she speaks about the 'portrait of a perfect sanctity'.

Notes

105 Cf. text, p. 71, Note 113. We assume that this is an original expression of Claudine, although there is a strong allusion in this thought to Heb. 1:3 - 'He is the radiant light of God's glory and the perfect copy of his nature.' Christ is to be seen as the perfect image of God, in other words the perfect pattern of sanctity for those who are baptised; and their aim should be a continual interior renewal according to Christ the model of the new man. For references to the image of God in St Paul, see Col. 1:15, 1:17, 2:9, 3:10; 1 Cor. 11:7; 2 Cor. 4:4. This idea of the image of God plays a fundamental role in all aspects of the mystical life. Its essential character, in effect, is the progressive awareness of the presence of God dwelling in the soul. Now this presence in the soul is itself proportionate to the transformation of the soul into God, that is to the restoration of the image (icon). This title, image of God, is derived from the first chapters of Genesis (Gen. 1:27). And it is also characteristic of Pauline Christology; because it is found nowhere else in the New Testament. In Gen. 1:27, the first Adam was said to have been created in the image of God; and for St Paul it is Christ alone, risen from the dead, who has fully realised this image of the Father, and so is capable of assimilating the Christian to that image. Only the total awareness of her own unworthiness, of her own nothingness, as it were, to the point of seeing in herself 'an infinite abyss of all evil' (text, p. 117), could prepare the way for the complete restoration of the image of God in her. Here, as in the rest of the prayer, we find Claudine in total conformity with the central theme of Christian spirituality and, in her own spiritual experience, on the right road to perfection. This restoration can be envisaged in three different stages: in its beginning it is baptism, in that first realisation of it which is *apatheia*, the Purgative Way; secondly, it is a returning to the angelic knowledge through the dark night of the senses and concepts, which is contemplation, or the Illuminative Way; and thirdly, it is characterised by the superior degrees of this contemplation, which is the mystical life, the Unitive Way (cf. Daniélou, *Platonisme*, p. 177). It consists in effect of a participation in the divine nature. And the divine nature being infinite, this work in the soul is always open to growth. Indeed Claudine goes on to endorse this in the next few sentences when she speaks about being rendered 'completely divine in the interior'. It would have seemed, at the beginning of this prayer, that Claudine could have been considered among the moralists, so much did she insist on the acquisition of the virtues. However, she only practises these virtues out of the motive of love: it is because she loves Jesus Christ and wishes to show him that she desires to be like him and to make herself completely conformable to him, for example, in obeying him as he himself obeyed his Father, as his humanity subjected itself to his divinity. The theological perspicacity displayed in all of this prayer, and the ability to put it into simple words, comes to an astonishing conclusion at the end. In order to become conformed to Jesus Christ, she does not count so much on a continual mortification as on the Eucharist (as we shall go on to see), prayer and love, through which - as in the case of St Paul who, significantly, with all his emphasis on Christ, finally refers the Christian ultimately to the Creator, the Father (cf. Col. 3:10) - she is drawn, she says at the end of the prayer, into the bosom of the Father where her only occupation will be to contemplate, praise and love Christ. This whole prayer can only bespeak the exceptional quality of Claudine Moine's text both spiritually and theologically, and throw a more meaningful light on the apophatic aspects of her spirituality we have hitherto encountered (cf. text, pp. 70-1, Note 111 and 112); she has already prepared us for this: see text, p. 82, Note 147. In a word, the theology of the *kenosis* we find in St Paul's Epistle to the Philippians (chap. 2) is to my mind the dominant spirituality in this prayer.

106 In the more traditional sense, Claudine is expressing here her desire for divinisation. But transubstantiation is only a comparison. What is to be noted instead is the important place given to the Eucharist in her writings, that is the central role it played in her spiritual formation, and this without any detriment to the place of mental prayer in her life. From the moment God 'looked at' her, Claudine experienced for Communion a desire which continued to grow unceasingly, to the point of becoming a veritable torment for her on the days she was not allowed to approach the holy table. For unlike nowadays, when everyone goes to Communion as they wish, in Claudine's time the number of times you went to Communion was determined by your confessor; and it was an indication of how advanced you were spiritually. Very quickly, however, Claudine was admitted to the Communion table daily.

She considered the Eucharist to be the essential means of all spiritual growth; in fact she declared that she almost never 'received graces except through Holy Communion' (see text, p. 81). For calming the passions and practising the virtues, this means is more efficacious than all the asceticism in the world; it is the sovereign remedy for all evils and the source of all good for us. The soul that in humility and confidence nourishes itself with this sacrament, finds itself, in the end, entirely transformed. And the Eucharist is not only the means of arriving at this union of transformation; it is also its finished model, since, under the appearances of the host which remained unchanged, subsists a divine reality. At the time when these words were written, this prayer had already been heard by God. It would seem that this would have been the period when Claudine, the servant of God, was elevated to the spiritual marriage. She herself never uses this expression. She speaks only of a union or a transformation; but the descriptions she gives us of the effects realised in herself through grace correspond to that which all authors call 'transforming union' or 'spiritual marriage'. Claudine has already attributed this transforming union to the Eucharist (see text, p. 82). From the beginning of her spiritual life, as she hesitated to communicate as often as her desire to do so would have wanted, an interior voice encouraged her in these words: 'Go to God as you are, and he will make you that which he wishes you to be' (text, p. 81). For her, the Eucharist is not only the source of the whole mystical life, but also the supreme model of spiritual transformation (see text, pp. 81-4). The union which results from this cannot be considered as a dissolution of the personality; for a powerful exchange of love establishes itself then between God and the soul, always distinct from its Creator, even though it is considered to be deified. On the images of the Eucharist in Claudine Moine, see Jean Orcibal, 'La Couturière mystique', *La Vie spirituelle* (May 1960), pp. 533-9. For example, at Communion, Claudine sees Communion as a sea and she herself as a drop of water thrown therein in order to be lost (see text, p. 78). See the same idea in P. Guilloré, *Les Progrès de la vie spirituelle* (Paris, 1675), vol. 3, chap. 3; *Oeuvres spirituelles du P. Guilloré* (Paris, 1684), p. 587. On the Eucharist, as a sacramental means of attaining the greatest heights of the interior life, see the important work by Ephrem Longpré, 'Eucharistie et expérience mystique', in *Dictionnaire de spiritualité*, ed. M. Villier (Paris, 1932-), vol. 4, col. 1586-1621. In 1960 Longpré (died 1965) expressed his regret that he hadn't known Claudine before the appearance of his article. Although the Eucharist holds the primary place in her spiritual development, we must not forget the important role given to prayer in Claudine's life. One will recall how she consecrated an hour to prayer each morning, before going to Mass (see text, p. 86), and resumed it often again in the evening (p. 87). Her prayer is faithfully prepared the evening before with a reading of some kind; but more important in her opinion is the lengthy and more drawn-out preparation, which consists in leading a mortified and recollected life, and above in offering oneself totally to the good pleasure of God. She will later give a description of the states of prayer which constitute a new - and more profound - exposition of her spiritual journey from the time of the first favours to the Great Darkness: see text, pp. 203-15. Infused prayer for her produces multiple effects of which the first is a great aversion to sin (see text, p. 83), then mistrust of oneself (pp. 51, 72), confidence in God, humility, simplicity, docility, and peace above all. And the synthesis of her thinking would be: all prayer achieves its summit through the Eucharist; it is particularly at Holy Communion that the soul receives from its Saviour the greatest testimonies of love, and it is at this time that it forces itself, on its part, to give itself completely to him (text, p. 218).

107 Cf. John 6:57.

108 Cf. Gal. 2:20.

109 The palace of the Louvre, but used here in the plural: an unusual way of referring to it.

110 Cf. John 17:24.

111 Cf. text, p. 83.

112 In the manuscript the name 'Padua' is not complete.

113 St Anthony of Padua was a Franciscan.

114 The only convent of Franciscan nuns in the district of the Annonciade and St Louis was Ave Maria. This convent does not exist today; and the only memory of it is retained in the name of the road, Rue de l'Ave Maria.

Notes

115 Not an English word; but used in mystical language to indicate that the heart was pierced by love - the wound of love. It comes from the Latin verb *transverberare* (to pierce through). Consequently, in speaking about a supernatural action, we speak about 'piercing through the heart'. The word is used in this form among French writers in spirituality to refer to the ecstasy of love experienced by the soul when it is pierced by the wound of love. The most famous and well-known example of this is taken from the life of St Teresa of Avila (see below, Note 116). And this experience described by Claudine is almost a word-for-word repetition of that of St Teresa. This does strengthen the belief that Claudine was more than acquainted with the writings of St Teresa, and was also somewhat influenced by her: see Introduction, pp. 21-2.

116 Cf. *The Life of Saint Teresa of Avila*, translated by E. Allison Peers (first published in *The Complete Works of St. Teresa of Jesus*, London: Sheed & Ward, 1944; this independent edition published 1979, reprinted 1984), chap. XXIX, pp. 191-3. With this notion of the wound of love, we find ourselves once again face to face with a powerful evocation of the mystery of the Incarnation. We have already come across equally strong, human images in Claudine's relationship with Christ (see text, pp. 57, 61, 81). Love is God. And God is the divine archer who sends the chosen arrow, his only Son. Claudine's experience here is a continuation of that loving conversion of hers, that moment when God 'touched her'. 'O beautiful wound and sweet hurt', writes Gregory of Nyssa, 'through which life penetrates to the interior in clearing a way for itself through the rent (fissure) of the arrow as a door and a passage. For hardly does the soul feel itself to be smitten with the arrow of love, that already its wound is transforming itself into nuptial joy' (Gregory of Nyssa, *In Cantica Canticorum* (On the Song of Songs), Homily 4, PG 44, col. 852B; the translation is mine). Here Gregory is commenting on the words of our Lord: 'If anyone loves me he will keep my word, / and my Father will love him, / and we shall come to him / and make our home with him' (John 14:23). Other texts of Gregory will tell us of the profound purification this wound effects in us, and others still will speak about the wound of ecstasy in the soul as 'the exit of the Word of God': 'It [the soul] is smitten and wounded by the despair of never being able to obtain that which it desires. But this veil of sadness is taken away from it when it learns that the true possession of him whom it loves, is never to cease from desiring him' (Gregory of Nyssa, *In Cantica Canticorum* (On the Song of Songs), Homily 12, PG 44, col. 1037B; the translation is mine). This then is the meaning behind the word 'transverberation'.

117 Cf. text, p. 102, Note 40. We have already discussed the radicalism in Claudine's language with regard to the *apatheia* (cf. text, p. 114, Note 85; 117, Note 96; 120, Note 102; 121, Note 104). A close reading of her text will absolve her of any accusation in this regard. The description of 'transverbera-tion' in the previous section is ample proof that her spiritual experience was truly Christian and deeply rooted in incarnational theology. We must regard Claudine's experience of God as having been real also from the side of God. It was not just an intellectual experience stemming from her own powers to purify her own mind of everything created and transitory, hence the eradication and elimination of all the passions in order to see God; which would have been nothing less than the worst forms of gnosticism. The sense behind the words - 'destroying them [natural inclinations and passions] entirely' - must be seen in the context of God's particular help to her during times of temptation. In other words, something radical had to be done first so that evil could be eradicated from her so she could enjoy the happy result of seeing her natural passions savouring their union with the will of God. With the passions purified through *apatheia*, Claudine enters into what is called the *parresia* (cf. text, p. 60, Note 72) as the crowning of the *apatheia*, and finds again the freedom of her relationship with God: the soul dares anew to present itself before him, entering into his familiarity (p. 53). The appearance of the *parresia* is the culminating point of the *apatheia*, and marks also the end of the Purgative Way. It is the restoration of the soul into the paradise of the divine friendship (cf. Daniélou, *Platonisme*, p. 104). It is essentially the restoration of the image of God in us (cf. text, p. 121, Note 105); and in this state of the *parresia*, the soul turns to God with confidence: from a paradise lost the soul now comes to a paradise regained (cf. Daniélou, *Platonisme*, 103-15), removing all fear and being now at home with God.

118 Claudine does not spell out what these other desires are, as distinct from what she has referred to in the previous sentence as her natural inclinations and passions. As she stated earlier (cf. text, p. 60) that she had no more knowledge of her sins after she had confessed them, the ambiguity expressed here reflects something of that state of spiritual anaesthesia in which she is no longer that aware of distinctions between good and evil and the various passions of her soul. It would seem to be the beginning of the dark night of the spiritual senses.

119 Claudine is now entering the state we refer to as the Great Darkness. After her early lessons in the spiritual life during her adolescent years in the convent school at Langres (see text, pp. 44-5), and the reversals of fortune caused by the war (p. 46), she was already serving God with a generous heart when, sometime before the feast of All Saints 1642, she was 'touched' (see text, pp. 60, 75) by God (p. 51). Six months of infused favours from God followed (see text, p. 52), and these favours absorbed her completely; next came two years of temptations (see text, p. 56), followed by a period of progressive appeasement; then three years of great lights (see text, p. 67) which ended in the union of transformation (see text, p. 82; also, see text, p. 124). Finally the Great Darkness invaded her (see text, p. 127); but eventually let her soul dwell in a profound peace, arrived at through her experience of the weight of the divine action in her life.

120 Her benefactor.

121 Cf. Matt. 13:13. Ordinarily darkness designates the negative character of the mystical life, its transcendence with relation to thought. But to this aspect corresponds a positive reality: the mystical life is the domain of union and love. In referring to the 'mystical life' here, I do not intend to jeopardise the objectivity of our commentary by labelling Claudine too hastily as a mystic; but it does help to throw some light on the spiritual experience she is having. The three years of infused lights (see text, p. 67), manifesting the Trinity as well as the grandeur of God to her (see text, pp. 185-8), provoked - by their intensity - in Claudine's consciousness the effacement, or elimination of all creatures from her life. And soon God would hide himself from her, as in a cloud which will invade her soul little by little. Reflecting then on this evolution which was being produced in her, Claudine herself will show in the pages that follow how the passage from light to darkness was brought about in three stages (also, for a foretaste of these three stages, see text, pp. 75-7, where she speaks about the three states of her soul). First, Claudine was for many years no longer able to focus her attention on herself. The knowledge she had received of her own nothingness had as a consequence the effect of making herself disappear, as it were, from the domain of her own consciousness. Secondly, in the course of the second stage, the clear vision she had of God pushed aside, so to say, the external world as if into a sort of shadow. To the extent that she had use of them in order to work, Claudine still made use of her senses; but she did not experience any true sensation from them any more. Thirdly, God finally hid himself from her, and, except for very short intervals, all the supernatural lights she had disappeared. The soul is still full of affections, but does not discern any longer with actual knowledge what their cause or source is. All visions were taken from her; their effect, however, remained profoundly engraved on her soul, being part of her very being and finding themselves revivified at the slightest breath of the spirit. Later, Claudine will compare herself with a blind person who, introduced to a prince, can be assured of his presence without seeing him. God is present now in the soul, in as real a sense as a newly-conceived child is in a pregnant woman. As with Matt. 13:13, then, it is a seeing without seeing in so far as it is a real experience of God's love and not just an intellectual awakening to the knowledge of his existence: God is flesh and blood for Claudine, not a concept. Is this, then, what we must regard as a 'mystical' experience?

122 See text, p. 70, Note 111.

123 The days of fast and abstinence.

124 When she started to put wine into the water, to redden it.

125 In her little room: see text, p. 60. She is speaking about leaving her retreat and solitude where she had been for about three years. She is referring here to leaving that little room and going to live in her benefactor's house (see text, p. 64).

Notes

126 Cf. St Francis de Sales, '*Introduction à la vie dévote*', Preface, in *Saint François de Sales: Oeuvres* (Bibliothèque de la Pléiade), Editions Gallimard, Paris, 1969, p. 24. Recall that Claudine was given this book, the *Introduction to the Devout Life*, by Francis de Sales, by a Jesuit priest during the period of her convalescence after her accident: see text, p. 47.

127 See text, p. 77.

128 See text, p. 78. Claudine does not quote herself verbatim here. There are a few changes in the words she uses: a further indication that Claudine always wrote from memory.

129 This sentence must not be separated from the one preceding it. It is not the real destruction of creation that Claudine is asking for here, but that it would have no attraction in her life so that she would be free to give herself completely to her God. This is really her prayer for the fulfilment of her vocation to the hidden life.

130 See text, p. 65, Note 103. Cf. Plotinus, 'The flight of the alone to the Alone', *Enneads IV*. This is the notorious phrase in which Plotinus (204-70) defined the soul's possession or enjoyment of eternity: cf. Evelyn Underhill, *The Essentials of Mysticism* (London: J.M. Dent & Sons Ltd., 1920; reprint New York: AMS Press Inc., 1976), p. 64. Much negative criticism of the mystics almost always includes the charge that their experience of God is too personal and relies too much on personal satisfaction. Standing aloof from humanity, claiming a special knowledge of God, a special privilege of communion with him, these mystics are often represented as having an unsocial type of religion: that their spiritual experiences are personal and individual and that they do not share or value the more community-minded institutions of the Church to which they belong. Undoubtedly Claudine's words do refer to the mystic's need for solitude. But we must realise that the corporate experience of God always begins in a personal experience of God. So Claudine, who is never removed from complete obedience to the Church (see text, General Conclusion, p. 239), must be considered among those whose mission it is to step out of history, as it were, pushing us beyond the protective limits of the structure of the Church, and bring us back into direct touch with the pristine values of the Gospel. It is this simplicity which characterises the Christian realism we find in all great spiritual people: because they are in direct contact with God in Jesus Christ. It is understandable that the individual soul, overcome by the intensity of its experience, would want God for itself. And although the radicalism of the Christian life demands of us to give freely to others as God has given to us, it must be emphasised here that the more intense and authentic one's personal relationship with God is, the more it prepares one for the Christian commitment of love to others: 'But when the soul is wholly turned to God all people are equally dear to him, for he then feels no other cause for loving than God himself. So all are loved simply and sincerely, for God's sake as well as his own' (*The Cloud of Unknowing*, translated by Clifton Wolters, London: Penguin Classics, 1961, chap. 25, p. 93).

131 Perhaps the person in question here is the addressee of her writings, Father Castillon.

132 A scholastic term which could be translated here as 'likenesses'.

133 Notice here a certain Platonism in her use of language. The influence of Plato on Christian thinking and language - especially through the Neoplatonism of Plotinus (see above) and Philo (*ca.* 25-20 BC to after 41 AD) would also undoubtedly manifest itself in a doctrine of the soul that would countenance lower and higher orders of the soul's vision and return to the One, the absolute Godhead from which the soul originally came, or, to be more exact, fell.

134 See text, p. 127.

135 Cf. Guennou, *La Couturière mystique de Paris*, p. 298; Orcibal, *La Vie spirituelle*, p. 535.

136 See text, p. 70, Note 111.

137 The author of *The Cloud of Unknowing* says as much when he wants to get across the correct understanding of 'nowhere' and 'nothingness' in the soul's experience of God: 'Let go this Everywhere and this Everything in exchange for this Nowhere and this Nothing. Never mind if you cannot fathom this nothing, for I love it surely so much the better. It is so worthwhile in itself that no thinking about it will do it justice. One can feel this nothing more easily than see it, for it is completely dark and hidden to those who have only just begun to look at it' (*The Cloud of Unknowing*, pp. 142-3).

138 See text, p. 102.

139 A gentle reminder to us of the *apatheia*.

140 This distinction will make a fortune for Kant (1724-1804), 127 years later. See text, p. 160, where she speaks about seeing the visible and perceptible world with new eyes. But unlike Kant, Claudine will see the beauty of the created world as leading to the contemplation of God, the Creator (p. 160). In other words, Claudine would be thinking as St Paul did, when he said: 'And so we have no eyes for things that are visible, but only for things that are invisible; for visible things last only for a time, and the invisible things are eternal' (2 Cor. 4:18); see above, p. 84. Claudine's philosophical consciousness here should not surprise us much, seeing that the Cartesian revolution was in the very air she breathed. Descartes (1596-1650) had just published his *Discourse on Method* in 1637, five years before Claudine's arrival in Paris in 1642; and with her spiritual training of the Jesuits, with their emphasis on the Spiritual Exercises, Claudine was a child of her time and bound to have been influenced by the prevailing emphasis on method in seventeenth-century France. As there is a method for finding the truth, there must also be a method for becoming holy; so we see developing in the seventeenth century a certain cult of the inner life. But I believe that we must attribute this philosophical sensitivity of Claudine's above all to her spiritual maturity, which she demonstrates with great clarity as she moves on (see text, pp. 138-9). Here and elsewhere (see text, pp. 77-8, Notes 132, 133, 135) Claudine is firmly established in the Illuminative Way in her thinking.

141 The sentiments expressed here, and generally in the preceding pages, are a clear indication of the spiritual depth of Claudine's thinking and of the essentially Christian basis for it: our sanctification comes only from the loving and healing grace of the Cross of Christ (see text, p. 134). The mature progress Claudine herself has made in her spiritual life is evident from these pages, but always subject to the gratuitous grace of God in Jesus Christ.

142 See text, p. 77; p. 121, Note 104.

143 A proof of the healing power of God's love and grace. He will not remember our sins; he will wipe them all out: cf. Ezek. 18:23, 36:25-32; Hos. 11:8ff.; Ps. 78:38, 103:3. 'Though your sins are like scarlet, / they shall be as white as snow; / though they are as red as crimson, / they shall be like wool' (Isa. 1:18). Claudine's words point out that to obtain forgiveness, conversion is necessary. And a conversion of any real value must begin with an awareness of our own wretchedness: 'When a man is experiencing in his spirit this nothing in its nowhere, he will find that his outlook undergoes the most surprising changes. As the soul begins to look at it, he finds that all his past sins, spiritual and physical, which he has committed from the day he was born are secretly and sombrely depicted on it' (*The Cloud of Unknowing*, chap. 69, p. 143). See also text, p. 73. But Claudine had already gone far beyond this stage; the attachment to sin had been taken away from her. She even says that once she confessed her sins, she had no more knowledge of them (see text, p. 60). 'If memories of your past actions keep coming between you and God, or any new thought or sinful impulse, you are absolutely to step over them, because of your deep love for God; you must trample them down under foot. Try to cover them with the thick cloud of forgetting, as if they never had been committed, either by you or anyone else' (*The Cloud of Unknowing*, chap. 31, pp. 97-8). See text, p. 60, Note 72, for a discussion of the *epectasis* and St Paul's notion of forgetting the past and striving to what lies ahead (Phil. 3:13) as the secret of spiritual progress.

144 See text, p. 60.

145 See text, p. 73. Claudine is moved by the spirit, and her spiritual experience is not the result of some intellectual illuminism or of her own reasoning. It is important to mention this here, for it is fundamental in any assessment of the spiritual experience of Claudine Moine: she had a real experience of God. 'Hence we put first among our essentials [of mysticism] the clear conviction of a living God as the primary interest of consciousness, and of a personal self capable of communion with Him . . . his [the mystic's] communion with God is always personal in this sense: that it is communion with a living Reality, an object of love, capable of response, which demands and receives from him a total self-donation. This sense of a double movement, a self-giving on the divine side

answering to the self-giving on the human side, is found in all great mysticism' (Underhill, *The Essentials of Mysticism*, pp. 3-4).

146 See text, pp. 59-60, 72.

147 See text, p. 83. Here, and in the following sentence where Claudine admits that she considered her state to be common to everyone, she is sharing with most mystics an optimistic view of salvation. Claudine's optimistic view for man's salvation is reminiscent of Julian of Norwich's puzzlement with regard to the tension in her mind rising from the fact of God's love and the existence of sin: 'But Jesus, who in this vision informed me of all I needed, answered, Sin was necessary - but it is all going to be all right; it is all going to be all right; everything is going to be all right' (*Julian of Norwich: Revelations of Divine Love*, translated into modern English and with an introduction by Clifton Wolters, Penguin Classics, 1966, chap. 27, p. 103). Julian will go on to say that 'in every soul to be saved is a godly will that has never consented to sin, in the past or in the future' (ibid., chap. 37, p. 118); indeed, Claudine speaks about the will too, see text, p. 135. Although Julian goes so far as to say that she did not see sin, and that she believes that sin has no substance or real existence (ibid., p. 104) - something which would be a questionable stance to take in the eyes of the Church - her heterodoxy is typical of a certain kind of mystic who must struggle to fit theology to their personal spiritual experience. It is very unlikely that Claudine would have known about Julian (born towards the end of 1342 and died around 1416); but the similarities in thought between the English anchorite and the French dressmaker at least speak for the solidarity of the mystical experience.

148 Cf. text, pp. 77, 78, Note 136. Being directed by her Jesuit confessors, it is not surprising that Claudine had arrived at such an advanced stage of detachment - which is very central to Ignatian spirituality; although it must be kept in mind that the spiritual direction she received from the Jesuits was always in conformity with the movements of the spirit in herself: cf. text, pp. 61, 64, 90, 110. In one place she is recorded as having said that she regards herself as having been taught by God (text, p. 53).

149 Her benefactors.

150 Cf. above, Note 148. Claudine is moved by the spirit in everything she does.

151 Father Castillon.

152 Cf. text, pp. 64, 90, 110.

153 Cf. text, p. 62.

154 This new confessor is not identified.

155 Cf. text, p. 53, where Claudine speaks about writing a report for her confessor, Father Jarry, to let him know the state of her soul. She does not mention explicitly any other report; but she assures us of having proceeded in the same way every time she changed confessor (pp. 110-11); for it would be unreasonable to think that she would have acted otherwise, all the more so because the response given by all her confessors was the same, as one might judge from what she writes: ' but especially with regard to the direction of my heart and mind, they [her confessors] only said to me to follow in simplicity the attractions of God' (text, p. 111).

156 She was not considering anyone in particular to be her confessor.

157 This fifth confessor remains likewise unknown.

158 A total, then, of three years and nine months.

159 In reality, Father Castillon, her third confessor; but the first with regard to those whom she has just spoken of.

160 Perhaps Father Castillon, the addressee of her writings.

161 She is probably referring here to her writings, which she would never have written if it were not for the fact that she did so out of obedience to her confessor, Father Castillon, the priest in question.

162 Cf. text, p. 132, Note 140. To see things as they are is not to be understood here in the philosophical sense. The Illuminative Way, of which we have found the expression in the book of Ecclesiastes (cf. text, pp. 75, 77, 78. Notes 120, 132, 135, 137), has convinced the soul of the vanity of everything which is not God (cf. text, p. 78), and at the same time the soul's inability to reach God through the

natural forces of our intelligence: cf. Daniélou, *Platonisme*, p. 209. The soul has to be able to cry out like the Preacher, Qoheleth, 'Vanity of vanities . . . Vanity of vanities! All is vanity!' (Eccles. 1:2), see the vanity of the things of this world, be aware that it has been a victim of an illusion, an error, and that it has let itself be deceived by false appearances, not seeing things as they really are. The object of the Illuminative Way, then, is to redress one's judgement, to give a just appreciation of things, that is, above all, to see the error of judgement which causes one to overestimate the visible goods and to underestimate the real goods. Man was made for the invisible world; but he has been so immersed in the perceptible that his spiritual faculties have been darkened and he himself has lost the sense of his true nature: cf. Daniélou, *Platonisme*, p. 122. In his *Commentary on Ecclesiastes*, Gregory of Nyssa deals with this question of the vanity of creatures, or the visible world, and represents them as a dream, as an illusion (cf. Gregory of Nyssa, *In Ecclesiasten Salomonis*, PG 44, col. 629B; *In Cantica Canticorum*, PG 44, col. 996A-B; Daniélou, *Platonisme*, pp. 121-6). So the whole meaning of the visible world is not to be an end in itself, as if this is where the real world lies, but to be a symbol, that is a means of directing us to God, the invisible, but real, world. So, to see things as they really are, the science of being, is the privilege of the divinity, but also of the person who has God as his final end. In short, we are talking here about the contemplative who, having left the things of this world, the natural senses, can now examine terrestrial things, and, with a spiritual sense, see how they relate to their final end. Throughout all of this section, Claudine is speaking about the Illuminative Way, the way of the contemplative; and, as a result of God having 'touched' her (text, pp. 60, 75), the first stage the soul must go through that has been separated from sin and has recuperated its pristine serenity (*apatheia*) and boldness (*parresia*), is to disengage itself from the visible goods of the world and to attach itself to its invisible realities. Below, Claudine goes on to develop this further.

163 This is, of course, the complete opposite to what we would normally refer to as covetousness.

164 An extremely difficult passage to translate. The ellipsis has been added in order to indicate that the sentence does not seem to be completed. In the manuscript it is separated from the preceding sentence and the one that follows it by a full stop.

165 Claudine is beginning to develop here the notion of the spiritual senses. On this question, see Karl Rahner, 'Le début d'une doctrine des cinq sens spirituels chez Origène', *Revue ascétique et mystique* (1932), pp. 113-45. For, to a person who has learned the good use of all things through the means of a religious consideration of the world, and is persuaded of the vanity and instability of everything visible, the gates of knowledge and contemplation are opened (ibid., p. 132). See also Daniélou, *Platonisme*, pp. 222-52. In all of this section on the Great Darkness, Claudine is clearly describing the nature of the Illuminative Way which has for its essential objective the dissipating of the illusion of the perceptible pleasures and the giving back to one the taste for God. It is this experience of God which is at the heart of the mystical life. Consequently the doctrine of the spiritual senses, by which we become capable of savouring God, plays an essential role in this.

166 In this dark night of the soul, which Claudine is describing here, she is obliquely stating that she is being led by the spirit. In conformity with Jesuit spirituality of the 'mystical invasion' of the soul (Hugo Rahner, *Spirituality of St Ignatius Loyola*, translated by F.J. Smith, SJ, Westminster, Md, 1953, p. 47), Claudine comes across in all of this section on the Great Darkness as a perfect example of her Jesuit training (see text, p. 135, Note 136; p. 140, Note 156). It was under the direction of Father Castillon that Claudine was introduced to the Great Darkness. In this darkness she was no longer conscious of her body or her soul; for, to the gifts of God also follows a faith that 'is pure and stripped of light and feeling, except at intervals when it is given some small rays' (see text, p. 138). Looking into herself, Claudine does not know if this state is good or bad (see text, pp. 130, 134, 146). And she can surely doubt it, all the more because her natural inclinations are awakened again (see text, pp. 197 -8). The only thing that remains to her now is union in the night through mortification, patience and resignation, for she puts her sovereign contentment in doing in everything the will of God (see text, pp. 139-41, 199-200). Under the movement of the spirit alone, and taught by God alone (see text, pp. 160, 202), Claudine's spirituality does not belong to any particular school, but is a synthesis of many.

Notes

This particular characteristic of her spirituality is due to the excellent direction she received from the Jesuits (see text, p. 111). Because of her direct experience of being taught by God, Claudine was forced to go back to the simplicity of the Gospels, avoiding all the complications of theological schools often found in various manuals of spirituality. Claudine is stating simply that her schooling was directly from the spirit. This is borne out, I think, in the pages that follow, by the very fact that Claudine, having dealt with the Great Darkness, goes on to discuss love. Her 'abstract' stage (on the Abstract School of Spirituality, see Louis Cognet, *Histoire de la Spiritualité Chrétienne*, Paris: Aubier, 1966, pp. 233-73) is only a passing and purifying one - the dark night of the soul, as it were - on her journey to love.

167 Cf. text, p. 78, Note 137.

168 See the influence that this sentence exercised on Madame Acarie, otherwise known as Mary of the Incarnation (1566-1618), in A. du Val, *La Vie de la Soeur Marie de l'Incarnation*, 10th edition (Paris, 1647), p. 28.

169 Allusion to Luke 9:24.

170 Cf. text, p. 77.

171 Cf. Thomas Aquinas, *Summa*, Pt 1, q. 8, art. 3. Perhaps Claudine is inspired here by Thomas Deschamps: cf. *Le Jardin des contemplatifs* (Paris, 1605), p. 763; but more importantly by some sermon heard at the church of St Louis, for she could not have taken this phrase directly from St Thomas.

172 Claudine does not ask to die, but to escape from the sin of fragility.

173 The life of the Eucharist is understood in contrast here.

174 The domain of the instincts.

175 This was the prayer of St Francis-Xavier before his departure for India: cf. A. Brou, *Saint François-Xavier*, vol. 3 (Paris, 1912), p. 282. Claudine could have known this treatise through the preaching she heard at St Louis, or through A. Ribadeneira and A. du Val, *Les Fleurs des vies des Saints*, vol. 2, (Rouen, 1645), p. 722, col. 1; p. 731, col. 1.

176 A reminder of St Augustine, cf. text, p. 69, Note 109.

177 Cf. text, p. 43, Note 2. In the conversion, or change of heart that begins the spiritual life, the eyes are opened to visions beyond the span of average sight; in a sense one becomes one's own parent of a new life, born again in baptism: cf. Gregory of Nyssa, *De Vita Moysis* (On the Life of Moses), PG 44, col. 327B; *La Vie de Moïse*, Sources Chrétiennes 1, p. 32.

178 Cf. text, p. 61, Note 78.

179 Cf. text, p. 178, for the same idea. Also, cf. text, p. 168ff.

180 Cf. Luke 1:38.

181 Whether conscious of it or not, Claudine's clear reference here to the fact that Jesus's soul and humanity were distinct from his divinity is a strong indication of how authentic her Christology was. She could actually identify herself with Jesus, for he, although divine, is also human and has a human soul like one of us.

182 In keeping with the more incarnational side to her discourse evident here, one would expect Claudine to refer to 'Father' instead of 'God'.

183 The oxymoron, empty/full, is typical of the kind of language the mystics use in order to describe more effectively the soul's spiritual experience: see Daniélou, *Platonisme*, pp. 274-84. The spiritual awakening of Claudine's conversion is not a mere intellectual awareness, but could be best described as a watchful sleep in which she becomes aware of the fact that God was 'looking at' her: in her experience, then, God is real also from his side and is not merely the result of the pure activity of Claudine's mind. See text, p. 79, Note 139.

184 See text, p. 78, Note 137. It is in a passage like this where Claudine is most apophatic (see text, p. 70, Note 111) in her thinking, and it would lead one to wonder how this passage can be reconciled with the more Christ-centred ones that have gone before it which give a very vivid impression of the humanity of Jesus. All we can say is, that her experience of God in Christ must have been so real that

she needed no help from any outside source, be it conceptual or of the imagination, to experience this. Of course, this is the real life of the contemplative. And it is possible that Claudine is already writing here from her experience of the Unitive Way, which would explain why her language is not always that easy to understand and is thereby often subject to a wrong interpretation. Her text is not a treatise. So, a central characteristic of her text, and something we should be constantly aware of as we read it, is that, moved by the spirit (see text, p. 135, Note 148), her writings always reflect the state she is in at the time of writing. Her rejection of any image of God is her way of saying that she is already united with God in the knowledge that he loves her and will continue to love her.

185 In the French text, Claudine uses the phrase 'dresser ses intentions'. What she means by this is best found within the overall context of her ideas expressed in this section. As the rest of this paragraph indicates, Claudine seems to be saying that the rectitude of her intentions does not occur as the result of the pure activity of her own will. Avoiding the obvious dangers of voluntarism by going on to show how her delight in God was the result of a single glance at God, a simple sentiment that the soul was not even aware of, Claudine is strongly saying that every real experience of God comes from God's initiative who first 'looked at' her.

186 A certain Quietism could be detected in this sentence. It seems to me that Claudine's desire to show that it was love that moved her in all things suggests something of that tendency. But Claudine's analysis of the will is extremely important in this context, especially since, in the West, we are inclined to regard the will as facultative, in other words, as another intellect. She is by no means a voluntarist. Nor is she a quietist; for Claudine's reflection on the experience of God in her life is not a passive devotional contemplation with the extinction of the will and the withdrawal of the senses from all things; but, on the contrary, her will is totally engaged in loving God. Claudine is not being influenced unduly by any school of thought; showing the originality of her spirituality. Claudine goes on to verify this total absorption in God in the lines that follow, by explaining that, for her, the soul cannot act or operate except through the movement of the spirit of God and of Jesus Christ and his love. In this state, her will is completely one with the will of God.

187 Morally speaking; for the soul remains resolutely in an attitude of dependence with regard to the interior motion, for as long as this manifests itself. See text, pp. 223-6 where Claudine speaks about the ways in which God speaks to the soul and governs it.

188 In the pages that follow we shall see that Claudine's spiritual awakening was not merely intellectual, after the manner of the Greeks and Plato, but countenanced a real union with God. For the property of love is to effect union. All the following section, emphasising the primacy of love in experiencing God, is very important: it shows us above all how for Claudine the way of love and union is open, while that of knowledge or the intellect is closed. The primacy of love and therefore of the mystical life, which is the dominant character of her spirituality, is expressed here; and this love is essentially identified with the historical and mystical Christ. In fact, in the following account, 'Light', we shall see the relation that is established between the Eucharist and love: the Eucharist for Claudine is the sacrament of union, of love. There is then a peculiar relationship for her between the Eucharist and the mystical life. In one sense we can regard Claudine Moine as a mystic of the Eucharist. She herself states that she scarcely ever received graces except through Holy Communion (see text, p. 81). This fact alone removes any doubt in our minds about the Christian aspect of Claudine's spirituality.

189 It is in this indirect way by which Claudine exercises her hidden apostolate. See text, p. 77, Note 128.

190 See text, p. 70, Note 110.

191 Not the result of Quietism, but another way of referring to the primacy of love over knowledge in her spirituality.

192 Claudine then can not be accused of Illuminism, or the doctrines of those sixteenth-century Spanish heretics, known as the *Illuminati* (in Spanish they were known as the *Alumbrados*), who claimed special enlightenment in religious matters. Neither the repose of Quietism nor the enlightenment of the *Illuminati*, her spiritual experience of God can only be described as a knowledge of love,

the knowledge that God loves her and will continue to love her. She is sustained by that knowledge alone, and not by any favours she is conscious of having received from God. This then must be the darkness of mystical union, loving God because he is God, for his own sake, hence pure love.

193 See text, p. 68.

194 Remember the part played by choice in all spiritual conversions: see text, p. 51, Note 47.

195 'If I may use a funny example, I would suggest you do all you can to cloak your great and ungoverned spiritual urge; as though you were altogether unwilling that he [God] should know how very glad you would be to see him, to have him, to feel him . . . . One reason why I bid you hide from God the desire of your heart is this: I think it is a clearer way of bringing to his notice what you are aiming at, and it is more beneficial for you, and will sooner fulfil your desire, than any other sort of demonstration.' *Cloud of Unknowing*, pp. 115-6). Here, as in the case of Claudine, the suggestion is that we should hide our desires from God, to save us from having too physical an understanding of the spiritual life.

196 An allusion to S. of S. 3:1, 'Upon my bed by night I sought him whom my soul loves; I sought him, but found him not; I called him, but he gave no answer.'

197 See text, p. 138.

198 An obvious reference to the dark night of the senses spoken of in most works on contemplation.

199 See above, Note 196. The following passage from Gregory of Nyssa develops this same idea with incredible beauty: 'It [the soul] rises again and, by the spirit, travels through the intelligible and hypercosmic world, which it names city; where are found the Principalities, the Dominations and Thrones assigned to Powers; it goes through the assembly of celestial beings, which it names square, and their innumerable multitude, which it names way, looking [to see] if its Beloved is found among them. It traverses in its search the complete and entire angelic world; and as it does not find among the goods it encounters him whom it seeks, it says aside to itself: "Is it, at least, that these can be appreciated by the one whom I love?" But they remain silent to this question, and by this silence they make known to it [the soul] that he whom it seeks is inaccessible to them. Then, after having surveyed by means of the activity of the spirit the whole hypercosmic city, and not having recognised among the intelligible and incorporeal him whom it desires, leaving everything it finds, it recognises that which it seeks by the fact alone that it does not grasp what he is' (Gregory of Nyssa, *In Cantica Canticorum* (On the Song of Songs), PG 44, col. 893A-B; the translation is mine).

200 She must mean by this that she has spoken about it to someone, more than likely her confessor; but that she finds that she writes better about it than she speaks about it.

201 The reference here is obviously to her confessor, Father Castillon, the addressee of her writings: cf. text, p. 157.

202 The reason for this is that Christ has taken over completely in her life; and he is the only way for her.

203 Cf. text, pp. 111, 119, Notes 79, 98.

204 Cf. Tobit 5:12.

205 Cf. text, p. 76.

206 The antithesis set up here between death and existence postulates in the true Pauline fashion that true life never dies.

207 Cf. text, p. 54, for a similar attitude of Claudine with regard to the illusion of this life which, as she says, she only holds in name.

208 Cf. Jean-Baptise de Saint-Jure, *L'Homme spirituel*, Paris, 1646, p. 144. See Introduction for a discussion of this work as a probable source for Claudine. The passage in de Saint-Jure is as follows: 'As it is said, the tyrant Mezentius used to put living men who he wanted to die to lie with dead bodies.' We often hear something spoken of as being comparable to the action of Mezentius (Mezentian), a mythical Etruscan king, who bound living men to corpses and left them to die of starvation (cf. Virgil, *Aeneid*, viii, 485-8).

209 Allusion to 1 Cor. 15:55.

210 In other words, there was nothing in Claudine that could die, since she was already dead to all things, but alive to God. And it is to be expected that the inspiration behind this is again St Paul, 'Life to me, of course, is Christ' (Phil. 1:21). It must be understood that Claudine's whole desire for death is Pauline: 'I want to be gone and be with Christ' (ibid., 1:23-4), cf. p. 150.

211 See text, p. 70, Note 111, for a discussion of the *via negativa* in Claudine's spirituality.

212 Cf. S. of S. 8:6: 'Set me like a seal on your heart, / like a seal on your arm. / For love is strong as Death, / jealousy relentless as Shoel.'

213 Cf. Gen. 2:16, 3:19.

214 The underlying reference here may be to Rom. 8:32, 'Since God did not spare his own Son, but gave him up to benefit us all, we may be certain, after such a gift, that he will not refuse anything he can give.'

215 Cf. Rom. 6:5, 'If in union with Christ we have imitated his death, we shall also imitate him in his resurrection.'

216 Later she will refer to the last moment of her life as the end of her exile and the first moment which will put her in the full and perfect enjoyment of God; in a sense she hopes through the goodness and the merits of Christ to go directly to Heaven (see text, p. 149). But, as she goes on to explain in the following lines, here she is aware of the fact that she must render herself entirely subject to divine justice and believes that she will have to make satisfaction for all her sins in Purgatory.

217 Claudine comes here to the height of her abandonment to the will of God: if it is the will of God that we must die, then it is only in abandoning ourselves to this will that we live. One could regard all of this section as a commentary on St Paul's theology of death.

218 There is a full stop here in the manuscript. But the sentence is not completed; hence the ellipsis I have put here. A simple comma would also create difficulties.

219 The impossible suppositions, since the time of St Paul, are a way of explaining to God that one loves him above all things.

220 The reference is to 'precipice' in the previous paragraph.

221 This statement more than any other allays any fears one might have concerning the authentically Christian aspect of Claudine's spirituality: her spirituality is essentially Eucharistic and is centred on the humanity of Christ.

222 At this stage Claudine has arrived at a crucial moment in her writing about death, where life and death seem to be interchangeable in her thinking: the oxymoron, life/death, is now a more effective way of describing her spiritual experience, a literary device, no doubt, but it is well suited to the use of ecstatic language. For in the language that follows we shall see how Claudine, having shared the cup of Christ's suffering and been purified in *apatheia* (see text, p. 64, Note 100) to become the friend of God (see text, *parresia*, p. 138, Note 162), strives to explain the sufferings of ecstatic union - the two elements characteristic of ecstasy: in the first place, a transport out of oneself (that is, a passage from earthly things which are less good), and secondly, returning to the better (that is, to the divine things). As in the case of David in speaking about what he saw (2 Sam. 23:1-7), Claudine in the pages that follow will struggle with language to describe her mystical experience. And being, as I stated earlier, a mystic of the Eucharist (see text, p. 144, Note 188), Claudine will go on to show in the third account, 'Light', the special relation of ecstasy with the Eucharist, and in general the sacramental character of Christian mysticism (see text, pp. 170-8). It is Christ whom she loves. And bearing testimony to what she has seen ('you looked at me') in fact constitutes the very plan of her writings.

223 The reference here is to the Thirty Years War and the havoc it caused in the fortunes of her family (see text, p. 46, Note 16).

224 The copyist has probably passed over some words here, unless of course it is simply a question of Claudine's own oversight. The words supplied fit in, it seems to me, with the general meaning intended by the sentence.

225 Allusion to the vocation of Abraham (cf. Gen. 12:1). But whether Claudine was alluding to Abraham or not is beside the point; the fact is that it did happen, and this event is central to the whole spiritual journey of Claudine Moine.

Notes

226 There are reminiscences here of the prayers of the Offertory during Mass. Although, in Claudine's time, these prayers would have been said by the priest in Latin, it does not rule out the possibility that Claudine could have had in her possession a French missal of some sort.

227 Cf. text, p. 43, Note 2.

228 Cf. text, p. 149, Note 216.

229 The meaning intended here is, 'Be you "Saviour" to me!', for this is what the name 'Jesus' means in the Hebrew language.

230 This prayer, as indeed all the others that are found scattered throughout her text, merits much more commentary than I can give here. To take all the prayers composed by Claudine herself would make up a substantial volume of texts to be studied for their theological content. My personal view is that she is best as a spiritual writer when she moves into that element of her narrative. Her understanding of the mystery of redemption as centred on Christ comes across in this prayer with a poignancy that belies any questioning about the authentically Christian aspect of her thinking.

231 Cf. 2 Cor. 5:14.

232 Cf. text, p. 123, Note 115, for a description and discussion of the wound of love ('transverberation').

233 This is slightly ambiguous, because burning from love is often used by the mystics as a way of showing how profound their love is. Here again Claudine's language verges on the paradox. Or she could still be referring here to the state of the soul in Purgatory - there the soul does burn from the love of God.

234 The same ambiguity is found in this sentence. It is possible that Claudine is contrasting in her mind the state of Hell to the state of her own soul in Purgatory.

235 This refers to a devotional exercise from some meditation on death, perhaps from *The Spiritual Exercises of Saint Ignatius Loyola*.

236 Cf. Deut. 32:4, 'He is the rock, his work is perfect.' The French translation in the Louvain Bible (Rouen, 1648) reads as follows: 'Les oeuvres de Dieu sont parfaites.' (The works of God are perfect.)

237 Cf. text, pp. 83, 117; Note 94; p. 151, where she speaks about being put back in the state of innocence. Her repeated emphasis on the verb 'finish' is typical of Claudine's constant entreaty to God to complete within her some work he has already begun: a portrait of his Son (cf. text, p. 71).

238 As a result of her excessive desire to be with Christ, Claudine echoes here the same longing as St Paul: cf. Phil. 2:21-5.

239 This, then, would be more in line with St Paul's dilemma: 'I want to be gone and be with Christ, which would be very much better, but for me to stay alive in this body is a more urgent need for your sake.' (Phil. 1:23-5). Claudine begins to understand that staying alive in the body is what God wishes for her now: cf. text, p. 150.

240 This is a very frank confession on the part of Claudine, and is an indication that she has recognised certain dangers in her excessive desire to die.

241 A reference to the desire to die.

242 This whole paragraph is an astonishing confession of a writer, revealing the birth and nature of a work. The genesis of this work is exceptional: moved by the spirit, Claudine only wrote what God had revealed to her about herself. This last sentence is in reference to the fact that she wrote the first account (the most autobiographical account of the four) in the same way. And 'your Reverence' is that same Father Castillon, the addressee of her writings.

243 All this will be the object of the third account, 'Light'.

244 See the fourth account, 'On Prayer'.

245 The absence of the final full stop in the manuscript here could indicate that this last sentence has not been completed.

Light

1 Cf. text, p. 69, Note 108.

2 Cf. text, p. 51, Note 48.

3 Cf. text, p. 132.

4 Cf. de Saint-Jure, 'Notre-Seigneur est un livre en tout le cours de sa vie', *Le Livre des Eluz* (Paris, 1643), p. 2.

5 Franche-Comté (Claudine's homeland) was submitted to the Spanish Inquisition, being then a territory of Spain, whereas France, in this respect, was a more liberal regime as a result of the Edict of Nantes (1598).

6 The name given from about the middle of the sixteenth century to the Protestants of France.

7 As a boarding student in a religious house, or convent school.

8 Cf. Matt. 13:13; Mark 4:12; Luke 8:10; Isa. 6:9.

9 Cf. text, p. 138, Note 166; text, p. 202.

10 Cf. text, p. 65, Note 104.

11 Not unlike in the Revelations of Julian of Norwich, Claudine begins more and more to use this phrase, 'I saw'. The first revelation of Julian of Norwich begins, 'And at once I saw . . .' (cf. *Julian of Norwich: Revelations of Divine Love*, translation by Clifton Wolters, Penguin Classics, 1966, p. 66). The whole of this third account of Claudine broadly resembles the revelations of Julian.

12 This means that he could deny us the Beatific Vision.

13 Cf. text, p. 69, Note 109. Allusion to St Augustine.

14 Cf. 1 Cor. 1:25. St Paul here wants to show that the foolishness of the Cross can only be understood through the excessive love Christ has for us.

15 Cf. text, p. 70, Note 111. Claudine uses this word constantly in order to describe the state of *kenosis* the soul must go through so as to progress spiritually. The stripping of self is the central meaning conveyed in the French use of the word, 'anéantissement'. Her mention of St Paul in the following sentence endorses this spiritual interpretation of the word.

16 Cf. Phil. 2:7.

17 Allusion to 1 Sam. 3:10.

18 Cf. text, pp. 52, 61, 64, 107.

19 Cf. Matt. 2:14-21.

20 Claudine, from Franche-Comté, would have regarded herself to be in a foreign land in Paris, and therefore considered herself to be in exile.

21 The reference to 'room' here is a recollection of the time when she lived alone.

22 Cf. Luke 2:49.

23 Claudine seems to be suggesting that his divinity was so hidden, as a result of such a perfect *kenosis*, that his humanity was not aware of it.

24 Cf. Matt. 17:1-8; Mark 9:2-9; Luke 9:28-36.

25 Claudine uses one word to express this idea, 'passible'. The present French meaning of the word would be 'punishable' by a fine, for example. In this context it could be a transliteration into French of the Latin verb *patior* (to undergo pain). I have translated it as 'capable of experiencing pain'. As part of the common French vocabulary she uses, we often find, sprinkled here and there throughout her text, words and concepts that are of a very technical and theological kind. While Orcibal thinks that many of the images she uses come from the Rhineland mystics (see Orcibal, in 'La couturière mystique', *La Vie spirituelle*, p. 537), I feel that for her theological vocabulary, as in this case I believe, we must look to her confessors as the source, or to the many learned sermons she would definitely have heard in the church of St Louis.

26 His hidden life.

27 In the manuscript there is a blank here; perhaps the text is incomplete.

28 Of course it is not correct to use here the 'first', for the simple reason that Christ died at the age

of 33. It is only a detail, but the linguistic implications would be that Christ lived for another thirty years or so. Of course Claudine did not intend this.

29 Cf. text, pp. 65, 129.

30 Claudine uses the word 'extorsion', but I do not think that she intends this - she probably means the torture that is sometimes involved in the act of extortion.

31 And besides, she says she only committed faults of fragility since the time she had been 'touched' by God: cf. text, p. 96.

32 Throughout this section, Claudine seems to be inspired by the Pauline theology of the Cross: cf. Rom. 6:5-11; 1 Cor. 1:18.

33 Cf. Eph. 4:22-4.

34 Cf. Num. 21:8-9.

35 The word Claudine uses here is 'braverie', which is not to be found in present-day French usage. I have translated it as 'ostentation', referring to the affectation with which people act who place a lot of importance on the beauty of clothes.

36 The French word used here is 'litière'; and the phrase Claudine uses is 'à faire litière de tous les biens et richesses de ce monde' (literally: to make litter of all the goods and riches of this world). This is simply an indication of Claudine's use of the language of the day, and in particular certain language that was used in literary circles of the time. After all, she said that she read many romances and comedies when she was young (see text, p. 45). A closer study of Claudine's vocabulary from the literary side of things would indeed be very rewarding; but this is a study I have not carried out in this translation in any great depth. I leave this for another time. In fact, in the pages that follow, you will find much of the vocabulary of the time of Louis XIII, in authors such as Descartes, Racine, Corneille, etc. We shall be reminded much, throughout this section, of the Christian ideals we find portrayed in Corneille's *Poleucte*, for example.

37 This sentence could easily be the subtitle to Corneille's Christian tragedy *Poleucte*. We should not be surprised, then, to find such words in Claudine as: grandeur, courage, generosity, heart, honour, glory, virtue, vanquish, generous and magnanimous hearts, etc. Claudine came to live in Paris in 1642 (see text, pp. 50-1, Notes 38, 40), in the Marais quarter of the city, just when Corneille's works were being staged in the Théâtre Marais - *Poleucte, Horace, Cinna*: all works in which Corneille was trying to portray on stage the noble virtues of Christianity, while, ironically, Claudine, not too far away, was living them in fact. This, of course, speaks for the spirituality of the hidden life. The point to be emphasised here is that Claudine, despite the fact that she retained very obviously her own individuality in her spiritual life, was also the product of a very definite spiritual trend in seventeenth-century France. Notwithstanding her very personal spiritual experience, it was unlikely she would get through her life without being influenced both in her thinking and in her language by the theological and spiritual trends of the time. We shall see an example of this later when she discusses the Jansenist work of Antoine Arnauld, *De la fréquente communion*. So, as in the works of Corneille, we see here in Claudine a profound sense of human nature, with its supreme conflicts and the tragic alternatives to which they lead, and which, at moments of great crisis, take on exceptional significance. A strong ethical element is conspicuous in all these problems; they primarily concern the moral conscience; the victory at stake is the full mastery of the will over circumstances, and over the sources of weakness that we carry within ourselves. It is a question here of the clashes between passion and duty, and this works itself out mainly in terms of decisions of the soul, subordinated in everything to this pure and dominating issue. In *Poleucte*, for example, it is a war between attachment to a creature and the exclusive claim of Heaven. These alternatives are presented with an incisive neatness which leaves no room for equivocation. They liberate in us whatever idealistic urge there may be, and stimulate us to live nobly. The very atmosphere of Corneille's plays breathes the heroic grandeur Claudine herself asks for in her own life. Self-mastery, which thus appears as the epitome of virtue, includes duty under all its forms: subservience to a high ideal, whether honour, loyalty, or faith; to 'glory', or to feminine pride in chastity - all of which we see lived to the full in the life of Claudine. See Introduction, pp. 15, 22.

38 Cf. 1 Cor. 1:18.

39 Cf. text, p. 161, Note 12.

40 It is obviously the transcendent God she is thinking about here; but we have to be careful in exaggerating this, because it would be very difficult to reconcile this notion of God with the God of Christianity. Take, for example, the following words of St Thomas Aquinas as a good illustration of the dangers in this thinking: 'To sorrow over the miseries of others does not belong to God' (*Summa*, Pt 1, q. 21, art. 3). When we think of the words of the Psalmist, 'Yahweh Sabaoth, bring us back, / let your face smile on us and we shall be safe' (Ps. 80:3), and Claudine's own personal experience of God 'you looked at me', we are confident that the source for Claudine's thinking here must come from some learned sermon she heard and not from her own understanding of the question.

41 Seeing less his bodily pains, and seeing less his virtues, is an oblique reference on Claudine's part to the spiritual journey of the soul that experiences through darkness the progressive indwelling of Christ in the soul (cf. text, p. 127, Note 121). Earlier, Claudine speaks about God's creatures being small shares, or tributaries in his divine perfections (text, p. 160). She is also pointing to the experience of God through the spiritual senses (cf. text, p. 138, Note 165). The first systematic expression of this doctrine (the doctrine of the spiritual senses) is found in Origen. A remarkable passage, from his *Contra Celsum* 1:48, states: 'Anyone who looks into this subject more deeply will say that there is, as the Scripture calls it, a certain generic divine sense which only the man who is blessed finds on this earth. Thus Solomon says: "Thou shalt find a divine sense" (Prov. 2:5). There are many forms of this sense: a sight which can see things superior to corporeal beings, the Cherubim or Seraphim being obvious instances, and a hearing which can receive impression of sounds that have no objective existence in the air, and a taste which feeds on living bread that has come down from heaven and gives life to the world (John 6:33). So also there is a sense of smell which smells spiritual things, as St Paul speaks of "a sweet savour of Christ unto God" (2 Cor. 2:15), and a sense of touch in accordance with which John says that he has handled with his hands "of the Word of life" (1 John 1:1). The blessed prophets found this divine sense, and their vision and hearing were spiritual; in a similar way they tasted and smelt, so to speak, with a sense which was not sensible. And they touched the Word by faith so that an emanation came from him to them which healed them. In this way they saw what they record that they saw, and they heard what they say they heard, and their experience was similar when, as they recorded, they ate the roll of a book which was given them.' (This translation is taken from Henry Chadwick's *Origen: Contra Celsum*, Cambridge University Press, 1953, paperback edition 1980, p. 44.) Claudine's experience, her spiritual testimony, was - to use the words of Origen above - recording what she saw. What kind of seeing was it? For Origen, it would seem that God can be experienced by a spiritualisation of the natural senses, particularly that of sight (vision) - a rather intellectual interpretation of the spiritual life, influenced by Plato. In other words, man's own powers of contemplation bring him to God. It is completely different for Gregory of Nyssa. For him there is no vision of God, but only an experience of the presence of God, that is that God is grasped as a person in an existential contact beyond all intelligence and finally in a relation of love (Daniélou, *Platonisme et Théologie Mystique*, Paris: Aubier/Editions Montaigne, 1944, p. 232). The great revolution brought about by Gregory is to have inverted the previous order and to have affirmed the priority of knowledge through darkness over knowledge through vision. This is what establishes the Christian tradition of the mystical experience. And we have to say that Claudine would seem to be rooted definitely in that tradition. The direct vision of the divine essence is impossible to man. It would completely bedazzle him. What is accessible to man is the knowledge of God through the participation in him he possesses in the supernatural life. It is essentially the result of grace, God's completely gratuitous gift of himself, and not man's own powers of vision. God 'looked at' Claudine, and her whole life was changed. In her writings she bears testimony to what she saw and felt - a real experience of God. This is developed in the pages that follow, particularly in the section on the Eucharist, where she maintains she received all her graces from God. Two important stages in Claudine's spiritual journey are baptism and the Eucharist. We have already seen the parallelism that exists between baptism and the first stage of the

soul's journey to God (text, p. 43, Note 2). We find again the same parallelism for the Eucharist: considered as bread, we see it as the divine sweetness in the purgative journey of this life; and finally the comparison between the deification operated through the Eucharistic wine and the summit of the mystical life - ecstatic inebriation, shows us the continuity of the parallelism (cf. Daniélou, *Platonisme*, p. 245). Claudine can rightly be called a mystic of the Eucharist, for her whole spiritual life was lived out from one Communion to the next.

42 The experience described here, and which is a cessation of the activity of the corporeal senses, is seen as a consequence of a participation in the death of Christ at baptism. Baptism gives to the Christian life its rhythm of death and resurrection, which must be ratified at all stages of its development. These elevated graces are nothing but a blossoming of the baptismal grace that is constantly renewed in the Eucharist.

43 Claudine actually uses the word 'dos' (dowries). One could translate it as 'gift'. But it is not unlikely that the idea of spiritual marriage was already in her thinking as she wrote these words.

44 Cf. text, p. 178. St Paul says: 'ever since we heard about your faith in Christ Jesus and the love that you show towards all the saints because of the hope which is stored up for you in heaven' (cf. Col. 1:4-5). Endowed with the dowries of glory, which she speaks of above, and the body itself in some way having become completely spiritualised and no longer having any feeling or affection for the things of the world, Claudine rejoices in the pleasant expectation of eternal goods, delighting the senses of the soul with the fragrance of hope. This sentence, and the rest of this section, is of great interest for the fusion it brings about between the idea of the spiritual senses and the progressive communication of the Word with the soul. In other words, the spiritual life is an on-going process and is presented as much as a hope as an experience, the hope of future things, more as a promise than as a presence. It is the Word itself which offers itself to our desires under the names of justice, truth, sanctification, redemption; it is above all that same bread that comes down from Heaven in the Eucharist. So Christ, dwelling in the soul, is relished by the soul, and his image is being formed there through the virtues. The soul is at the same time satisfied and yet always hungry. This is precisely the place of the Eucharist in Claudine's spirituality: her spiritual progress depended on it. With the Eucharist we have arrived at the summit of the doctrine of the spiritual senses. This summit can be interpreted either as eternal life or as that pretasting of eternal life which, in relation to the Eucharist, is ecstasy, future grace. On the question of spiritual progress, *epectasis* (Phil. 3:13), cf. text, p. 60, Note 72.

45 Sometimes to the countryside: cf. below, p. 183. But the word 'often' creates some difficulties here, admittedly, even if one were to delete it. For Claudine stated earlier in effect that, except for the times she went out to go to church, she had not gone out ten times within the past ten years (cf. above, p. 103). Either she does not include in that number her personal visits - where she accompanied her benefactor, above all after 1654 - or else the word 'souvent' (often) must be interpreted with discretion (cf. Guennou, *La Couturière mystique de Paris* (Paris: Editions du Cerf, 1959, LXXXII, p. 268) or in a different way. If, for example, 'often' could also refer to 'feel myself drawn to prayer', another translation is possible: 'up to the point even, that when Madame took me on a visit with her, it often happened to me to feel myself moved to prayer'. But, of course, the initial discrepancy still remains.

46 Cf. text, p. 166.

47 This consideration was prompted earlier when she referred to her journey to the country in the carriage of Madame (text, p. 168).

48 Cf. text, p. 102.

49 Allusion to St Paul, cf. 2 Cor. 3:4-6.

50 Remember her words of conversion (text, p. 51).

51 Cf. 2 Cor. 2:10, 'In persona Christi'. The Bible of Louvain, the one that Claudine would have had, if she had any at all (1648 edition), translates this passage from St Paul, 'in the person of Christ'. Indeed, all this section seems to get its inspiration from St Paul.

52 This entire passage is an incredibly simple and beautiful description of the contemplative life. As

a reward of her conversion 'you looked at me', Claudine now enjoys to the full the contemplation of the one she loves; and the same attitude is found in S. of S. 4:1-2, 'How beautiful you are, my love,/ how beautiful you are! / Your eyes, behind your veil, are doves; / your hair is like a flock of goats / frisking down the slopes of Gilead.'

53 Cf. John 15:26. But Claudine's writings as a whole are Johannine in so far as they also bear testimony to what she has seen. Cf. also, 1 John 1:1-4. Seeing and bearing testimony is what characterises the entire work of Claudine Moine. For a more detailed discussion of this, see Introduction.

54 Cf. Gal. 4:19.

55 Cf. John 14:26, 16:12-13.

56 She uses the word 'verité'. She wishes to convey here the meaning that there is evidence for the efficacy of this sacrament, that is that in fact it carries out, or effects what it signifies; as she goes on to explain.

57 This is the language used in the twenty-third session of the Council of Trent concerning the real presence of Christ in the Eucharist; it says that Christ in the Eucharist, is truly, really and substantially present: see Session XXIII, chap. IV, canon 2; *Enchiridion Symbolorum*, Denzinger, 883.

58 It is indeed the word 'faibles' (weak) which Claudine uses in the text of the manuscript, followed by a comma. But the copyist could easily have been mistaken. For, in another passage, which is a complete parallel to this one (cf. text, p. 84), one finds the word 'fables' ('fables' also in English). The word 'fable' would be more in keeping with the meaning of the sentence here. Elsewhere, Claudine uses the expression 'fables ou des pures rêveries' (foolishness and mere reveries): see text p. 76..

59 This has definitely a seventeenth-century ring to it; and we recall immediately the whole Cartesian revolution which placed so much emphasis on finding the method that led to the truth. As there was a method for finding truth in the seventeenth century, there was also a method for becoming holy. Consequently we see an amazing upsurge of the cult of the inner life in the spiritual renewal of seventeenth-century France: cf. Henry Bremond, 'La Conquête mystique', *Histoire littéraire du sentiment religieux en France*, vol. 3, (Paris: Bloud et Gay, 1926-32), p. 4. But neither of these tendencies is what inspired Claudine, as she goes on to explain in the lines that follow.

60 Cf. text, p. 78.

61 As she beheld other people receiving Communion.

62 On feast days when there would be large numbers of people receiving Communion.

63 The phrase Claudine uses is 'par accompagnement'. The concept itself is a beautiful, though dangerously courageous way of emphasising the centrality of Christ; because one could take from it that the other two persons had not the same importance in the Trinity. But of course Claudine does not intend this. It is an ambiguous statement that needs some further clarification. With all the theological ambiguities present in it, the innocent meaning comes across that the Father and the Spirit remain lovingly in the background while the Son is being presented to the world. It definitely illustrates Claudine's profound Christological sense.

64 The copyist probably forgot the word 'seulement' (only), which the text demands.

65 See Introduction for more information about the sermons preached at St Louis.

66 The bread and wine.

67 Claudine uses the word 'anéantissement', which is definitely taken from the spiritual vocabulary of the time (cf. text, p. 70, Note 111) to indicate that state of the soul when emptied of all concepts and affections. 'Nothingness' would be another way of describing this state. It pertains very much to the *apophatic* school of spirituality, and in seventeenth-century France to the so-called Abstract School of Spirituality. Cognet defines the essential spirituality of the Abstract School as a 'voluntary extinction of all notional activity, in order to reach directly the divine essence, bypassing every created intermediary, even the humanity of Jesus Christ' (Louis Cognet, *Histoire de la Spiritualité Chrétienne*, Paris: Aubier, 1966, p. 244). Obviously Claudine does not fit into that category of mystic, particularly since the humanity of Christ is very central to her spirituality; which is emphasised in the

preceding pages. But her constant use of the word (cf. text, p. 161, Note 15) shows that she was exposed somewhat to its spiritual meaning. In this context, of course, as she goes on to point out, she is thinking of the *kenosis* (Phil. 2:7-8) of Jesus Christ, a stripping and a denial we must all practise in order to find our true glory. The soul rids itself of itself; but this does not come about through the pure activity of the mind - through one's own efforts - in order to see God. This would be pure Platonism, a constant threat to authentic Christian spirituality. One is rid of oneself only as a result of being filled with God - a gratuitous gift of himself to us, the effect of grace. This state of *kenosis*, of course, or annihilation, if you wish, can result from the suffering we encounter in life. This creates humility, which in the Christian sense is one with this experience of nothingness. It is in this second sense that Claudine understands the state of 'anéantissement'.

68 For a comment on the spiritual use of the English word 'awe': 'That quivering of the whole being, that sacred horror one experiences, or which one should experience, and still more, at the thought alone of the approaches of God. Horror, I say, in the latin sense, and not terror. There is an abyss between the two' (cf. Bremond, *Histoire littéraire*, vol. 3, p. 37). There is something of this in Claudine's understanding of 'loving respect' in the presence of God.

69 Here we are being introduced to the theological controversy of the seventeenth century; and undoubtedly Claudine is repeating here what she heard in some sermon or other. Attending the church of St Louis, and having the Jesuits from there as her confessors, she could not but have been influenced by the theological controversy of the time concerning the Eucharist that took place between the Jesuits and the Jansenists. In the following pages she has much to say on the well-known Jansenist treatise of Antoine Arnauld, *De la fréquente communion*, which attacked the Jesuits' position by stating that frequent communion was wrong. Claudine, of course, would have taken the Jesuits' position that frequent communion was right. She has already introduced this question earlier: see text, p. 81.

70 Antoine Arnauld (1612-94), the great spokesman of Jansenism among the secular clergy, took clerical orders in 1638 and was ordained in 1641. Then he went to Port-Royal, where he studied Augustinian theology. He is known as 'Le Grand Arnauld' of Jansenism who came into conflict with the Jesuits in 1643 when he published *De la fréquente communion*. Censored by the Sorbonne in 1656, around the time when Claudine was writing, he remained in retirement until the 'paix de l'Eglise' in 1668. Jansenism, the name, comes from Cornelius Jansen (1585-1638). He was born in Holland and studied at Louvain, Paris and Bayonne. He was appointed professor at Louvain, and later, in 1636, became Bishop of Ypres. His massive work, *Augustinus*, was published posthumously in 1640 - two years before Claudine came to Paris - and became the central point of controversy between the Jesuits and his own followers. This is the background to the following pages of Claudine.

71 Claudine is not able to say if she was 'touched' by God in 1642 or 1643: see text, p. 51, Note 45.

72 Cf. above, Note 70. Arnauld's own work occasioned about twenty works of controversy between 1644 and 1645.

73 Generally the adversaries of the Jansenists used the word 'party' to designate them.

74 She means that she does not have an academic knowledge of the doctrine discussed.

75 An interesting description of the times, when theological issues were no longer held behind the closed doors of the Sorbonne to be discussed only there, but were debated openly on the streets, as it were. A good example of this popularisation of theology is to be found in Pascal's *Provincial Letters*, in which he brings to the public notice the debate on grace between the Jesuits and the Jansenists: cf. *Lettres écrites à un provincial*, chronology and introduction by Antoine Adam (Paris: Garnier-Flammarion, 1967), pp. 35-47. One might see it as pamphleteering at its best.

76 Father Jarry or Father de Sesmaisons: see text, pp. 61-2. It would be useful to recall here that Claudine's writings, after she had written the first account (which was essentially autobiographical and must be seen as the historical account of her life), do not continue as a chronological narrative of her life: the three accounts that follow consist of a continuous reflection on the first. We see here how she has already gone back in her mind to an event of the past, and is now commenting on it, or seeing it in a new light. This is a particular feature of Claudine's writing.

77 The doctrine of the Jansenists about frequent communion that was found in Arnauld's book on the subject, criticising - as Arnauld would understand it - the lax approach of the Jesuits.

78 Jansenist objection.

79 The Jansenist doctrine.

80 This is to be taken as a rhetorical statement. One realises that Claudine wishes to stretch the point that it is more important to say Mass, despite one's imperfections, than not to say Mass. The entire paragraph is an indirect argument on Claudine's part.

81 This countenances the theology of sacrifice so strongly present in French spirituality of the seventeenth century; and it would fit in spiritually with the notion of 'anéantissement' spoken of above (Note 67). We normally regard Cardinal Pierre de Bérulle (1575-1629) as the founder of what is referred to as the French School of Spirituality: see Bremond, *Histoire littéraire*, vol. 3, p. 4. And central to this school of spirituality was its understanding of sacrifice. Sacrifice involves a complete death to all that is human. Charles de Condren (1588-1641), the second Superior General of the Oratory, was one of the great exponents in the French School of Spirituality ('Ecole Française') of this notion of death to everything that is human, a complete annihilation of self, so that the soul may be filled with Christ: cf. *Lettres du Père Charles de Condren*, published by Paul Auvray and André Jouffrey, priests of the Oratory, Paris, Les Editions du Cerf, 1943, pp. 339-40. Condren says that the idea of sacrifice is one of the essential duties of religion and therefore most perfectly witnessed to in the life of the priest: cf. C. Condren, *L'Idée du sacerdoce et du sacrifice de Jésus-Christ* (Paris, 1677; 1901 edition), pp. 35, 38-41. Claudine indeed goes on to say as much in the following sentence. She was undoubtedly influenced in her thinking by the prevailing French spirituality of the seventeenth century. But in this context she merely wants to point out that it is more important for the priest to offer the sacrifice of the Mass than to wait until he is perfect to do so, which of course would never happen. She is really speaking against the Jansenist doctrine.

82 Cf. above, Note 81. In the wake of the Protestant reform, and with the emergence of Jansenism, certain schools of thought of the early years of the Church emerge again; and in this case we think of the whole movement of Donatism, which placed such importance on sanctity as a condition for the valid administration of the Sacraments. In all of this, Claudine comes out as very strongly Catholic in her thinking.

83 The Jansenists.

84 This sentence is taken from Thomas à Kempis' *Imitation of Christ*, 'A devout call to Holy Communion', Book 4, chap. 1, translated into modern English by Edgar Daplyn, FRLS (London: Sheed & Ward, 1952), p. 157. But the Jansenists used this for their own purposes.

85 Cf. John 8:50-4.

86 Reference to God in the previous sentence.

87 This is Claudine's answer to the rhetorical question she posed earlier: see above, Note 80.

88 The French here is 'suppôt divin' (divine henchman). Present-day French does not use this expression, except as 'suppôt du diable' (fiend, hell-hound). But the expression 'suppôt divin' now forms part of the technical vocabulary of theologians to teach that, in the Incarnation, a divine person assumed a human nature.

89 Allusion to Matt. 22:14, 'For many are called, but few are chosen.' Claudine is obviously taking a very rigid interpretation of this passage from Matthew; and it is interesting that she does not seem to have any ideas on the subject. She is very different indeed from Julian of Norwich who says that Jesus, in a vision, informed her that 'Sin was necessary - but it is all going to be all right; it is all going to be all right; everything is going to be all right' (Julian of Norwich, *Revelations*, p. 103).

90 Again, a very rigid interpretation of Matt. 22:14. What about Abraham and his appeals to God for Sodom and Gomorrah (cf. Gen. 18:32-3)? There has been a very strong tradition among certain Fathers of the Church that, in God's own time, everyone will be saved, including the devil. We think in particular of Origen.

91 Claudine is anxious to point out in this paragraph that salvation is from God and not from

ourselves; and who is to be saved cannot be determined by human reasoning or ingenuity: it is the gratuitous gift of God to us in Christ. This accounts for her rigid interpretation of Matt. 22:14 and perhaps her belief in the need for frequent communion.

92 Cf. Matt. 4:4.

93 Cf. above, Note 57.

94 Cf. Luke 23:34.

95 Cf. 1 Cor. 11:27.

96 This is Claudine's summing up, as it were, of the whole question concerning *De la fréquente communion* of Antoine Arnauld, what in fact she thinks about the whole matter of frequent communion; although she does not mention the book specifically in her writings. Despite her confessor's invectives against Port-Royal (a celebrated Cistercian abbey, a few miles south-west of Paris, which became the centre of the Jansenist reform), which she ignores (cf. Guennou, *La Couturière*, p. 163), Claudine is not content to treat of the whole matter - as in *Question s'il est meilleur de communier souvent que rarement* of Father de Sesmaisons (see Introduction), her confessor - as a question just of tepidity of sensibility. Curiously enough, like Arnauld himself, but for different reasons, she sides with the point of view of conduct; where how you have acted, and not how you feel is important, as indicated in these words: 'The only necessary disposition' (cf. Orcibal, *La Vie spirituelle*, p. 537).

97 Cf. text, p. 174.

98 Presumably the meaning must be that children are inclined not to give any consideration to small, hidden faults.

99 Cf. above, p. 141, Note 179; p. 168, Note 44. The beautiful expression of Claudine, 'serving an apprenticeship to that which I hope to do eternally', is a wonderful way of describing her authentic Christian spirituality, where hope is never destroyed, but in fact is the virtue leading to love. In everything she says about her spiritual experience, she follows St John in bearing testimony to the fact that she has seen Christ - 'those eyes of infinite and extraordinary mercy' (text, p. 51) - and has fallen in love with him and now hopes and longs for the day when she will spend all time and eternity with him. Unlike the Abstract School of Spirituality (cf. above, Note 67), which would find the humanity of Christ an obstacle, or at least a difficulty in the soul's experience of God, here Claudine's words are the antithesis of everything that is gnostic in Christian spirituality. For Claudine, the truth is not something we grasp on to with the power of our reasoning, but something we understand through love. Fundamentally, she is saying that it is Christ who saves; and that salvation is not through knowledge, but through love. The theological problem posed here is: how is participation itself the source of a thirst that gets greater and never seems to be satisfied? Claudine's words describe exactly the interior attitude which corresponds to the objective law of spiritual progress: stretched by the desire for celestial things to that which lies ahead (Phil. 3:13), the soul raises itself continuously above itself, seeking desperately for the one it loves (cf. S. of S. 3:1-2). Serving an apprenticeship to that which one hopes to do eternally, is an excellent way of describing souls as universes of grace that are in constant expansion.

100 Cf. text, p. 168, Note 40.

101 In the seventeenth century the Ottoman Empire was an ever-present threat to the West.

102 Claudine begins with 'you' here, leaving the previous phrase 'do you fear that' to be understood.

103 The French word here is 'attente'. The idea is more or less that of waiting for God; and it is related to the question of desire we spoke of above (Note 99). The progress of the soul, the constant moving ahead we also spoke of (*epectasis*) - to understand this is the supreme discovery of the soul: to lose the illusion of a state where one would have stopped and which could be considered as a possession; in reality this would be in contradiction with the nature itself of the rapports between God and the soul, which are rapports of waiting and liberality, waiting on the soul's part and generosity on God's part. For it is in this that consists the true vision of God, in so far as he who raises his eyes towards him never ceases desiring him. Here also we see gathered together all the stages of the spiritual life. They are

found between participation in Christ who is the principle of divine life - communicated at baptism - and the transcendence of the divine essence, which remains always inaccessible. The whole spiritual life is thus a prolongation of baptism, following through with the stripping, or shedding of the old man (cf. Eph. 4:22-3) right from his culpable passions up to the passive purifications of the mystical life, and at the same time putting on Christ and being transformed into him (cf. Daniélou, *Platonisme*, p. 309). Cf. Rom. 8:22-4, 'From the beginning until now the entire creation, as we know, has been groaning in one great act of giving birth; and not only creation, but all of us who possess the first fruits of the Spirit, we too groan inwardly as we wait for our bodies to be set free.'

104 Cf. text, p. 61.

105 Cf. text, p. 61.

106 She is referring here to the state of annihilation her soul entered into afterwards, when she was unaware of the things that were happening around her.

107 Cf. text, p. 59.

108 Cf. Exod. 3:14.

109 Cf. Isa. 40:15 - 'See, the nations are like a drop on the pail's rim, / they count as a grain of dust on the scales.' For parallels here between Claudine and Catherine of Genoa, see Introduction; also, cf. Orcibal, *La Vie spirituelle*, p. 534.

110 Cf. Wisd. 2:20.

111 Allusion to Descartes, *Discourse on Method*, in which he speaks about clear and distinct ideas as his way of arriving at the truth, that is that he would state nothing he was not absolutely sure about: cf. *Discourse on Method*, in The Philosophical Works of Descartes, translated by Elizabeth S. Haldane and G.R.T. Ross, 1911, reprinted 1979 (Cambridge: Cambridge University Press, 1979), vol. 1, p. 92. It is not at all improbable that Claudine would have known about Descartes, and indeed unconsciously use a certain language of his that was in vogue at the time. In seventeenth-century France, the emphasis on method in philosophical circles also had an influence on spirituality (see above, Note 59; text, p. 210, Note 15.)

112 Here, and in the rest of this paragraph, we see an important stage in Claudine's spiritual life described and a central point of the spiritual life in general. Many spiritual writers, and Gregory of Nyssa in particular, have recourse to the oxymoron as the most effective way of describing the spiritual experience (cf. above, p. 79, Note 139), and in this case we can think of the unmoved mover. For a discussion of this, see Daniélou, *Platonisme*, pp. 291-307. The oxymoron is essentially linked to the notion of spiritual progress (see above, Note 44). Thus, for the soul there is at the same time an element of stability, of possession, which is participation in God, and an element of movement, which is always the infinite gap between that which the soul possesses of God and that which God is, infinitely distant and transcendent (cf. Daniélou, *Platonisme*, p. 305).

113 For a discussion of *apatheia*, see text, p. 64, Note 100. What follows is a description of the state of *apatheia* in the soul.

114 See text, pp. 127ff.

115 'Jesus Christ' designates the Son of God 'made man'. There where the holy humanity is missing, there indeed is God the Son, but not 'Jesus Christ'. Claudine's statement here, of Christ not being present, risks many dangerous interpretations, the most serious of all being the accusation of Gnosticism, as if she were making a very clear distinction between her direct relationship with God and her relationship with Jesus Christ. But that is not what she is saying; she is merely pointing out that the union she feels with God through the very food she eats is essentially different from her union with Jesus Christ in the blessed Sacrament of the altar.

116 Claudine wishes to bring out here the following meaning: those religious people, who are supposed to give everything up for God, give greater value to a house, or a material thing, than they do to their God.

117 The reference here is to the sermons preached in the church of St Louis, renowned in the seventeenth century for its great preachers. In the early part of that century, when religious oratory began to flourish, preachers often seemed to have regarded their sermons as opportunities for the

wanton display of their art and erudition. Perhaps they were encouraged in this by their audiences. So important was the sermon in the seventeenth century, and particularly in France, that it was considered to be a literary genre of its own, inspired more by the rigid rules of the art of rhetoric than by any pastoral concern for preaching the Word of God to the people. We have only to recall the great sermons of Bossuet (1628-1702) and Fénelon (1651-1715) to see how developed and refined a literary genre the sermon had become in religious thought of seventeenth-century France.

118 Among the great preachers in later years, we must not forget the great Bourdaloue who preached in the church of St Louis; and among the distinguished people who came to listen to him, we must recall the famous Madame de Sévigné. Still in the world of hypothesis with regard to the identity of Claudine's benefactors (cf. Guennou, *La Couturière*, LXXXII, pp. 265-8), Father Guennou shared with me his views that it is quite possible that Claudine knew the young Madame de Sévigné, alias Marie de Rabutin-Chantal (1626-96), and that the 'well-known' house (see above, p. 63, Note 94) she stayed in could easily have been that of the family with which the young Marie de Rabutin-Chantal lived as a young girl: cf. text, p. 63, Note 93. This is a very fascinating hypothesis indeed; but there is no definite proof for this.

119 A clear indication of the seriousness with which the preachers regarded the sermon. However, there was a great call for reform, the main objection to this ingenuity being that it obscured the real purpose of the sermon, which was to persuade. So we see St Vincent de Paul, who praises the direct but powerful language of the New Testament, calling preachers back to their duty, urging them to abandon the false rhetoric of display.

120 In all of this, Claudine appears to have been very well acquainted with the world of the sermon.

121 The text of the manuscript, probably altered, is as follows: 'qu'en se cachant les uns des autres pour commettre leurs crimes, qu'ils auraient honte d'avoir des témoins de leurs actions, et qu'ils n'en ont pas'. To arrive at my translation I have had to change 'en se cachant' to 'se cachent', and 'qu'ils auraient' to 'ils auraient'.

122 Cf. text, p. 65, Note 103; p. 130, Note 130.

123 Cf. text, p. 51.

124 Cf. Acts 17:28.

125 Cf. above, Note 113.

126 It is difficult to discern what Claudine means by this. Maybe 'evil spirits' is intended!

127 This is when she took care of her benefactors' house when they went to the country: see text, p. 64. This is indeed saying a lot about the sturdy character Claudine must have had. People placed much trust in her. It must not be forgotten that she left her hidden life at various times to come and help her benefactors in their need. And although she says above that she remained insensible to human respect, that is indifferent to the respect that human beings showed her, for she was a mystic of the hidden life, her spirituality was in no wise lacking in sensitivity to the apostolate of prayer and the apostolic life of the Church: cf. text, pp. 76, 144. For a treatment of the mystic's involvement in the world, see Underhill, 'The Mystic and the Corporate Life', *The Essentials of Mysticism* (New York: AMS Press, 1976), pp. 25-43.

128 If Claudine was already established in the house of her benefactors, as it seems, the event of which she is speaking happened then in 1649, the year in which the feast of the Trinity fell on 30 May. These lights having lasted two years (cf. text, p. 186), in this case the Great Darkness would not have reached its definitive phase until towards the month of May 1651: cf. text, p. 127, Note 119.

129 Cf. Thomas Aquinas, *Summa*, pt 1, q. 3, art. 2. A good example of being influenced by what she heard in some sermon or other; one cannot say that the language used throughout this passage is the form this revelation of the Trinity took for Claudine. More accurately, Claudine is using borrowed, technical language here in order to put across what she herself understands by the Trinity from the interior.

130 Although one could say that this section of her writings is the less engaging spiritually for the reader, Claudine's use of such language does show at least that her reflections on her own spiritual

experience did extend her mind into many areas of theological investigation; and even though she doesn't always succeed in this, her use of such technical language does not obfuscate her own internal vision of the Trinity that she received from God.

131 This unexpected interpolation points to the fact that 'Claudine had given thought to the whole question of the Trinity, and possibly accounts for her use of the technical language above (text), which in itself would be an indication that she probably did some reading for her little project. This shows at least that Claudine was used to putting her thoughts into writing.

132 Father Castillon, Rector of the College of Orléans since the last days of 1648. Obviously we have not got this written account of Claudine's on the Trinity; but it would seem to have been a separate work from the one here. She was already residing with her benefactors when, the day or the vigil of the feast of the Trinity (probably in 1649 or 1650), having sat at table with the rest of the people of the house, the vision of the mystery which the liturgy had celebrated that day was divinely presented to her. This insight stayed with her for about two years, during which time she composed the work on this mystery. For a moment she thought of sending it to Father Castillon in the provinces (one will recall that he resided at Orléans from the end of 1648 to the summer of 1651, then at Rennes to September of 1652: see text, p. 136, Notes 151-2), then, changing her mind, she destroyed it, on the approval of the confessor she had at the time.

133 This expression could have been taken from Benoît de Canfield's *La Règle de Perfection*, 7th edition (Paris, 1633), p. 294; see also Orcibal's recent publication, *Benoît de Canfield: La Règle de Perfection/The Rule of Perfection* (cf. text, p. 70, Note 111). The same expression is also found in *L'Entrée à la divine sagesse* by Father Maur de l'Enfant-Jésus (Paris, 1652), p. 162. Father Maur was Prior of the Carmelites of the old observance at Bordeaux; and his work contains many themes and expressions familiar to Claudine: ocean, divine abyss, Purgatory, the primacy of love, the work of art which God wishes to create in those who serve him, etc.: cf. ibid., pp. 47, 55, 106, 141, 161. However, if need be, it is sufficient for an identity of sources in Claudine to explain these resemblances by referring to Catherine of Genoa and de Saint-Jure (see Introduction) and how they were influenced by de Canfield.

134 Allusion to St Augustine. Cf. text, p. 69, Note 109.

135 God is under no obligation to us in this.

136 Claudine uses the plural here, 'les enfers' (Hells), perhaps she is referring to the state of many souls in Hell!

137 This is a confession that Hell is not absolute in her thinking.

138 Cf. text, pp. 67-8.

139 Cf. text, p. 124.

140 A reminder of the good spiritual direction Claudine received from her Jesuit confessors: cf. text, p. 111.

141 Unlike the case of St Teresa of Avila who suffered a great deal on account of the bad spiritual direction of some of her confessors.

142 Cf. text, p. 169, Note 48; cf. also p. 102.

143 Cf. Isa. 33:17 - 'Your eyes will see the King in his beauty; they will behold a land that stretches afar.' Seeing the glory of God, and bearing testimony to it is what characterises the writings of Claudine Moine; cf. text, p. 51, 'those eyes of infinite and extraordinary mercy'. But her journey to that vision is through darkness (cf. text, p. 127, Note 121). After all, Moses asked to see the glory of God (cf. Exod. 33:18-23) and all he saw was the back of God. Gregory of Nyssa uses this in his life of Moses to show that the true way to the knowledge of God is through darkness (*La Vie de Moïse*, Sources Chrétiennes 1, pp. 257-9). For the theme of darkness is Gregory's spirituality, see Daniélou, *Platonisme*, pp. 190-9; *Glory to Glory*, translated by H. Musurillo with introduction by Daniélou (London, 1962) - translation of extracts mainly from the life of Moses and the Commentary on the Song of Songs, pp. 26ff; and 'Mystique de la ténèbre chez Grégoire de Nysse', *Dictionnaire de Spiritualité*, ed. M. Viller (Paris, 1932), vol. 2, col. 1872ff.

144 A difficult passage to translate. The French is 'que je suis par pur amour'. A possible meaning could be, 'that I exist through pure love'.

145 Cf. text, p. 44, Note 4.

146 The word 'content', passed over, it seems, by the copyist, has been supplied here according to the parallel passages where it is found each time: cf. text, pp. 61, 233.

147 Notice here how she makes no distinction between God and her confessor as the addressee of her writings. By the end of her writings the change will have become complete, in so far as, writing under obedience to her confessor, she sees it as God's will that she declare all the mercies he granted her in secret.

148 For an earlier mention of the spiritual senses, cf. text, p. 138, Note 165.

149 She is referring to the dangers in too great a physical understanding of the spiritual life. Cf. *The Cloud of Unknowing*, translation by Clifton Wolters, London: Penguin Classics, 1961, p. 116.

150 She is saying here that she considers it a great grace that God deprives us of these consolations early on in our spiritual life.

151 Cf. text, p. 51.

152 Despite this humble confession, we have to attribute to Claudine the temperament of an exceptional writer: cf. Orcibal, *La Vie spirituelle*, p. 535.

153 Here Claudine goes through a self-analysis which serves as a commentary on the dangers encountered in the contemplative life. For similar comments, see *The Cloud of Unknowing*, chap. 45, pp. 113-4.

154 Cf. S. of S. 8:6, 'Set me like a seal on your heart, / like a seal on your arm. / For love is strong as Death, / jealousy relentless as Sheol.' Cf. text, p. 147, Note 212.

155 Father Castillon.

156 To be held in contempt.

157 Cf. Matt. 6:8.

158 This is a completely biblical sentiment, found at the beginning of Ps. 51 (the Miserere); and which Claudine knew by heart: cf. text, pp. 86, 108.

159 Cf. text, p. 70, Note 111; p. 127, Note 122.

160 Cf. text, pp. 108-9.

161 Cf. text, p. 51.

162 Cf. text, p. 147ff.

163 Cf. text, p. 51, Note 48.

164 As in the case of her comments on Antoine Arnauld's *De la fréquente communion* (see text, pp. 172ff), Claudine is also touching here upon a very controversial issue debated in seventeenth-century France, namely the question of sufficient grace. For a discussion of this in the seventeenth century and an almost vitriolic attack on the Jesuits' theology of grace, see Pascal's *Lettres écrites à un provincial*, in which he derides the Jesuit understanding of sufficient grace with the memorable words, 'grâce suffisante . . . qui n'est pas suffisante' (p. 47). Claudine of course would have been influenced by the Jesuits in her understanding of sufficient grace: she accepts that there is such a reality.

165 A remarkable statement that lays claim to having been taught by God alone (cf. text, p. 53). This can only be appreciated by a reader open to the exceptional beauty and quality of this text; also, cf. text, p. 135, Note 148. The only construction we can put on such an absolute statement, and not feel incredulous as to its truthfulness, is that Claudine is referring obliquely to the fact that she belongs to no school of spirituality: she was led by the spirit. This is what makes this text extraordinary.

On Prayer

1 Prayer. Unlike Teresa of Avila in her treatment of prayer (cf. *The Life of St. Teresa of Avila*, translated by E. Allison Peers, London: Sheed & Ward, 1944 and 1979, reprint 1984, pp. 62-118), and many more like her who lay great stress in their treatment on the methodological aspects of prayer - that is following the usual rules laid down for meditation and the like - Claudine will place greater emphasis on prayer as essentially contemplation. 'Prayer', says Gregory of Nyssa, 'is the contemplation of invisible things.' (Gregory of Nyssa, *De Oratione Dominica* (On Sunday Prayer), PG 44, col. 1124B). Also on prayer, Evagrius of Pontus writes: 'If you are a theologian, you will truly pray, and if you pray, you are a theologian.' (Evagrius of Pontus, *De Oratione 60*, PG 79, col. 1179). In another place (*Century 5:26*, PO 28, pp. 186-7) the same Father of the Church says something to the effect that the theologian is the person who has seen God, for if you haven't seen him you can't speak about him. A theologian in her own right in so far as she is bearing testimony to what she has seen, Claudine will see prayer as the result of the fact of having been touched by God, and therefore of having discovered the realities of the divine life. In this final account of her writings (which is much more peaceful and irenic than the other three), when her vision is complete, she enters into the true world of contemplation, not just through a purification of her intelligence, but more importantly through a purification of her heart; for high fantasy fails her when she finds herself touched directly by the hand of God. Through love, more than through knowledge, prayer for Claudine Moine will be a rediscovery of that intimacy with God: cf. text, p. 53; p. 138, Note 162. So we shall see the precedence of love over knowledge in her following description of prayer as a contemplation of the beloved of her heart: cf. text, p. 220, Note 38.

2 The two years she spent in the convent at Langres.

3 Moved. God takes the initiative and the soul is guided by a sort of instinct, cf. text, p. 135. Every idea of 'agitated' in the modern sense of the word is to be excluded.

4 An ambiguous statement. It can only mean that Claudine wishes to unite herself to Christ in order to praise God the way he (Jesus) does.

5 For meditation.

6 Cf. *The Spiritual Exercises of Saint Ignatius Loyola*, Week 1, Exercise 1, Prelude 1, by Louis J. Puhl, SJ (Chicago: Loyola University Press, 1951), p. 25. It speaks about a mental representation of the place.

7 Cf. text, p. 182, Note 111.

8 Cf. 1 Sam. 3:10. Cf. text, pp. 117, 162.

9 Her confessor, Father Castillon.

10 See Introduction for a discussion of the same attitude of obedience in the life of St Teresa of Avila with regard to her writings.

11 She now sees with the eyes of faith.

12 Allusion to John 20:29, 'Happy are those who have not seen and yet believe.'

13 This very discrete concession given to knowledge is also an indirect criticism of its dangerous excesses in the spiritual life. The true Christian gnosis is knowing that God loves us and will continue to love us. Too much emphasis in the West, it could be argued, has been placed on the will as if it were another intellect, that is regarding the will as facultative. This, it seems to me, has been detrimental to spirituality. Christian spirituality is essentially a putting on of Christ, as St Paul says: 'to put on the Lord Jesus' (cf. Gal. 4:19). So Christian perfection cannot be a special knowledge possessed by an inner few of selected people. The way to love is open to everyone. Many movements in spirituality, Albigensian in the Middle Ages and Quietism (cf. text, p. 143, Note 186) in seventeenth-century France, for example, have manifested this aberration, which is an imbalance, a misrepresentation of the Christian life, because it places the following of Christ chiefly in the region of knowledge rather than in the region of love and life. In modern times it sometimes takes the form of an obsessive devotion to the higher ways of prayer, of depth psychology, or the new theology, pursuits which,

because of their nature, are for only a few chosen persons and not the masses (cf. John Dalrymple, *Theology and Spirituality*, Cork: The Mercier Press, 1970, p. 46). So Claudine's spiritual experience was not only a purification of the intelligence, an intellectual awakening, but also a purification of the heart (cf. above, Note 1). And in fact her conversion, 'you looked at me', was indeed a purification of the heart: God first loved her, and now she uses her intelligence to contemplate that love in herself. We read in *The Cloud of Unknowing*: 'Only he himself is completely and utterly sufficient to fulfil the will and longing of our souls. Nothing else can. The soul, when it is restored by grace, is made wholly sufficient to comprehend him fully by love. He cannot be comprehended by our intellect or any man's - or any angel's for that matter. For both we and they are created beings. But only to our intellect is he incomprehensible: not to our love.' (*The Cloud of Unknowing*, translation by Clifton Wolters, London: Penguin Classics, chap. 4, pp. 62-3). Claudine goes on in the next sentence to clarify this further.

14 Touched by God, Claudine's experience of God is not the projection or end product of her own reasoning, her own imagination, which would be Illuminism (cf. text, p. 145, Note 192). Not seeing any light - or reason - that might be the cause of the love in her heart, is a proof that God is as real from his side as he is from Claudine's perception of him: her experience of God does not remain within her own conception of him but in fact corresponds to an actuality outside of itself.

15 See above, p. 132, Note 140; p. 182, Note 111. This allusion to Descartes's clear and distinct ideas (cf. René Descartes, *Discourse on Method*, The Philosophical Works of Descartes, vol. 1, translated by Elizabeth S. Haldane and G.R.T. Ross, Cambridge University Press, first edition 1911, reprinted 1979, p. 92) is undoubtedly an indirect reference to the prevailing philosophy of seventeenth-century France in its highly individual quest for truth, as outlined in *Discours de la méthode* (1637), but at the same time a rather gentle yet strong criticism of the possibility of such rationalistic tendencies to have any apprehension of God. The accommodation of Stoic ideas to Christian moral teaching in seventeenth-century France led theologians to incorporate into the Christian doctrine of the Fall - as a result of which reason became a source of error and the passions, attracting the will, a cause of sin - the Stoic notion that the principle of 'right reason' and a knowledge of natural law are found in all people, which makes virtuous action possible despite the tragedy of original sin. This 'Christian Stoicism' dominated many moral treatises of the first part of the seventeenth century. But with Descartes, this 'right reason', which originally included both intuitive intellect and moral will, and enabled man to control his passions in accordance with God's purposes, was already being divided into 'reason', reduced to its analytical and critical functions, and will, considered as an autonomous faculty (cf. above, Note 13) which puts the promptings of reason into action. In this sense reason becomes the faculty which is rooted in self-interest rather than the faculty which has an intuitive apprehension of God's will. This thinking reached its culmination in Descartes, *The Passions of the Soul* (1649): see above, The Philosophical Works of Descartes, vol. 1, pp. 329-427. His theory of the passions is a marvellous example of the extreme point reached by the optimistic ethical humanism of the seventeenth century. It bears a marked resemblance to that of Corneille's stage heroes (cf. text, p. 167, Note 37), for whom, in their cult of glory, passion is a manifestation of personal energy and an exigence of personal development. In the pages that follow, and indeed earlier where she also speaks about the passions of the soul (cf. text, p. 64, Note 100; p. 102, Note 40; p. 141, Note 177), Claudine clearly testifies to the supremacy of love over knowledge as the hallmark of a true Christian experience of God. She will end this section (text, p. 212), by setting up a certain antithesis between the rational creature and a Christian, and saying that she intends to be ruled by the lights of faith and no longer by the lights of reason. In this fourth written account of Claudine's spiritual experience, she resembles Dante somewhat in his *Paradiso* where, confessing that his vision was greater than his speech could show (cf. Dante Alighieri, *The Divine Comedy, Paradiso: 1, Italian Text and Translation*, Bollingen Series LXXX, translated, with a commentary, by Charles S. Singleton, Princeton/New Jersey: Princeton University Press, 1975, second printing, with corrections, 1977, Canto XXXIII, lines 55-6), he says that, through abounding grace, he presumed to fix his look through the eternal light

so far that all his sight was used up, and that in its depth he saw gathered together there, bound by love in one single volume, that which is dispersed throughout the whole universe (ibid., lines 82-7). He was experiencing the Trinity, in which, as in a knot (line 91), he now saw the meaning of all existence. Speech is scant indeed, and how feeble is one's conception when it is a question of relating such wonderful things. In all of this fourth account, 'On Prayer', Claudine is struggling desperately with language to tell us, like Dante (ibid., line 145), that it is not reason that makes the world go round, but that it is love that moves the sun and the other stars; see text, pp. 83-4.

16 Cf. text, p. 71, Note 113; p. 121, Note 105.

17 Cf. text, p. 65, Note 103; p. 130, Note 130.

18 Cf. text, p. 172, Note 67, for a discussion on the word 'anéantissement' and the Abstract School of Spirituality.

19 Cf. above, Note 15.

20 The most sacred point of the Temple in Jerusalem, where only the High Priest penetrated once a year, was called the Holy of Holies (cf. 1 Kgs. 6:19ff.).

21 Cf. text, p. 153, Note 237.

22 Cf. S. of S. 2:16.

23 Cf. text, p. 45.

24 For the same sentiments, cf. text, pp. 121-2; see also pp. 219-20.

25 'that obedience wishes' is a reference to the fact that she is writing under obedience to her confessor, Father Castillon.

26 Cf. Luke 2:51; Phil. 2:8.

27 Cf. text, p. 51, 'you looked at me'.

28 This does not mean intellectual in so far as it is in contrast to the real, in other words that the visions were abstract. She really intends to say 'interior' here.

29 Speaking of beauty is significant, for it denotes her real experience of God in contrast to the more intellectual awakenings of other forms of spirituality: 'How beautiful you are, my Beloved, / and how delightful! / Your eyes are doves.' (S. of S. 1:15)

30 'You have ravished my heart, / my sister, my promised bride, / you ravish my heart / with a single one of your glances, / with one single pearl of your necklace' (S. of S. 4:9). Remember Claudine's own words in describing her conversion: 'with those eyes of infinite and extraordinary mercy, you looked at me' (text, p. 51, Note 46).

31 Cf. John 13:8-9.

32 Cf. Ps. 110:4; Heb. 5:6.

33 Allusion to Matt. 21:12-13, and to parallel passages.

34 Cf. Gal. 2:20; text, p. 121.

35 Cf. Rom. 8:35.

36 Cf. text, p. 239.

37 See the Ambrosian hymn of Te Deum: 'Quos pretioso sanguine redemisti.' Cf. text, p. 215, Note 24.

38 Cf. S. of S. 2:5; 5:8.

39 'I am my Beloved's, / and his desire is for me' (S. of S. 7:10). Cf. above, Note 30.

40 Cf. Matt. 7:7; Luke 11:9.

41 See Introduction for discussion of the question of being obedient to her confessor in writing for him about the favours God granted her, and how it relates to a similar attitude in the life of St Teresa of Avila.

42 Cf. text, p. 119, where the references to interior words indicated in Note 98 are to be clarified later by pp. 139, 217, 238.

43 To be held in contempt.

44 Notice here the mastery with which is expounded the notion of 'spiritual infancy', such as Claudine herself had lived it.

Notes

45 Like many writers of the seventeenth century in France who were conscious of the great changes taking place then, Claudine expresses the same sensitive awareness when she refers to the confusion of the century. The word 'century' carries with it here a certain preciousness.

46 The negative here, 'not obliged', makes this sentence rather ambiguous when connected with the preceding one. I think the meaning must be that even the silent person, not accustomed to speaking (that is the one who is not obliged by his ministry and special vocation to speak a great deal), must also watch out for the dangers of the tongue, even in speaking about spiritual matters.

47 Cf. Jas. 3:2.

48 Cf. text, p. 186, Note 133.

49 Cf. Matt. 6:10.

50 Cf. text, pp. 204-5.

51 'For I tell you truly that the devil has his contemplatives as God has his' (*The Cloud of Unknowing*, chap. 45, p. 114); see text, pp. 73, 96.

52 Fabulous reptile (also cockatrice) hatched by serpent from cock's egg, blasting by its breath or look; figuratively a glance, evil eye, person or thing that blasts. It would be interesting to know where Claudine found this image.

53 Allusion to Augustine: cf. text, p. 69, Note 109.

54 The word used is 'déportement', which is not what is meant by the context. The word 'comportement' (behaviour) would seem to be intended.

55 See Introduction for a discussion of Claudine's written accounts as comprising a spiritual testimony.

56 Cf. Rom. 13:13.

57 Cf. text, p. 77, Note 131.

58 'The guardian of Israel / does not doze or sleep' (Ps. 121:4). This brings us back to Claudine's own words of conversion 'you looked at me', and the nature of the spiritual awakening experienced. Hers was not a mere intellectual awakening; she saw Christ, and, for her, in seeing Christ she saw God, and in loving Christ she knew God. This entire paragraph highlights the language of love used by Claudine to bear testimony to what she has seen. Again we will come across the oxymoron - sleep/ awake - as the best way to explain the spiritual life, the soul's final vision of God, for she goes on to say that while she sleeps between the arms of God she longs incessantly to see him fully and openly. Seeing while you sleep is undoubtedly mystical language; for he who dreams sees, and after the dream the passion remains imprinted and the rest is forgotten by the mind; so it was with Dante in the final image he experienced of God; because he says that, although his vision had almost wholly faded away, the sweetness that was born of it still dropped within his heart (cf. *Paradiso*, XXXIII, 58-63). In a sense it is love taking over from knowledge; as St Paul says: 'In short, there are three things that last: faith, hope and love; and the greatest of these is love' (1 Cor. 13:13). Our souls can afford to sleep, because the guardian of Israel is always looking after us - he neither slumbers nor sleeps (see above). If the soul were to depend on its intellectual faculty alone to know and love God, it could never afford to sleep; for then the soul would exist no more. But only the language of love can understand that the soul can sleep, forgetting self and all things in order to place itself in the 'full and perfect enjoyment of God for ever'. Cf. text, p. 151, Note 222; p. 144, Note 188; p. 142, Note 183; p. 79, Note 139.

59 Cf. text, p. 149, Note 216.

60 As in the expression 'reprendre ses esprits' (to come to, to regain consciousness), the use of 'esprits' here can only refer to 'the whole of the soul's conscious self', untrammelled by the body.

61 Cf. text, pp. 64-5, 70-1, 127ff.

62 Cf. text, p. 124, Note 117, for a note on the *parresia*; p. 98, Note 23.

63 The mention of St Teresa for the second time (cf. text, p. 111, Note 46 for the first mention) is a strong indication that Teresian spirituality had some influence on Claudine. See Introduction for further discussion of this question.

64 The source must be some sermon or other, or perhaps her confessor.

65 Cf. text, p. 171, Note 57.

66 Cf. text, p. 68.

67 Cf. Luke 12:49.

68 Cf. text, pp. 76-7, 144; p. 185, Note 127.

69 Father Castillon.

70 Cf. text, p. 121, Note 106.

71 Cf. Gen. 32:27.

72 The gift of tears.

73 Prayer.

74 Another indication of the influence of St Teresa of Avila. Teresa ends her *Interior Castle* with a similar declaration (*Interior Castle*, translated and edited by E. Allison Peers, Image Books, 1961, p. 235).

75 The prayer of Simeon in the Temple: cf. Luke 2:29-32.

76 In keeping with Johannine inspiration in her writings, that is, bearing witness to what she has seen (cf. 1 John 1:1-4), and as a result of her having written out of obedience, Claudine could quite legitimately make John's words her own: 'This is the evidence of one who saw it - trustworthy evidence, and he knows he speaks the truth - and he gives it so that you may believe as well.' (John 19:35)

77 Father Castillon.

78 Cf. text, p. 149, Note 216.

79 Cf. John 20:30.

80 In 1648. Cf. text, p. 64, Note 98; also, in particular, p. 110, Note 76.

81 In 1652. Cf. text, p. 137.

82 Cf. text, p. 83.

83 As a mystic of the Eucharist, the image of Christ has been fully restored in the soul of Claudine Moine.

84 Notice here how she has moved from addressing her confessor to addressing God directly.

85 Cf. text, p. 51.

86 Cf. *Interior Castle*, p. 23.

Selected Bibliography

Historical and literary source material for the work translated in this book is still in its infancy. Accordingly, what follows is not intended as an exhaustive bibliography of the history of this text. I begin first of all with reference to the two separate publications of the French edition and the historical source material used in its preparation. I then draw attention to those primary sources mentioned in the text and those which patient research has discovered and informed guesses have identified. Finally, secondary sources of ancient and modern authors are listed, first as an indication of the literary sources for my own thought as I translated the French edition, and secondly as a guide to further reading as I now introduce the first English translation of MS 1409, 'Notes spirituelles par une Demoiselle, datées du 17ᵉ siècle', from the archives of La Société des Missions Etrangères in Paris.

Editions and historical source material

Ma Vie secrète: Claudine Moine. Preface by Cardinal Garrone, edited and presented by Jean Guennou, Paris: Desclée et Cie, 1968.
La Couturière mystique de Paris, Claudine Moine: Relations Spirituelle. Preface by Cardinal Garrone, edited and presented by Jean Guennou, Paris: Téqui, 1982.

Annales du premier Monastère de l'Annonciade Céleste de Paris (Archives of the Annonciade de Langres), vol. 1.
Bournon, F. *Rectifications et additions à l'histoire de la ville de Paris de Lebeuf.* Paris: 1890.
Coudriet de Châtelet, Abbès. *Histoire de la Seigneurie de Jonville.* Besançon: 1864.
- *Histoire de Jussey.* Besançon: 1876.
de Guilhermy, F. *Inscriptions de la France du 5ᵉ au 18ᵉ siècle*, vol. 1. Paris: 1873.
de Hansy, D. *Notice historique sur la paroisse royale Saint-Paul-Saint-Louis.* Paris: 1842.
de Menorval, E. *Les Jésuites de la Rue Saint Antoine, l'église Saint-Paul-Saint-Louis et le Lycée Charlemagne.* Paris: 1892.
Dictionnaire historique et géographique ecclésiastique, vol. 3, Paris: 1924.
Directoire pour les novices du Monastère Sainte-Ursule de Langres. Lyon: 1642.
Dufour, V. *Le Charnier de l'ancien cimetière Saint Paul.* Paris: 1866.
Garnier, A. 'Les misères de la ville de Langres et de la campagne langroise: 1610-40', *Les Cahiers Haut-Marnais* (Chaumont, 1948).
Guennou, Jean. *La Couturière mystique de Paris.* Paris: Editions du Cerf, 1959.
Jimenez, J. 'Précisions biographiques sur le P. L.L.', *Archivum Historicum Societatis Jesu*, XXXIII (1964), pp. 318-20.
Lazare, F. and L. (eds.) *Dictionnaire administratif et historique des rues et monuments de Paris.* Paris: 1855.
Lefèvre d'Ormesson, O. *Journal*, vol. 1. Paris: 1860.
Monnier, Louis. *Histoire de la ville de Vesoul.* Vesoul: 1909.
Orcibal, Jean. 'La Couturière mystique de Paris', *La Vie spirituelle* (Paris, May 1960), pp. 533-9.
Plond, L. *La Maison professe des Jésuites de la Rue Saint Antoine.* Paris: 1956.

Vincent, F. *Histoire des famines à Paris*. Paris: 1964.
Wedgwood, C.V. *The Thirty Years War*. London: Jonathan Cape, paperback edition, 1964 (first published 1938).

Primary sources

Acarie (*alias* Mary of the Incarnation), Madame. See A. du Val, *Vie admirable de la Soeur Marie de l'Incarnation*, Paris, 1621; for reference to this work, see 10th edition, *La vie de Soeur Marie de l'Incarnation*, Paris, 1647.

Angela of Foligno. *L'Esperienza di Dio Amore: il libro di Angela da Foligno*. Translation, introduction and notes by Salvatore Aliquò, Rome: Città Nuova Editrice, 1973.

Arnauld, Antoine. *De la fréquente communion*. Paris: 1643.

Augustine, St. *The Confessions of St. Augustine*. Translation, with introduction and notes by John K. Ryan. New York: Image Books, 1960.

Binet, E. *Abrégé des vies des principaux fondateurs des religions de l'Eglise*. Anvers: 1643.

Castillon, André. *Desseins de Jésus-Christ dans l'institution de Saint Sacrement de l'Autel*. Paris: 1669.

- *Les Merveilles de l'amour de Jésus-Christ dans le Saint Sacrement de l'Autel*. Paris: 1669.

Catherine of Genoa, St. *La Vie et les Oeuvres spirituelles de Sainte Catherine Adorny de Genes*. Published by the Carthusian monks of Bourg-Fontaine in 1597, this French translation of Catherine's writings was often re-edited: see the edition of 1627 for references to this work. This first translation into French appeared in Paris in 1598 and, because of its widespread distribution, was considered important. Cattaneo Marabotto, Catherine's spiritual director, had gathered all that Catherine revealed to him and used it in composing her *Life*, as well as two treatises, the *Purgatory* and the *Dialogue*: see *Libro de la vita mirabile e dottrina santa de la beata Catarinetta da Genoa*, Genoa: 1551; Florence: 1568. On the life and doctrine of Catherine, one must consider as essential and paramount the work of F. von Hugel, *The Mystical Element of Religion as Studied in St Catherine of Genoa and her Friends*, 2 vols., London: 1909. For modern English translations of the principal works: see *Catherine of Genoa: Purgation and Purgatory, The Spiritual Dialogue*, in The Classics of Western Spirituality, translation and notes by Serge Hughes, introduction by Benedict J. Groeschel, OFM, CAP. New York: Paulist Press, 1979.

de Canfield, Benoît. *Reigle de perfection, contenant un bref et lucide abrégé de toute la vie spirituelle réduite à ce seul point de la volonté de Dieu*. Paris: C. Chastellain, 1609. For reference to this work: see *Benoît de Canfield: La Règle de Perfection/The Rule of Perfection*. Critical edition, published and annotated by Jean Orcibal, Bibliothèque de l'Ecole des Hautes Etudes, vol. LXXXIII. Paris: Presses Universitaires de France, 1982.

de Saint-Jure, Jean Baptiste. *L'Homme spirituel, où la vie spirituelle est traitée par ses principes*, Paris: 1646.

- *De la connaissance et de l'amour du Fils de Dieu, Notre-Seigneur Jésus-Christ*, Paris: 1634.

- *Le Livre des Eluz, Jésus-Christ en Croix*, Paris: 1643.

- *Méditations sur les plus grandes et les plus importantes vérités de la Foy*, Paris: 1643.

- *Les trois filles de Job*, Paris: 1646.

- *Maître Jésus-Christ enseignant les hommes*, Paris: 1649.

de Saint-Nicolas, Donatien. *La Vie, les maximes et partie des oeuvres du vénérable Jean de Saint-Samson*. Paris: D. Thierry, 1651.

de Sales, Charles-Auguste. *Histoire du B. François de Sales*. Lyon: 1634.

de Sales, St François. *Introduction à la Vie dévote*, Lyon: 1608. For reference to this work: see *Saint François de Sales: Oeuvres*, Bibliothèque de la Pléiade, Paris: Editions Gallimard, 1969, pp. 19-317.

Deschamps, Thomas. *Le Jardin des contemplatifs, parsemé de fleurs d'amour divin*. Paris: N. Du Fossé et P. Chevalier, 1605.

de Sesmaisons, Pierre. 'Question s'il est meilleur de communier souvent que rarement'. Refuted by Antoine Arnauld, this text serves as the basis of his commentary and target of his attack in his treatise *De la fréquente communion*, Paris, 1643. For reference to this work, see the 4th edition of *De la fréquente communion*, Paris: chez Antoine Vitré, 1644. Also, this text by de Sesmaisons is summarised by Father Rapin, a Jesuit (see *Mémoires du P. Rapin*, vol. 1, Paris: 1865, p. 30), who maintained that the *Question* was an extract from Molina's book, *L'Instruction des prêtres*, which appeared in France in Lyon, in 1640.

Du Val, André. *Vie admirable de la Soeur Marie de l'Incarnation*, Paris: 1621. For reference to this text: see *La Vie de Soeur Marie de l'Incarnation*, 10th edition, Paris: 1647.

Guilloré, P. *Les Progrès de la vie spirituelle*, Paris: 1675. See *Oeuvres spirituelles du P. Guilloré*, Paris, 1684, p. 587.

Jansen, Cornelius. *Augustinus*, 1640.

Lallemant, Louis. *Doctrine spirituelle*, published in Paris in 1694 by Father Pierre Champion. The best edition of the *Doctrine spirituelle* is by A. Pottier, Paris, 1936. Also by Pottier, see *Le P. Louis Lallemant et les spirituels de son temps*, 3 vols., Paris, 1927-9. For a very exact reproduction of the text of 1694: see *La Vie et la doctrine spirituelle du Père Louis Lallemant*, Introduction and Notes by François Courel, SJ. Paris: Club du livre religieux, Desclée De Brouwer, 1959. For excellent and precise biographical indications, see Jimenez, J. 'Précisions biographiques sur le P. L.L.', in *Archivum Historicum Societatis Jesu*, XXXIII (1964), pp. 269-332.

Marie-Agnès Dauvaine, Mère. *La Vie de la Vénérable Mère Marie-Agnès Dauvaine*, Paris, 1675.

Maria Magdalena dei Pazzi, St. *Opere*, Florence, 1893; *Oeuvres*, edited by D. Anselme Bruniaux, 2 vols., Paris, 1873. For reference to this Italian mystic, see M. Vaussard, *Sainte Marie Madeleine de Pazzi*, 3rd edition, Paris: 1925. For further possible similarities between the writings of Claudine and those of Maria Magdalena dei Pazzi, it would be useful to see *Extases et lettres*, translation by M.M. Vaussard, Paris: Editions du Seuil, 1946.

Martin, S. *Les Fleurs de la solitude*, Paris: 1652.

Maur de l'Enfant-Jésus, Father. *Entrée à la divine Sagesse, comprise en plusieurs traittés spirituels qui expliquent les plus profonds secrets de la théologie mystique*, Paris: 1652; Bourdeaux: J. Mongiron-Millanges, 1652.

- *Le Royaume intérieur de Jésus-Christ dans les ames*, 2nd edition, Paris: D. Thierry, 1664.

- *Théologie chrestienne et mistique, ou Conduite spirituelle pour arriver bien-tost au souverain degré de la perfection*, Bourdeaux: J. Mongiron-Millanges, 1651.

Orcibal, Jean. *Benoît de Canfield: La Règle de perfection/The Rule of Perfection*. Bibliothèque de l'Ecole des Hautes Etudes, vol. LXXXIII. Paris: Presses Universitaires de France, 1982.

Puhl, Louis J., SJ. Ignatius Loyola, St. *The Spiritual Exercises of Saint Ignatius Loyola*, Chicago: Loyola University Press, 1951.

Ribadeneira, Pedro A. *Flos Sanctorum: Primera parte del Flos Sanctorum, o libro de las vidas de los Santos . . . escrita por el P. Pedro de Ribadeneira*, 2 vols. Madrid: 1624; for the French translation, see A. Ribadeneira and A. du Val, *Les Fleurs des vies des Saints et fêtes de toute l'année, suivant l'usage du calendrier romain réformé, recueillies par le R.P. Ribadeneira . . . auxquelles ont été ajoutées les vies de plusieurs Saints de France par M. André du Val . . . revues . . . et remises en état de perfection selon la traduction d'espagnol en français de M. René Gautier*, 2 vols. Rouen:1645 -46.

Surius, Lawrence. *De Probatis Sanctorum historis*. Cologne: 1570-5.

Teresa of Avila, St. See *The Life of St Teresa of Avila*, translated and edited by E. Allison Peers, London: Sheed & Ward, 1944 and 1979, reprint 1983; also *Interior Castle*, translated and edited by E. Allison Peers, New York: Image Books, 1961.

Thomas à Kempis. *The Imitation of Christ*. Translation into modern English by Edgar Daplyn, FRSL. London: Sheed & Ward, 1952.

Vaussard, M. *Sainte Marie Madeleine de Pazzi*, 3rd edition, Paris: 1925; also *Extases et lettres*, translation by M.M. Vaussard, Paris: Editions du Seuil, 1946.

Secondary sources

Athanasius, St. *Life of Antony*. The Nicene and Post-Nicene Fathers, vol. 4, 1891 (reprinted Grand Rapids/Michigan: Wm B. Eerdmans Company, 1982), pp. 195-22; for a more recent English translation, see 'The Life of Antony', translation and introduction by Robert C. Gregg, in *Athanasius: The Life of Antony and the Letter to Marcellinus* (The Classics of Western Spirituality), New York: Paulist Press, 1980.

Bernard of Clairvaux, St. *On the Song of Songs 1*, Sermons 1-20. Kalamazoo/Michigan: Cistercian Publications, Inc., 1981.

Bouchereaux, Suzanne-Marie. *La Réforme des Carmes en France et Jean de Saint-Samson*. Etudes de Théologie et d'Histoire de la Spiritualité, vol. XII. Paris: Librairie Philosophique J. Vrin, 1950.

Bremond, Henri. *Histoire littéraire du sentiment religieux en France*, 12 vols. Paris: Bloud et Gay, 1916-32.

Brou, A. *Saint François Xavier*. Paris: 1912.

Chadwick, Henry. *Origen: Contra Celsum*. Cambridge: Cambridge University Press, 1953; paperback edition, 1980.

Clement of Alexandria, St. *The Stromata* (Miscellanies). The Ante-Nicene Fathers, American reprint of the Edinburgh edition (Grand Rapids/Michigan: Wm B. Eerdmans Company, 1983), vol. 2, pp. 444-567.

The Cloud of Unknowing and Other Works. Translated into modern English with an introduction by Clifton Wolters. Penguin Books, 1961; reprinted with *The Epistle of Privy Councel*, *Dionysius' Mystical Teaching*, and *The Epistle of Prayer*, 1978.

Cognet, Louis. 'La Spiritualité moderne: 1. L'Essor, 1500-1650', in *Histoire de la Spiritualité Chrétienne*, vol. 3, Paris: Editions Aubier-Montaigne, 1966.

Corneille. *Le Cid*, 1636.

- *Poleucte*, 1643.

Council of Trent, The. Session XXIII, chap. IV, canon 2, in *Enchiridion Symbolorum*, Denzinger, 883.

Dalrymple, John. *Theology and Spirituality*. Cork: Mercier Press, 1970.

Daniélou, Jean. *Platonisme et Théologie Mystique: Doctrine spirituelle de Saint Grégoire de Nysse*. Paris: Aubier/Editions Montaigne, 1944. See also: *Grégoire de Nysse: La Vie de Moïse*, Sources Chrétiennes 1, Paris: Les Editions du Cerf, 1955, 1968; *From Glory to Glory*, translation by H. Musurillo with introduction by Daniélou (London, 1962) - translation of extracts drawn mostly from Gregory of Nyssa's *The Life of Moses* and his *Commentary on the Song of Songs*; 'Mystique de la ténèbre chez Grégoire de Nysse', in *Dictionnaire de Spiritualité*, ed. M. Viller (Paris, 1932), vol. 4, col. 1872ff.

Dante. *Dante Alighieri, The Divine Comedy: Paradiso, 1: Italian Text and Translation*, translated, with a commentary, by Charles S. Singleton, Bollingen Series LXXX, Princeton/New Jersey: Princeton University Press, 1975.

- *Paradiso, 2: Commentary* (ibid.).

de Condren, Charles. *L'Idée du sacerdoce et du sacrifice de Jésus-Christ*. Paris: 1677.

- *Lettres du Père de Condren*, published by Paul Auvrey and André Jouffrey, priests of the Oratory, Paris: Editions du Cerf, 1943.

Descartes, René. *Discourse on Method*. The Philosophical Works of Descartes, translated by Elizabeth S. Haldane and G.R.T. Ross, 1st edition 1911, reprinted 1979, Cambridge: Cambridge University Press, 1979, vol. 1, pp. 79-130.

- *The Passions of the Soul*, ibid., pp. 329-427.

Dionysius, Pseudo-. *De Mystica theologica*. In Patrologia Graeca 3, ed. J.P. Migne (Paris, 1844-55), col. 997-1064. See also: *Dionysius' Mystical Teaching*, translated in modern English with an introduction by Clifton Wolters, in *The Cloud of Unknowing and Other Works*, Penguin Classics, 1978. For a recent English translation of the complete works of Pseudo-Dionysius, see *Pseudo-*

Selected Bibliography

Dionysius: The Complete Works, translation by Colm Luibheid, The Classics of Western Spirituality, New York: Paulist Press, 1987 (*The Mystical Theology*, ibid., pp. 133-141).

Evagrius of Pontus. *Century 5:26*, see *Les six Centuries des Képhalaia gnostica d'Avagre le Pontique*, ed. with translation from the Syriac version by A. Guillaumont, in Patrologia Orientalis 28 (ed. R. Graffin and F. Nau, Paris, 1903-), vol. 1 (Paris, 1958). See also Evagrius' treatise on prayer: *De Oratione*, 60, in Patrologia Graeca 79, ed. J.P. Migne (Paris, 1856-66), col. 1165-1200.

Evdokimov, Paul. *L'Orthodoxie*. Paris: Delachaux et Niestlé, 1965.

Festugière, A.J. *L'Enfant d'Agrigente*. Paris: 1942.

Gregory of Nyssa, St. *La Vie de Moïse*. Sources Chrétiennes 1, ed. H. de Lubac and Jean Daniélou (Paris, 1942-), Paris: Editions du Cerf, 1968, with introduction, critical text and translation by Jean Daniélou (a reproduction of Daniélou's 1955 edition of the same text).

- *De Vita Moysis* (On the Life of Moses), Patrologia Graeca 44, col. 327A-430D.
- *In Psalmos*, PG 44, col. 431A-616B.
- *In Ecclesiasten Salomonis*, PG 44, col. 615C-754C.
- *In Cantica Canticorum*, PG 44, col. 755A-1120A.
- *De Oratione Dominica*, PG 44, col. 1120-1193.
- *De Beatitudinibus*, PG 44, col. 1193B-1302B.

Hausherr, Irenée. *Le Leçons d'un contemplatif: Traité de l'Oraison d'Evagre le Pontique*. Paris: Beauchesne, 1960.

Hopkins, Gerard Manley. 'That Nature is a Heraclitean Fire and of the Comfort of the Resurrection', *Poems and Prose of Gerard Manley Hopkins*, selected with an introduction and notes by W.H. Gardner, Penguin Books, 1953, 1963.

Jaeger, Werner. *The Theology of the Early Greek Philosophers*. Oxford: Oxford University Press, 1960; first published by Clarendon Press, Oxford, 1947; reprinted by Greenwood Press, Westport/ Connecticut, 1980.

Julian of Norwich. *Julian of Norwich: Revelations of Divine Love*. Translated into modern English and with an introduction by Clifton Wolters, Penguin Classics, 1966.

Lemaire, H. *Les Images chez Saint François de Paris*. Paris: 1962.

Longpré, Ephrem. 'Eucharistie et Expérience mystique', *Dictionnaire de Spiritualité*, ed. M. Viller (Paris, 1932-), vol. 4, col. 1586-1621.

Louth, Andrew. *The Origins of the Christian Mystical Tradition: From Plato to Denys*. Oxford: Clarendon Press, 1981.

Moschus, John. *Jean Moschus: Le Pré Spirituel*. Introduction and translation by M.-J. Rouet de Journel, SJ. Sources Chrétiennes 12, ed. H. de Lubac and Jean Daniélou (Paris, 1942-), Paris: Editions du Cerf, 1946.

Origen. *Origen: An Exhortation to Martyrdom, Prayer and Selected Works*. Translation and introduction by Rowan A. Greer, preface by Hans Urs von Balthasar. The Classics of Western Spirituality, New York: Paulist Press, 1979.

Parias, L.H. Writing in *La France Catholique*, Paris, 22 January 1960.

Pascal. *Pensées*. Introduction by T.S. Eliot. New York: Dutton, paperback, 1958.

- *Lettres écrites à un provincial*. Chronology and introduction by Antoine Adam. Paris: Garnier-Flammarion, 1967.

Philo. *On Abraham*, XIV, 62. Translated by F.H. Colson, Loeb Classical Library. Cambridge, Massachusetts: Harvard University Press, 1935.

Plato. *The Republic*, Book 7, 515C. Penguin Classics, translated with an introduction by Desmond Lee, 2nd edition (revised), 1955-74, p. 318.

Plotinus. *Enneads* 4, vii.

Poullier, Louis. 'Consolation Spirituelle', in *Dictionnaire de Spiritualité*, ed. M. Viller (Paris, 1932), vol. 2, col. 1617-1634.

Racine. *Esther*, 1689.

Rahner, Karl. 'Le début d'une doctrine des cinq sens spirituels chez Origène', *Revue ascétique et mystique* (1932), pp. 113-45.

Rahner, Hugo. *Spirituality of St. Ignatius Loyola*. Translated by F.J. Smith, SJ. Chicago: Loyola University Press, 1953.

Thomas Aquinas, St. *Summa*, pt 1, q. 3, art. 2; pt 1, q. 21, art. 3.

Underhill, Evelyn. *The Essentials of Mysticism*. London: J.M. Dent & Sons Ltd/New York: E.P. Dutton & Co., 1920; reprinted, New York: AMS Press Inc., 1976.

Virgil. *Aeneid*, viii, 485-8.

von Hügel, F. *The Mystical Element of Religion as Studied in Saint Catherine of Genoa and her Friends*. London: 1909, 2 vols.

INDEX of BIBLICAL PASSAGES
Preface and Introduction

Text

OLD TESTAMENT

Index of Biblical Passages

GENERAL INDEX

Preface, Introduction and Text

sophical, 278n140; primary interest of, 278n145.

consolation(s), 15, 91 and 266n2, 106, 122, 180, 187, 195 and 297n150, 197, 205, 224; to serve without, 106.

contemplation, 78, 146; of divine mysteries, 46; mystical, 77; superior degrees of, 273n105; passive devotional, 282n186; man's powers of, 288n41.

contemplative, the, 280n162, 281n184; experiences, 255n46.

contempt, 70, 105, 144, 168, 188, 191, 196-7, 206, 208, 218, 231-2.

contentment, 149, 215.

contrition, 98, 135.

controversy, 291nn70 and 72; theological, 11, 246n25, 291n69.

conversion, 17, 23, 33, 38-9, 44, 237, 242n2, 255n46, 257n61, 281n177; words of, 301n58.

Corneille, 15, 287nn36 and 37.

courage, 23, 98, 122, 154, 162, 166-7, 258n67.

Couture-Sainte-Catherine, Rue, *see Annonciade*.

covetousness, 114, 121, 138, 233.

Creator, The, 161; vanity of, 279n162; creation, 85; *see also* God.

Cross, (the), 47, 52, 55, 57-9, 70, 85, 97-8, 106, 121, 134, 154, 165-8, 177; Pauline theology of, 287n32; depth of the mystery of, 167.

crucifixion,165.

Dames de la Charité, 257n58.

damned, (the), 51, 73, 159, 201.

Dante, 3, 34, 301n58.

darkness, 77 and 264nn129 and 132, 127 and 276nn119 and 121, 140, 146, 182, 191, 195, 296n143; into the light, 261n110; experience through, 288n41; the great, 15, 17, 27, 264n130, 280nn165 and 166, 295n128.

day, special, 88.

Dauvaine, Agnès, 26; *Dauvaine, La Vie de la Vénérable Mère Marie-Agnès*, 26-7.

dead, to rise from among the, 147.

death, 29, 32, 35-6, 61, 147-53, 157, 161, 164-7, 170, 175-6, 188, 196, 201, 207, 239; and existence, 147; desire for, 284n210; St. Paul's theology of, 147, 284n217; abandonment with regard to, 148.

de Canfield, Benoît, 262n111, 296n133.

de Choisy, Abbé, 5, 19.

de Condren, Charles, 292n81.

de Coulanges, Philippe, 259n93.

De la fréquent communion, 14 and 246n25, 28; regarding the treatise, 172; *see also* Communion, Holy.

de Saint-Jure, Father, 25-6, 28-30, 247n38.

de Sesmaisons, Father (Pierre), 9 and 245n16, 28, 62, 64.

de Sévigné, Madame, 12.

Deepening, 19, 90-1, 264n130; deepening spiritual commentary, 33, 38.

delight(s), 191, 218-19, 227.

demons, 73, 95, 97, 99, 101, 106, 117, 185, 223, 237.

departure, 48.

dependence, 140-1, 143-4, 225; Supreme, 150.

deprivation, interior, 139.

Descartes, 132n140; *Discourse on Method*, 294n111; Cartesian revolution, 278n140.

desire(s), 5, 151-4, 157, 165, 179, 188, 196, 200-1, 213-4, 217, 224, 233, 236-7, 239; of devotion, 227; for divinization, 273n106; for death, 284n210; for religious life, 45; complete elimination of, 268n36; inflamed, 236; intense, 104.

desolation, 205, 266n2.

despair, 52 and 256n49, 56, 95, 187; temptation of, 261n106.

destitution, 57.

detachment, 109, 264n128, 279n148; total, 109.

Devil, the, 43, 95, 117, 120, 122-3, 176 and 292n90, 187, 231 and 301n51.

devotion(s), 56, 63, 88, 92, 94, 99, 103, 108, 110-11, 115, 122-4, 129, 132-4, 138, 146, 148, 165, 171, 174, 186, 194-8, 220, 228, 238; exercise(s) of, 195, 197-8, 200, 207-8, 232; the guardian angels of, 227; appearance of, 235.

die, to win or, 102.

dignities, 163-4, 181.

Dijon, 49, 243n11.

direction, spiritual, 279n148, 296nn140 and 141; of souls, 237.

director(s), spiritual, 24 and 246n36, 30.

discipline, 89.

discretion, necessary, 238.

disdain, 26, 111, 130; self- 206.

disposition(s), 229, 237, 239; fruits and, 176; for prayer, 227, 229; of mind, 232.